Stockholm

timeout.com / stockholm

51

69

Contents

204

Introduction

Home to about one million locals, Stockholm is one of Europe's more petite capitals, but the fun-size nature of the Nordic city makes it a stress-free place to visit. Although they're spread across 14 islands, Stockholm's attractions are easily accessible from one another: the royal buildings and medieval squares of the old city are a pleasant stroll from the cult cafés in creative Södermalm, and a delightful ferry ride from the world-class museums on Djurgården and Skeppsholmen. Those opting for public transport will find it clean, safe and ruthlessly efficient, and if you happen to get lost, you'll struggle to find a Stockholmer who doesn't speak great English.

The single factor that has the biggest impact on any trip to Sweden is the weather. On the coldest winter days, Stockholm becomes a snowy wonderland, with residents skating across its frozen waterways or gathering to drink hot mulled wine at outdoor craft markets. Yet the limited daylight means that many residents hunker down at home as soon as darkness sets in. Summertime, by contrast, sees the city bursting into life: locals swim and picnic late into the night, while others cut loose in rooftop cocktail bars or at seasonal music festivals.

Whenever you choose to visit, Stockholm's postcard-perfect waterfronts, spice-hued buildings and abundant green spaces have obvious appeal. But while these natural and historic riches create a stunning backdrop, the Swedish capital is also a fast-growing, modern city that's increasingly luring in visitors with impeccable design and technology, forward-thinking fashion and a thriving international food scene.

Riddarholmen

ABOUT THE GUIDE

This is one of a series of Time Out guidebooks to cities across the globe. Written by local experts, our guides are thoroughly researched and meticulously updated. They aim to be inspiring, irreverent, well-informed and trustworthy.

Time Out Stockholm is divided into five sections: Discover, Explore, Experience, Understand and Plan.

Discover introduces the city and provides inspiration for your visit.

Explore is the main sightseeing section of the guide and includes detailed listings and reviews for sights and museums, restaurants & cafés ⑩, bars ⑩, and shops & services ⑩, all organised by area with a corresponding street map. To help navigation, each area of Stockholm has been assigned its own colour.

Experience covers the cultural life of the city in depth, including festivals, film, LGBT, music, nightlife, theatre and more.

Understand provides in-depth background information that places Stockholm in its historical and cultural context.

Plan offers practical visitor information, including accommodation options and details of public transport.

Hearts

We use hearts ♥ to pick out venues, sights and experiences in the city that we particularly recommend. The very best of these are featured in the Top 20 (*see p10*) and receive extended coverage in the guide.

Maps

A detachable fold-out map can be found on the inside back cover. There's also an overview map (*see p8*) and individual streets maps for each area of the city. The venues featured in the guide have been given a grid reference so that you can find them easily on the maps and on the ground.

Prices

All our **restaurant listings** are marked with a krona symbol category from budget ⓦ to blow-out ⓦⓦⓦⓦ, indicating the price you should expect to pay for an average main course: ⓦ = under 200kr; ⓦⓦ = 200kr -300kr; ⓦⓦⓦ = 300kr-500kr; ⓦⓦⓦⓦ = over 500kr.

A similar system is used in our **Accommodation** chapter based on the hotel's standard prices for one night in a double room: **Budget** = under 800kr; **Moderate** = 800kr-1,300kr; **Expensive** = 1,300kr-2,000kr; **Luxury** = over 2,000kr.

Discover

Cobblestone street in Gamla Stan

7

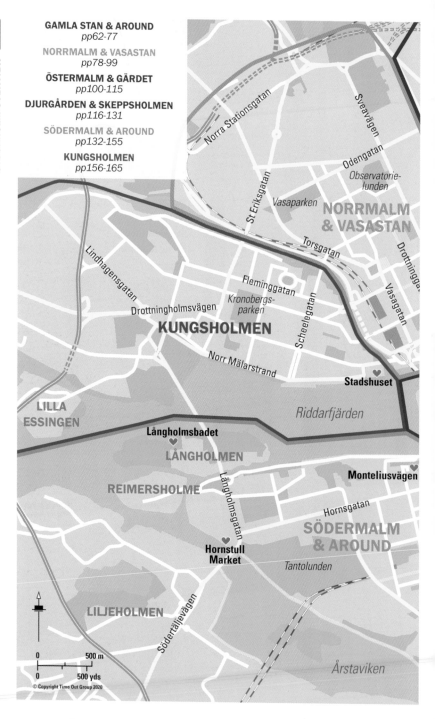

Norra Stationsgatan

Sveavägen

Norra Stationsgatan

Odengatan

Observatorie-
lunden

St Eriksgatan

Vasaparken

**NORRMALM
& VASASTAN**

Torsgatan

Drottningga-

Lindhagensgatan

Flemminggatan

Vasagatan

Kronobergs-
parken

Drottningholmsvägen

Scheelegatan

KUNGSHOLMEN

Norr Mälarstrand

♥
Stadshuset

**LILLA
ESSINGEN**

Riddarfjärden

Långholmsbadet
♥

LÅNGHOLMEN

Monteliusvägen ♥

REIMERSHOLME

Långholmsgatan

Hornsgatan

**SÖDERMALM
& AROUND**

♥
**Hornstull
Market**

Tantolunden

LILJEHOLMEN

Södertäljevägen

0   500 m

0   500 yds
© Copyright Time Out Group 2020

Årstaviken

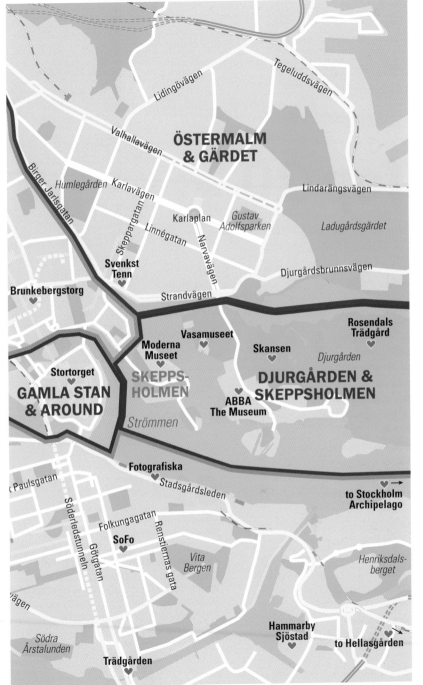

Lidingövägen

Tegeludsvägen

Valhallavägen

ÖSTERMALM & GÄRDET

Birger Jarlsgatan

Humlegården Karlavägen

Lindarängsvägen

Karlaplan

Gustav Adolfsparken

Ladugårdsgärdet

Skeppargatan

Linnégatan

Narvavägen

Svenkst Tenn ♥

Djurgårdsbrunnsvägen

Brunkebergstorg ♥

Strandvägen

Rosendals Trädgård ♥

Vasamuseet ♥

Moderna Museet ♥

Skansen ♥

Djurgården

Stortorget ♥

SKEPPS-HOLMEN

DJURGÅRDEN & SKEPPSHOLMEN

GAMLA STAN & AROUND

ABBA The Museum ♥

Strömmen

Fotografiska ♥

Stadsgårdsleden

Paulsgatan

to Stockholm Archipelago →

Söderledstunneln

Folkungagatan

Renstiernas gata

SoFo ♥

Vita Bergen

Götgatan

Henriksdals-berget

vägen

Södra Årstalunden

Hammarby Sjöstad ♥

to Hellasgården ♥→

Trädgården ♥

Top 20

*Museums, markets and meatballs – we
count down the city's finest*

01

Monteliusvägen *p149*

You can breathe in one of the most
stunning views in Stockholm from
the wooden Monteliusvägen walkway,
which runs along the cliffs of northern
Södermalm. It looks out across the
Riddarfjärden bay, taking in the
distinctive black rooftops of Gamla Stan.

02

Stortorget *p70*

The Gamla Stan neighbourhood is touristy, but there's a reason its main square – the oldest in Stockholm – remains so popular. The former medieval marketplace is lined with some of the city's most historic buildings and hosts pop-up food and handicraft stalls around Christmas.

03

Stockholm archipelago *p174*

If you're visiting Stockholm during the summer, taking a boat to one of the city's 30,000 archipelago islands is a must. Fjäderholmarna and Vaxholm make for popular day trips, while Grinda and Björno offer more greenery and seclusion.

04

SoFo *p137*

The buzzing bars, restaurants and coffee shops in this district teem with young creatives, who buy their clothes from the area's thriving second-hand stores and independent boutiques. The name 'SoFo' is a nod to the area's location (south of a street named Folkungatan) and its similarities with the hip Soho/SoHo districts in London and New York.

05

Fotografiska *p139*

Stockholm's premier photography museum is housed in an art nouveau industrial building that was converted in 2010. Alongside regularly changing exhibitions by leading Swedish and international talents, there's an excellent shop and an eating area with panoramic views.

06

Rosendals Trädgård *p127*

For a taste of the Swedish countryside, head to this idyllic biodynamic garden in the middle of Djurgården. Alongside fruit and vegetable beds, and wildflower meadows, there's a popular greenhouse café that uses produce grown on site.

07

Fika *p47*

Fika is the word for the Swedish ritual of taking a break to enjoy a coffee, often with a cinnamon bun or slice of cake. Coffee is decent in the majority of Stockholm cafés, which increasingly cater to healthy-living locals by offering milk substitutes alongside raw and gluten-free sweet treats. Try Pom and Flora in the Södermalm district (*see p97*) or Café Pascal in Vasastan (*see p95*).

08

Moderna Museet *p130*

The greats of 20th-century art are on display in this purpose-built gallery surrounded by former naval buildings. Once you've had your fill of culture, head to the museum restaurant for top-notch nosh and even better views.

09

Brunkebergstorg *p85*

Edgy hotels and panoramic bars are the focal point of this newly revamped neighbourhood, where Spotify and Facebook have their Nordic headquarters. TAK (*see p89*) is one of the bars to see and be seen – be prepared for long queues for the rooftop terrace when the sun is shining.

10

Vasamuseet *p125*

This museum contains the awe-inspiring and incredibly well-preserved remains of the 17th-century Vasa warship. It sank off the coast of Stockholm on its maiden voyage in 1628 but was salvaged in the 1960s. The Vasa Museum has been one of the city's most popular attractions since it opened in 1991.

11

Swedish meatballs *p42*

Sweden's most famous traditional dish is meatballs served with mashed potato, lingonberry jam and a thick gravy. It's easy to find on the menu in touristy areas, but for a high-end experience try Operabaren (*see p88*) or head to Meatballs for the People or Kvarnen in Södermalm to avoid the crowds (*see p141*).

12

Långholmsbadet *p153*

The small island of Långholmen is something of a green retreat and is home to one of Stockholm's most popular inner-city swimming spots. With a modest sandy front, it's surrounded by flat rocks and a grassy bank where locals love to picnic.

13

Trädgården *p199*

The mother of outdoor clubs in Stockholm, Trädgården sprawls beneath a giant concrete bridge between May and early September. Alongside a massive courtyard where headline DJs and live acts perform, it boasts a burger shack, table tennis tables and several bars.

14

ABBA The Museum *p121*

The ABBA museum is a don't-miss for fans of the supergroup, which remains one of Sweden's most successful exports. It's an interactive attraction that allows visitors to experience what it would feel like to be the fifth member of the band.

15

Stadshuset *p161*

The city's huge red-brick City Hall dates back to 1923, and its 106-metre (350-foot) turret affords marvellous views of the Riddarfjärden bay and Gamla Stan. The Nobel Prize banquet is held here every December.

16

Skansen *p122*

This open-air museum and animal park contains more than 150 traditional Swedish buildings – houses, shops, churches, classic cafés and workshops. It's also home to brown bears, moose, wolves and other Scandinavian animals.

17

Hornstull Market *p51*

On summer weekends, locals flock to Hornstull on Södermalm for second-hand fashion, vintage bargains and foodie treats at the hugely popular market. Thrifty fashionistas will find plenty of other flea markets (*loppis*) and second-hand clothing boutiques around town.

18

Hellasgården *p171*

Embrace the Nordic ritual of sweating it out in a sauna at Hellasgården, a recreation area inside Nacka nature reserve. You can cool off with a dip in Lake Källtorp. Brave locals do this year-round; a hole is drilled into the ice when it freezes over.

19

Svenskt Tenn *p111*

Stockholm's most famous interiors shop isn't a place for those on a budget, but it's a must-visit for a lesson in Swedish design heritage. Started by pewter artist ('*tenn*' means 'pewter') Estrid Ericson in 1924, the brand is most famous for its bold textile designs.

20

Hammarby Sjöstad *p155*

Off the beaten path for many travellers, this former industrial wasteland turned award-winning urban eco district is worth a visit for its impressive energy-saving modern architecture and pristine waterfront cycle lanes. To quench your thirst, make a stop at craft beer bar Nya Carnegiebryggeriet, which specialises in seasonal releases and limited-edition brews.

WE'LL TELL YOU WHERE TO GO

Wherever you're exploring, we've got the insider insight on the world's best destinations.

 TIMEOUT.COM/STOCKHOLM

Time Out
THE BEST OF THE CITY

Itineraries

*Make the most of every Stockholm minute with
our tailored tours of the city*

ESSENTIAL WEEKEND

Budget 1000kr-2000kr per day
Getting around if you don't want to
walk, buy a 24-hour travelcard (130kr) for
public transport, which will cover you for
subway, bus, tram and ferry journeys for
one day. To cover the whole weekend, a
72-hour travelcard costs 260kr.

DAY 1

Morning

Colourful **Stortorget** (*see p70*), at
the heart of Stockholm's medieval old
town (Gamla Stan) is the perfect spot
to fuel up for the day with a coffee and
cinnamon bun, before beating the
crowds who descend on this historic
area's ever-popular winding cobbled
streets. **Chokladkoppen** (*see p73*)
is an institution, or try the Grillska
Huset restaurant inside **Stockholms
Stadsmission** (*see p140*). There are
several stand-out Scandinavian gift
shops nearby, including **Iris Hantverk**
(*see p77*), **Charlotte Nicolin** (*see
p76*) and a branch of the cult rainwear
store **Stutterheim** (*see p145*), but if
you want to maximise your sightseeing
opportunities, then make time for the
13th-century **Storkyrkan** (*see p71*)
before buying a ticket to explore the
official residence of the royal family,
Kungliga Slottet (*see p67*). It's a vast
complex but the **Livrustkammaren** is
one of the highlights (*see p69*).

Gamla Stan and the Royal Palace

Rosendals Trädgården

Afternoon

Weave out of the inner old town on to Skeppsbron, from where you can catch the ferry (*see p237*) to the large green island of Djurgården. From the dock, it's a peaceful 20-minute walk to **Rosendals Trädgården** (*see p127*), a blooming biodynamic garden with a tasty ecological greenhouse restaurant. After a lunch pitstop among the many flowerbeds and vegetable patches, head to one of the island's diverse selection of museums, from **Vasamuseet** (*see p125*), which houses an incredible 17th-century wooden warship that sank on its maiden voyage in 1628, to the interactive poptastic **ABBA The Museum** (*see p121*).

If your legs aren't too tired, stroll back into the city centre via the boat-lined waterfront Strandvägen; it's buzzing with bars, especially during the summer months.

ABBA The Museum

Evening

Now you're well placed to sample the gastronomic treats of the **Östermalm** district. Go high end with the seasonal tasting menu at **Gastrologik** (*see p107*) or get a simpler fix at New York-style bistro **Kommendören** (*see p108*) or from one of the mini-restaurants inside **Östermalms Saluhall** (*see p112*). Opera buffs have a choice of three eateries in the grand surroundings of the **Kungliga Operan** (*p205*), followed by an evening performance, while party people can choose from the selection of classy bars around well-heeled Stureplan, such as the buzzing late-night brasserie **Riche** (*see p109*). A little further south, re-vamped **Brunkebergstorg** (*see p85*) offers rooftop terraces, creative cocktails and weekend DJs at the likes of **TAK** (*see p89*) and **Stockholm Under Sjärnorna** (*see p197*).

Fotografiska

DAY 2

Morning

Head straight to contemporary photography museum **Fotografiska** (*see p139*), close to Slussen, which serves daily pastries and an extensive sustainable brunch on Sundays, accompanied by panoramic waterfront views towards the old town and Djurgården island. Once you're full, explore Fotografiska's stunning exhibition space – it's a huge art nouveau industrial building dating back to 1906, with regularly changing collections on themes ranging from fashion and wildlife to war and social challenges.

Fotografiska

View from Montellusvägen

Afternoon

After your morning culture fix, wander south-west into the creative **SoFo** district (*see p137*), a compact shopping heartland that combines good-quality vintage thrift stores with emerging boutique brands and iconic Swedish fashion houses, such as Acne and Nudie Jeans. It's an area brimming with tasty eateries too. Choose between the offerings at **Urban Deli** (*see p142*) and **Katarina Ölkafé** (*see p143*); the latter, on one of the neighbourhood's slightly calmer streets, serves top-notch pastrami sandwiches and four styles of mac 'n' cheese, plus a strong selection of cold draft beers.

Take a break from the bustle in nearby **Vitabergsparken** or by popping your head into the domed, yellow **Katarina Kyrka** (*see p138*). Alternatively, continue your shopping tour with a saunter towards Slussen, up the busy thoroughfare of Götgatan. It's packed with high-street brands and design stores; watch out for fashionistas speeding through on their bikes.

From Slussen, head west along Hornsgatan towards **Monteliusvägen** (*see p149*), a raised wooden walkway that almost guarantees Insta-worthy snaps of one of the most stunning views of the city, looking out across the Riddarfjärden bay towards Gamla Stan. If time and weather allow, continue towards **Skinnarviksberget**, slightly further west, A rockier hilltop with an equally impressive panorama, it's frequented by young Stockholmers popping prosecco and sipping beer on long summer evenings.

Urban Deli

Debaser Strand

Katarina Kyrka

Evening

For dinner, stay in the same neighbourhood for a date at **Häktet** (*see p148*), an edgy modern restaurant inside a former 18th-century jail for petty criminals who couldn't afford to pay their bail. A five-minute walk away, there's a cluster of laid-back bars just south of Mariatorget square, where you can round-off the evening. Try **Racamaca** (*see p151*) or **Morfar Ginko** (*see p151*) for starters. Still got more to give? Jump on the red subway line or take the no.4 bus to Hornstull and prepare yourself for some late-night dancing at **Laika** (*see p200*) or **Debaser Strand** (*see p198*).

BUDGET BREAK

Budget 400kr-600kr per day
Getting around You can complete this whole itinerary on foot, but if you don't want to walk, buy a 24-hour ticket for the public transport system (130kr). Otherwise, single journeys cost 32kr on a pre-loaded SL card, or 45kr on the SL mobile app.

Changing the Guard

Morning

Start your day on the raised wooden decking by **Monteliusvägen** (*see p149*) with a takeaway coffee or cinnamon bun from a branch of Pressbyrån, such as the one at Slussen subway stop. From here, you can enjoy one of the best free views in the city, overlooking Stockholm's old town and the Riddarfjärden bay. Continue along the Monteliusvägen until the path finishes and then loop back towards Slussen via the eastern end of Hornsgatan to check out the high-quality thrift stores, run by the Swedish Red Cross (Röda Korset) and the charity Stockholms Stadsmission. You'll also find a selection of browsable art galleries. Stop off at **Falafelbaren** (*see p148*) to pick up a flavour-packed Lebanese falafel box to save for a picnic if the weather is fine.

Once you reach Slussen, keep walking north into Gamla Stan. You don't have to pay a single entrance fee to get a sense of this area's history; there are plenty of outdoor statues and monuments in among the spice-hued townhouses. Squeeze yourself along Mårten Trotzigs gränd, Stockholm's narrowest street, and pass by the royal palace to watch the free **Changing the Guard ceremony**, which takes place at 12.15pm most weekdays and at 1.15pm on weekends (*see p67*). Nearby, the tiny island of Hegeandsholmen is home to the Swedish parliament, the **Riksdag** (*see p69*), which you can tour for free. On the eastern side of the island, the **Stockholms Medeltidsmuseum** (*see p71*) is also free to visit and retells everyday stories about Stockholmers' lives during the Middle Ages.

Falafelbaren

Falafelbaren

Moderna Museet

Trädgården

Afternoon

Continue north from Hegeandsholmen across the pedestrian Riksbron. If you haven't yet stopped for a bite to eat, walk towards Drottninggatan for a selection of affordable Nordic chain cafés, such as Espresso House and Joe and the Juice. There are two stand-out free museums in the city centre; if you're not fussed about visiting every gallery, you could just about squeeze both into an afternoon. Follow Strömgatan eastwards along the waterfront, past the Kungliga Operan, to reach the **Nationalmuseum** (*see p84*), a huge 19th-century building that houses Swedish and international art and design from the Middle Ages to the present day. A short walk east on Skeppsholmen island, the **Moderna Museet** (*see p130*) is a small but impressive contemporary art museum with works by the likes of Picasso, Dalí and Pollock. Once gallery fatigue sets in, stroll along the mile-long path around the island for gorgeous views of yacht-lined Strandvägen, Gamla Stan, Djurgården and northern Södermalm. Add on the adjacent islet of **Kastleholmen**, with its distinctive red-turreted citadel, if you have time. A fun public transport boat ride from northern Skeppsholmen will take you back to Gamla Stan.

Evening

The Slussen area offers a couple of high-quality places for a decent budget evening meal. Mexican canteen **La Neta** (*see p142*) is home to some of the best tacos in the city, while **Creperie Fyra Knop** (*see p141*) is a rustic, candle-lit restaurant where you can get a filling savoury pancake dinner for the price of a sandwich in some of Stockholm's priciest gaffs. Nearby **Carmen** (*see p143*) is one of the city's most legendary dive bars, but you'd do better to budget for a few extra kronor per beer in the bars of **SoFo** (*see p137*). Pick your favourite spot around trendy Nytorget square to get a real taste of Södermalm's beating heart. If you're planning to stay out late during summer, head to outdoor club **Trädgården** (*see p199*). Alcohol isn't cheap here, but entry is usually free before 8pm at weekends and all night during the week. Arrive early – you won't be the only one hoping to skip the fee. The venue transforms into a smaller house and techno club, **Under Bron**, between September and April.

FAMILY DAY OUT

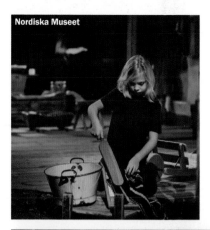
Nordiska Museet

Budget 3000kr-4000kr. If you're going to visit a lot of museums, consider investing in a Stockholm Pass (2156kr for two adults and two children).
Getting around Public transport is free for under-sevens at all times and free for up to six children under 12 with a paying adult from noon on Friday to midnight on Sunday. Bus travel is also free for a single adult with a pram/pushchair and buses graciously bow to street level for easy access.

Morning

Djurgården island is the place to head if you've got children: it's packed with museums and attractions, and it has plenty of green space where kids can run around. Start your day at **Skansen** (*see p122*), a 'living' historic village and animal park that contains more than 150 traditional Swedish buildings, brought to life by actors. It also has brown bears, elk, wolves and other Scandinavian animals. If you need a snack or lunch, there's both a family-friendly canteen and a picnic area. There are no restrictions if you want to have a picnic on any of the grassy areas around Djurgården, but you'll need to stock up in advance, as there is no proper supermarket on the island.

Junibacken

Skansen

Afternoon

Skansen is just a short walk from both **Junibacken** (*see p124*), a mini outdoor theme park devoted to wild-child storybook character Pippi Longstocking, and **Nordiska Museet** (Sweden's museum of cultural history; *see p124*), which has a playhouse themed around life in the Swedish countryside. Both also have cafeterias that are popular with families. **Gröna Lund** (*see p122*), Sweden's oldest amusement park, is perched on the edge of Djurgården with fantastic views across the water and plenty of family-friendly rides, although it's only open between May and September. A winter alternative might be **Tekniska Museet** (*see p114*), Sweden's popular interactive museum of science and technology, which is a 30-minute walk from Skansen in Ladugårdsgärdet. Or, get a tram back into the city centre and then hop on the green subway to Skanstull, where **Eriksdalsbadet** (*see p138*) has a selection of indoor swimming pools and splash pools (as well as seasonal outdoor pools). There's a popular playground, outdoor gym and skate park at **Rålambshovsparken** (*see p160*) where older kids can let off steam.

Tekniska Museet

Kulturhuset Stadsteatern

Kulturhuset Stadsteatern

Evening

In family-friendly Stockholm, most cafés and mid-range restaurants are willing to accommodate children, but space for prams can be limited. Budget restaurant chain **Vapiano** (se.vapiano.com) has several spacious branches in the city centre, including one in Gamla Stan, and offers a children's menu and smaller portions of its main dishes. Look out for family-friendly puppet performances by the Marionetteatern at the **Kulturhuset Stadsteatern** (*see p205*), or, if you're after a child-free evening, try nanny.nu and hemfrid.se, which offer babysitting services in a range of languages.

When to Visit

Stockholm by season

Spring

March to May is the driest time of the year in Stockholm. Bars and cafes start opening their terraces (although blankets and heaters are usually still needed) and locals tend to be a little chirpier than you'll find them during the long, dark winter. On the other hand, the city's spring weather is sometimes fickle; snow could still make an appearance, or days might be gloomy and chilly. Seasonal highlights include the canopy of pale-pink cherry blossoms in Kungsträdgården park, Hornstull's weekly food and vintage **market** (see p51) and **Kulturnatt** (see p182), an annual free celebration of music, art and literature.

Cherry blossoms in Kungsträdgården park

Summer

Stockholm is at its liveliest between the end of May and the beginning of September, when temperatures can hit 25°C (occasionally even 30°C) and the sun sets late into the evening. Swedes clock off from work as early as possible to enjoy a beer or a glass of rosé on board the city's floating bars, and they spend their weekends sailing, hiking and barbecuing in the archipelago. The biggest national festival of the year, **Midsommarafton** (see p183), takes place around the summer solstice at the end of June. Swedes don flower crowns, dance around maypoles and drink schnapps. Many people head out to their summer cottages for the celebrations and remain away from the capital for up to a month, so July isn't the best time to mingle with the locals. August, by contrast, is the busiest month of the year for al fresco social events, from park gigs and theatre performances to cinema screenings.

Summer in the archipelago

Midsummer celebrations at Skansen

Autumn

For a technicolour Stockholm experience, visit during autumn, when the capital's iconic ochre and terracotta buildings are offset by the red and golden leaves on the tree-lined walkways. During September and October, there is still plenty of light, but you'll also get to experience how cosy Stockholm becomes once the sun goes down: windows are lit with candles, and log fires crackle in bars and restaurants. Two of the city's longest-running cultural events, **Stockholm Jazz Festival** (see p184), and **Stockholm Film Festival** (see p185) take place during this period. Mid to late November is one of the bleakest times of the year, with short days and rarely any snow to brighten up the surroundings.

Autumn on Djurgården

Stockholm Film Festival

Stortorget Christmas market

Winter

Exploring Stockholm in the winter can be like stepping into a luxury Christmas card: a blanket of soft snow, real fir trees twinkling with lights and the smell of hot mulled wine wafting through the air at seasonal markets (see p54). But it might also mean not feeling your fingers in temperatures of -20°C, or trudging through melting brown slush if you arrive between snow dumps. It's dark too: in December the sun sets before 3pm. Hiring ice skates or cross-country skis is a popular way to embrace the cold, once the days start getting longer.

Stockholm Today

A small city with big ideas

Stockholm has been busier than ever in recent years, charming visitors with its medieval streets, immaculate parks and waterfront promenades, but the city is also a fast-growing urban capital that's quickly become a magnet for innovative start-ups and global talent.

The pace of change is evident at a glance in the number of cranes piercing the skyline. Building companies are rushing to keep up with the demand for office and housing space, while the ongoing redevelopment of the Slussen transport hub has resulted in an unsightly construction zone that tourists will be cropping out of their photos for several years yet.

At the same time, Stockholm is grappling with the long-term impact of the national government's decision to take in record numbers of asylum seekers at the height of Europe's refugee crisis, with ongoing debates about how best to integrate these newcomers into the workforce and society.

View of Riddarholmen from Ivar Los Park *p149*

But despite its challenges, Stockholm has retained its reputation as a city where quality of life is the most important measure of success. Buoyed by a strong welfare state and a keen focus on sustainability, Swedes have a near-genetic preoccupation with work-life balance.

A start-up hub

Sweden has long punched above its weight in international business. Few other destinations with a population of ten million can lay claim to such big household names in fashion, design and technology (think IKEA, H&M, Ericsson and Electrolux), alongside a reputation as a leading exporter of music, from ABBA and Roxette to Swedish House Mafia and Avicii.

In the last decade, a burgeoning tech scene in the Swedish capital has cemented the Nordic nation's reputation for innovation. Spotify's co-founders Daniel Ek and Martin Lorentzon launched their now-global music streaming business in Stockholm in 2006. By 2015, the city could boast more billion-dollar companies per resident than anywhere outside Silicon Valley: it's the birthplace of Skype, gaming companies Mojang and King, and digital payment giants iZettle and Klarna. The start-up sector continues to grow exponentially, thanks to a strong and increasingly international entrepreneurial community, rising interest from both Nordic and global investors, government-backed funding programmes and a boom in co-working spaces.

If that sounds abstract, just chat to a local about the apps they're using. Stockholm is frequently used as a test bed for fresh ideas and tech-savvy Swedes love to be early adopters. Hyped start-ups that began their journeys in Stockholm include European electric scooter company Voi, popular food-waste app Karma and common-interest friend-finding platform Panion.

A burgeoning tech scene has cemented the Nordic nation's reputation for innovation

Spotify's co-founder Daniel Ek launched the music-streaming service in Stockholm.

Greta Thunberg

Changing the world one Friday at a time

Born in Stockholm in 2003, teenage climate activist Greta Thunberg began her campaign to force governments to cut carbon emissions in September 2018 by skipping class to protest outside the Swedish parliament, the Riksdag. Her actions quickly inspired other Swedish schoolchildren and went on to spark a global movement, with pupils around the world missing school on Fridays and sharing their experiences on the hashtag #FridaysForFuture. In December 2018 Thunberg made international headlines speaking at the UN Climate Change COP24 Conference. She went on to deliver addresses to EU leaders in Brussels, to the World Economic Forum in Davos and to the UK Parliament. In August 2019, she sailed across the Atlantic in a carbon-neutral yacht in order to attend the UN Climate Action summit in New York. Her example prompted a global climate protest in which four million people in well over 100 countries took part. Despite her global reach, Greta Thunberg still turns up to protest with local activists whenever she can, holding a large painted placard reading 'Skolstrejk för klimatet' (School strike for climate).

Sustainability star?

The world's climate crisis was a hot issue in both national and city politics in Stockholm years before local teen activist Greta Thunberg initiated the global 'School strike for climate' movement (www.schoolstrike4climate.com) in 2018 (*see above*). Swedes have a deep-rooted concern for nature, based on an appreciation of their country's abundance of lakes and forests and on the popularity of outdoor activities, from hiking and sailing to ice skating and skiing. Although, Greta Thunberg has highlighted that even Sweden – a country with a reputation for championing green projects – still has work to do in terms of cutting carbon emissions, the nation's capital deserves recognition for its programmes to protect the environment. Stockholm was the first place to be labelled a European Green Capital by the European Commission in 2010, largely thanks to its joined-up city planning, which ensures a focus on sustainability at every step when it comes to new housing or infrastructure projects. Tap water is clean and high quality; locals are avid recyclers, and, in 2019, the World Health Organization ranked Stockholm as having the lowest levels of air pollution of any capital city in Europe. The left-leaning Social Democrat Party and its junior coalition partner the Greens, which have led the national government since 2014, are committed to ensuring the country is carbon neutral by 2045.

The welfare safety net

Most Stockholmers enjoy a high standard of living, in part due to nationwide policies designed to promote economic development, distribute wealth more evenly and support gender equality. Under the so-called Swedish Model, taxes pay for unemployment insurance, free education, heavily subsidised childcare and 480 days of paid parental leave that can be split between a child's parents. Swedish unions are powerful and help regulate working conditions by making agreements with employers' organisations and industries. Swedes are guaranteed at least five weeks holiday a year, and just one per cent of the population regularly works more than 50 hours a week, according to the OECD (Organisation for Economic Co-operation and Development). Meanwhile Swedish economic policy

The Swedes' deep-rooted concern for nature is based on an appreciation of their country's natural assets and makes them generally willing advocates of green initiatives.

embraces international competition and a flexible labour market.

Yet, although the lowest jobless rate in a decade was recorded in January 2019 and the economy is stable, the Swedish Model has come under fire from multiple directions in recent years. Right-leaning campaigners and a growing consumer class have called for lower income taxes, increased privatisation of public services and stricter rules for collecting welfare payments. Those on the left argue that the gap between the rich and the poor is widening and have raised concerns about future tax reforms and about maintaining workers' rights in the age of the gig economy. A complex housing crisis, linked to long queues for sought-after rent-controlled apartments, a thriving black subletting market and, until recently, spiralling property prices, has made it increasingly difficult for many to afford to live in Stockholm and other major Swedish cities.

A complex housing crisis has made it increasingly difficult for many to afford to live in Stockholm

Cranes and building sites are a common sight in this rapidly developing city.

Immigration and integration

Debates about living standards in Sweden have also been fuelled by an increase in immigration. National stereotypes of tall, blonde natives with braided hair or long beards are increasingly outdated, with a quarter of the population now identified as having been born abroad or as having two foreign-born parents. The Nordic nation took in more asylum seekers relative to its population size than any other EU country during the peak immigration year of 2015, with refugees from troubled corners including Syria, Iraq, Afghanistan, Eritrea and Somalia seeking shelter here. The perceived squeeze on access to public services and accommodation led to the anti-immigration Sweden Democrat Party increasing its share of the vote for the fourth election in a row in 2018, although the country's other main parties refused to bring it into any coalition government.

Sweden took in more asylum seekers relative to its population size than any other EU country during the peak immigration year of 2015.

High-profile crimes, including a terror attack in central Stockholm in April 2017 that killed five people, and tensions in vulnerable neighbourhoods with high immigrant populations, such as Rinkeby and Tensta, have grabbed global headlines in recent years. But, while Sweden's peaceful image has taken a battering from international media, the number of deadly shootings in the capital actually dropped in 2018, and Stockholm remains one of Europe's safest capitals according to the The Economist Intelligence Unit's Safe Cities Index. Nevertheless, debates continue about how best to integrate and support Sweden's newest residents. The unemployment rate among residents born abroad stood at around 19 per cent in January 2019, compared to a national average of less than seven per cent. Perversely, Sweden's Migration Agency has been criticised for rejecting work permit extensions and deporting highly skilled foreign workers, often based at tech companies in Stockholm, on the basis of small administrative errors made during their residency.

Despite political tensions, support for the European Union is stronger than ever among Swedes

Despite political tensions connected to the European migration crisis, support for the European Union itself is stronger than ever among Swedes. A 2018 poll for Swedish public service broadcaster SVT indicated that 77 per cent of Swedes view ongoing membership as a good thing, with analysts suggesting that the UK's struggles with Brexit are a core reason for many in Sweden to back the status quo.

Cultural norms

Stockholmers tend to view themselves as slightly more cosmopolitan and sophisticated than the average Swede, embracing the latest trends in fashion and music as well as tech. But the capital's residents remain creatures of habit when it comes to Swedish celebrations and traditions (*see p180*), and the cultural norms of balance and moderation also persist. The concept of *lagom* (which roughly translates as 'just enough') pervades daily life; it is sometimes interpreted as a lifestyle ideal that supports a stereotypical image of Swedes caught in a never-ending cycle of coffee-and-pastry breaks and brisk walks. However, its essential message encourages people to be content with what they've got. Meanwhile, Jantelagen, or the 'law of Jante', is a cultural compass that discourages Swedes from being showy about individual successes or possessions. If you want to make friends with a Stockholmer, you're unlikely to win them over by bragging about your latest promotion. In fact, all small talk with strangers is typically kept to a minimum. That said, as a visitor to Sweden's capital you shouldn't struggle to connect with locals if you're looking for help or advice. Swedes are among the best in the world at English as a second language and usually jump at the chance to practise, especially with native speakers – although their all-round modesty means they don't always grasp why so many tourists and immigrants keep falling in love with their quiet northerly country and its fast-evolving capital.

Jantelagen is a cultural compass that discourages Swedes from being showy about individual successes or possessions

Stockholmers tend to view themselves as slightly more cosmopolitan and sophisticated than the average Swede, embracing the latest trends in fashion and music as well as tech.

Eating & Drinking

Stockholm's thriving contemporary food scene proves that Swedish cuisine is so much more than meatballs

While some residents can still remember a time when fish and boiled potatoes dominated the city's menus, the Stockholm food scene has been transformed over the past few decades by the demands of its well-travelled citizens and by an increase in immigration. The range of international tastes available now runs from Mexican street food to Bangladeshi curries. Conversely, New Nordic cuisine, based on Scandinavian culinary heritage and locally sourced ingredients, has also made its mark.

TAK *p89*

Gone fishing

If you are after a classic Swedish cuisine experience, herring – called *sill* on the west coast and *strömming* in Stockholm – is a great place to start. It used to be the staple food of the Swedish diet. Today, this little fish is still much loved and always on the menu, at venues ranging from the cheapest lunch restaurant to the poshest luxury establishment. For lunch, it's often blackened (*sotare*) and served with mashed potatoes, melted butter and lingonberry sauce. A plate of pickled herring (*inlagd strömming*) and new potatoes with special soured cream (*gräddfil*) will make any Swede foggy-eyed. Pickled herring is a prominent feature on a traditional Swedish *smorgasbord*, available in restaurants around Christmas and Easter (start with this, before moving on to the meats), while *gravad strömming* (pickled herring cured with a mustard sauce) is indispensable for celebrating Midsummer. It's served with some beer and *kalled snaps*, a liqueur distilled from potato or grain mash and flavoured with caraway seeds. **Oaxen Slip** (*see p128*) has an innovative pickled herring selection as part of its Sunday brunch menu.

Red kräftor (crayfish) are eaten everywhere when the season starts in August, with crayfish parties galore (preferably outside under a full moon). Cooked with huge amounts of dill, they're an unmissable treat. Try them in traditional style at **Sturehof** (*see p109*), which hosts crayfish events throughout the season. Other fishy treats include *toast Skagen*, a delicious starter of prawns with mayonnaise, lemon and dill, served on toasted rye bread; *lax* (salmon); *gravlax* (salmon cured with sugar and salt), and *torsk* (cod) from the west coast. Though more and more scarce, cod is a vital part of Swedish culinary tradition. At Christmas it is prepared as *lutfisk*: salted and air-dried, then soaked in lye, which transforms it into something that looks and tastes nothing like fish. It's served with peas, butter and a béchamel sauce.

♥ **Best traditional Swedish cuisine**

Den Gyldene Freden *p75*
Classic high-end Swedish dining.

Meatballs for the People *p141*
A contemporary take on a Swedish staple.

Operabaren *p88*
Quality food and impeccable service in sumptuous surroundings.

Pelikan *p142*
Old-fashioned beer hall with a trad menu.

♥ **Best budget eats**

Creperie Fyra Knop *p141*
Cheap, cheerful and atmospheric.

Falafelbaren *p148*
These organic, gluten-free falafels are, arguably, the best in town.

Lily's Burger *p163*
American-style burgers 'n' fries 'n' shakes.

Meno Male *p163*
No-frills neighbourhood pizza joint.

Shaka Shaka *p150*
Pretend you're in Hawaii at this poke bowl cafe.

Meat and two veg

Swedish *köttbullar* (meatballs) are, of course, a speciality, immortalised by the Swedish chef in *The Muppet Show* and made increasingly popular by their prevalence in IKEA canteens around the world (*see p42* Swedish meatballs). A variation is *kåldolmar* (stuffed cabbage rolls), made by wrapping cabbage leaves around minced pork. Other popular meat-based dishes to look out for on menus include *pytt i panna*, diced and fried meat and potatoes, adorned with a fried egg and pickled beetroots, and *rimmad oxbringa*, lightly salted brisket of beef.

Game, such as *älg* (elk) and *rådjur* (roe deer), is conspicuous in the autumn, usually roasted and served with potatoes, lingonberries and a cream sauce. **Ekstedt** (Humlegårdsgatan 17, 08 611 12 10, ekstedt.nu) in Östermalm is one of the most innovative places to try game in the city: the adventurous kitchen takes inspiration from centuries-old techniques, including the use of birch logs for cooking.

In the know
Tipping

It is not standard practice to tip in Swedish restaurants or bars. A service cost of 10 to 15 per cent is added automatically to most bills and locals don't usually offer any extra. In part, this is due to heavily unionised waiting staff being paid more than in many other places in Europe. Sweden's increasingly cash-free economy is also a factor: since many places now refuse payment with notes and coins, it's trickier to leave a little extra on your table when you depart. However, you can request to add a tip when paying by card, and this is becoming more common, especially in fine-dining restaurants that attract an international crowd.

EATING & DRINKING

Falafelbaren

EATING & DRINKING

❤ Meatballs

Although Sweden has a thriving international food scene, the country's most famous traditional dish is one of Stockholm's must-try food experiences. Meatballs, called *köttbullar* in Swedish, are typically made of minced beef or pork (or both) and served with mashed potato, lingonberry jam and a thick gravy. They're a fantastic comfort food, whether sampled at a classic Stockholm restaurant or bought frozen from the supermarket on a cold winter's evening. Despite their global association with Sweden, in recent years there has been a lively debate about where meatballs originate from. The country's official Twitter account @sweden (disappointingly disbanded in 2018), claimed that the Swedish way of serving them is actually based on a recipe King Charles XII brought home from Turkey in the early 18th century as a way of helping to boost relations between the two countries. Others have noted that similar recipes existed in Ancient Chinese cooking and during Roman times. One of the most inventive places in Stockholm to try meatballs with a contemporary twist is **Meatballs for the People** (*see p141*), which serves reindeer, chicken and veggie versions. Popular traditional spots include **Operabaren** (*see p88*), **Kvarnen** (*see p141*) and **Pelikan** (*see p142*). Or you can do as the locals do and sample them in the canteen at a Swedish IKEA store after a long day's shopping.

Meatballs for the People

Café Pascal

Make room for the mushroom

As well as potatoes, lingonberries and dill, you'll find that many Swedish dishes feature foraged wild mushrooms – especially chanterelle (*kantarell*), which can be found all over Sweden. Look out for mushroom *kroppkakor*, old-school potato dumplings that hail from southern Sweden. They're traditionally made with pork and onions, but the tasty mushroom-filled variety sometimes appears as a vegetarian option in restaurants. **Dirty Vegan** (*see p141*) uses mushrooms to create vegan burgers and fritters.

What's for breakfast?

Fermented milk products, such as yoghurt and soured milk, are traditional breakfast foods in Sweden, and often appear in hotel breakfast buffets, as do hard-boiled eggs, linseeds, cereals and breads, smoked salmon and gravlax, pastries – and, if you're lucky, fried cinnamon bread. Bread in Sweden is

❤ Best coffee spots

Café Pascal *p95*
Popular Vasastan java joint.

Il Caffè *p140*
Hang out with Södermalm's hipsters.

Chokladkoppen *p73*
Unmissable hot chocolate in a prime location.

Kaffeverket *p96*
Monochrome decor is the perfect backdrop to great food and coffee.

normally excellent, and ranges from dark, dense rye breads to buttery cake-like bread, the ever-popular sourdough, as well as lots of varieties of crispbread (*knäckebröd*). Bakeries have enjoyed a resurgence in recent years, with quality traditional and more inventive seasonal loaves available for sale at the likes of **Fabrique** (*see p73*) and **Bröd and Salt** (*see p148*).

Eating out

Although Copenhagen is the better-known foodie destination in the region, a growing number of Stockholm restaurants have received global recognition for their culinary prowess and have been awarded Michelin stars. These include **Gastrologik** (*see p107*), run by dynamic duo Jacob Holmström and Anton Bjuhrs, which works exclusively with Swedish produce, and **Sushi Sho** (*see p97*), an intimate Tokyo-inspired sushi bar with head chef Carl Ishizaki at its helm.

Eating out in Stockholm remains pricey by European standards but grabbing a bite with friends during the week has recently become a much more popular pastime, resulting in a boom in budget restaurants and home-delivery options. What's more, many of the city's top restaurants offer lunchtime menus (called *Dagens lunch*) at a fraction of the cost of an evening meal. **Gondolen** (*see p143*) and **TAK** (*see p89*) offer especially good-value deals (see *also right* In the know).

Swedes love to plan ahead, which means that the restaurants of the moment are often packed, and it can sometimes be a battle to find a free table. For popular places, you should always book in advance, especially for Fridays and Saturdays. Many restaurants only accept online reservations, either via their own websites or via the popular booking site **The Fork** (www.thefork.se). Punctuality is a source of national pride in Sweden, so make sure you arrive on time for your reservation. Be aware,

Gastrologik

Hobo *p231*

In the know
Food karma

In a capital that champions start-ups and sustainability, it's perhaps no surprise that Stockholm is the birthplace of the Karma food app (https://karma.life), which allows restaurants and cafés to cut down on food waste by selling off surplus meals. It has taken off in 150 towns and cities across Sweden, as well as in London and Paris, and is a good way to experience meals from some of Stockholm's top restaurants on a budget.

too, that many restaurants close in July (and sometimes for the first half of August).

There is a relaxed dress code in all but the very smartest establishments in Stockholm. Children are welcome in most places and many eateries provide high chairs and kids' menus. All restaurants are smoke-free. Many restaurants will have a version of the menu in English, but at the ones that don't, staff are normally happy to translate. For food terms, *see p246* Vocabulary.

♥ **Best waterfront bars**

Ångbåtsbryggan *p109*
Sip your sundowner surrounded by luxury yachts.

Mälarpaviljongen *p164*
Kick back, relax and drink in the view.

Nyfiken Gul *p142*
Barbecue hotspot.

Solstugan *p164*
Laid-back clifftop watering hole.

Mälarpaviljongen

Drink it all in

When it comes to drinking, few capitals in Europe are as expensive as Stockholm, where high taxes on alcohol can push a pint of beer up to 80 kronor (€7.60), even in the most run-of-the-mill pubs. However, the pleasure of sipping a sundowner on one of the city's waterfront terraces or enjoying a cosy winter tipple in a Scandi-chic hotel lounge usually makes up for the price tag. Wine is popular by the glass but is pricey by the bottle, costing a minimum of 300 kronor (€28) and up to 1000 kronor (€95) in fancier places. For cheaper deals on alcohol, head to the bar around 4pm, when numerous pubs offer happy hour deals on beer and house wines. If you're a fan of fizz, **Folkbaren** (*see p148*) in Södermalm and **Bongo Bar**

In the know
Alcohol rules & regulations

The legal drinking age in Sweden is 18, although some bars and clubs have a minimum entry age of 21. By law, venues have to offer food service to qualify for an alcohol licence; this even applies to music festivals, which means you can only drink alcohol in areas of a festival site where food is served. You have to be 20 to buy alcohol at the state-run off-licences (known as *Systembolaget*). Supermarkets are not permitted to sell alcohol apart from beer with an alcohol content of less than 3.5% (known as *följköl* or *lättöl*).

(*see p110*) in Östermalm are loved by locals for serving discounted early-evening cava.

Beers in Sweden are ranked by alcohol content: *starköl* (over 4.5%) means 'strong beer' and is what you'll typically get as a draft beer on tap. There's also *folköl* (2.25%-3.5%) and *lättöl* (less than 2.25%), which are the only forms of alcohol sold in supermarkets (*see p45* In the know). You'll find a wide selection of pale ales and artisan options in many bars, as well as alcohol-free (*alcoholfri*) and gluten-free (*glutenfri*) beers, which are increasingly popular with clean-living locals.

Many Stockholmers enjoy an excuse to drink a glass or more of *bränvinn* (schnapps) to celebrate a national festival, a birthday or just a sunny afternoon. Schnapps comes in many varieties, highly flavoured with native herbs and spices such as caraway, aniseed, coriander and fennel. The traditional way to drink it is to fill the first glass to the brim, the second only halfway. Before downing, it's customary to sing a *snapsvisa* ('schnapps ditty').

Taking it in turns to buy a round of drinks, as is common in the UK and other Anglophone countries, is not a Swedish custom. If you offer to get the beers in for new local friends, don't expect them to return the favour.

♥ **Best cocktail bars**

At Six *p89*
Classy cocktails and knowledgeable bar staff.

Grand Hotel *p229*
An atmospheric setting and impeccable service.

Pharmarium *p76*
Creative mixology in a former pharmacy.

TAK *p89*
A top terrace in happening Brunkebergstorg.

TAK

Grand Hotel

❤ Fika

Café culture in Sweden is as rich as the coffee the natives consume by the gallon. As the pub is to the Brits, so the café is to the Swedes. The Swedes are among the world's top coffee consumers and, unlike the take-out cup culture prevalent elsewhere, they like to sit down with friends, families or colleagues for their cup of java, often accompanied by a sweet treat. This laid-back and sociable ritual is known as '*fika*'. If you're not in a hurry, take your time and pick a spot with a view, such as **Chokladkoppen** (*see p73*) in Gamla Stan or the panoramic cafe at **Fotografiska** gallery (*see p139*).

Most cafés in Sweden serve the usual range of lattes and cappuccinos. Stockholmers were early adopters of the trend for choosing soya, oat, lactose-free or coconut milk instead of dairy, so don't be afraid to ask for these options. However, in the more traditional *konditori*, coffee may be restricted to the filtered variety and there are fewer milk choices. You'll also find it hard to get a cup of British-style tea, with many cafés only offering fruit and herbal varieties. The exceptions to this are the city's more exclusive hotels, such as the **Grand** (*see p229*) and **At Six** (*see p229*), as well as design store **Svenskt Tenn** (*see p111*), all of which serve afternoon tea.

To accompany your coffee, all cafés serve a selection of biscuits, cakes and sandwiches. The *kanelbulle* (cinnamon bun) is a typical treat, as is the *chokladboll* (a golf ball-sized concoction made of oatmeal, sugar, coffee, cocoa and butter, and normally covered in coconut flakes). Many cafés also serve delicious Swedish cheesecakes (*ostkaka*). Watch out, too, for seasonal favourites: at Christmas time treat yourself to a *lussekatt* (a saffron-flavoured bun) and, in the run-up to Easter, look out for the magnificent *semla*, a truly epic creation of pastry, almond paste and whipped cream.

Café Pascal *p95*

Shopping

Home-grown fashion labels and minimalist design stores abound,
alongside a thriving second-hand scene

Sweden's reputation for cool, contemporary design and cutting-edge, uncomplicated fashion means that Stockholm is a great place to purchase stylish, often understated clothes and homewares, with many shops channelling sleek, minimalist interiors and artful displays. There are hundreds of stores to choose from, with mainstream big-name brands rubbing shoulders with luxury global names, small boutiques and vintage markets.

Stockholm has several major shopping districts, which largely reflect the overall vibe of the surrounding neighbourhood. Glitzy Östermalm is best for exclusive and world-famous labels, while Södermalm hosts the bulk of the city's edgier boutiques, packed with up-and-coming labels suitable for its creative yet aspirational crowd. It's also Stockholm's second-hand hub, mixing vintage record stores with charity-run clothing shops and outdoor markets. Norrmalm has the largest selection of mainstream mid-range chains, alongside one of Europe's finest department stores, NK, which dates back to 1915 and oozes old-world charm. Gamla Stan is mostly a source of tourist tat, but its narrow, cobbled streets are also home to a few retail gems, including antique stores and homeware boutiques.

Designtorget *p92*

Fashion favourites

Sweden's best-known global brands have a strong presence on home soil. You'll find branches of H&M across the city, alongside the group's other popular fashion labels Cos and Weekday, as well as womenswear stores &OtherStories and Monki. Shopaholic Swedophiles in search of the country's most famous denim company, **Acne Studios**, will want to visit flagship location in Södermalm as well as its outlet in Vasastan (*see p91*). Acne merchandise is also available at Sweden's largest department stores **Åhlens City** (*see p91*) and **NK** (*see p93*). These stores are great places to check out other Swedish fashion staples, such as **Whyred** (*see p93*), J.Lindeberg (www.jlindeberg.com), Tiger of Sweden (www.tigerofsweden.com) and Filippa K (www.filippa-k,com), if you don't want to trek between individual branches around the city. Other cult brands to look out for include **Hope** (*see p92*), a fashion-forward gender-neutral label that, in 2017, was one of the first well-known Swedish brands to mark all clothing with both men and women's sizes; contemporary rainwear company **Stutterheim** (*see p145*), and outdoor gear specialist **Fjällraven** (www.fjallraven.com), which is the brand behind the iconic *Kånken* backpacks that have become ubiquitous around the world in recent years.

SoFo (*see p137*) in Södermalm is the best focal point for fashion fans seeking lesser-known ateliers and cutting-edge labels. Notable stores here are **Nudie Jeans** (*see p145*), whose products are designed to be worn without washing for six months and come with a free repairs for life; **Swedish Hasbeens** (*see p145*) the country's much-hyped ecological clog chain, and streetwear store **SneakersnStuff** (*see p145*). **Grandpa** (*see p144*), a large fashion and accessories store, is the best one-stop shop in the area, selling mens- and womenswear collections from both Nordic and international designers.

❤ **Best fashion boutiques**

Acne *p91*
Denim delights.

Grandpa *p144*
One-stop fashion for all.

Sandqvist *p152*
Bags of quality.

Stutterheim *p145*
Great gear for bad weather.

Sandqvist

Grandpa

In the know
Opening hours

High street stores are typically open from 10am until 7pm or 8pm Monday to Saturday in the city centre, while some shopping malls have later opening hours. Many shops are also open on Sundays, typically from 11am or noon until 6pm. Supermarket opening hours are more generous, with most open between 7am and 10pm or 11pm seven days a week.

❤ Hornstull Market

Hornstulls Strand 1-13, Södermalm (www. hornstullsmarknad.se/info-english). T-bana Hornstull. **Open** *Apr-Sept 11am-5pm Sat, Sun. Closed Oct-Mar.* **Map** *p147 G13.*

Stockholm fashion hounds delight in hitting Hornstull's waterfront on weekends between April and October, where stylish locals sell off second-hand clothing at the area's compact but popular market. Here, beneath brightly coloured bunting, you can source anything from weathered leather jackets and snow boots to winter-ready ice skates or scissored denim shorts. Other sellers use the market to sell vintage homeware items ranging from antique razors and shoehorns to lamps and cutlery. Thanks to Sweden's long history of fashion and design, the quality of items is usually high. Some weeks you'll also find creative locals showcasing their own new designs, from T-shirts and babygros to greetings cards and posters. You'll also want to eat your way around the varied food trucks, which serve up gourmet burgers, veggie curries, Mexican-style tacos and the like.

Although some of the hype surrounding Hornstull has shifted to these accompanying food trucks in recent years, it is the clothing stalls that are the key to Stockholmers' shopping habits, as symbols of a deep nationwide love affair with recycling and rehoming garments. Green-thinking, thrifty Swedes have been fans of flea markets (called *loppis* in Swedish) for decades.

Pop-up *loppis* are a common sight across Stockholm in spring and summer time, usually advertised a few weeks in advance on social media. The suburbs of Midsommarkransen (*see p154*) and Bagarmossen host some of the busiest. Hornstull is also home to the annual **Återvinningsfesten** market (www. atervinningsfesten.se), one of the biggest second-hand events in Europe which takes place on the last Sunday in May each year and sees hundreds of stalls sprawling across the suburb.

Other places to source well-preserved vintage clothing in Stockholm include **Beyond Retro** (*see p151*) in Södermalm, and **Arkivet** (*see p98*) in Vasastan. There are also numerous impressively organised charity shops run by **Stockholms Stadsmission** (www.stadsmissionen.se), the **Red Cross** (www.rodakorset.se) and **Myrorna** (www.myrorna.se), which donates profits to the Salvation Army. You never know what you might find...

Design delights

If you're looking to take home a taste of Sweden's globally admired homeware and design output, two must-visit outlets are **Designtorget** (*see p92*) and **Granit** (*see p144*), which stock relatively affordable portable items, including glassware and kitchenware, trays, textiles and stationary. Both have several locations around the city. **Lagerhaus** also has a decent collection for the thriftiest of shoppers.

Stockholm's more high-end design boutiques are well worth a visit, even if you don't have the funds for shopping and shipping their wares. **Nordiska Galleriet** (*see p112*) in Norrmalm, open since 1912 with three floors of stylish armchairs, lamps, rugs, shelves and tables, is a fun place to fantasise about your dream Scandi-style apartment. In Östermalm, the bold prints at **Svenskt Tenn** (*see p111*) challenge the idea that Swedish design always has to be minimalist, while **Dusty Deco** (*see p112*) features vintage furniture and lighting

❤ **Best design stores**

Designtorget *p92*
Covetable and portable homewares.

Granit *p144*
Simple, affordable, stylish essentials.

NK *p93*
Classic Swedish department store.

Nordiska Galleriet *p112*
Furnish your fantasy apartment.

Svenskt Tenn *p111*
Fabulous fabrics by Josef Frank.

Stutterheim *p145*

SWEDISH MELANCHOLY AT ITS DRIEST

from Swedish and global heavyweights.
For more information on Sweden's
design history (*see p222*).

Of course, a round-up of Swedish design
shopping isn't complete without mentioning its
best-known flat-pack furniture brand: **IKEA**. If
you're sticking around long enough to furnish
an apartment, or simply fancy tasting the
bargain meatballs in its on-site canteen, there
are two giant IKEA complexes in Stockholm's
outer suburbs (Kungens Kurva and Barkaby) as
well as a kitchen design concept store in the city
centre (Regeringsgatan 65).

Tasty treats

Stockholm has a handful of fabulous
delicatessens, where you can stock up on
non-perishable traditional Swedish treats to
take home: lingonberry sauce (*lyngonsylt*),
cinnamon snaps (*pepperkakor*), pickled herring
(*sill*) or crispbread (*knäckebröd*). **Paradiset**
(Sweden's answer to America's Whole Foods
Market) has a store in the basement of NK (*see*

♥ Best delicatessens

Eataly *p92*
Italian treats in a landmark
building.

Meatballs for the People
p141
Takeaway deli meals
take the sweat out of self-
catering.

Östermalms Saluhall *p112*
Classic food hall featuring
the best produce.

ROT Butik & Kök *p145*
Perfect picnic pitstop.

Urban Deli *p142*
Shop for delicious fresh
produce or tuck in to the
restaurant's own offerings.

Nordiska Galleriet

Stockholm's Christmas Markets

Where to get your festive retail fix

Although Stockholm's Christmas markets can't compete with the likes of Tallin, Vienna or Budapest in terms of scale, they are charming shopping spots where you can get into the seasonal spirit each year. They typically sell Scandinavian souvenirs, such as Christmas gnomes, reindeer rugs and woollen socks and mittens, alongside foodstuffs including jams, cheese, smoked meats and spices. It is traditional to browse the stalls while drinking *glögg* (Swedish mulled wine) and snacking on *pepparkakor* (gingerbread snaps).

Open-air museum **Skansen** (see p122) hosts one of the most popular markets, although you have to pay the standard entry fee to gain access. Here, you'll be greeted by staff dressed in traditional costumes. **Stortorgets Julmarknad** (www.stortorgetsjulmarknad.com) in the Old Town, which has been running since 1915, is another of the best-known locations and is free to visit. At the Christmas market in **Kungsträdgården** (see p83) you can test out the ice rink after you've done your shopping. All of these markets are usually open from late-November until just before Christmas. Note that they close in the early evening; Stockholm doesn't have a late-night market scene.

You'll also find numerous pop-up markets on various weekends during December. These vary from year to year but have previously included a lakeside market outside **Drottningholm Palace** (see p168) and **Långholmens Julmarknad** (https://langholmen.com/aktiviteter/julmarknad) in the grounds of a former prison (see p152). A quirkier place to source gifts is Sweden's largest university for arts, crafts and design in **Telefonplan** (see p154), where students organise their own annual Christmas market, usually on the first weekend in December, selling creative contemporary posters, canvases, textiles, jewellery and cards.

p93) as well as branches in Södermalm and Sickla. **Urban Deli** (*see p142*) and **ROT Butik & Kök** (*see p145*) are also a good bet. These stores are also where to source top-quality ready-to-heat meals – a great option if you're renting an apartment in the city and want to save money on eating out. They also stock more contemporary offerings from vegan raw bars to dried blueberries.

For gift-boxed sweet snacks, NK has an in-house chocolatier, or try **Gamla Stan's Polkagriskokeri** (*see p77*), **Östermalm's Saluhall** (*see p112*), or branches of **Chokladfabriken** (Chocolate Factory) around the city. Sweden's biggest chocolate brand, Maribou, can be found in most supermarkets and convenience stores.

Svenskt Tenn *p111*

Shopping malls

Stockholm has a surprisingly large selection of shopping malls, which, for the most part, are minimalist, spacious, warm and well-lit. These can be a good choice if you're short

Granit *p144*

NK *p93*

on time and keen to check out a range of Swedish and international labels during your visit, or if you're in need of an indoor activity on a harsh winter day.

In Norrmalm, **Gallerian** (Hamngatan 37, www.gallerian.se) is best for high-street brands, while **MOOD** (Regeringsgatan 48, www.moodstockholm.se) plays host to slightly flashier fashion and design stores, alongside several beauty salons where you can get a pricey blow-dry, manicure or lash-lift. **Sturegallerian** (Stureplan 4, Östermalm, www.sturegallerian.se) has an even more exclusive feel. For a more low-key experience, try the smaller **Skrapan** (Götgatan 78, https://skrapan.se) or **Bruno** (*see p144*) malls in Södermalm, which are each home to a cluster of budget to mid-range Nordic brands.

Further afield in Solna, the largest shopping centre in the Stockholm district, **Mall of Scandinavia** (www.mallofscandinavia.se) has more than 220 stores. It's a ten-minute journey on the commuter train from Stockholm City. You can also reach discount shopping hub **Stockholm Quality Outlet** (https://qualityoutlet.com) in Barkaby by commuter train; it sells unsold items from premium brands' earlier collections.

In the know
Read all about it

Swedes' exceptional grasp of English and the slow uptake of e-readers for such a usually tech-savvy country mean that Stockholm has a range of bookstores selling English-language material. The **English Bookshop** (Södermannagatan 22, Södermalm, 08 790 55 10, www.bookshop.se) is the largest and also hosts events and readings in English. Branches of **Pocket Shop** (www.pocketshop.se) throughout the city sell current bestsellers in English while **Hedengrens** in Sturegallerian (*see p112*) is an independent store that stocks books in English, French, German, Spanish, Italian, Danish, Portuguese and Norwegian. You can usually find something in English in the city's many second-hand thrift stores too.

Explore

Skeppsbron, Gamla Stan

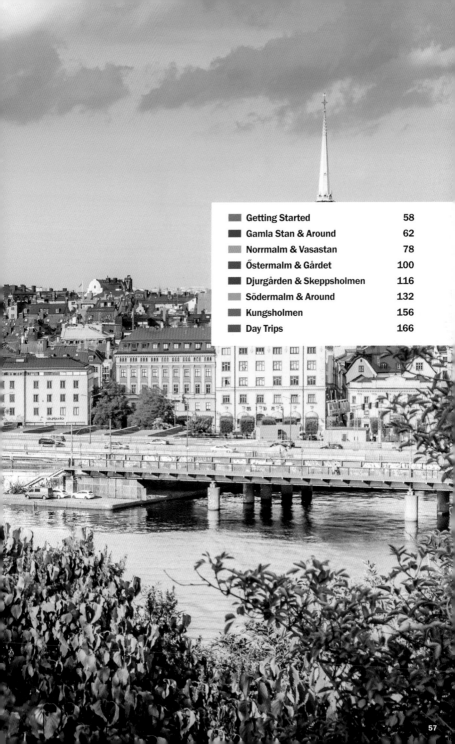

Getting Started

Stockholm is a capital on the water, spread across different islands that are cleverly connected by bridges, tunnels and ferries. Fourteen islands make up the city centre proper, which links Sweden's third-largest lake, Lake Mälaren, with the Baltic Sea. These inner islands are not to be confused with the Stockholm archipelago, a sprawling collection of around 30,000 more sparsely inhabited islands and islets that begins a few miles east of the capital.

Despite its topography, Stockholm is relatively compact, and it's easy to walk between many of the most popular attractions. It's also a bike-friendly city. When you do need public transport, the city's underground network is usually the fastest option.

❤ **Best views**

Fotografiska café *p139*
Big picture windows offer panoramic views.

Kastellholmen *p129*
Enjoy Djurgården views from the cliffs of this tiny island.

Monteliusvägen *p149*
The boardwalk gives spectacular views of Gamla Stan.

Västerbron *p160*
Climb this large bridge for a postcard-perfect cityscape.

❤ **Best gardens**

Bergianska Trädgården *p115*
Botanists and picnickers love this botanical garden.

Rosendals Trädgärd *p127*
Organic gardens with an idyllic café and a botanical shop.

Stora Henriksvik *p154*
The garden of the old-school Långholmen Café.

Tantolunden allotments *p146*
Much-coveted allotment gardens on Södermalm.

Mårten Trotzigs Gränd *p66*

An overview of the city

For this guide, we begin in the city's historic core, **Gamla Stan** (*see p62*), meaning 'Old Town', which dates back to medieval times. Its labyrinth of cobbled streets is home to some of Stockholm's best-loved sights, such as Stortorget (*see p70*) – the capital's oldest square – and the Royal Palace.

Across the water to the north, **Norrmalm** (*see p78*) is Stockholm's central shopping and business district. This area includes the recently revitalised Brunkebergstorg neighbourhood (*see p85*), which boasts some of the city's best boutique hotels and panoramic bars.

To the east of Gamla Stan, **Djurgården** (*see p116*) is a green island oasis that packs in many of the Swedish capital's premier tourist attractions. Among them are the world class Vasamuseet (*see p125*), which houses a jaw-dropping 17th-century warship, and ABBA The Museum (*see p121*).

Södermalm (*see p132*), south of the city centre, is where Stockholm's most creative crowd hangs out, in organic cafés, craft beer bars and vintage stores. By contrast, **Östermalm** (*see p100*), in the north-east, is the land of plenty for well-heeled residents who frequent its prestigious restaurants and fancy boutiques, or moor their yachts along Strandvägen, one of the city's poshest streets.

Kungsholmen (*see p156*) to the west is a calm, largely residential area, but you won't want to miss its most iconic building, Stadshuset (City Hall; *see p161*), or a scenic stroll along its tree-lined waterfront boulevard, Norr Mälarstrand.

Beyond the city centre, there are attractions to discover in Stockholm's outer suburbs, such as Telefonplan and Sundbyberg, which are rapidly evolving to cater to the city's fast-growing cosmopolitan population. And finally, our **Day Trips** chapter (*see p166*) covers the islands of the Stockholm archipelago to the east, as well as castles and historic towns to the north and west.

In the know
Running the city

Stockholmers love to run. To participate in the jogging craze, visitors can join a guided tour with a sporty local through **Run With Me Stockholm** (www.runwithme. world/stockholm) or take part in regular free social events hosted by running clubs including **Ssideline City Run Club** (SSidelineCity.com), **Mikeller Run Club Stockholm** (mikellerrunningclub.dk/ chapters/stockholm-2) and **Adidas Runners Stockholm** (www.adidas.com.vn/ adidasrunners/community/stockholm).

In the know
Cards not cash

Beware that Stockholm is almost entirely cash-free, with many cafés, restaurants, hotels and tourist attractions refusing to take notes and coins. If your bank charges for international card transactions, consider investing in a prepaid debit card instead.

Getting around

Stockholm's compact centre is a pleasure to walk around. Bikes and electric scooters come in handy for roaming further afield. There's a popular public bicycle-share scheme, plus numerous bicycle hire outlets and app-based scooter rental agencies – for all, *see p238*. Some city centre hotels such as **Downtown Camper** (*see p231*) and **Hobo Hotel** (*see p231*) also offer bikes for guests.

The city's metro system, **Tunnelbana** (T-bana for short) is fast, efficient and operates through the night at weekends. Major bus routes run round the clock, seven days a week. Trams, commuter trains and ferries also connect the capital's various districts. All these services are operated by the same company, **Storstockholms**

Lokaltrafik (SL), so you can easily switch between different transport modes. SL has an easy-to-use app that provides precise information on how best to connect between destinations; you can choose whether you are travelling immediately or select a later time or date. The same functions are available online at www.sl.se.

Tickets must be bought in advance, from self-service machines available at underground stations and major bus stations, or Pressbyrån convenience stores. A single journey up to 75 minutes costs 45kr. If you are planning frequent trips, it is usually better value to buy a plastic SL card and top up with credit, or buy a 24-hour, 72-hour or weekly pass.

▶ *For more information on all of Stockholm's transport options, see p235 Getting Around.*

Information and visitor passes

The main tourist office is **Stockholm Visitor Centre**, which is located inside the city's public cultural centre, Kulturhuset Stadsteatern (*see p244*), close to the central station. **Royal Djurgården Visitor Center** (*see p124*) offers a special tourist information service for Djurgården island.

Ocean Bus Estelle

There's good news for budget-conscious visitors to Stockholm: admission to the main exhibition spaces at more than a dozen public museums is completely free, including the Nationalmuseum (*see p84*), the Swedish Museum of Natural History (*see p115*) and Moderna Museet (*see p130*). This means that the major pre-paid card for tourists, the **Stockholm Pass** (www.stockholmpass.com) makes most sense for those visitors who are planning to go to several eligible fee-paying attractions or to enjoy multiple boat and bus tours (*see below*). The adult pass costs 669kr for one day, 929kr for two days, 1129kr for three days or 1479kr for five days, with reductions for under-16s. It can be bought online and downloaded directly to your phone or collected in person from the Stockholm Visitor Centre, from Strömkajen or from the Royal Djurgården Visitor Center.

Tours

Hop-on, hop-off bus tours run by **Stromma** (www.stromma.se) and **Red Sightseeing** (www.redsightseeing.com) are a popular way to see the main sights if you have limited time. They call at major attractions and have multilingual audio guides on board. The Stromma services are included with the Stockholm Pass (*see above*). Stromma also offers hop-on, hop-off boat services and longer tours by boat to major archipelago ports, which give a sense of the geography of this watery city. The amphibious **Ocean Bus Estelle** (oceanbus.se) tours Stockholm's main sites by both land and water.

Otherwise, the compact city centre is perfect for exploring on foot. Free guided walking tours in multiple languages are offered by **Free Tour Stockholm** (freetourstockholm.com). Fans of Swedish crime writer Stig Larsson can follow in the footsteps of his characters on the Millennium Trilogy walk, while the **100 Point Challenge** is a unique self-guided walking tour that combines race, game and quiz elements (*see p66*). **Rent a Bike** (*see p238*) offers guided cycling tours of the city; see the website for details.

In the know
Rush hour

Stockholmers typically enjoy a short working day compared to workers in many other European countries, leaving the office between 4pm and 5.30pm. It's best to avoid T-Centralen station during these times and also between 7am and 9am in the morning – this is when the station is at its busiest and the so-called 'stress tunnel' between the different metro lines is at its most congested.

Gamla Stan & Around

Gamla Stan – meaning 'Old Town' – is where the embryonic city was formed more than 750 years ago. The island straddles the strategic gateway between the global reaches of the Baltic Sea and the expansive inland trade routes of Lake Mälaren. Many of its structures stand on foundations from the 17th and 18th centuries, packed into narrow, meandering cobbled streets that today echo with the footfalls of tourists and the lucky few who are residents. The Swedish royal family have had their 'official' home here for hundreds of years, and the immense Kungliga Slottet (Royal Palace) is still the main sight.

Two islets lie to the north and west of Gamla Stan: Helgeandsholmen is the site of the Swedish Parliament, while Riddarholmen houses government buildings along its cobbled streets.

♥ **Don't miss**

1 Stortorget *p70*
Stockholm's prettiest public square.

2 Livrustkammaren *p69*
Suits of armour and royal history.

3 Nobelmuseet *p69*
Learn about the history of the famous prizes.

4 Riddarholmskyrkan *p69*
One of the city's most distinctive churches.

5 Mårten Trotzigs Gränd *p66*
The narrowest street in the Swedish capital.

6 Changing the Guard *p67*
A rare dose of pomp and ceremony in this egalitarian-minded city.

PALATIVM
ORDINIS
EQVESTRIS·

...ENTIA· CLARIS·MAIORVM·EXEMPLIS·A...

GVSTAVO...

Riddarhuset *p66*

GAMLA STAN

Before Stockholm sprawled out on to neighbouring farmland, the whole city was limited to this small island, referred to historically as 'the city between the bridges'. A fortress was built on the island's north-eastern shore around the 11th century, but there's no record of an actual city on Gamla Stan until Birger Jarl's famous letter of 1252, which mentioned the name 'Stockholm' for the first time (*see p213*). The island city grew into a mess of winding streets and ramshackle houses until most of the western half burned down in 1625. City planners finally crafted a few right angles and tore down the crumbling defensive wall around the island to make room for waterfront properties for the city council.

The old fortress of Tre Kronor, which stood on a hill at the highest point in Gamla Stan, was ravaged by a fire in 1697, leaving only the north wing. Royal architect Nicodemus Tessin the Younger was tasked with designing a new royal palace in its place, with a Roman Baroque exterior. The architect Carl Hårleman completed Tessin's work on the **Kungliga Slottet** in 1754.

The low, yellow-brown building is imposing rather than pretty; its northern façade looms menacingly as you approach Gamla Stan over the bridges from Norrmalm. A square central building around an open courtyard is flanked by two wings extending to the west and two more to the east. Between its eastern wings lie the gardens of Logården, and between the curved western wings is an outer courtyard; the ticket/information office and gift shop are located in the south-western curve. The southern façade with its triumphal central arch is the most attractive; it runs along Slottsbacken, a large open space that slopes up from Skeppsbron and the water to the back of **Storkyrkan**. It was left undeveloped to make it easier to defend the palace.

Although the palace is the official residence of the royal family, the King and Queen live west of the city at Drottningholm Palace (itself well worth a visit; *see p168*).

Visitors are welcome to roam around the sumptuous **Representationsvåningarna** (Royal Apartments) and museums: the **Museum Tre Kronor** explores the history of the palace, while the **Skattkammaren** (Treasury), **Livrustkammaren** (Royal Armoury) and **Gustav III's Antikmuseum** (Museum of Antiquities) show off its prized possessions. The limited opening hours and sheer size of the place mean that you'll probably have to visit a couple of times if you want to see it all. The **Kungliga Myntkabinettet** (Royal Mint Collection), which was formerly housed on Slottsbacken, has been moved to the Swedish History Museum in Östermalm (*see p106*).

There are plenty of other sights on Gamla Stan apart from the Royal Palace. At the top of Slottsbacken stands the imposing yellow bulk of Stockholm's de facto cathedral, **Storkyrkan** (Great Church), the scene of royal weddings and coronations. The obelisk in front of the church, designed by Louis Jean Desprez, was erected in 1799 as a memorial to those who fought in Gustav III's war against Russia in 1788-90. Trångsund, the street at the front of the church, leads down to Gamla Stan's main square, **Stortorget** (*see p70*).

Gamla Stan's main thoroughfares of Västerlånggatan, Österlånggatan, Stora

---

♥ Time to eat & drink

Coffee break
Chokladkoppen *p73*

Classic lunch
Tradition *p75*

Cocktails with atmosphere
Pharmarium *p76*, Tweed *p76*

Swedish fine dining
Den Gyldene Freden *p75*

♥ Time to shop

Fashion whatever the weather
Rain Store by Stutterheim *p77*

Creative homewares
Charlotte Nicolin *p76*, Iris Hantverk *p77*

Sweet treats
Gamla Stans Polkagriskokeri *p77*

Geek-tastic books and more
Science Fiction Bokhandeln *p77*

In the know
Getting around

Many of the narrow, cobbled streets of Gamla Stan and Riddarholmen are pedestrianised, so the whole area is best explored on foot. All branches of the city's red and green subway lines call at Gamla Stan station, which is on the west side of the island. Buses stop on the area's main traffic thoroughfares: Munkbroleden and Skeppsbron.

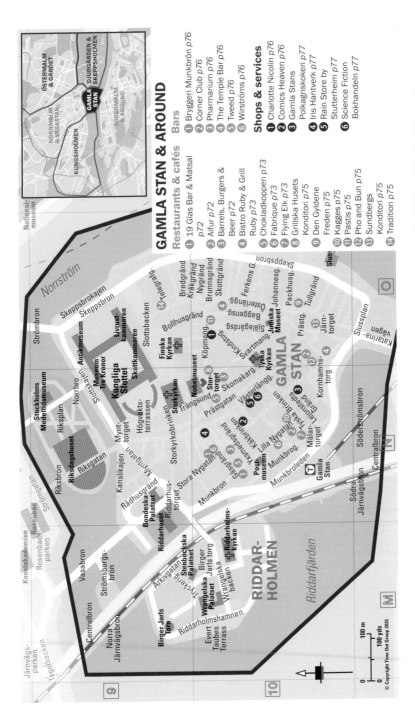

GAMLA STAN & AROUND

Restaurants & cafés
1. 19 Glas Bar & Matsal p72
2. Aifur p72
3. Barrels, Burgers & Beer p72
4. Bistro Ruby & Grill Ruby p73
5. Chokladkoppen p73
6. Fabrique p73
7. Flying Elk p73
8. Grillska Husets Konditori p75
9. Den Gyldene Freden p75
10. Kagges p75
11. Pastis p75
12. Pho and Bun p75
13. Sundbergs Konditori p75
14. Tradition p75

Bars
1. Bryggeri Munkbrön p76
2. Corner Club p76
3. Pharmarium p76
4. The Temple Bar p76
5. Tweed p76
6. Wirströms p76

Shops & services
1. Charlotte Nicolin p76
2. Comics Heaven p76
3. Gamla Stans Polkagriskokeri p77
4. Iris Hantverk p77
5. Rain Store by Stutterheim p77
6. Science Fiction Bokhandeln p77

© Copyright Time Out Group 2020

100 m
100 yds

65

Combining race, game and quiz elements, 100 Point Challenge (www.100pointchallenge.com/stockholm) is a unique sightseeing tour that encourages visitors to explore Stockholm while learning about the city's history and culture. The challenge starts at Svartmangatan 18 in Gamla Stan, with many of the clues taking you through some of this area's most scenic spots.

Nygatan and Lilla Nygatan run north–south along the island. Crowded **Västerlånggatan** draws tourists to its many small shops, while the parallel street – narrow, curving **Prästgatan** – is a quiet alternative to the hubbub and far more atmospheric, giving you a much better idea of life in the crowded medieval city. At the southern end of Västerlånggatan is **Mårten Trotzigs Gränd**, the city's narrowest street at only 90 centimetres wide. You'll notice it from the number of tourists gathered around its entrance, taking snaps of the photogenic steep steps. Just down from here is **Järntorget**, another of the island's main squares, where you can sit outdoors and enjoy the excellent cakes and pastries of **Sundbergs Konditori**.

There are only a handful of hotels on Gamla Stan; two of them – the **Victory Hotel** (www.thecollectorshotels.se) and the **Scandic Gamla Stan** – are located on Lilla Nygatan, as is the surprisingly interesting **Postmuseum**. On nearby Stora Nygatan (nos.10-12) you can visit the **Forum för Levande Historia** (Stora Nygatan 10, 08 723 87 50, www.levandehistoria.se, closed Sun, free), a government exhibition centre and library focusing on human rights, racism and genocide.

The island's churches include the **Tyska Kyrkan** (German Church) and the **Finska Kyrkan** (Finnish Church) – proof of Sweden's long connections with its European neighbours. The latter is housed in a 1640s building opposite the Kungliga Slottet; originally a ball-games court for the palace, it has been the religious centre of the Finnish community since 1725.

Gamla Stan also contains a number of beautiful palaces, all former homes of the aristocracy. On the island's north-western corner is the lovely **Riddarhuset** (08 723 39 90, www.riddarhuset.se), built in the second half of the 17th century as the seat of the Swedish nobility; they governed the country from here until parliamentary reforms in 1866. The palace is still owned by the Swedish nobility but is open to visitors for an hour a day (11am-noon Mon-Fri, 60kr, 40kr reductions). Come to admire the coats of arms (more than 2,000 in all), signet collection and early 17th-century chair with ivory engravings. Another way to see inside is to attend a concert by the **Stockholm Sinfonietta**. Also on Riddarhustorget is **Bondeska Palatset**, designed by Tessin the Elder in the 1660s; it has been the seat of the Supreme Court since 1949. Just to the south of Riddarhuset, a bridge crosses from Gamla Stan to the island of **Riddarholmen**.

Riddarholmen

Cut off from Gamla Stan by several lanes of traffic and a narrow canal, the tiny island of Riddarholmen to the west is a sanctuary of cobbled streets, 17th-century palaces and lovely water views. Several of the island's palaces are today used by the Swedish courts and government authorities. They are seldom open to the public but taking a walk to view their exteriors is highly recommended.

Riddarholmen's main attraction is the medieval brick church, **Riddarholmskyrkan**. Next to the church is **Birger Jarls Torg**, with an 1854 statue of Stockholm's founder, Birger Jarl, at its centre, and the huge white **Wrangelska Palatset** to the west. Constructed as a nobleman's residence in the mid 17th century, the palace was extensively rebuilt a few decades later by Tessin the Elder, under its new owner, Field Marshal Carl Gustaf Wrangel. The palace became the home of the royal family for several years after the Tre Kronor fire of 1697 (see p216). On the other side of the square is the well-preserved, pink-coloured **Stenbockska Palatset**, built in the 1640s by state councillor Fredrik Stenbock, but extended and renovated in succeeding centuries.

Down by the water on **Evert Taubes Terrass**, you'll find one of the best views in Stockholm, looking out across the choppy water of Riddarfjärden and towards the shores of Lake Mälaren. The terrace is named after the much-loved Swedish poet and troubadour Evert Taube (who died in 1976); there's a bronze sculpture of him, lute in hand, near the water. It's also a prime spot to celebrate the arrival of spring on Walpurgis Night, with a bonfire by the water and communal singing. Author and dramatist August Strinberg was born here in 1849; a plaque in Swedish on a nearby wall commemorates the site of his birth.

North along the waterfront, on Norra Riddarholmshamnen, is the distinctive circular **Birger Jarls Torn**, the only remnant of the defensive fortifications built by Gustav Vasa around 1530 (along with part of the Wrangelska Palatset). The tower was given its name in the 19th century when it was mistakenly thought to have been built under Birger Jarl 600 years earlier. It's not open to the public.

Helgeandsholmen

Helgeandsholmen is the tiny oval-shaped island that's connected to the southern end of Norrmalm and the northern end of Gamla Stan by two bridges: a pedestrian one at the western end and a road bridge at the eastern end. The **Riksdagshuset** (Parliament Building; Riksgatan 3, 08 786 48 62, www. riksdagen.se) dominates the whole western half of the island. As you walk north, the new Parliament Building is to your left and the old one to your right, joined by two stone arches. The older section, completed in 1905, was designed by Aron Johansson, with two chambers for a bicameral Parliament, Baroque motifs and a grand staircase. At the same time, he also designed a curved stone building across the street for the Bank of Sweden. After the country changed over to a unicameral system in 1971, the bank moved out, the roof was flattened, and the Parliament's new glass-fronted debating chamber was built on top. The Parliament is open for guided tours year round. You can also sit in the public gallery when Parliament is in session and listen to debates. For more information, refer to the very detailed website (with text in Swedish and English).

Beneath the lawns at the other end of the island, the **Stockholms Medeltidsmuseum** provides a fascinating insight into life in medieval Stockholm.

Sights & museums

Judiska Museet

Själagårdsgatan 19 (08 30 15 00, http:// judiskmuseet.se). T-bana Gamla Stan. **Open** *11am-5pm Tue, Wed, Sat, Sun; 11am-8pm Thur; 11am-4pm Fri. Guided tours in English 2pm Tue-Sun.* **Admission** *100kr; 80kr reductions; free under-19s.* **Map** *p65 O10.*

Following a relocation from the Vasastan district in 2016, the Jewish Museum is now housed inside the oldest preserved synagogue in Stockholm. The museum's revamped core exhibition focuses on the history and culture of Jews living in Sweden. Combining interactive exhibits and traditional displays, it tells the story of Sweden's first Jewish communities and some of the challenges they have faced since then. There are also art installations, including a moving collection of handwritten letters by German Jews seeking asylum in Sweden during World War Two.

Kungliga Slottet

Slottsbacken 1 (08 402 61 00, royalpalaces. se/english). T-bana Gamla Stan or bus 2, 43, 55, 76, 96. **Representationsvåningarna, Museum Tre Kronor, Skattkammaren** *Oct-Apr 10am-4pm daily. May-Sept 10am-5pm daily (Royal Apartments may close for official engagements; check online for details).* **Gustav III's Antikmuseum** *May-Sept 10am-5pm daily. Closed Oct-Apr.* **Admission** *160kr; 80kr reductions; free under-7s. Free with SC.* **Map** *p65 N9.*

You'll need more than one visit to see all the attractions at the palace. Buy the combined ticket (rather than individual tickets for each attraction), which provides admission to everything except the Livrustkammaren.

In the know
♥ Changing the Guard

The **Högvakten** (Royal Guard) has been stationed at the Royal Palace since 1523, and the Changing the Guard ceremony is a popular tourist attraction. It takes place daily in summer (12.15pm Mon-Sat, 1.15pm Sun) and three times a week in winter (12.15pm Wed and Sat, 1.15pm Sun), when around 20 soldiers in full livery go through their paces in the palace's outer western courtyard to the sound of a marching band. The whole thing lasts about 40 minutes.

Kungliga Slottet p67

Gustav III's Antikmuseum
Entrance on Lejonbacken (Slottskajen).

This museum of Roman statues and busts, in two halls in the north-east wing of the palace, has been laid out to look exactly as it did in the 1790s when King Gustav III returned from Italy with the collection, which includes *Apollo and His Nine Muses* and the sleeping *Endymion*. The repairs and additions made to the statues at the time have been left intact, as well as the odd combinations of pieces, such as table legs on fountains. Nothing is labelled, in accordance with the period, so you should try and take the 20-minute tour (conducted in English) or borrow a pamphlet if you want to make the most of your visit.

Museum Tre Kronor
Entrance on Lejonbacken (Slottskajen).

A boardwalk built through the palace cellars, along with several models, enables visitors to see how war, fire and wealth have shaped the palace as it is today. An old well from the former courtyard, a 13th-century defensive wall and the arched brick ceilings are evidence of how the palace was built up around the fortress that was once there. Panels describe life within the castle, archaeological discoveries and building techniques.

Representationsvåningarna
Entrance in western courtyard.

The Royal Apartments occupy two floors of the palace and are entered by a grand staircase in the western wing. Since it's the stories behind the rooms and decorations that make the palace especially interesting – such as Gustav III's invitation to aristocrats to watch him wake up in the morning – taking a guided tour is highly recommended. Banquets are held

several times a year in Karl XI's Gallery in the State Apartments on the second floor. Heads of state stay in the Guest Apartments during their visits to the capital, and for this reason part or all of the palace may be occasionally closed. Downstairs in the Bernadotte Apartments, portraits of the current dynasty's ancestors hang in the Bernadotte Gallery. Medals and orders of various kinds are awarded in the Apartments of the Orders of Chivalry, and paintings of coats of arms decorate its walls. Until 1975, the monarch opened parliament each year in the Hall of State, and directly across from this lies the Royal Chapel with pew ends made in the 1690s for the Tre Kronor castle. Services are held every Sunday, and all are welcome to attend.

Skattkammaren
Entrance on Slottsbacken.

The regalia of past Swedish royal families sparkles behind glass, with orbs, sceptres and crowns in adults' and children's sizes. The crowns are still in use for the monarch's inauguration and were present at the wedding of Carl Gustav and Silvia. The museum also contains Gustav Vasa's etched sword of state from 1541, the coronation cloak of Oscar II and the ornate silver baptismal font of Karl XI.

In the know
Standing small

At just 15cm tall, *Järnpojke* (Iron Boy) is the smallest public monument in Stockholm. Located just behind the **Finska Kyrkan** (Finnish Church, *see p66*) in Gamla Stan, the sculpture was created in 1954 by Swedish artist Liss Eriksson. Its shiny head is testament to local superstition that stroking the statue will bring good luck.

♥ Kungliga Slottet: Livrustkammaren

Slottsbacken 3 (08 402 30 30, www. livrustkammaren.se). T-bana Gamla Stan or bus 2, 43, 55, 76, 96. **Open** *Sept-Apr 11am-5pm Tue, Wed, Fri-Sun; 11am-8pm Thur. May, June 11am-5pm Tue-Sun. July, Aug 10am-6pm Tue-Sun.* **Admission** *Free.* **Map** *p65 O9.*

The Royal Armoury is one of the palace's best museums – don't miss it. Founded in 1633, it is Sweden's oldest museum and is stuffed full of armour, weapons and clothes from the 16th century onwards. The museum is housed in the palace's former cellars, which were originally used for storing potatoes and firewood. With wonderfully descriptive texts, the museum's first room shows what a bloody and dangerous business being a king once was. It contains the masked costume King Gustav III wore when he was assassinated in 1792, and the stuffed body of Streiff, the horse that Gustav II Adolf was riding when he was killed in battle in 1632. Don't overlook the glass jar preserving the stomach contents of one of the conspirators to Gustav III's murder. Other rooms display splendid mounted knights, suits of armour, swords and muskets. Two rooms of clothes and toys – including a miniature carriage – describe the lost childhoods and early responsibilities of the royal children. The ceremonial coaches lie beneath the main floor, in another hall.

♥ Nobelmuseet

Stortorget 2 (08 534 81 800, www. nobelmuseum.se). T-bana Gamla Stan or bus 2, 3, 43, 53, 55, 76, 96. **Open** *June-Aug 9am-8pm daily. Sept-May 11am-5pm Tue-Thur; 11am-8pm Fri; 10am-6pm Sat, Sun. Guided tours (in English) June-Aug 10.15am, 11.15am, 1pm, 3pm, 4pm, 6pm daily. Sept-May 11.15am, 1pm, 3pm Tue-Sun.* **Admission** *120kr; 80kr reductions; free under-18s. Free with SC. Free Sept-May 5-8pm Fri.* **Map** *p65 N10.*

The Nobel Museum opened in 2001 to commemorate the centenary of the Nobel Prizes. Although the museum is not particularly large, its two theatres and an 'e-museum' bombard you with enough information to keep you entertained for a while. There are short films about the laureates, television clips about the prizes and audio recordings of the acceptance speeches, including that of Martin Luther King, Jr in 1964. Alfred Nobel's books, lab equipment and two packs of dynamite are displayed in a side room, along with his death mask and a copy of the first page of his four-page will, which called for the creation of the prizes. An exhibit on the Nobel banquet includes a glassed-in table setting and videos of the event.

High profile plans to move the museum into a new purpose-built venue were put on ice in 2018 after a Swedish court ruled that the proposed design was too large for the capital's picturesque waterfront.

▶ *For more on the Nobel Prize, see p74 The Noblest of Them All.*

Postmuseum

Lilla Nygatan 6 (08 436 44 39, www. postmuseum.se/en). T-bana Gamla Stan or bus 3, 53. **Open** *11am-4pm Tue-Sun.* **Admission** *80kr; free under-18s. Free with SC.* **Map** *p65 N10.*

Life-size scenes depicting more than 360 years of the Swedish postal service make the main exhibit of this museum unexpectedly enjoyable. A mounted postal carrier, a farm boy running with the mail and a postal train wagon, among other tableaux, illustrate the effect that the postal service has had on people's lives over the centuries. From 1720 until 1869, the city's only post office was housed on this spot. Lilla Posten downstairs includes a miniature post office for kids, and the gift shop sells stationery and, of course, stamps.

♥ Riddarholmskyrkan

Kungligaslottet, Riddarholmen (08 402 61 00, royalpalaces.se/english). T-bana Gamla Stan or bus 3, 53. **Open** *May-Sept 10am-5pm daily. Oct-Apr 10am-4pm daily.* **Admission** *50kr; 25kr reductions; free under-7s. Free with SC. No cash.* **Map** *p65 M10.*

The black lattice-work spire of Riddarholmskyrkan is one of Stockholm's most distinctive sights, visible from all over the city. Construction of a monastery for Franciscan monks first began on the site in the late 13th century. The church's benefactor, King Magnus Ladulås, is buried in the church along with 16 other monarchs, including Gustav III, Gustav II Adolf and Gustav V, the last to be buried here in 1950. Additions have been made to the church over time, in part to make room for more graves, since an estimated 500 to 1,000 people are buried in its floors and vaults. The southern wall was moved back in the 15th century; the tower was added in the late 16th century, and work began in 1838 on the current cast-iron spire after lightning struck the original. Colourful plaques of the Serafim order, which is awarded to Swedish nobility and visiting heads of state, decorate the walls of the church.

Riksdagshuset

Riksgatan 3, Helgeandsholmen (08 786 40 00/020 349 000, www.riksdagen.se). T-bana Kungsträdgården or bus 43, 62, 65.

❤ Stortorget

T-bana Gamla Stan. **Map** *p65 N10.*

Butter-, chilli- and mint-coloured
townhouses dating back to the Middle
Ages, an 18th-century fountain surrounded
by cobblestones and an imposing palatial
building combine to make this Stockholm's
most Instagrammable square. A former
market place and the focal point of the
city's Old Town (Gamla Stan) for 800
years, Stortorget has witnessed some of
the key moments in Stockholm's history,
including suffrage demonstrations by the
disenfranchised working class in the 1800s.
Most infamous, however, was the *Game-
of-Thrones*-esque Stockholm Bloodbath
of 1520, in which more than 80 noblemen,
priests and burghers were hanged or
decapitated in the square at the command
of the Danish king, Christian II. Look out for
the cannonball in the façade of Stortorget
7, on the corner with Skomakargatan. It is
said to have been fired at Christian II at the
time of the Bloodbath, but in fact was placed
there much later as a joke, probably in 1795
by a furniture dealer named Grevesmühl.

The most notable building on the square
is the former **Börhuset** (Stock Exchange),
designed by Erik Palmstedt in the late
18th century to replace an older town hall.
The building now houses the high-tech
Nobelmuseet (*see p69*), which tells the
history of the esteemed Nobel Prizes. The
Nobel Library and the Swedish Academy
(which decides who will be the laureate
for the Nobel Prize in Literature) also
occupy the building.

Palmstedt also designed the 1778 well in
the centre of the square. Due to the land
rising, the well dried up in the 19th century
and was moved to Brunkebergstorg in
Norrmalm, but it was moved back to its
original position in the 20th century.

These days Stortorget is a magnet for
tourists, who descend on the square's cafés:
Chokladkoppen and **Kaffekoppen** at the
western end are the best (*see p73*). It's
also renowned for its Christmas market
(*see p54*), featuring local delicacies
and handicrafts; the market is best
experienced after dark when the square
is lit by a twinkling fir tree and the golden
glow of oil candles dotted outside the
bars and restaurants.

Open *(guided tours only) mid June-mid Aug noon, 1pm, 2pm, 3pm Mon-Fri. Mid Sept-June 1.30pm Sat, Sun.* ***Admission*** *free.* ***Map*** *p65 N9.*

Free 50-minute guided tours of the Riksdagshuset (Parliament Building) are given in Swedish and English. The guides are exceptionally well-informed, and the tour is interesting enough – if you don't mind a little education. You'll see the modern semi-circular main chamber; at the front is a large tapestry, *Memory of a Landscape* by Elisabet Hasselberg Olsson, woven in 200 shades of grey. Beneath the chamber lies the former bank hall, now a lobby for the parliamentarians. In the old building, where the tour begins and ends, visitors are shown the grand former main entrance with its marble columns and busts of prime ministers, as well as the old dual chambers (now used as meeting rooms).

Stockholms Medeltidsmuseum

Strömparterren 3, Norrbro, Helgeandsholmen (08 508 31 620, www.medeltidsmuseet. stockholm.se). T-bana Kungsträdgården or bus 57, 65. ***Open*** *noon-5pm Tue, Thur-Sun; noon-8pm Wed. Guided tours July, Aug 2pm Tue-Sun.* ***Admission*** *Free; tours 50kr.* ***Map*** *p65 N9.*

During an excavation of Helgeandsholmen during the late 1970s, archaeologists discovered thousands of artefacts from medieval Stockholm. The site was earmarked for the construction of a new parking garage for MPs but, instead, Parliament decided to build an underground museum to store and display the archaeological finds. The Medieval Museum informs visitors about the emergence and medieval development of Stockholm through more than 850 objects, a hidden passage to the castle and a 14th-century cemetery wall.

▶ *The museum also runs 90-minute guided tours of Gamla Stan (2500kr-3,500kr per group); book by phone in advance (9am-noon Tue-Fri).*

Storkyrkan

Storkyrkobrinken, Trångsund 1 (08 723 30 00, www.stockholmsdomkyrkoforsamling. se). T-bana Gamla Stan or bus 2, 3, 43, 53, 55, 76, 96. ***Open*** *Oct-Apr 9am-4pm daily. May, Sept 9am-5pm daily. June-Aug 9am-6pm daily.* ***Admission*** *60kr; 50kr reductions; free under-18s & for service or prayer. Free with SC. Guided tours 1250kr-1500kr.* ***Map*** *p65 N9.*

Dating from the mid 13th century, 'the Great Church' is the oldest congregational church in Stockholm and the site of past coronations and royal weddings. A huge brick church with a rectangular plan, it's been extended and rebuilt numerous times. Between 1736 and 1742, its exterior was renovated from medieval to Baroque to match the neighbouring palace, and in 1743 the tower was raised to its current height of 66m (216ft). Inside, the style is primarily Gothic with Baroque additions – such as the extravagant golden booths designed for the royal family by the palace architect Tessin the Younger. The main attraction is Bernt Notke's intricately carved wooden statue, *St George and the Dragon*, which is decorated with authentic elk antlers. The statue symbolises Sten Sture's victory over the Danes in a battle in 1471 and was given to the church by Sture himself in 1489. (A bronze copy of the statue can also be found in Köpmantorget, not far from the church.) Don't miss the famous *Parhelion* painting, which shows an unusual light phenomenon – six sparkling halos – that appeared over Stockholm on 20 April 1535. It's one of the oldest depictions of the capital, though the painting is a 1630s copy of the earlier original. From July to mid August, theology students give guided tours (in Swedish and English) of the church's tower, which involves climbing 200 steps on narrow wooden staircases for an amazing view of the black roofs of Gamla Stan.

Tyska Kyrkan

Svartmangatan 16A (08 411 11 88, www. svenska kyrkan.se/deutschegemeinde). T-bana Gamla Stan. **Open** *11am-3pm Fri, Sat; 12.30-4pm Sun.* **Admission** *30kr; 20kr reductions; free under-10s.* **Map** *p65 O10.*

At the height of the Hanseatic League in the Middle Ages, when Stockholm had strong trade links with Germany, many German merchants settled in this area of Gamla Stan. They originally worshipped at the monastery on what is now Riddarholmen but moved to St Gertrude's guildhouse after its expansion in the 1580s. Baroque renovations in 1638-42 gave the German Church its present appearance; its tower was rebuilt after a fire in 1878. Tessin the Elder designed the royal pews, and Jost Henner created the richly decorated ornaments and figures on the portal. The church is best viewed from Tyska Brinken, where the tower rises up 96m (315ft) from the narrow street. At the church's summer concerts, you can listen to a replica of a 17th-century organ, constructed for the church in 2004 at a cost of ten million kronor. There's also a café here in summer.

Restaurants & cafés

19 Glas Bar & Matsal ⓦ ⓦ ⓦ ⓦ

Stora Nygatan 19 (08 723 19 19, www.19glas. se). T-bana Gamla Stan or bus 3, 53. **Open** *noon-midnight Tue-Sat.* **Map** *p65 N10* ❶ *Contemporary*

The size of a living room, 19 Glas used to be able to host just 19 guests (hence the name); coming here is still a bit like visiting someone at home. The menu changes each night – a four- or seven-course journey into whatever locally produced ingredients the owner has found that day. The wine list is nicely put together, and the two-course set lunch is good value.

Aifur ⓦ ⓦ

Västerlånggatan 68 (08 20 10 55, aifur.se). T-bana Gamla Stan or bus 2, 43, 55, 76, 96. **Open** *5-11pm Mon-Thur; 5pm-1am Fri, Sat.* **Map** *p65 O10* ❷ *Swedish*

Taking its name from a Viking ship, Aifur serves up historic dishes including roast chicken with apple cider gravy and pikeperch, the most typical fish dish found on a Viking table. You can wash your dinner down with a cup of mead, a Viking beverage created by fermenting honey, water and grains. Best experienced during winter, this is a dark underground restaurant, lit up by atmospheric candles.

Barrels, Burgers & Beer ⓦ

Stora Nygatan 20 (08 10 00 03, barrels.se). T-bana Gamla Stan or bus 2, 43, 55, 76, 96. **Open** *4-11pm Mon-Wed; 11.30am-11pm Thur; 11.30am-midnight Fri, Sat; 11.30am-9pm Sun.* **Map** *p65 N10* ❸ *American*

Classic juicy patties made with locally sourced meat and served inside fluffy homemade buns dominate the menu at this affordable burger joint with a rustic charm. There's always an innovative 'burger of the month' on offer too, as well as decent veggie and vegan options. As its name suggests, a roster of artisan beer choices is available. But this isn't a place to linger: it's a popular spot with long wooden tables crammed tightly together.

Bistro Ruby & Grill Ruby

*Österlånggatan 14 (08 20 57 76/60 15, www. grillruby.com). T-bana Gamla Stan or bus 2, 43, 55, 76, 96. **Open** Bistro Ruby from 5pm Mon-Sat. Grill Ruby from 11am daily; brunch noon-4pm Sat, Sun. **Map** p65 O10* ④
French/North American

These two sister restaurants set out to combine Paris and Texas. Bistro Ruby offers European formality in a pleasant environment ideal for a quiet chat. The menu goes from classic French to more modern Mediterranean influences, and it's all well-cooked, tasty and not overworked. Next door, Grill Ruby is noisier and more fun, and it's all about the meat, so vegetarians should steer clear. With each cut you get a wide choice of tapas, salsas and other accompaniments. The weekend brunch is recommended.

♥ Chokladkoppen

*Stortorget 18 (08 20 31 70, www. chokladkoppen.se). T-bana Gamla Stan or bus 2, 3, 43, 53, 55, 96. **Open** Winter 10am-10pm Mon-Thur; 10am-11pm Fri; 9am-11pm Sat; 9am-10pm Sun. Summer 9am-11pm daily. **Map** p65 N10* ⑤ *Café*

Just how good can a hot chocolate really be? To find out, skip Gamla Stan's tourist traps and head for this place on Stortorget, the charming square at the centre of Gamla Stan. Colourful Chokladkoppen has a trendy feel and a traditional interior, and it's popular with Stockholm's gay crowd. The laid-back service suffers at weekends when it gets ridiculously busy. In summer, the tables

outside are a prime spot. It also serves fantastic cakes and snacks – don't miss the utterly divine white chocolate cheesecake.

▶ *Next door, sister café Kaffekoppen (no.20, www.cafekaffekoppen.se) has a similarly cosy feel and serves decent savoury dishes.*

Fabrique

*Lilla Nygatan 12 (08 20 81 44, www.fabrique. se). T-bana Gamla Stan or bus 3, 53. **Open** 7.30am-6pm Mon-Fri; 8am-5pm Sat, Sun. **Map** p65 N10* ⑥ *Bakery café*

This successful bakery mini-chain sells superior sandwiches, buns and pastries, as well as a range of quality fruit juices and yoghurts. The interior of the corner building is entered from Schönfeldts Gränd, and has a clean industrial look, with white wall tiles, chequered floors and vintage tables and chairs. **Other locations** throughout the city; check the website for the full list.

Flying Elk

*Mälartorget 15 (08 20 85 83, www.theflyingelk. se). T-bana Gamla Stan. **Open** 5pm-midnight daily. **Map** p65 N10* ⑦ *Gastropub*

With the same owners as the Michelin-starred Frantzén, this Old Town gastropub with chunky wooden tables is a solid bet in an area crowded with tourist traps. British influences are evident in both the atmosphere and the menu, but the place still allows space for some local interpretation: 'God Save the Elk' is the unofficial slogan, and dishes include the likes of posh fish and chips with curry *remoulade*, pan-fried local char with new potatoes, and an Eton mess that definitely isn't for purists. Camden Town Brewery beer is on offer, while Asian food is the speciality on Sundays.

Riddarholmen

The Noblest of Them All

The life and legacy of Alfred Nobel

Born in Stockholm in 1833, Alfred Nobel spent his teenage years in Russia and early adulthood in the USA. On returning to Sweden, the chemist, engineer and inventor devoted himself to the study of explosives, inventing dynamite, which he patented in 1867. Upon his death in 1896 he bequeathed his huge fortune (around 1.8 billion kronor in today's money) as an endowment to humanity. His last will specified that the generated interest 'shall be annually distributed in the form of prizes to those who, during the preceding year, shall have conferred the greatest benefit on mankind'. He specified five categories: Physics, Chemistry, Medicine, Literature and Peace. The first prizes, set at 150,782 kronor, were awarded in 1901.

The Nobel Prizes today are still each field's most prestigious annual award. The Peace Prize is awarded in Oslo, Norway, while the other prizes are awarded in Stockholm on 10 December (the anniversary of Nobel's death) in the Stockholm Concert Hall, with a Nobel banquet, attended by the Swedish royal family, taking place in Stockholm City Hall. Each recipient receives around 10 million kronor from the Nobel Foundation.

The Nobel Prize for Literature was cancelled in 2018 following months of infighting and a string of resignations within the Swedish Academy, after the husband of one of its members was involved in a sex assault scandal in the wake of the #MeToo movement. The Nobel Foundation decided to award two prizes for literature in late 2019 to make up for the cancellation.

Famous laureates

Malala Yousafzai, who was shot in the head for campaigning for girls' rights to education in Pakistan, became the youngest laureate to receive an award when she picked up the Peace Prize in 2014. Bob Dylan was the first songwriter to be given the Literature prize in 2016, although he didn't pick up his award or give his obligatory lecture until the following year. Other famous Nobel laureates include Marie Curie (Physics 1903, Chemistry 1911); Rudyard Kipling (Literature 1907); Albert Einstein (Physics 1921); Alexander Fleming (Medicine 1945); Martin Luther King, Jr (Peace 1964); Nelson Mandela (Peace 1993); Doris Lessing (Literature 2007); and Barack Obama (Peace 2009). Literature Prize winner Jean-Paul Sartre declined the award in 1964, in keeping with this philosophy of rejecting all official honours.

The most notorious Nobel Prize recipient, however, is Fritz Haber, dubbed the 'father of chemical warfare'. Haber received the 1918 Chemistry Prize at the end of World War I, during which he had developed chlorine gas, which killed thousands in the trenches in Belgium. Other controversial laureates include Egas Moniz, who won the 1949 prize in medicine for his discovery of the lobotomy. More than 60 years later, people continue to lobby for the posthumous revocation of his prize, citing the misuse of his procedure, which condemned patients to a near zombie-like existence. Henry Kissinger and Lê Duc Tho (the latter declined the prize) were awarded the Peace Prize for negotiating a ceasefire between North Vietnam and the US in 1973, despite hostilities still occurring. Two Norwegian Nobel Committee members resigned over the award.

Nobel by numbers

Nobel laureates 935 individuals, 27 organisations
Female laureates 52
Youngest laureate Malala Yousafzai (17 years; Peace 2014)
Oldest laureate Arthur Ashkin (96 years; Physics 2018)
(Source: The Nobel Foundation, 2018)

Alfred Nobel

Grillska Husets Konditori Ⓦ

Stortorget 3 (08 684 23 364). T-bana Gamla Stan or bus 2, 3, 43, 53, 55, 71, 76, 96. **Open** *Café 9am-6pm Mon-Fri; 9am-4pm Sat; lunch served 11am-2pm Mon-Fri. Bakery 8am-6pm Mon Fri; 9am-4pm Sat.* **Map** *p65 N10* ⑧
Bakery café

This café and bakery in a corner of Stortorget is run by a charitable group that works with the homeless. For a real treat, walk through the downstairs café and follow signs to the tranquil first-floor terrace, which is one of Gamla Stan's best-kept secrets. Spend your change on the good-value pastries and friendly service on offer here, and make a difference.

💙 Den Gyldene Freden ⓌⓌⓌⓌ

Österlånggatan 51 (08 24 97 60, www. gyldenefreden.se). T-bana Gamla Stan or bus 2, 43, 55, 76, 96. **Open** *11.30am-midnight Mon-Fri; 1-11pm Sat.* **Map** *p65 O10* ⑨
Traditional Swedish

This first-class restaurant is housed in an 18th-century building owned by the Swedish Academy, and the dimly lit interior lends a suitably grandiose atmosphere to a meal here. Since it first opened in 1722, large sections of Stockholm's cultural elite have dined here – singer-poet Carl Michael Bellman, painter Anders Zorn and singer-composer Evert Taube were regular customers. As you'd expect, the menu is stocked with traditional Swedish dishes, including smoked reindeer, meatballs and plenty of herring and salmon.

Kagges ⓌⓌⓌ

Lilla Nygatan 21 (08 796 81 02, www.kagges. com). T-bana Gamla Stan. **Open** *5-10pm Wed-Sun;* **Map** *p65 N10* ⑩ *Contemporary*

This small cosy bistro specialises in New Nordic cuisine, with a seasonal frequently changing menu, focused around small sharing plates. It's run by dynamic duo Kalle Lindborg and Douglas Tjärnhammaralm, who branched out on their own after working in some of Sweden's top restaurants. Kagge's corner location was previously occupied by Swedish celebrity chef Björn Frantzén's Michelin-starred restaurant Frantzén, which has relocated to Norrmalm.

Pastis ⓌⓌ

Baggensgatan 12 (08 20 20 18, www.pastis. se). T-bana Gamla Stan or bus 2, 43, 55, 76, 96. **Open** *from 4pm Mon-Wed; from 11.30am Thur, Fri; from noon Sat, Sun.* **Map** *p65 O10* ⑪ *French*

Favoured by locals, this cute corner bistro in the heart of the Old Town serves up a good selection of French classics (*bouillabaisse*,

steak tartare, foie gras, beef *bourguignon*) from a charming old building. There are outdoor tables in summer.

Pho and Bun Ⓦ

Kornhamnstorg 51 (08 23 32 10, phobun.se). T-bana Gamla Stan or bus 2, 43, 55, 76, 96. **Open** *11am-10pm Mon, Tue; 11am-11pm Wed-Fri; noon-11pm Sat; noon-10pm Sun.* **Map** *p65 O10* ⑫ *Vietnamese*

This relaxed Vietnamese restaurant serves up healthy soups, noodles and rice dishes, including a wide range of vegetarian options. Portions are large, while prices are modest by Stockholm standards. The drinks menu is limited but includes a small selection of decent beers from South-East Asia. Outdoor seating during summer offers a great location from which to people-watch, overlooking Lake Mälaren and a popular commuter cycle path.

Sundbergs Konditori Ⓦ

Järntorget 83 (08 10 67 35). T-bana Gamla Stan or bus 2, 3, 43, 53, 55, 71, 76, 96. **Open** *10am-8pm daily.* **Map** *p65 O10* ⑬ *Café*

This place has served hot coffee from a copper samovar for more than 200 years. Believed to be Stockholm's oldest *konditori*, it was founded in 1785 by Johan Ludvig Sundberg. According to local lore, King Gustav III had a secret passageway from the Kungliga Slottet straight to the bakery. Don't expect newfangled frappuccinos and smoothies here: come to Sundbergs for traditional cakes and atmosphere. This is a good starting point for navigating the curiosities and cobbles of nearby Västerlånggatan, Gamla Stan's busiest street.

▶ *For ice-cream and fresh waffles, stop at nearby Café Kåkbrinken (Västerlånggatan 41, 411 61 74).*

💙 Tradition ⓌⓌ

Österlånggatan 1 (08 20 35 25, www. restaurangtradition.se/gamla-stan/). T-bana Gamla Stan or bus 2, 43, 55, 76, 96. **Open** *11.30am-11pm Mon-Fri; 4-11pm Sat; 4-10pm Sun.* **Map** *p65 O9* ⑭ *Swedish*

This restaurant juxtaposes classic Swedish fare with a modern minimalist Scandinavian interior. The homemade meatballs are the star of the show, alongside other traditional dishes such as toast Skagen (shrimp toast with bleak roe) and breaded Baltic herring served with potato mash. It's especially good value at lunchtime, offering a range of filling daily deals that are up to a third cheaper than main meals on its evening menu.

Bars

In the Old Town, most of the bars are situated around Kornhamnstorg or Järntorget. For DJ bars, music venues and clubs, *see p195.*

Bryggeri Munkbrön

Lilla Nygatan 2 (076 770 85 86). T-bana Gamla Stan, bus 3. **Open** *4-11.45pm Mon; 4-11pm Tue, Wed; 4pm-1am Thur-Sat.* **Admission** *free; minimum age 18.* **Map** *p65 N10* ❶

This cavernous centuries-old beer hall sprawling across a huge cellar was completely refurbished and reopened under new ownership in April 2019. It's designed for beer nerds, with a small selection of ales brewed on site and a choice of European and American beers also available on tap.

Corner Club

Lilla Nygatan 16 (08 20 85 83, www.cornerclub. se). T-bana Gamla Stan or bus 2, 43, 55, 76, 96. **Open** *from 5pm Wed-Sat.* **Admission** *free; minimum age 18.* **Map** *p65 N10* ❷

Nordic design fans will love the vibe at this small upmarket bar. Here, you can sip on fancy cocktails from sleek black bar stools that set off a minimalist grey interior. It's expensive, but you get what you pay for: carefully crafted drinks shaken and stirred by experienced mixologists. This is part of the Frantzen Group, owned by the Michelin star-winning chef Björn Frantzen.

♥ Pharmarium

Stortorget 7 (08 20 08 10, pharmarium. se). T-bana Gamla Stan or bus 2, 3, 53, 55, 76, 96. **Open** *4.30-11pm Mon, Tue, Sun; 4.30pm-midnight Wed, Thur; 4.30pm-1am Fri, Sat.* **Map** *p65 N10* ❸

Creative craft cocktails infused with herbs and spices are the staple at this low-lit, luxurious venue that's a popular date spot for well-heeled locals. Pharmarium takes its name from Stockholm's first pharmacy, which opened on this spot in 1575; eagle-eyed visitors will spot Latin words for traditional medicinal ingredients on the dark wooden panels by the bar. There's also a food menu, which features small plates designed to complement each drink.

The Temple Bar

Kornhamnstorg 55 (08 20 40 48, www. thetemplebar.se). T-bana Gamla stan. **Open** *11am-3am daily.* **Map** *p65 O10* ❹

Outdoor seating is the big draw at the Temple Bar during warmer weather. The interior lacks the charm of many of this area's more rustic-style locations, with red walls and plenty of fake leather on display. But it's a friendly place where you can watch sports and catch decent live music for free, including soul, blues, slow jazz and funk. The Jamnation band, which performs every other Thursday, usually draws a lively crowd.

♥ Tweed

Lilla Nygatan 5 (08 506 40 082, www. tweedbar.se). T-bana Gamla Stan or bus 2, 43, 55, 76, 96. **Open** *5pm-1am Tue-Sat.* **Map** *p65 N10* ❺

You can enjoy more than a dozen types of gin from the comfort of classic Chesterfield leather sofas at this atmospheric high-end saloon bar with a British twist. The decor is a nod to turn-of-the-century gentleman's clubs, complete with dark wooden panels, red and white tartan walls, and lamps. The extensive drinks list includes a range of whiskies, wines and cocktails.

Wirströms

Stora Nygatan 13 (08 21 28 74, www. wirstromspub.se). T-bana Gamla Stan or bus 2, 43, 55, 76, 96. **Open** *2pm-midnight Mon; 2pm-1am Tue-Thur; noon-1am Fri, Sun; 11am-1am Sat.* **Map** *p65 N10* ❻

This sprawling Irish pub is something of a rabbit warren, offering regular free live music in its 17th-century cellar and large screens that show most major international rugby, football and cricket matches. It's a firm favourite with local expats, with a huge selection of globally sourced beers and spirits.

Shops & services

♥ Charlotte Nicolin

Köpmangatan 3 (08 21 66 66, charlottenicolin. com). T-bana Gamla stan. **Open** *11am-5pm daily.* **Map** *p65 O10* ❶ *Gifts & souvenirs*

This interior design boutique is named after its artist owner, who specialises in tasteful animal portraits that are printed on to trays, cushions, mugs, aprons and other household accessories. Many of the motifs are based on Nordic animals, such as elk, deer, wolf, hare and hedgehog.

Comics Heaven

Stora Nygatan 23 (08 20 25 16, www. comicsheaven.se). T-bana Gamla stan. **Open** *10am-6.30pm Mon-Fri; 10am-6pm Sat; 11am-5pm Sun.* **Map** *p65 N10* ❷ *Books & games*

Comic- and cartoon-lovers will consider this an Aladdin's cave. It's stocked with English-language Marvel and DC superhero comics, American indie publications and Manga. There are also Swedish titles and a selection

of books and boardgames. If you need help or inspiration, the nerdy staff here really know their stuff.

❤ Gamla Stans Polkagriskokeri
Stora Nygatan 44 (08 10 71 82, www. gamlastanspolkagriskokeri.se). T-bana Gamla stan. **Open** *10am-6pm Mon-Sat; 11am-5pm Sun.* **Map** *p65 N10* ❸ *Sweets*

Candy fans will adore this retro sweet store. It takes its name from its staple product, red-and-white peppermint *polkagris* (rock candy) made by hand on site and based on a 19th-century recipe. The shelves are also stacked with assorted types of fudge, caramel and Liquorice.

❤ Iris Hantverk
Västerlånggatan 24 (08 698 09 73, www. irishantverk.se). T-bana Gamla Stan or bus 2, 43, 55, 76, 96. **Open** *10am-6pm Mon-Fri; 11am-4pm Sat; noon-4pm Sun.* **Map** *p65 N10* ❹ *Gifts & souvenirs*

This design company has been hand-making cleaning brushes since the 19th century. These days, the range spans high-duty brooms to body brushes and toilet plungers. Many of the items are produced by visually impaired craftspeople. Brightly coloured ceramic plates and bowls, linen towels and organic beauty products are also on sale in this beautifully arranged store.

❤ Rain Store by Stutterheim
Västerlånggatan 40 (stutterheim.com). T-bana Gamla stan. **Open** *10am-late daily.* **Map** *p65 N10* ❺ *Fashion*

Specialising in cult rubber raincoats in a rainbow of colours, this is one of several stores named after the company's founder, Alexander Stutterheim. A former copywriter, the entrepreneur launched the fashion firm in 2010 after struggling to find stylish all-weather gear. If you're lucky he might pop in during your visit: he owns an apartment in Gamla Stan.

❤ Science Fiction Bokhandeln
Västerlånggatan 48 (08 21 50 52, www.sfbok. se). T-bana Gamla stan. **Open** *10am-7pm Mon-Fri; 10am-6pm Sat; noon-5pm Sun.* **Map** *p65 N10* ❻ *Gifts & souvenirs*

A treasure trove for anyone with a penchant for dragons, vampires, aliens or ninjas. This science-fiction bookstore also sells video games alongside a growing body of non-fiction work about artificial intelligence, published in both Swedish and English.

Norrmalm & Vasastan

Many visitors to Stockholm arrive in Norrmalm, zooming in on the Arlanda Express to its terminal next to Central Station. Stepping out from here, they are confronted by the functionalist concrete buildings that dominate the area. Most of downtown Norrmalm resulted from a massive 'renewal' campaign in the 1960s, in which nearly all of the district's older buildings were torn down in favour of boxy office spaces. This isn't the prettiest part of the city, but there are treasures to be found, particularly around the recently revamped Brunkebergstorg district, which is home to a cluster of boutique hotels and panoramic bars.

Much of Vasastan (formerly Vasastaden), to the north of Norrmalm, was built in the late 1800s to accommodate Stockholm's growing population. Aside from its main thoroughfares of Sveavägen, Odengatan and St Eriksgatan, the area has stayed primarily residential, but you'll find several beautiful parks and a slew of good-quality independent restaurants.

❤ **Don't miss**

1 Brunkebergstorg *p85*
Stockholm's new inner-city sweet spot.

2 Nationalmuseum *p84*
Sweden's largest museum.

3 Kulturhuset Stadsteatern *p84*
A hub for culture vultures.

4 Gustaf Vasa Kyrka *p94*
Beautiful Baroque church with a dominating 60-metre (197 feet) dome.

5 Stadsbiblioteket *p95*
Browse the shelves and marvel at the architecture in the circular reading room.

St Jacobs Kyrka *p86*

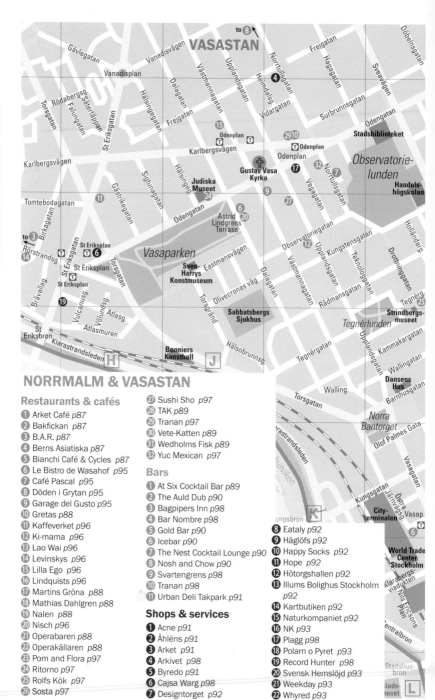

NORRMALM & VASASTAN

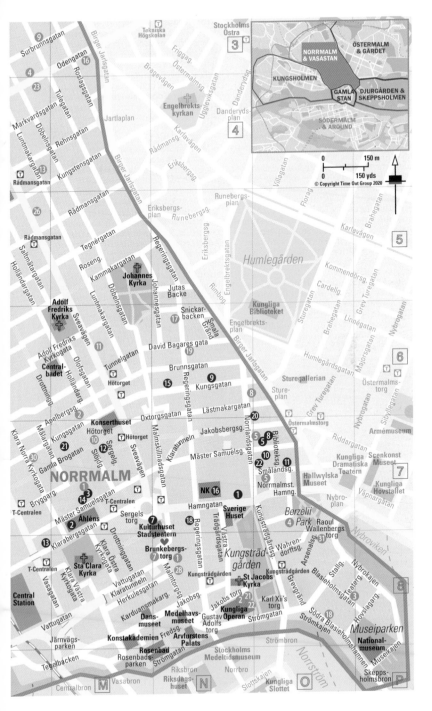

NORRMALM

In Stockholm's early years, the city government discouraged construction on Norrmalm out of fear that an enemy attacking Gamla Stan would take shelter in the buildings. In the early 16th century Gustav Vasa tore down many of Norrmalm's structures but, by 1602, the district had grown to such an extent that it was declared a separate city. This independence lasted until 1637, when Norrmalm was absorbed into its larger neighbour. Under Gustav II Adolf, the wooden buildings of the district were razed once again to be replaced by more uniform stone streets. Central Station opened on the edge of the district in 1871, attracting industries and workers to the area, and redevelopment in the 1880s turned southern Norrmalm into Stockholm's business district. In the 1960s, Norrmalm was again redeveloped by the city's planners, resulting in the concrete-laden streets you see today.

Stockholm Central Station (*see p236*) is an ornate 19th-century building with its main entrance on Vasagatan. Those wanting to head straight into the very heart of the shopping district should follow **Klarabergsgatan** east from Central Station towards Sergels torg. But, to see the water and the more picturesque areas of Norrmalm, head south on the eastern side of Vasagatan; swing round the corner when you reach the Sheraton Stockholm Hotel and walk one block up Jakobsgatan to avoid the horrible tangle of highways and viaducts. The nearby **Konstakademien** (Royal Academy of Art), on parallel Fredsgatan, occupies a renovated palace designed by renowned Swedish Baroque architect Tessin the Elder in the 1670s.

Many of Sweden's government departments are nearby, such as the two buildings – one light orange and the other red – called **Rosenbad**, which house the offices of the prime minister. A stone walkway and bicycle path follow the northern shore of **Norrström** from Rosenbad to the tip of the Blasieholmen peninsula. East on Fredsgatan is **Gustav Adolfs torg**, named after King Gustav II Adolf, who greatly expanded the city in the early 17th century; a statue of the king stands in the centre of the square. Nearby, there are Mediterranean antiquities in the **Medelhavsmuseet** and dance costumes in the **Dansmuseet**.

On the square's eastern flank is the grand **Kungliga Operan** (*see p205*), which was styled after the Royal Palace in the late 19th

Gustav Adolfs torg

❤ Time to eat & drink

Cinnamon bun pitstop
Gretas *p88*, Kaffeverket *p96*

Light lunch
Arket Café *p87*, Café Pascal *p95*, Martins Gröna *p88*

Crafty cocktails
At Six *p89*, The Nest Cocktail Lounge *p90*

Stylish supper
Lilla Ego *p96*, OperaBaren *p88*, TAK *p89*

❤ Time to shop

Fash pack favourites
Acne *p91*

Nordic design
Designtorget *p92*, NK *p93*

All-weather gear
Häglöfs *p92*, Naturkompaniet *p92*

Tasty treats
Cajsa Warg *p98*, Eataly *p92*, Hötorgshallen *p92*

In the know
Getting around

Stockholm's major transport hubs – Central Station, City Station and Cityterminalen – are clustered together in close proximity to each other on the western edge of Norrmalm. They are connected by tunnels and escalators to T-Centralen on the underground network; all branches of the blue, red and green metro lines pass through here and there are multiple entry and exit points at ground level; Sergels torg is the busiest. Once you're in Norrmalm, you'll join throngs of pedestrians on the area's shopping streets. To get to Vasastan take the green metro line or a commuter train to Odenplan. Vasastan is a compact neighbourhood that can easily be explored on foot, but bus 4 connects Odengatan to Sankt Eriksplan if needed.

century, with a splendid chandelier-strewn gold foyer 28 metres (92 feet) long. The original opera building, where King Gustav III was assassinated in 1792, looked exactly like **Arvfurstens Palats**, the building across from it, which was constructed in the 1780s and is now used by the Ministry for Foreign Affairs. The Opera House contains several restaurants, varying in splendour and price; the fanciest, and one of Sweden's best-known, is **Operakällaren**. From the front of the Opera House you get a beautiful view across the water towards Kungliga Slottet (the Royal Palace); behind the opera house stands the earthy red Gothic structure of **St Jacobs Kyrka** (St Jacob's Church).

The rectangular park of **Kungsträdgården** (King's Garden) stretches north from here. This is a popular venue for open-air events and food fairs. In winter, there's an ice rink. Originally a vegetable garden for the royal castle in the 15th century, the park later developed into a pleasure garden and opened to the public in the 18th century. A century later, French-born King Karl XIV Johan tore out the trees, erected a statue of his adoptive father, Karl XIII, and converted the garden into a field for military exercises. After his death it was turned back into a park. The statue of Karl XII – his finger pointing to his old battlegrounds in Russia – was added in 1868 near the water. Two tree-lined avenues shade the restaurants and glassed-in cafés along the park's western and eastern edges. At the top end of the park is a shallow pool with three fountains.

East of the Opera House, meanwhile, is the **Blasieholmen** peninsula, which pokes out into the water towards Skeppsholmen. At the end of this spur of land stands the imposing limestone façade of Sweden's largest art museum, the **Nationalmuseum**, which reopened in 2018 following a huge refurbishment. Strömkajen, in front of the five-star **Grand Hôtel** (*see p229*), is the boarding point for sightseeing boats and ferries to the archipelago. Another wharf for ferries to the archipelago, Djurgården and Hammarby Sjöstad is located on the other side of the peninsula at the small harbour of Nybroviken.

Nearby, overlooking the lawns of Berzelii Park, is **Berns Salonger** (*see p195*), a legendary venue since the 1860s. It's still a nightlife favourite; its magnificent salons, gilded and topped with crystal chandeliers, now host one of Stockholm's largest restaurants, **Berns Asiatiska**, along with several bars.

The crowded thoroughfare of **Hamngatan** crosses the top of both Berzelii Park and Kungsträdgården. The street's highlight is **NK**, Sweden's first and most exclusive department store. For cheaper shops, try the **Gallerian** mall just up the street. A couple of blocks west along from NK is **Sergels torg**. This two-level area of glass, concrete and underground shops was built after the bulldozer extravaganza of the 1960s. The sunken modernistic square of black-and-white triangles is a popular spot for political demonstrations; the tall glass tower surrounded by fountains in the middle of the traffic island was designed by sculptor Edvin Öhrström in 1972.

Architect Peter Celsing was responsible for **Kulturhuset**, the seven-storey structure that stands on the south side of Sergels torg like a great glass wall. Built in the early 1970s and renovated in 2019-20, it's home to Stockholm's main **tourist office** (*see p244*), one of the city's biggest theatres, **Stadsteatern** (*see p205*), as well as Sweden's only comic book library, **Serieteket**. Take the escalators up to the galleries on the upper floors to check out one of the many temporary art exhibitions and the view from **Cafe Panorama**.

Several main streets converge on Sergels torg, including Klarabergsgatan and Sveavägen. The block-long, **Åhléns** department store occupies the north-west corner of the former, with another entrance on the permanently heaving pedestrian street of Drottninggatan, which is home to numerous Nordic high-street brands, including H&M, Arket and Clas Ohlson. Just south of Sergels torg, behind Kulturhuset Stadsteatern, is **Brunkebergstorg** (*see p85*), a compact inner-city neighbourhood that's become the heart of the city's style and tech scenes.

North from Sergels torg, five glass office buildings stand in a row towards the open space of Hötorget; built in the 1950s, they're city landmarks – whether people want them to be or not. **Hötorget** is home to an outdoor market largely selling fruit, flowers and bags. It's overlooked by **Haymarket** (*see p230*), an art deco-inspired hotel which occupies the former PUB department store. The indoor food hall, **Hötorgshallen**, bustles beneath the **Filmstaden Sergel** multiplex (*see p190*). On another side stands the **Konserthuset** (*see p204*), Stockholm's main concert hall. Regarded as a prime example of Swedish neoclassical style, the 1926 building was modelled on the temples of ancient Greece by the architect Ivar Tengbom; the artworks inside depict figures and scenes from Greek mythology. Tengbom's son, Anders, renovated the building in 1972 to improve the acoustics. Einar Forseth (who also decorated the Golden Hall at the Stadshuset) created the floor mosaics in the entrance hall and main foyer, and Carl Milles sculpted the bronze statue of Orpheus near the front steps.

Further north on Drottninggatan, **Centralbadet** is a lovely, art nouveau bathhouse built in 1905, with café tables in its pretty front courtyard. Nearby, **Dansens Hus** (*see p207*) is the capital's main venue for modern dance. To the east of Dansens Hus, on Sveavägen, stands the classical **Adolf Fredriks Kyrka**. It has a Greek cross plan and a beautifully painted ceiling; assassinated prime minister Olof Palme is buried in the cemetery here. On the corner of Drottninggatan and Tegnérgatan is the building in which Swedish author August Strindberg spent the last four years of his life. His apartment is now home to the **Strindbergsmuseet** – a must for fans of Sweden's greatest writer. On Drottninggatan, near the museum, a few of Strindberg's famous quotes have been printed on the street in Swedish, and there's a statue of him in the small park of **Tegnérlunden** to the west.

Sights & museums

Dansmuseet

Drottninggatan 17 (08 441 76 51, www. dansmuseet.se). T-bana T-Centralen or bus 43, 62, 65. **Open** *11am-5pm Tue-Fri; noon-4pm Sat, Sun.* **Admission** *120kr; 80kr reductions; free under-18s.* **Map** *p80 M8.*

Stockholm's Dansmuseet (Dance Museum) displays costumes from Swedish and Russian ballets, paintings and sketches related to dance, and traditional masks and costumes from Africa, Thailand, China, Japan and Tibet. Rolf de Maré, who managed the Swedish Ballet in Paris in the 1920s, opened the museum in the French capital in 1933. When the museum closed in the 1940s, the contents relating to Swedish and non-European dance were relocated to Stockholm. The collection is small but well presented. A variety of free dance films is also screened regularly. Be sure to visit the well-stocked café too.

Konstakademien

Fredsgatan 12 (08 23 29 25, www. konstakademien.se). T-bana Kungsträdgården or T-Centralen, or bus 43, 62, 65. **Open** *11am-5pm Tue-Fri; noon-4pm Sat, Sun.* **Admission** *Free* **Map** *p80 M8.*

Sweden's Royal Academy of Fine Arts was founded by King Gustav III in 1773 and moved into its current premises in 1780. Today you can see a permanent collection of paintings and sculptures dating back to the 18th century, a large collection of letters and manuscripts written by Swedish artists, and temporary special exhibitions showcasing the work of contemporary academy members. The venue's terrace bar is also very popular in summer.

♥ Kulturhuset Stadsteatern

Sergels torg (information 08 506 20 212, library 08 506 20 348, www. kulturhusetstadsteatern.se). T-bana T-Centralen or bus 52, 56, 59, 65. **Open** *11am-7pm Mon-Fri, 11am-5pm 'Sat, Sun.* **Admission** *free.* **Map** *p80 M7.*

Kulturhuset, or the House of Culture – designed by Peter Celsing – is one of the most prominent modern buildings in Stockholm. Reopening in October 2020 after renovations, it includes theatres that host film screenings, debates and poetry readings; galleries for art and photography exhibitions; a library (with a wide selection of foreign newspapers); several cafés; the city's main tourist information centre, and a roof terrace with an impressive view. Daily events (including a growing number in English) are tailored to different tastes and age groups. For details of theatre and other performances at the Kulturhuset Stadsteatern, *see p205.*

Medelhavsmuseet

Fredsgatan 2 (010 456 12 98, www. medelhavsmuseet.se). T-bana Kungsträdgården or bus 43, 62, 65. **Open** *11am-8pm Tue-Fri; 11am-5pm Sat, Sun.* **Admission** *Free.* **Map** *p80 N8.*

Artefacts from Greece, Rome, Egypt and Cyprus are housed in the Museum of Mediterranean Antiquities. Displayed in the main hall are a variety of busts and statues, while other rooms contain Islamic art, early medical instruments, ancient sarcophagi and a reconstruction of an Egyptian tomb. The Gold Room, a vault holding ancient wreaths of gold, is open during visiting hours. The second-floor Bagdad café serves Mediterranean specialities for lunch.

♥ Nationalmuseum

Södra Blasieholmshamnen 2 (08 519 54 300, www.nationalmuseum.se). T-bana Kungsträdgården or bus 2, 62, 65, 76, 96. **Open** *11am-7pm Tue, Wed, Fri-Sun; 11am-9pm Thur.* **Map** *p80 P9.*

Sweden's largest museum features both Swedish and international art and design from the Middle Ages to the present day. The building itself, designed in 1866 to look like a northern Italian Renaissance palace, remains a Stockholm landmark. The creation of the Nationalmuseum was the largest governmental investment in culture in 19th-century Sweden, and although its collection may not be as impressive as some of Europe's big art museums, there are works by Rembrandt, Rubens, Gauguin, Goya and Degas, as well as substantial collections of 17th-century Dutch, 18th-century French and 18th/19th-century Swedish art, plus a huge

❤ Brunkebergstorg

T-bana T-Centralen. **Map** *p80 N8.*

In the 19th and early 20th centuries, Brunkebergstorg was a prominent meeting place in the city, with hotels and bars frequented by high society. However, swingeing demolition and development in the 1960s and '70s saw its belle epoque buildings replaced by concrete blocks, and it became a neglected intersection, sandwiched between the Riksbank on one side and government offices on the other.

Then, in 2016, city planners, architects and investors came together with a plan to redevelop this dormant space behind Gallerian, one of Stockholm's most central shopping malls. The aim was to restore Brunkebergstorg to its position at the heart of a reinvigorated city centre. Brutalist buildings from the 1970s were revamped and extended, with minimalist architecture, acres of glass and green rooftop gardens, while the central space was redesigned (by local landscape architects Nivå), with street furniture, fountains and cherry trees.

The newly revived inner-city neighbourhood has attracted a cluster of high-end boutique hotels and top-notch bars and eateries. It's also become a hub for Stockholm's mushrooming tech community: Swedish music-streaming giant Spotify moved its headquarters here in 2018, global giants Facebook and Microsoft have offices in the area, and it is home to WeWork, a hub for many of the city's most promising digital start-ups.

Of the much-hyped hotels that have opened here since 2016, **Hobo Hotel** (*see p231*) has an industrial-chic vibe and hosts regular gigs, exhibitions and panel discussions; **At Six** is an elegant design hotel known for its cocktails (*see p89*), while **Downtown Camper** (*see p231*) scores points for its rooftop pool and a rosta of outdoor activities. Food-wise, **TAK** (*see p89*), an Asian-Swedish fusion restaurant next to Hobo Hotel, is the star of the show. Next to TAK is **Stockholm Under Stjärnorna** (*see p197*), one of the best panoramic bars in the city, with long queues to get up to the sprawling outdoor terrace during summer months. You'll spot young workers in expensive trainers making good use of the daily lunch deals in the neighbourhood, while at night the bars and restaurants pull in a diverse range of Stockholmers and tourists, curious to try out the many culinary treats and cocktails on offer.

At Six Cocktail Bar

Norrbro

collection of 20th-century Scandinavian design pieces. The museum reopened in October 2018 after a five-year refurbishment project that included installing a new state-of-the-art climate control system to allow the museum to exhibit more climate-sensitive works, creating a sculpture garden courtyard and opening a restaurant designed by award-winning architects Gert Wingårdh and Erik Wikerstål.

Sta Clara Kyrka

Klarabergsgatan 37 (08 411 73 24, clarakyrka. se). T-bana T-Centralen or bus 53, 56, 59, 65, 69. **Open** *8am-5pm Mon-Fri; 5-7.30pm Sat; 10am-5pm Sun.* **Admission** *free.* **Map** *p80 M8.*

The copper spire of this brick church across from Central Station rises from a cluster of dull, box-like 1960s buildings. Sta Clara Kyrka was one of many churches built in the late 16th century during the reign of Johan III, who had a Catholic wife and a love of architecture. He decided to build here in the 1570s as it was the site of a former convent torn down in the Reformation. Dutch architect Willem Boy designed the church, and Carl Hårleman, who also completed the interior of the Kungliga Slottet (*see p67*), redesigned its roof and spire after a fire in the mid 18th century. Inside the sunlit church, the ceiling is painted with biblical scenes. The congregation gives out bread and coffee to the needy, so the graveyard and nearby steps are often occupied by homeless people.

St Jacobs Kyrka

Västra Trädgårdsgatan 2 (08 723 30 00, www.svenskakyrkan.se/stockholms domkyrkoforsamling/st-jacobs-kyrka).
T-bana Kungsträdgården or bus 43, 62, 65. **Open** *11am-5pm Mon-Wed, Sat; 11am-6pm Thur, Fri, Sun. Worship in English 6pm Sun.* **Admission** *free.* **Map** *p80 N8.*

This red church overlooking Kungsträdgården was commissioned in 1588 by King Johan III. The project was abandoned four years later when Johan died but was resumed in 1630 and completed in 1643. The church is named after the patron saint of pilgrims, who is depicted in the sandstone sculpture above the southern entrance carrying a walking staff. The church underwent several interior renovations in the 19th century, including the addition of five stained-glass panels behind the altar, depicting scenes from the New Testament.

Strindbergsmuseet

Drottninggatan 85 (08 441 91 70, www.strindbergsmuseet.se). T-bana Rådmansgatan or bus 59, 65. **Open** *Sept-June noon-4pm Tue-Sun. July to mid Aug 10am-4pm Tue-Sun. Closed Christmas.* **Admission** *75kr; 50kr reductions; free under-19s. Free with SC. Guided tours 20kr (phone 08 411 53 54. ahead to book).* **Map** *p80 L6.*

Sweden's most celebrated writer, August Strindberg, moved into an apartment in the Blå Tornet (Blue Tower) in 1908; it was his last home and is now a museum. Much of it is taken up with temporary exhibits on Strindberg as a writer, dramatist, photographer and painter, but his tiny apartment is the main reason for visiting. An air of reverence pervades the space: you have to put white slippers over your shoes to protect the floor, and his bedroom, study and sitting room are preserved as they

were at the time of his death, his pens still neatly lined up on his writing desk. It's an atmospheric and moving place: you can just imagine the ailing playwright standing on the balcony to greet a procession of well-wishers on his last birthday, 22 January 1912. He died just a few months later, on 14 May, aged 63.

Restaurants & cafés

♥ Arket Café
Arket, Drottninggatan 53 (08 566 40 240, www.arket.com). T-bana T-Centralen. **Open** *8am-8pm Mon-Fri; 10am-7pm Sat; 11am-6pm Sun.* **Map** *p80 M7* ❶ *Café*

Inside the flagship store of one of Sweden's fastest-growing fashion labels, Arket, this vegetarian cafe has been a hit with in-the-know Stockholmers since opening in 2018. Here you'll find filling wraps and salads, as well as pastries prepared at the on-site bakery. The menu was created by chef Martin Berg, one of the early proponents of the New Nordic food movement, and champions seasonal ingredients sourced from local producers.

Bakfickan
Kungliga Operan, Karl XIIs torg (08 676 58 00, www.operakallaren.se). T-bana Kungsträdgården or bus 2, 43, 62, 76, 96. **Open** *11.30am-10pm Mon-Thur; 11.20am-11pm Fri; noon-11pm Sat; noon-5pm Sun.* **Map** *p80 N8* ❷ *Traditional Swedish*

In the Opera House, alongside Operakällaren (*see p88*) and Operabaren (*see p88*), you'll find Bakfickan, the little brother of the trio that shares the same giant kitchen. Head here for

quality traditional Swedish fare if the more upscale opera establishments are too pricey or stiff for your taste.

B.A.R.
Blasieholmsgatan 4A (08 611 53 35, www.restaurangbar.se). T-bana Kungsträdgården or bus 2, 62, 65, 76, 96. **Open** *11.30am-2pm, 5pm-1am Mon-Fri; 4pm-1am Sat.* **Map** *p80 O8* ❸ *Seafood*

This seafood restaurant has its own aquarium, from which customers can select something for their dinner plate. The day's fish options are listed on a blackboard, with other dishes available from the à la carte. The quality of the cooking is generally reliable, while the long bar is ideal for pre-drinks, especially if you fancy hobnobbing with the city's fashionable set.

Berns Asiatiska
Berzelii Park (08 566 32 767, www.berns.se). T-bana Kungsträdgården or bus 2, 52, 55, 62, 69, 76, 96. **Open** *11.30am-1am daily.* **Map** *p80 O7* ❹ *Asian*

Sir Terence Conran transformed this jaw-dropping grand ballroom into a restaurant at the turn of the millennium. The food is crossover pan-Asian cuisine, ranging from sushi to ramen pork broth and crispy sweet chicken. It's served in medium-size portions, designed to be shared. The set menu is good value if you're struggling to choose.

Bianchi Café & Cycles
Norrlandsgatan 16 (08 611 21 00, bianchi.cafe). T-bana Östermalmstorg. **Open** *11am-10pm Mon, Tues; 11am-11pm Wed, Thur; 11am-midnight Fri, Sat; 11am-5pm Sun.* **Map** *p80 O7* ❺ *Café*

Cycling enthusiasts can get a bike and caffeine hit at this cosy café with leather sofas and mosaic floors, which serves a range of classic pasta, pizza and salad dishes, alongside daily specials and delicious pistachio ice cream for dessert. Stylish Italian Bianchi bikes, apparel and accessories (all for sale) decorate the space, and there's a cycle repair workshop adjacent to the restaurant.

♥ Gretas ⓦ
Haymarket Hotel, Hötorget (08 517 26 700, www.scandichotels.com). T-bana Hötorget. **Open** *8am-8pm Mon-Thur; 8am-9pm Fri; 10am-9pm Sat; 10am-6pm Sun.* **Map** *p80 M7* ⑩ *Café*

This 1920s-themed pink bistro cafe is named after the late Swedish actress Greta Garbo, who worked in the building when it was a department store, before she was famous. Despite being inside the Haymarket hotel, it's a popular spot with locals. The avocado sandwich is its trademark breakfast dish; lunch is made up of daily specials and a small selection of regular dishes, including soup and salad. This is also a great spot to enjoy afternoon tea. Outdoor tables spill on to Hötorget during the summer.

♥ Martins Gröna ⓦ
Regeringsgatan 91 (08 411 58 50, www.martinsgrona.com). T-bana Hötorget or bus 2, 43, 96. **Open** *11am-2pm Mon-Fri.* **Map** *p80 N6* ⑰ *Vegetarian*

This small, unpretentious vegetarian restaurant is a pleasant, relaxed place to eat lunch in the city centre. Each day there's a choice of just two dishes (or you can have a mix of both), served with home-baked bread and tea or coffee. It's not sophisticated fare – hearty stews are popular – but it's tasty and filling. Try to avoid the noon rush.

Mathias Dahlgren ⓦⓦⓦⓦ
Grand Hôtel, Södra Blasieholmshamnen 6 (08 679 35 84, www.mathiasdahlgren.com).

T-bana Kungsträdgården or bus 2, 43, 55, 62, 65, 76, 96. **Open** *Food bar noon-2pm, 6pm-midnight Mon-Fri; 6pm-midnight Sat. Closed mid July to mid August.* **Map** *p80 08* ⑱ *Contemporary*

Mathias Dahlgren is one of Sweden's most respected chefs and the critics' darling. His Grand Hôtel restaurant is a two-room affair: Matbaren, with one Michelin star, is a contemporary bistro serving seasonal dishes including plenty of meat and fish, while Rutabaga, is a world-class vegetarian restaurant which opened in 2017. You will need to book several weeks in advance to get a table at either, although Matbaren has several drop-in seats at the bar.

Nalen ⓦⓦ
Regeringsgatan 74 (08 505 29 201, www.nalen.com). T-bana Hötorget or bus 1, 2, 43, 56, 96. **Open** *11am-3pm, 4-10pm Mon; 11am-3pm, 4-11pm Tue-Fri; 5-11pm Sat.* **Map** *p80 N6* ⑲ *Traditional Swedish*

This restaurant shares space with an old jazz haunt (*see p196*), but it's worth scouting out even if you're not a music fan. Nalen offers classic Swedish cuisine with the best of native ingredients, such as reindeer, pike-perch and herring, at reasonable prices. Staff are attentive, and the Irish coffee comes highly recommended.

♥ Operabaren ⓦⓦⓦ
Kungliga Operan, Karl XIIs torg (08 676 58 08, www.operakallaren.se). T-bana Kungsträdgården or bus 2, 43, 55, 62, 76, 96. **Open** *11.30am-11pm Mon-Thur; 11.30am-midnight Fri; 12.30pm-midnight Sat.* **Map** *p80 N8* ㉑ *Traditional Swedish*

Operabaren is one of the city's true treasures – and perhaps the finest place to come for traditional Swedish meatballs. Sitting on the old leather sofas and admiring the magnificent Jugendstil interior is like travelling back in time. Service from the white-jacketed waiters is impeccable; prices are fair, and the food never disappoints.

Operakällaren ⓦⓦⓦⓦ
Kungliga Operan, Karl XIIs torg (08 676 58 00, www.operakallaren.se). T-bana Kungsträdgården or bus 2, 43, 55, 62, 76, 96. **Open** *6pm-1am Tue-Sat.* **Map** *p80 N8* ㉒ *European*

Operakällaren is one of Sweden's best European restaurants, with one Michelin star and a history and Opera House setting to match. The restaurant was created in the 1960s by legendary chef Tore Wretman, who, more than any other person, is responsible for turning the Swedes into foodies. These days, Stefano Catenacci, who also catered

2017. The large restaurant serves a fusion of Swedish and Asian flavours. There's also an exclusive private dining room, Unn, located inside TAK, which seats just eight guests. For drinkers, there are carefully crafted cocktails and a decent range of wines and beer, all of which can be enjoyed with a view over the Royal Palace and Lake Mälaren. Bear in mind that you may have to queue for this privilege in fine weather.

Vete-Katten ⓦ
Kungsgatan 55 (08 20 84 05, www.vetekatten. se). T-bana Hötorget or bus 1, 56, 59, 91. **Open** *7.30am-8pm Mon-Fri; 9.30am-7pm Sat, Sun.* **Map** *p80 L7* ㉚ *Café*

This old-fashioned tearoom serves classic Swedish patisseries, including *prinsesstårta* (a cream-filled cake encased in green marzipan). You can also buy biscuits, bread, cinnamon, vanilla and cardamom rolls, plus home-made ice-cream. The café's pretty courtyard has outside tables in the summer.

Wedholms Fisk ⓦⓦⓦ
Nybrokajen 17 (08 611 78 74, www. wedholmsfisk.se). T-bana Kungsträdgården or bus 2, 52, 62, 76, 96. **Open** *11.30am-2pm, 6-11pm Mon; 11.30am-11pm Tue-Fri; 5-11pm Sat.* **Map** *p80 O8* ㉛ *Seafood*

The standard of seafood in Stockholm is high, and it's especially high at Wedholms Fisk. Located close to the waterfront in the heart of the city, this is a classic restaurant, both in terms of the decor and cuisine. Dishes are simple and unfussy: when fish is this good, it needs little doing to it. If fish isn't your thing but you've somehow ended up here, there's also a daily vegetarian and meat dish, and a popular cheese platter.

Bars

Other stand-out bars include the Candier Bar at the **Grand Hotel** (*see p229*) and fabulous terrace nightspot **Stockholm Under Stjärnorna** (*see p197*).

♥ At Six Cocktail Bar
At Six Hotel, Brunkebergstorg 6 (08 578 82 800, https://hotelatsix.com). T-bana T-Centralen. **Open** *4pm-midnight Mon, Tue; 4pm-12.30am Wed; 4pm-1am Thur, Fri; 3pm-1am Sat; noon-11pm Sun.* **Map** *p80 N8* ①

The huge, polished cocktail bar inside art and design hotel At Six serves up creative signature drinks alongside light bites. The staff here really know their stuff, so don't be shy about asking for recommendations if the range seems overwhelming. If you're with a large group, the Punch Bowls are for sharing.

for Princess Madeleine's wedding, is at the helm of a frequently changing menu. This is a luxury establishment on all counts – food, service and wine. The prices are equally spectacular.

♥ TAK ⓦⓦⓦ
Brunkebergstorg 4 (08 587 22 080, tak.se). T-bana T-Centralen. **Open** *11.30am-2.30pm, 5pm-midnight Mon-Fri; noon-midnight Sat.* **Map** *p80 N8* ㉘ *Asian*

A minimalist Nordic-Japanese interior, eclectic Eurasian cocktails and a terrace sprouting with greenery and bold soft furnishings – these are just some of the carefully curated details that made this venue an instant hit when it opened in summer

The Nest Cocktail Lounge

The Auld Dub

*Holländargatan 1 (08 679 77 07, theaulddub. se). T-bana Hötorget or bus 1, 56, 59. **Open** 11am-1am Mon-Thur, Sun; 11am-3am Fri, Sat. **Map** p80 M6* ②

Still known to many locals by its previous name, the Dubliner, this is as close as you'll come to a traditional Irish pub in Stockholm, with numerous beers on tap and a lengthy whiskey list. It's fairly rowdy, and most of the bar staff – a mix of Aussies, Brits and Irish – speak English only. But it's a fun place to head if you're looking for a sociable crowd. The stage hosts covers bands and traditional Irish acts, and there's a big screen for major sporting events.

Gold Bar

*Nobis Hotel, Norrmalmstorg 2-4 (08 614 10 00, www.nobishotel.se). T-bana Östermalmstorg or bus 2, 43, 52, 55, 62, 69, 76, 96. **Open** 5pm-1am Mon-Thur; 4pm-1am Fri, Sat; 5pm-midnight Sun. **Map** p80 O7* ⑤

Nobis Hotel's (*see p229*) exquisitely designed Gold Bar has been the place for international fashionistas for nearly a decade. The bar is buzzing on Friday and Saturday nights with a glamorous crowd that includes both hotel guests and locals. Cocktails are a speciality here, including a top-notch Martini-based selection. Decent Italian bar snacks help to soften the punch of the drinks.

Icebar

*Hotel C Stockholm, Vasaplan 4 (08 505 63 520, www.icebarstockholm.se). T-bana T-Centralen or bus 1, 53, 65, 69. **Open** Mid May to mid Sept 11.15am-midnight Mon-Thur, Sun; 11.15am-1am Fri, Sat. Mid Sept-*

*mid May 3pm-midnight Mon-Thur, Sun; 3pm-1am Fri, Sat. **Admission** 199kr incl 1 vodka drink; 99kr under-18s. **Map** p80 L7* ⑥

You can be as cool as you like about this slightly gimmicky attraction, designed by the people behind the Icehotel in Jukkasjärvi in the far north of Sweden, but the minute you don your silver high-tech poncho and sip from your ice glass, you'll be giggling and snapping photos with the rest of them. This tiny sub-zero bar, maintained at a chilly -4°C (23°F), is in a corner of the Nordic C Hotel. With 20 minutes of chilling usually enough for most, the turnover is high. Loud music and fine Absolut shooters (one included in the steep entrance fee) keep spirits high. If you're part of a large group, it's wise to book (online or by phone) in advance.

♥ The Nest Cocktail Lounge

*Downtown Camper by Scandic, Brunkebergstorg 9 (08 517 26 300, www. scandichotels.se). T-bana T-Centralen. **Open** 4-10pm Mon-Thur, Sun; 2pm-1am Fri, Sat. **Map** p80 N8* ⑦

With stunning views over Stockholm's rooftops, the Nest is a cosy cocktail bar on the top floor of the Downtown Camper hotel. Crammed with soft furnishings, it gets much of its calm atmosphere from being next to the hotel's wellness centre. You can take the lift up from the main reception, even if you're not a hotel guest. For a more pub-like vibe, visit the Campfire bar and restaurant on the ground floor.

Nosh and Chow

Norrlandsgatan 24 (08 503 38 960, www. noshandchow.se). T-bana Östermalmstorg.

Open 11am-midnight Mon, Tue; 11am-2am Wed-Fri; 4pm-2am Sat. Map p80 N6 ⑧

This vibrant cocktail bar and restaurant draws a mix of affluent media types and corporate graduates. The interior was designed by Catalan architect Lázaro Rosa-Violán, famed for developing equally swish spots in Barcelona and around the world. An outdoor courtyard is usually open year-round, thanks to a fire and heaters.

Urban Deli Takpark

Urban Deli, Sveavägen 44 (08 425 50 020, www.urbandeli.org). T-bana Hötorget or bus 1, 56, 59. Open Apr-Sept 3-11pm Mon-Fri; 11.30am-11pm Sat, Sun. Closed Oct-Mar. Map p80 M6 ⑪

Open in summer only, Urban Deli Takpark is a low-key rooftop beer garden. It's lively and always busy, so come early to secure a seat in time for a sundowner. Access is via the lifts at the back of Urban Deli, the bar, cafe, restaurant and delicatessen complex on the ground floor. A firm favourite with locals, Urban Deli also has popular branches in Södermalm and in the suburb of Sickla.

Shops & services

Norrmalm's most upmarket shopping streets are located close to the border with Östermalm – head, in particular, to **Mäster Samuelsgatan** and **Biblioteksgatan** for mid-range and designer brands. For the cheaper chain shops, meanwhile, try busy, pedestrianised **Drottninggatan**, one of Stockholm's longest streets.

♥ Acne

Hamngatan 10-14 (08 20 34 55, www.acnestudios.com). T-bana Östermalmstorg or bus 2, 43, 55, 59, 62, 76, 96. Open 10am-7pm Mon-Fri; 10am-6pm Sat; 11-5pm Sun. Map p80 N7 ❶ *Fashion*

Cutting-edge Swedish fashion label Acne started out as an advertising agency, became a jeans manufacturer and is now an all-round design studio, although it's still best known for its innovative denim. This branch is located in a former bank building where a robbery and hostage situation took place in 1973. **Other locations** Norrmalmstorg 2, Norrmalm (08 611 64 11); Nytorgsgatan 36, Södermalm (08 640 04 70).

▶ *The Acne Archives store in Vasastan (Torsgatan 53 , 08 30 27 23) is a must for fans of the label, selling samples and items from past collections. There's also an Acne Outlet store at Barkarby Outlet (Majorsvägen 2-4, 08 760 53 09).*

Åhléns

Klarabergsgatan 50 (08 676 60 00, www.ahlens.se). T-bana T-Centralen or bus 52, 56, 59, 65. Open 10am-9pm Mon-Thur; 10am-7pm Sat; 11am-7pm Sun. Map p80 M7 ❷ *Department store*

You can't get much more central than Åhléns, which is located in a massive brick building next to Sergels torg. It's an excellent mid-range department store with a good cosmetics and perfume section, a nail bar and a well-stocked homeware department. The clothing departments for men, women and children stock threads by Swedish designers and international labels. Exercise fans will be impressed by the range of active wear.

Arket

Drottninggatan 53 (08 566 40 240, www.arket.com), T-bana T-Centralen. Open 10am-8pm Mon-Fri; 10am-7pm Sat, 11am-6pm Sun. Map p80 M7 ❸ *Fashion*

Part of the Swedish H&M group, Arket launched its first store in London in 2017, with the goal of offering timeless and long-lasting fashion choices for a wide age range. This Stockholm branch opened the following year and offers a high-end shopping experience, with tall grey shelves perfectly stacked with a rainbow of basic jerseys, shirts and socks. There's a homeware section selling a limited range of crockery and utensils.

Byredo

Mäster Samuelsgatan 6 (08 525 02 615, www.byredo.com). T-bana Östermalmstorg or bus 2, 55, 59, 62, 96. Open 11am-6.30pm Mon-Fri; 11am-5pm Sat. Map p80 O7 ❺ *Perfume*

The Byredo fragrance house was founded in 2006 by Ben Gorham, and has achieved enormous success in its short lifespan (it's one of the bestselling perfume brands at London's Liberty department store). The company creates perfumes, bodycare products, home fragrances and accessories – the Bibliothèque candle is utterly divine.

♥ Designtorget

Kulturhuset Stadsteatern, Sergelgången 29, Sergels torg (08 21 91 50, www.designtorget.se). T-bana T-Centralen or bus 52, 56, 59, 65. **Open** *10am-8pm Mon-Fri; 10am-7pm Sat; 11am-6pm Sun.* **Map** *p80 N7* ❼ *Design/homewares*

The concept of Designtorget is that promising new designers can sell their work on a commission basis alongside established companies. At this branch you'll find an assortment of jewellery, household goods, ceramics, textiles and furniture, as well as some original gifts. **Other locations** throughout the city.

♥ Eataly

Biblioteksgatan 5 (08 400 17 500, www. eataly.se). T-bana Östermalmstorg, bus 69. **Open** *9am-10pm Mon, Tue; 9am-11pm Wed, Thur; 9am-midnight Fri; 11am-midnight Sat; 11am-10pm Sun.* **Map** *p80 O7* ❽ *Food & drink*

This deli market and food hall is housed inside a spacious building that was formerly one of Stockholm's oldest cinemas. On sale are Italian store cupboard classics, ranging from pasta and olive oil to artisan sweets and regional condiments. There's also a decent range of fresh vegetables, meat, fish and cheese, as well as delicious fluffy bread baked on site in a wood-fired oven. If you want to eat as well as shop, the food hall has several sit-down eateries serving pizza, pasta and aperitivi, plus a mozzarella bar and a traditional Italian coffee shop.

♥ Häglöfs

Kungsgatan 10 (08 611 67 20, www.haglofs. com). T-bana Östermalmstorg or bus 2, 55, 96. **Open** *10am-7pm Mon-Fri; 10am-5pm Sat; noon-4pm Sun.* **Map** *p80 N6* ❾ *Fashion*

Founded in 1914, this stylish Swedish outdoor clothing brand has more recently won plaudits for its focus on social sustainability. The Fair Wear Foundation, an independent, non-profit organisation, gave the company its Inspiration Award in 2018 for rapidly improved conditions for workers in its garment factories. Alongside clothing for adults and children, Häglöfs sells a decent range of backpacks, although its equipment selection is more limited.

Happy Socks

Mäster Samuelsgatan 9 (08 611 87 02, www. happysocks.com/se). T-bana Östermalmstorg or bus 2, 55, 96. **Open** *10am-7pm daily.* **Map** *p80 O7* ❿ *Fashion*

This Swedish sock brand, known for its bright and bold designs, has grown exponentially since its launch more than a decade ago. Its socks and tights are stocked in shops all around the city, but this is the brand's original standalone store. Since 2014, the label has also been selling popular colourful underwear lines.

Hope

Smålandsgatan 14 (070 962 31 79, www. hope-sthlm.com). T-bana Östermalmstorg or bus 2, 52, 55, 62, 96. **Open** *10am-7pm Mon-Fri; 10am-6pm Sat; noon-5pm Sun.* **Map** *p80 O7* ⓫ *Fashion*

Hope is a stylish Swedish label created and run by the designers Ann Ringstrand and Stefan Söderberg, catering to women and men. It's characterised by well-made, modern utility wear, with influences including vintage uniforms and traditional jackets. This flagship store stocks the full collection. **Other locations** Odengatan 70, Vasastan (08 410 64 123); Götgatan 34, Södermalm (08 410 64 123).

♥ Hötorgshallen

Hötorget Sergelmalmstorg 29 (08 23 00 01, www. hotorgshallen.se). T-bana Hötorget or bus 1, 56, 59. **Open** *10am-6pm Mon-Thur; 10am-7pm Fri; 10am-4pm Sat.* **Map** *p80 M7* ⓬ *Food hall*

A visit to Hötorgshallen is a culinary trip around the world. Built in the 1950s, the hall was renovated in the 1990s and its international character has grown along with immigration to Stockholm. You can buy everything from Middle Eastern falafel to Indian spices, as well as fantastic fish and meat, and there are several good places to grab lunch. Outside there's a bustling fruit, vegetable and flower market on Hötorget, which first opened in the 1640s.

Illums Bolighus Stockholm

Klarabergsgatan 62 (08 718 55 00, www. illumsbolighus.se). T-bana T-Centralen. **Open** *10am-7pm Mon-Fri; 10am-6pm Sat; 11am-6pm Sun.* **Map** *p80 L8* ⓭ *Furniture/ homewares*

This is the Stockholm branch of the historic Danish furniture and interior design store chain, founded in 1926. Stock includes upmarket furniture, ceramics, glass and lighting fixtures by renowned Scandinavian designers.

Kartbutiken

Mäster Samuelsgatan 54 (08 20 23 03, www. kartbutiken.se). T-bana T-Centralen or bus 53, 56, 59, 65, 69. **Open** *10am-6pm Mon-Fri; 10am-4pm Sat; noon-4pm Sun.* **Map** *p80 M7* ⓮ *Books & accessories*

This travel specialist has a good range of maps, guidebooks, travel accessories, atlases and globes, as well as marine charts for the more intrepid traveller.

♥ Naturkompaniet

Kungsgatan 26 (08 24 19 96, www. naturkompaniet.se). T-bana Hötorget or bus 1, 56, 291. **Open** *10am-7pm Mon-Fri; 10am-5pm Sat; noon-4pm Sun.* **Map** *p80 N6* ⓯ *Outdoors*

Everything you need for that camping weekend, from clothing and boots to mushroom foraging equipment and travel guides. Naturkompaniet, whose symbol is a bear, is a core stockist of Swedish brand Fjällräven, famous both for its outstanding quality and timeless 1970s cut; a huge range of the brand's trendy colourful Kånken backpacks are on display here. There are several other locations around the city; see the website for details.

💚 NK

Hamngatan 18-20 (08 762 80 00, www.nk.se). T-bana Kungsträdgården or Östermalmstorg, or bus 2, 43, 52, 55, 62, 69, 76, 91. **Open** *10am-8pm Mon-Fri; 10am-6pm Sat; 11am-5pm Sun.* **Map** *p80 N7* **16** *Department store*

Eternally elegant, Nordiska Kompaniet is one of the city's most treasured institutions. The famous revolving sign on the roof – with the letters NK on one side and a clock on the other – is visible from all over town. A sort of Swedish Selfridges, it's a first-class store, particularly good for clothes (lots of Scandinavian labels), Swedish souvenirs (crafts, homewares and glassware in the basement) and gourmet food. There's a decent in-house supermarket, a books section with a good selection of fiction titles in English, and a concession of Swedish stationery brand Bookbinders – established in 1927, and selling some of the best-quality paper, books, boxes and folders in Stockholm.

Polarn o Pyret

Hamngatan 37 (08 735 33 24, www. polarnopyrét.se). T-bana Östermalmstorg or bus 2, 52, 55, 62, 69, 59, 76, 96. **Open** *10am-8pm Mon-Fri; 10am-6pm Sat; 11am-6pm Sun.* **Map** *p80 N7* **18** *Children's fashion*

Polarn o Pyret (the Pal & the Tot) became famous in the 1970s when its striped, long-sleeved T-shirts dressed a generation of kids. With a retro revival in the new millennium, today's grown-ups and children can be seen sporting Polarn o Pyret's soft fabrics and simple styles, including, of course, stripes. **Other locations** Gallerian, Hamngatan 35, Norrmalm (08 411 22 47); Västermalmsgallerian, Kungsholmen (08 653 57 30); Fältöversten, Karlaplan 13, Östermalm (08 660 62 75); Ringen, Götgatan 98, Södermalm (08 642 03 62).

Svensk Hemslöjd

Norrlandsgatan 20 (23 21 15, www. svenskhemslojd.com). T-bana Östermalmstorg. **Open** *10am-6pm Mon-Fri; 11am-4pm Sat; noon-4pm Sun.* **Map** *p80 N6* **20** *Crafts/homewares*

Founded in 1899, Svensk Hemslöjd (Swedish Handicrafts) is the place to head for hand-made Swedish homewares, textiles, yarns and traditional gifts, with a wide range of cushions, wool blankets, candleholders and superior Dala horses. You can also buy everything you need to make your own.

Weekday

Drottninggatan 63 (08 411 29 70, www. weekday.com). T-bana Hötorget or T-Centralen, or bus 1, 56, 59. **Open** *10am-7pm Mon-Fri; 10am-6pm Sat; 11am-5pm Sun.* **Map** *p80 M7* **21** *Fashion*

This is Stockholm's biggest stockist of Swedish brand Cheap Monday, known for its cool, well-cut cheap jeans. Other items sold here are equally stylish and affordable, featuring sharp silhouettes and edgy graphics. All Weekday stores are spacious and full of energy. **Other location** Götgatan 21, Södermalm (08 642 17 72).

Whyred

Smålandsgatan 20 (08 660 01 70, www. whyred.se). T-bana Östermalmstorg or bus 2, 55, 96. **Open** *10am-7pm Mon-Fri; 10am-5pm Sat; noon-4pm Sun.* **Map** *p80 O7* **22** *Fashion*

This flagship of the stylish Swedish clothes brand features well-cut clothes for men and women, with extremely desirable takes on urban classics such as the parka jacket, chelsea boots and chinos. Tasteful tones, stripes and quality materials feature heavily. **Other location** Bruno, Götgatsbacken 36, Södermalm (*see p144*).

VASASTAN

Tegnérgatan marks the border between Norrmalm and Vasastan. You'll find a good selection of pubs, restaurants and antiques shops east of Tegnérlunden park. Head north on tree-lined Sveavägen – designed to look like a Parisian boulevard – to reach the south-east corner of the hillside park, **Observatorielunden**. On the park's eastern side is the grand **Handelshögskolan** (Stockholm School of Economics), designed by Ivar Tengbom, who was also architect of the Konserthuset. Up the steep steps on top of the hill is the observatory building, which dates back to the 18th century and was the source of the Swedish meridian that controlled timekeeping throughout the country until the Greenwich meridian became the international standard in 1884. For the moment, the public can only access the observatory's **Himlavalvet Café** (11am-5pm daily).

Standing proudly at the park's north-east corner, Gunnar Asplund's bright orange **Stadsbiblioteket** (Stockholm Public

Library) is one of Sweden's best-known architectural works, instantly identifiable by its round central building. Several blocks north on Sveavägen is the quiet, hilly park of **Vanadislunden**.

If you head west from the library along busy Odengatan, you'll reach the triangle-shaped **Odenplan** square, bordered by the beautiful Baroque **Gustaf Vasa Kyrka** and surrounded by the rumble of passing buses. The main entrance to Odenplan's metro and commuter train station is a futuristic structure with a white sloping roof; it featured in Swedish director Ruben Ostlund's Oscar-nominated satirical drama *The Square* in 2018.

Two blocks further west is the green retreat of **Vasaparken**, with outdoor summer cafés and a football field/ice-skating rink, depending on the season. The easternmost section of the park was recently renamed **Astrid Lindgren's Terrace** after the author of the Pippi Longstocking children's books, who died in 2002; she lived just across the street. At the western end of the park is the bustling intersection of St Eriksplan; to the south is the shiny contemporary **Sven-Harrys Konstmuseum**, a privately owned art museum, as well as high-end apartments.

The neighbourhood of **Birkastan**, west of St Eriksplan, was built during the early 20th century for the working classes, but now attracts all-comers to its charming cafés and restaurants around Rörstrandsgatan, especially during the summer when the street is pedestrianised. If you take St Eriksgatan south, you'll end up on Kungsholmen.

Sights & museums

Bonniers Konsthall

Torsgatan 19 (08 736 42 48, www. bonnierskonsthall.se). T-bana St Eriksplan or bus 3, 70, 77, 94. Open noon-8pm Wed; noon-5pm Thur-Sun. Admission 100kr; 80kr reductions; free under-26s & to all on Fri. Map p80 J6.

This contemporary art gallery was founded by the late Jeanette Bonnier, part of the family behind the Bonnier Group, one of Scandinavia's biggest media concerns. Bonniers Konsthall is one of the group's non-profit ventures. There's a programme of talks, artists in conversation and innovative exhibitions of international and Swedish art.

♥ Gustaf Vasa Kyrka

Karlbergsvägen 1-5 (08 508 88 600, www. svenskakyrkan.se/gustafvasa). T-bana Odenplan or bus 2, 40, 65. Open usually 11am-6pm Mon-Thur; 11am-3pm Fri-Sun. Admission free (concerts & activities free-100kr). Map p80 J4.

Completed in 1906, this white church in the Italian Baroque style is, without doubt, Vasastan's most beautiful building, its striking 60m (200ft) dome rising high above Odenplan. Inside, the spectacular 1731 altarpiece is Sweden's largest Baroque sculpture, originally created for Uppsala Cathedral. It depicts Jesus on the cross in

Gustaf Vasa Kyrka

Stadsbiblioteket p95

front of a relief of Jerusalem. The ceiling frescoes in the dome show scenes from the New Testament.

❤ Stadsbiblioteket

*Sveavägen 73 (biblioteket.stockholm.se). T-bana Odenplan. **Open** 10am-9pm Mon-Thur; 10am-7pm Fri; 11am-5pm Sat, Sun. **Admission** free. **Map** p80 L4.*

This landmark 1920s orange building is a paradise for bibliophiles and architecture addicts alike. It contains upwards of 400,000 novels, textbooks, plays, poems and reference materials in multiple languages, many of them stacked from floor to ceiling around its iconic cylindrical reading tower. The room's three-level design comes courtesy of Swedish architect Gunnar Asplund, whose goal was to allow visitors to browse the shelves without having to seek out help from librarians. You might feel a bit sheepish taking photos in here, but the regular bookworms and students that frequent the place are used to passing tourists. To photograph the rotunda's exterior from the best angle, head to the large rectangular pond on Sveavägen, designed by the same architect as the library.

Sven-Harrys Konstmuseum

*Eastmansvägen 10-12 (08 511 60 060, www. sven-harrys.se). T-bana Odenplan or St Eriksplan or bus 3, 4, 40, 53, 69. **Open** 11am-7pm Wed; 11am-9pm Thur; 11am-7pm Fri; 11am-5pm Sat, Sun. **Admission** 120kr; 90kr reductions; free under-19s. **Map** p80 J5.*

This six-storey art museum and exhibition space opened in spring 2011 in an impressive purpose-built building near Vasaparken – a five-minute walk away from Bonniers Konsthall (*see p94*). Swedish building contractor Sven-Harry Karlson has amassed a personal collection of 20th-century Scandinavian art over some 40 years, and

it's these works that form the basis of the museum. Upstairs is a restaurant and some upmarket apartments.

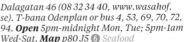

Restaurants & cafés

Le Bistro de Wasahof ⓦ ⓦ ⓦ

*Dalagatan 46 (08 32 34 40, www.wasahof. se). T-bana Odenplan or bus 4, 53, 69, 70, 72, 94. **Open** 5pm-midnight Mon, Tue; 5pm-1am Wed-Sat. **Map** p80 J5 ❻ Seafood*

This restaurant acts as a second home to writers, actors, singers and well-dressed wannabes. A bar and bistro, its main contribution to the culinary scene is its seafood – including imported oysters from France and the Swedish west coast. Next door at no.46, hipper sibling **Musslan** (08 32 34 40, www.musslan.se) specialises in *moules frites* and serves a younger crowd.

❤ Café Pascal ⓦ

*Norrtullsgatan 4, (08 31 61 10, cafepascal. se). T-bana Odenplan or bus 4, 53, 69, 70, 72, 94 **Open** 7am-7pm Mon-Thur; 7am-6pm Fri; 9am-6pm Sat, Sun. **Map** p80 K4 ❼ Café*

Run by three siblings with a passion for coffee, Café Pascal has partnered with three Swedish roasteries specialising in organic, fair trade and downright tasty grains. It also serves up buns, pastries, hearty soups and sandwiches. The exposed brickwork and hanging tungsten light bulbs create an edgy yet homely vibe, although it can be hard to get a table in the lunchtime crush.

Döden i Grytan ⓦ ⓦ

*Norrtullsgatan 61 (08 32 50 95, www. dodenigrytan.se). T-bana Odenplan or bus 2, 40, 65. **Open** 11am-2pm, 5.30-11pm Mon-Fri; noon-midnight Sat; noon-10pm Sun. Kitchen closes 11pm Mon-Sat; 9.45pm Sun. **Map** p80 J3 (off map) ❽ Italian*

Don't let the strange name (Death in the Pot) or dead-end street location put you off – this is a welcoming neighbourhood Italian with friendly service and great food. The focus is on first-class meat – *bistecca Fiorentina, salsiccia* in all shapes and sizes, *pasta all'amatriciana* – and the portions are enormous. The same family runs another excellent Italian, nearby **Den Gamle och Havet** (Tulegatan 27, 08 661 53 00, www.dengamleochhavet.se), which means 'the Old Man and the Sea'.

Garage del Gusto ⓦ

*Västmannagatan 54 (08 30 32 80, www. garagedelgusto.com). T-bana Odenplan. **Open** 5-11pm Tue-Fri; 6-11pm Sat. **Map** p80 K4 ❾ Italian*

Simple and unpretentious pasta is the staple at Garage del Gusto, which aspires to offer the

NORRMALM & VASASTAN

kind of down-to-earth experience you'd get eating at an Italian grandmother's home. The friendly owners encourage diners to mingle. *Aperitivi* are offered during the early evening (times vary depending on the day), which means you get a simple snack of meat, cheese and bread when you buy a drink.

❤ Kaffeverket ⓦ

Sankt Eriksgatan 88 (08 31 51 42, kaffeverket. nu). T-bana St Eriksplan or bus 3, 4, 42, 72, 77. Open 7am-6pm Mon-Fri; 9am-6pm Sat, Sun. Map p80 H5 ⑪ *Café*

Scandinavian minimalism fans will love this monochrome coffee shop, where hanging black lamps offset white-tiled walls and benches covered in soft sheepskin rugs. Alongside a mouth-watering selection of cakes and pastries, it serves rustic sandwiches, fresh salads and a small selection of warm dishes. There's top-notch coffee and a wide range of teas, juices and smoothies too.

Ki-mama ⓦ

Observatoriegatan 13 (08 33 34 82, https:// kimama.restaurant). T-bana Odenplan or bus 2, 40, 65. Open 11am-9pm Mon-Fri; 1-9pm Sat, Sun. Map p80 K5 ⑫ *Japanese*

This top sushi spot offers a good selection of fish, cut in the regular Swedish size (ie too big to eat in one bite), and reasonable prices. Ki-mama is deservedly popular among locals, although more for lunch than dinner, due to its early closing time and lack of an alcohol licence. Ramen dishes are also on the menu.

▶ *Ki-mama's sister restaurant, Ramen Ki-mama (Birger Jarlsgatan 93, 08 15 55 39), serves up noodle soups and ramen, and has an alcohol licence.*

Lao Wai ⓦⓦ

Luntmakargatan 74 (08 673 78 00, www. laowai.se). T-bana Rådmansgatan or bus 43, 59. Open 11am-2pm, 5.30-10pm Mon-Sat. Kitchen closes 9pm. Map p80 L4 ⑬ *Asian/ Vegetarian*

One of Stockholm's best vegetarian restaurants is slightly hidden away in a simply decorated space, but it's well worth seeking out. The base is Chinese, but with influences from several other Asian cuisines. Try the Jian Chang tofu (smoked tofu with shiitake mushrooms, sugar snap peas and fresh spices). The tea menu is also spectacular.

Levinskys ⓦ

Rörstrandsgatan 9 (08 30 33 33, www. levinskys.se). T-bana St Eriksplan or bus 3, 4, 42, 72, 77. Open 11am-10pm Mon-Thur; 11am-11pm Fri; 11.30am-10.30pm Sat; 11.30am-10pm Sun. Map p80 G5 ⑭ *Café*

If you've got a smoothie craving, head to Levinskys (try the blueberry and banana). Alongside the usual salad, sandwich and cake offerings, Levinskys offers tasty homemade burgers, as well as weekend brunch.

▶ *For dessert, pop round the corner to Stockholms Glasshus (Birkagatan 8, 30 32 37, www.glasshus.se) for home-made ice-cream in flavours you'd previously only dreamed about.*

❤ Lilla Ego ⓦⓦ

Västmannagatan 69 (08 27 44 55, lillaego. com). T-bana Odenplan or bus 2, 42, 69, 70. Open 5-11pm Tue-Sat. Map p80 J4 ⑮ *Contemporary Scandinavian*

The contemporary Scandinavian interior (bare-brick walls, white wooden chairs, sheepskin throws) gives this small neighbourhood restaurant a cosy, honest and hopeful vibe. And the food is fantastic, combining top-notch seasonal ingredients with skilful technique and passionate creativity. The frequently changing menu is written on the wall and might include the likes of pickled herring with egg yolk and swede, lamb with celeriac, or turbot with a seafood broth; the chefs engage with the diners by sometimes serving the dishes themselves. Lilla Ego is very popular, so book in advance – or try for a seat at the bar.

Lindquists ⓦ

Odengatan 27 (08 411 59 55, www.lindquists. nu). T-bana Rådmansgatan or bus 42, 53. Open 7am-7pm Mon-Fri; 8am-6pm Sat, Sun. Map p80 M3 ⑯ *Bakery café*

One of a dying breed of old-school bakery-cafés, Lindquists is as traditional as they come. Divided into two sections – a takeaway bakery/pâtisserie counter and a sit-down café area kitschly decorated with pictures of the Swedish royal family – it's a great spot for traditional Swedish delicacies such as *semlor* (cream-filled buns). The passionfruit cheesecake is also heavenly.

Nisch ⓦⓦⓦ

Dalagatan 42 (08 94 91 13, www. nischrestaurant.com). T-bana Odenplan or bus 40, 53, 69. Open 6-11pm Tue-Sat. Map p80 J5 ⑳ *Contemporary Scandinavian*

All guests at Nisch (previously called Smörgåårteriet until a revamp in 2018) are served a seven-course tasting menu, which promises to pick the best from Sweden's sea, fields and forest, depending on the season. Wine pairing is an important and highly enjoyable part of any meal here, and the excellent list includes lots of organic bottles. Service is polite and friendly.

Pom and Flora ⓦ
Odengatan 39 (073 371 38 19, pomochflora.
se). T-bana Rådmansgatan or bus 4, 42, 53.
Open *7am-4pm Mon-Fri; 9am-4pm Sat, Sun.*
Map *p80 L4* ㉓ *Brunch café*

All-day breakfast is the core theme at Pom
and Flora, which boasts some of the best acai
and vegan protein bowls in the city, as well
as pimped-up porridges and open toasted
sandwiches. There's plenty of floor space,
which means it's often packed with stylish
young families enjoying their long parental
leave. **Other location** Bondegatan 64,
Södermalm (076 249 67 01).

Ritorno ⓦ
Odengatan 80-82 (08 32 01 06, www.ritorno.
se). T-bana Odenplan or bus 4, 53, 69, 70, 72,
94. **Open** *Sept-June 7am-10pm Mon-Thur;*
7am-8pm Fri; 8am-6pm Sat; 10am-6pm Sun.
July-Aug 7am-6pm Mon-Fri; 8am-6pm Sat;
10am-6pm Sun. **Map** *p80 J5* ㉔ *Café*

Time stands still at this 1950s café, where
beautiful old jukeboxes are still in working
order. The regulars voiced a collective outcry
when a revamp was suggested, so the battered
leather sofas and kitsch decor remain.
Ritorno offers everything from traditional
shrimp sandwiches to calorie-dripping
Danish pastries.If you don't drink coffee, try
the apple soda Pommac. The café doubles as a
gallery and the paintings on show are for sale.

Rolfs Kök ⓦ ⓦ
Tegnérgatan 41 (08 10 16 96, www.rolfskok.
se). T-bana Rådmansgatan or bus 59, 65.
Open *11.30am-1am Mon-Fri; 5pm-1am Sat,*
Sun. **Map** *p80 L5* ㉕ *Swedish*

A favourite haunt for lunching business
executives, this Stockholm design classic
is well worth a visit for both the interesting
food (a mix of traditional and contemporary
Swedish) and decor. Chairs hang on the grey
concrete walls, ready to be quickly taken
down if more diners arrive. Solo eaters are
lined up at the long bar overlooking the
open kitchen. East Asian ideas combine with
southern European tricks, and the creative
somersaults usually succeed, making a visit
to Rolfs Kök always a treat. Owner-chef
Johan Jureskog also runs AG Restaurang in
Kungsholmen (*see p160*).

Sosta ⓦ
Sveavägen 84-86 (www.sosta.se). T-bana
Rådmansgatan or bus 59. **Open** *8am-6pm*
Mon-Fri; 10am-5pm Sat. **Map** *p80 L5* ㉖
Espresso bar

This standing room-only espresso bar is
known all over Sweden for its extraordinary
coffee and low prices – although some say it's
as famous for the well-dressed baristas who

make the *doppios* and serve the *cornettos*. Try
the focaccia or the home-made strawbery
sorbet, and you'll realise that Sosta is perhaps
the closest you'll get to Italy in Scandinavia.

Sushi Sho ⓦ ⓦ ⓦ ⓦ
Upplandsgatan 45 (08 30 30 30, www.
sushisho.se). T-bana Odenplan or bus 40, 53,
69. **Open** *5-11pm Tue-Fri; 1-11pm Sat.* **Map**
p80 K5 ㉗ *Japanese*

This intimate sushi bar was the first Asian
restaurant in Sweden to get a Michelin
star. Its head chef, Carl Ishizaki, spent two
decades perfecting his unique twist on
some of Japan's most classic recipes before
investing in his own tiny 20-seat venue. Here,
customers experience 15 of his signature
dishes in one sitting via a seasonal tasting
menu, scribbled up on a giant chalkboard, in
a relaxed, friendly atmosphere.

Tranan ⓦ ⓦ
Karlbergsvägen 14 (08 527 28 100, www.
tranan.se). T-bana Odenplan or bus 2, 4,
40, 65, 96. **Open** *11.30am-11pm Mon-Wed;*
11.30am-midnight Thur, Fri; noon-11pm Sat,
Sun. **Map** *p80 K4* ㉙ *Modern European*

Once a working-class pub, Tranan has
changed dramatically to reach out to the
professionals who now inhabit Vasastan. The
transformation has been managed well, and
Tranan has become one of the city's classic
eating holes, serving Swedish and European
comfort food which you're encouraged to
round off with a dessert or a glass of sherry.
There's a trendy bar in the basement (*see p98*).

Yuc Mexican ⓦ ⓦ
Norrtullsgatan 15 (08 30 00 81, yuc.se).
T-bana Odenplan or bus 2, 4, 40, 65, 96.
Open *5-10pm Mon, Sun; 5-11pm Tue;*
5pm-midnight Wed, Thur; 4pm-1am Fri;
5pm-1am Sat. **Map** *p80 K4* ㉜ *Mexican*

This Mexican restaurant with a modern-
industrial style always draws a lively crowd.
It's common to hear Spanish-speakers here,
tucking into a menu of *taquitos*, ceviche
and tacos, all of which are designed to be
shared. A sister branch, **Yuk LatAsian** on
Jakobsbergsgatan, close to Hötorget station,
fuses Mexican and Peruvian cuisine with
eastern flavours. The bar, where you can
order bar snacks, has an extensive tequila-
based cocktail list and a tropical vibe, thanks
to the bright and bold decor, regular DJs
playing Latin music and a holiday-happy
international crowd.

Bars

In the north-west of the district, rooftop bar
Arc at Blique by Nobis hotel (Gävlegatan 18,

www.bliquebynobis.se) is a rarity in
this part of the city.

Bagpipers Inn

*Rörstrandsgatan 21 (08 31 18 55, www.
bagpipers.se). T-bana St Eriksplan or bus 42,
72.* **Open** *4-11pm Mon, Tue; 4pm-1am Wed,
Thur; 3pm-1am Fri; 2pm-1am Sat; 2-11pm
Sun.* **Admission** *free. Minimum age 18.* **Map**
p80 G5 (off map) ❸

The bartenders have been known to wear kilts
at this Scottish-themed pub decked out in dark
wood and green paint, with knick-knacks from
the Highlands. There's a decent selection of
beer, with around a dozen brews on tap, many
from the UK and Ireland. The crowd consists
mainly of thirtysomethings and out-of-
towners drawn by the cosy atmosphere.

Bar Nombre

*Odengatan 36 (08 612 14 20, barnombre.se)
T-bana Odenplan.* **Open** *5-11pm Mon, Tue;
5pm-1am Wed, Thur, Sat; 4pm-1am Fri;
5-10pm Sun.* **Map** *p80 L3* ❹

Packed with Spanish-influences, this is a
stylish but laid-back option for those in
search of a simple glass of wine, cava or beer.
There's rustic furniture and velvet-red decor,
while vintage prints and newspapers plaster
an entire wall. You can soak up your drinks by
ordering the scrummy tapas plates on offer.

Svartengrens

*Tulegatan 24 (08 612 65 50, www.
svartengrens.se). T-bana Rådmansgatan or
bus 6, 61, 67, 72, 94.* **Open** *5-11pm Tue, Sun;
5pm-midnight Wed, Thur; 5pm-1am Fri, Sat.*
Map *p80 L3* ❾

The bar at Svartengrens, a meat-heavy
neighbourhood restaurant, is a winner if
you're looking for a calm venue where you
can savour your drinks slowly. You can book
a table here even if you're not eating. Handcrafted cocktails, a range of micro-brewed
beers and plenty of fine wines served by the
glass are on offer. Enjoy the bold wall art
while you sip on your tipple.

Tranan

*Karlbergsvägen 14 (08 527 28 100, www.
tranan.se). T-bana Odenplan or bus 2, 4,
40, 65, 96.* **Open** *11.30am-11pm Mon-Wed;
11.30am-midnight Thur, Fri; noon-11pm Sat,
Sun.* **Map** *p80 K4* ❿

In the basement of the well-respected Tranan
restaurant (*see p97*), this decades-old bar
combines minimalist chic with the cosy feel
of a cellar. A DJ spins as twentysomethings
congregate around the sturdy wooden tables.
Never too surprising, Tranan still manages
to hold its own as one of the most enduring
haunts in Stockholm.

Shops & services

For the **Acne Archives** shop, *see p91.*

Arkivet

*Norrtullsgatan 33 (072 969 20 00, arkivetsthlm.
se). T-bana Odenplan.* **Open** *11am-6pm Mon-
Fri; 11am-4pm Sat; noon-4pm Sun.* **Map** *p80
K3* ❹ *Second-hand fashion.*

High-end second-hand clothing is sold at
Arkivet, a symbol of Stockholm's strong
sustainable fashion economy. Open since 2017,
the idea is that regular customers bring in
items they no longer wear but could imagine
someone like them buying. They then earn a
commission if the stock is sold, which can be
put towards other clothing. Brands here vary,
but you're likely to find Swedish labels such as
Filippa K, Acne and Tiger of Sweden, alongside
more mid-range options. There's a second
store on Nybrogaten in Östermalm.

♥ Cajsa Warg

*Sankt Eriksplan 2 (08 33 01 20, www.
cajsawarg.se). T-bana Sankt Eriksplan or bus
4.* **Open** *7.30am-9pm Mon-Fri; 9am-9pm Sat,
Sun.* **Map** *p80 H5* ❻ *Delicatessen.*

Stockholm foodies adore this delicatessen,
named after Anna Kristina Warg, who was
a chef in the city during the 18th century. It
sells organic fruit and vegetables, sauces and
cheeses alongside quality store-cupboard
treats from Swedish lingonberry jam and
gingerbread biscuits to picholine olives and
handmade pasta. You can request items to
be gift-boxed. Cajsa Warg is also the perfect
place to pick up healthy ready-to-heat meals,
if you've rented an apartment.

Plagg

*Odengatan 75 (08 31 90 04, www.plagg.se).
T-bana Odenplan or bus 2, 4, 40, 65.* **Open**
*10am-6.30pm Mon-Fri; 11am-4pm Sat; noon-
4pm Sun.* **Map** *p80 K4* ⓱ *Fashion*

At Plagg, the smart-looking 21st-century woman
gets classy clothing from designers such as
Denmark's DAY/Birger et Mikkelsen or Sweden's
Filippa K. The selection is larger than you might
think, given the size of the shop. **Other locations**
St Eriksgatan 37, Kungsholmen (08 650 31 58);
Rörstrandsgatan 8, Vasastan (08 30 58 01).

Record Hunter

*St Eriksgatan 70 (08 32 20 23, www.recordhunter.
se). T-bana St Eriksplan or bus 3, 4, 49, 77,
94.* **Open** *noon-6pm Mon-Fri; 11am-4pm Sat;
noon-4pm Sun.* **Map** *p80 G5* ⓳ *Music*

One of Stockholm's best second-hand record
stores, in terms of scope, friendliness and
prices. Every genre is stocked, and there are
bargains aplenty. Be sure to inspect records
carefully for scratches.

Hagaparken

Explore a romantic royal garden

Hagaparken, just north of Vasastan, is a popular outdoor destination with lawns, meandering paths, scenic waterside views and assorted pavilions. It's the 18th-century legacy of King Gustav III and architect Fredrik Magnus Piper, who wanted to create a romantic English-style garden. Today, the park is part of a broader Stockholm national park, christened **Ekoparken** (www.ekoparken.org) in 1995 by the Swedish parliament. Tagged as the world's first national park within a city, Ekoparken consists of 27 square kilometres (ten square miles) of land and water, cutting a diagonal green swathe across the city from the island of Djurgården in the south-east to Ulriksdals Palace in the north-west.

In Haga's northern section, is the **Fjärilshuset** (fjarilshuset.se, 10am-5pm daily, admission 90kr-175kr), a conservatory full of exotic butterflies and tropical rainforest vegetation. There's also an aquarium with reef sharks here – **Haga Ocean**. To the south, three colourful copper tents form **Koppartälten**. Built as Gustav III's stables and guards' quarters, one now houses a café. The ruins of a palace left incomplete after Gustav III's assassination in 1792 are east of the tents.

Sweden's current king, Carl XVI Gustaf, was born in nearby **Haga Slott** (08 402 60 00, www.kungahuset.se), a castle now converted into a hotel and conference centre. Other royal buildings include the waterfront **Gustav III's Paviljong** (08 402 61 30, www. royalcourt.se), with Pompeii-style interiors by 18th-century interior decorator Louis Masreliéz, which is open for guided tours during the summer). You can also test the acoustics in the outdoor **Ekotemplet**, which was originally used as a summer dining room. The 18th-century obsession with the exotic is evident in the Chinese pagoda and Turkish pavilion in the south of the park. A small island nearby has been the burial place of Swedish royalty since the 1910s.

At the southern tip of Hagaparken, enjoy a meal or brunch at **Haga Forum** (Annerovägen 4, 08 833 48 44, https://hagaforum.se, ⓦ), a bus terminal turned modern restaurant with a terrace overlooking the park and water. Neighbouring **Stallmästaregården** (08 610 13 01, stallmastaregarden.se, ⓦⓦⓦ) is a fancier alternative; inside the buttercup-yellow wooden walls of the city's oldest surviving inn is one of Sweden's top design hotels with a fine dining restaurant.

Across the E4 highway to the west is **Norra begravningsplats** (Vårvindsvägen), an elaborate 19th-century cemetery featuring sculptures by Swedish artists. Alfred Nobel, August Strindberg and Ingrid Bergman lie amid its hedges and landscaped hills.

▶ *Entrance at Gustav IIIs Paviljong (visithaga.se). Bus 515 or 57 to Haga norra (for the north of the park) or Haga södra (for the south).*

Ekotemplet

Östermalm & Gärdet

This urban playground for the rich, beautiful and somewhat famous is a shopper's paradise by day and party central for glamour-seeking Stockholmers by night. The main focus is the bustling square of Stureplan, at the centre of which stands the concrete rain shelter known as Svampen (Mushroom). Strandvägen, the waterfront boulevard that runs towards Djurgården, is lined with grand, late 19th-century apartments that gaze down upon a long line of luxury yachts and vibrant floating bars during the summer months.

The district to the east of Valhallavägen is known as Gärdet. It encompasses a swathe of undeveloped grassy parkland called Ladugårdsgärdet, or 'the field of barns', which, until 1885, gave its name to all the land east of Norrmalm. However, as more affluent people moved into the neighbourhood, the agricultural association became less desirable, and Östermalm was adopted as the name for the built-up area closest to the city centre.

Recently the docks on the eastern edge of Gärdet, overlooking Lidingö, have been the focus for a massive redevelopment programme that will transform former industrial land into sustainable housing and businesses.

❤ **Don't miss**

1 Svenskt Tenn *p111*
Iconic Swedish design shop.

2 Hallwylska Museet *p105*
The eccentric home of Count and Countess von Hallwyl.

3 Bergianska Trädgården *p115*
Botanical gardens in a picturesque setting.

4 Tekniska Museet *p114*
Gadgets galore for kids and adults.

Sturegallerian *p104*

ÖSTERMALM & GÄRDET

Restaurants & cafés

1. Arnold's *p106*
2. Brasserie Elverket *p107*
3. Brasserie Godot *p107*
4. Café Saturnus *p107*
5. Djurgårdsbrunn *p114*
6. Gastrologik & Speceriet *p107*
7. Halv Grek plus Turk *p108*
8. Kommendoren *p108*
9. Konditoriet *p108*
10. Miss Voon *p108*

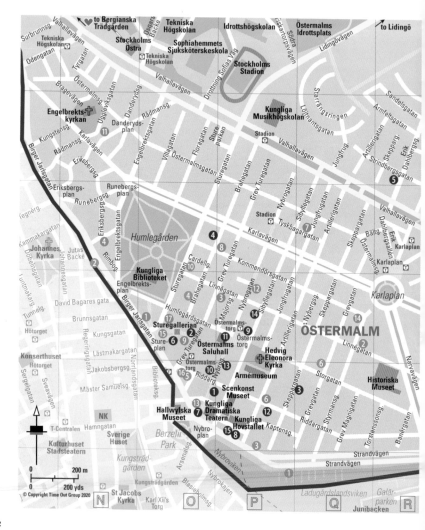

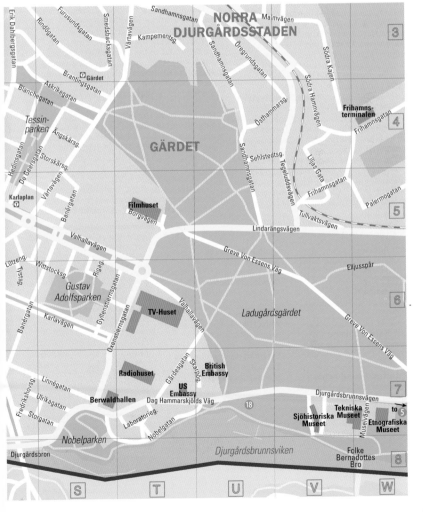

ÖSTERMALM

Stureplan is the city's most upmarket shopping area. The ultra-posh **Sturegallerian** shopping mall borders the square; as well as designer boutiques, it houses the exclusive art nouveau **Sturebadet** bathhouse (08 545 01 500, www.sturebadet.se). Shopaholics can spend a few happy hours trawling the surrounding streets, notably the lower end of Birger Jarlsgatan, where you'll find international designer fashion boutiques, classy jewellery, fancy cosmetics and swish sportswear galore.

Cinderella and Strömma Kanalbolaget ferries depart from **Nybroviken** for destinations in Lake Mälaren and the archipelago. Classics by Strindberg and Shakespeare are performed in the **Kungliga Dramatiska Teatern** (*see p206*), an ornate white marble building facing Nybroplan square and one of Stockholm's leading theatres. Nearby is the idiosyncratic **Hallwylska Museet**.

If you walk up Sibyllegatan, to the right of the theatre, you'll pass three buildings constructed by royal commission. Bread for the soldiers of the royal army was baked at the Kronobageriet, which today houses the **Scenkonst Museet** (Swedish Museum of Performing Arts). The royal family's horses and cars are still kept in the **Kungliga Hovstallet**, the huge brick building to the right of the bakery. Further up is the unusual **Armémuseum**, where the royal arsenal used to be stored. Behind this lies 17th-century **Hedvig Eleonora Kyrka**, the former place of worship for the royal navy, which now holds regular classical music concerts.

To catch a glimpse of the Östermalm upper classes, head to Östermalmstorg opposite the church. When the first plans for Östermalm were drawn up back in the 1640s, sailors and craftsmen lived around this square. Nowadays, expensive boutiques sell clothes and home accessories, and the pavements are teeming with mink-clad elderly women walking small dogs. On the corner of the square is **Östermalms Saluhall**, a dark red-brick building constructed in 1888 and long the flagship of the city's market halls. It's due to reopen after renovations in 2020.

Östermalm's main green space is **Humlegården**, the site of the king's hop gardens back in the 16th century and today a pleasant and very popular park, with the **Kungliga Biblioteket** (Royal Library) on its southern bank. Theatre performances are held in the park in summer. Further up Karlavägen, on a hill overlooking the city, looms the tall brick tower of **Engelbrektskyrkan**. Designed by leading Jugendstil architect Lars Israel Wahlman and opened in 1914, the church has an amazingly high nave – supposedly the tallest in Scandinavia.

For another kind of high life, follow the water's edge from Nybroplan along grand Strandvägen. Look out for the two classic interiors shops – **Svenskt Tenn**

❤ Time to eat & drink

Best beers
Mikkeller *p110*, Tudor Arms *p110*

Cake heaven
Mr Cake *p108*, Sturekatten *p109*

New Nordic cuisine
Gastrologik *p107*, Speceriet *p108*

Waterfront sundowner
Ångbåtsbryggan *p109*, Hotel Diplomat *p110*

❤ Time to shop

Cheese to please
Androuët *p110*

Chocolate factory
Ejes Chokladfabrik *p114*

Local labels
Anna Holtblad *p110*, Scampi *p113*

Swedish design classics
Malmstenbutiken *p112*, Svenskt Tenn *p111*

In the know
Getting around

The subway station serving this area is Östermalmstorg, and from here it's easy to reach most of the neighbourhood's main sights on foot. Stureplan, the main shopping and nightlife district, is also within walking distance of Hötorget subway station on the green line and Kungsträdgården on the blue line. Buses 1 and 2 are the main bus routes passing through Stureplan. To visit Gärdet, the branch of the red line in the direction of Ropsten is your best bet. Stockholm University, Bergianska Trädgården and Naturhistoriska Riksmuseet are on the red line branch that ends at Mörby Centrum.

Sturebadet

(*see p111*) and **Malmstenbutiken** – perfect for kitting out the swish late 19th-century residences that line this street. Until the 1940s, sailing boats carrying firewood from the archipelago islands used to dock on the quayside at Strandvägen; some of these vintage boats – with labels by each one – are now docked on its southern edge.

At the end of Strandvägen is the bridge leading over to leafy Djurgården (*see p114*), and north from there, on Narvavägen, is the imposing **Historiska Museet**; it's Sweden's largest archaeological museum, with an exceptional collection of Viking artefacts.

Strandvägen is part of an esplanade system mapped out for Östermalm in the late 1800s by city planner Albert Lindhagen. The project was only partially implemented but includes the broad boulevards of Valhallavägen, Narvavägen and Karlavägen – the last two radiating out from the fountain and circular pond (added in 1929) at Karlaplan. The central section of **Karlavägen** is dotted with sculptures by various international artists, and at its eastern end are the headquarters of Swedish national radio and television. The buildings were designed by Erik Ahnborg and Sune Lindström, who were also responsible for the **Berwaldhallen** concert hall (*see p204*) next door, home of the Swedish Radio Symphony Orchestra and Radio Choir.

Beyond the TV and radio buildings, on the border with Gärdet, is **Diplomatstaden**, a complex of grand mansions that house most

of the city's foreign embassies, including those of the UK and USA. The adjacent park next to the water is named after Alfred Nobel, scientist, inventor and founder of the famous prizes.

Sights & museums

Armémuseum

Riddargatan 13 (08 519 56 301, www. armemuseum.se). T-bana Östermalmstorg or bus 54, 69. **Open** *Sept-May 11am-8pm Tue; 11am-5pm Wed-Sun. June-Aug 10am-5pm daily.* **Admission** *free.* **Map** *p102 P7.*

Since 1879, the Army Museum has been housed in the former arsenal, an impressive white pile built in the 18th century. The story of Sweden at war, rather than its military infrastructure, is the museum's dominant theme, which may seem odd since Sweden has avoided conflict for the last 200 years. But with 1,000 years of history on show, exhibited over three floors, you soon learn that the Swedes were once a bloody and gruesome lot; it's certainly not all uniforms and gleaming weaponry. Life-size (and lifelike) tableaux, such as a woman scavenging meat from a dead horse and doctors performing an amputation, show the horrific effects of war on both soldiers and civilians. The main exhibition begins on the top floor with the Viking age and the Thirty Years War and continues below with the 20th century. The ground-floor area houses an artillery exhibit and a restaurant. If you miss the highly recommended guided tour in English, the front desk provides a detailed pamphlet, also in English.

▶ *The Royal Guard marches off from the museum (summer only) for the changing of the guard (see p67) at the Kungliga Slottet.*

❤ Hallwylska Museet

Hamngatan 4 (08 402 30 99, www. hallwylskamuseet.se). T-bana Östermalmstorg or Kungsträdgården, or bus 54, 69. **Open** *Jan-June, Sept-Dec noon-4pm Tue, Thur, Fri; noon-7pm Wed; 11am-5pm Sat, Sun. July, Aug 10am-4pm Tue-Sun. Guided tours see website for details.* **Admission** *free.* **Map** *p102 O7.*

Enter the opulent world of Count and Countess Walther and Wilhelmina von Hallwyl in one of Stockholm's most eccentric and engaging museums. This palatial residence was built as a winter home for the immensely rich couple in 1898. Designed by Isak Gustav Clason (architect of the Nordiska Museet), it was very modern for its time, with electricity, central heating, lifts, bathrooms and phones. The Countess was an avid collector of items that she picked up on her travels around Europe, the Middle East and Africa; these include everything from paintings and furniture to silverware and armoury. She always planned that the house should become a museum and donated the building and its collections to the Swedish state in 1920. Her vision became a reality in 1938 when the Hallwyl Museum was opened to the public, eight years after her death. The house has been preserved exactly as it was left, and situated among the *objets d'art* are personal peculiarities, including a chunk of the Count's beard and a slice of their wedding cake. For a taste of how the other half used to live, the guided tour takes you through an assortment of 40 incredibly lavish rooms and is led by extremely informative guides dressed up as butlers and maids.

Historiska Museet
Narvavägen 13-17 (08 519 55 600, www. historiska.se). T-bana Karlaplan, tram 7 or bus 67, 69, 76. **Open** *June-Aug 10am-5pm daily. Sept-May 11am-5pm Tue, Thur-Sun; 11am-8pm Wed. Audio guide 30kr.* **Admission** *free.* **Map** *p102 R7.*

Objects from the Stone Age to the 16th century are displayed in the Museum of National Antiquities, Sweden's largest archaeological museum. The plain design of this 1940 building – the façade looks like a tall brick wall with a door – gives no indication of the treasures within. To see the best exhibits, enter the darkened hall on the ground floor, where an impressive collection of Viking rune stones, swords, skeletons and jewellery is displayed. Detailed texts (in English) and maps describe the Vikings' economy, class structure, travels and methods of punishment. In the large halls upstairs, you'll find beautiful wooden church altarpieces, textiles and other medieval ecclesiastical artworks. Don't miss the basement, where the circular Guldrummet (Gold Room) displays more than 3,000 artefacts in gold and silver, from the Bronze to the Middle Ages. This collection was made possible by a unique Swedish law, more than 300 years old, which entitles the finders of such treasures to payment equal to their market value. In the foyer there's a copy of an Athenian marble lion statue – check out the Viking graffiti on its side. In 2019, Historiska Museet absorbed the collections of the Royal Mint that were previously held at the Kungliga Myntkabinettet in Gamla Stan.

Kungliga Hovstallet
Väpnargatan 1 (08 402 61 05, www. royalcourt.se). T-bana Östermalmstorg or bus 54, 69 or tram 7. **Open** *Guided tours only (English) mid Jan-mid June, mid Sept-mid Dec 1pm Sat, Sun. July-mid Aug 1pm, 3pm Mon-Fri, Sun. Late Aug 2pm, 3pm Mon-Fri,*

Sun. **Admission** *100kr; 50kr reductions.* **Map** *p102 P7.*

The royal family's own horses, carriages and cars are taken care of in this late 19th-century striped brick building designed by architect Fritz Eckert. The building is so vast that it occupies almost the entire block next to the Kungliga Dramatiska Teatern (*see p206*). A collection of 40 carriages from the 19th and 20th centuries (some still used on ceremonial occasions) stands in a long hall above the garage. Inside the garage are 11 cars, including a 1950 Daimler and a 1969 Cadillac Fleetwood. The stalls and riding arena may be empty if you visit in summer, as this is when the horses are 'on vacation'. This place may be a big hit with equestrian enthusiasts, but otherwise the tour is not particularly thrilling.

Scenkonst Museet
Sibyllegatan 2 (08 519 56 700, scenkonstmuseet.se). T-bana Östermalmstorg or bus 2, 54, 67, 69. **Open** *11am-5pm Tue-Sun.* **Admission** *140kr; 70kr reductions; free under-20s & free to all Wed.* **Map** *p102 P7.*

The Swedish Museum of Performing Arts received a full revamp in 2016, designed to make it more interactive and inter-generational, but its vast collections devoted to dance, music and theatre have been built up over a century, with the oldest items dating from the 1500s. Recent exhibitions included the Swedish Hall of Fame, a celebration of Sweden's pop history, and Sound Check, an installation designed to transform visitors into music producers. There is also a large performance space, a café and a shop.

Restaurants & cafés

For gourmet food hall Östermalms Saluhall, *see p112.*

Arnold's ⓦ ⓦ ⓦ
Biblioteksgatan 21 (08 519 42 154, www.restaurantarnolds.se). T-bana Östermalmstorg. **Open** *6pm-1am Tue-Sat.* **Map** *p102 O6* ❶ *Contemporary*

Open since early 2019, Arnold's aims to offer a luxurious experience to a broad and international clientele. The interior – from leopard-print chairs to crisp white tablecloths – has clearly been designed for social media-sharing. There's a well-stocked bar from which you can order cocktails, and the menu features rich dishes to be shared and eaten slowly, such as club steak or seared tuna, as well as lighter options, including papaya salad and salmon and poached egg.

Brasserie Elverket ⓦⓦ
*Linnégatan 69 (08 661 25 62, www.
brasserieelverket.se). T-bana Karlaplan
or bus 54.* **Open** *11am-9pm Mon-Thur;
11am-10pm Fri; 5-9pm Sat. Closed late June-
early Aug.* **Map** *p102 Q6* ❷ *Contemporary*

This busy bar-restaurant is in an old
electricity plant, together with the more
experimental stage of the Dramaten theatre.
The food served is modern crossover and
moderately priced, with a pre-theatre
menu and a selection of tapas, as well as a
popular weekend brunch. It's closed for a
month after midsummer, when the owners
retreat to the island of Gotland to run their
restaurant there.

Brasserie Godot ⓦⓦⓦ
*Grev Turegatan 36 (08 660 06 14, www.
godot.se). T-bana Östermalmstorg.* **Open**
*5-11pm Mon, Tue; 5pm-midnight Wed, Thur;
5pm-1am Fri, Sat.* **Map** *p102 P6* ❸ *French/
Swedish*

The bar is busy at weekends with rich
youngsters showing off designer bags and
parental credit cards, but it's worth pushing
past them to reach a formal but intimate
dining room where superb food – a mix
of French brasserie classics and modern
Swedish cuisine – is served. Both the seafood
(lobster, smoked shrimps) and meat dishes
(veal, spring lamb) are excellent. The steak
tartare is a highlight.

Café Saturnus ⓦ
*Eriksbergsgatan 6 (08 611 77 00, www.
cafesaturnus.se). T-bana Östermalmstorg.*
Open *7am-8pm Mon-Fri; 8am-7pm Sat, Sun.*
Map *p102 N5* ❹ *Café*

Sweden's Crown Princess Victoria has been
known to frequent this place, although the
famous cinnamon buns hardly need the royal
seal of approval: these gigantic pastries are out
of this world. You might have problems finding
Saturnus, though – there isn't a proper sign,
just a model of the planet hanging above the
entrance. It's close to independent cinema Zita
(*see p191*), so it's popular with cinephiles in the
evening and at weekends.

❤ Gastrologik ⓦⓦⓦⓦ
*Artillerigatan 14 (08 662 30 60, www.
gastrologik.se). T-bana Östermalmstorg.*
Open *6pm-1am Tue-Sat.* **Map** *p102 P7* ❻
New Nordic

Gastrologik, housed in a minimalist
space with white tablecloths and hanging
brass lamps, is among the wave of Noma-
influenced restaurants that have been
popping up around Scandinavia in recent
years. However, it's much more than an
imitation and has been awarded its own

Gastrologik

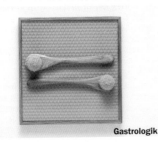

Gastrologik

Speceriet *p108*

Michelin star. An emphasis on seasonal ingredients is expected in a New Nordic restaurant, but this place takes it to the extreme. There is no written menu, because the ingredients are chosen on the day, depending on what's available and what's freshest. This will rule the place out for fussy eaters (though vegetarians and allergy sufferers can normally be accommodated), but it adds sensory engagement and a real element of surprise to the dining experience. Expert wine pairings complement the creative fish, seafood and meat dishes.

The owners of Gastrologik also have a *bakficka* (back pocket) in the same building: the more affordable and laid-back but just as successful **Speceriet** (www.speceriet.se).

Halv Grek plus Turk ⓌⓌⓌ

Jungfrugatan 33 (070 735 32 80, www. halvgrekplusturk.se). T-bana Karlaplan or Stadion. Open 6pm-late Mon-Sat. Map p102 Q5 ❼ *Middle Eastern*

Slightly off the beaten track and with an entrance marked by an easy-to-miss sign, it's worth the extra effort to find this gem of a restaurant. Born of a friendship between Greek and Turkish restaurateurs, the decor at Halv Grek plus Turk is modern Middle Eastern, accented with elegant lounge sofas, bright colours and soft lighting. The clientele is a mixed urban set, and the menu features an assortment of cold and hot meze dishes. Service is attentive, friendly and efficient.

Kommendoren ⓌⓌ

Kommendörsgatan 7 (08 661 67 00, www. kommendoren.se). T-bana Stadion or bus 1, 54, 69. Open 5-11pm Mon, Tue, Sun; 5-11.45pm Thur; 5pm-1am Fri, Sat. Map p102 P5 ❽ *American*

Channelling New York-style bistro vibes and serving American dishes ranging from fried chicken to barbecued ox, Kommendoren quickly became a firm neighbourhood favourite when it opened in 2015. The interior mixes diner-style booths that are ideal for small groups with a long communal table designed to encourage conversation between strangers, although most visitors remain on the reserved side. Saturday brunch here is a big deal, while the separate bar area is a popular post-work venue for local business people during the week.

Konditoriet Ⓦ

Sturegallerian, Stureplan (www.konditoriet. nu). T-bana Östermalmstorg. Open 8am-7pm Mon-Fri; 10am-6pm Sat; 11am-5pm Sun. Map p102 O6 ❾ *Bakery café*

Hold on to your purse strings – sweet-toothed tourists could blow their holiday budget at Konditoriet, purveyor of amazingly good cakes and pastries. It's all pink neon signage and gold countertops and can be found on the ground floor inside the luxurious Sturegallerian shopping centre. If the queue is long and you're looking for takeout, **Gateau**, a small bakery chain across the hallway, also sells tasty cakes, bread and coffee.

Miss Voon ⓌⓌⓌ

Sturegatan 22 (08 505 24 470, www. missvoon.se). T-bana Östermalmstorg or bus 1, 69. Open 6.30-10am, 11.30am-2pm, 5pm-1am Mon-Fri; 7-11am, 5pm-1am Sat; 8am-noon Sun. Map p102 O5 ❿ *Asian*

This Asian fusion restaurant serves half-portion dishes, designed to give guests the chance to experience a range of tastes and flavours. Choose between 15 savoury items on the menu, including bleak roe spring rolls, duck dumplings and lobster tacos. Sweet dishes include sorbet and chocolate fondant. There are large, round tables, perfect for bigger groups, but don't discount Miss Voon as a date venue; the vibe here is classy and there's a great cocktail bar at the entrance.

❤ Mr Cake Ⓦ

Rådmansgatan 12 (08 400 17 190, www. mrcake.se). T-bana Rådmansgatan or Tekniska Högskolan. Open 7.30am-6pm Mon-Fri; 9am-6pm Sat, Sun. Map p102 N4 ⓫ *Café*

Co-founded by award-winning Swedish pastry chefs Roy Fares and Mattias Ljungberg, this café is a wonderland for anyone with a sweet tooth. Alongside enormous slices of American-style sponge, you can order from a selection of pancakes, waffles and cheesecake. Savoury lunches are also served, with recent menus including falafel wraps, tofu bowls and chicken club sandwiches.

Nybrogatan 38 ⓌⓌⓌ

Nybrogatan 38 (08 662 33 22, www. nybrogatan38.com). T-bana Östermalmstorg. Open 7.30am-11pm Mon; 7.30am-midnight Tue-Thur; 7.30am-1am Fri; 10am-1am Sat; 10am-11pm Sun. Map p102 P6 ⓬ *Contemporary*

Billing itself as a friendly neighbourhood restaurant, Nybrogatan 38 truly delivers. It's a lot less stuffy than some of its local competitors, with a lively atmosphere and DJs on Friday and Saturday nights. None of this distracts from the top-quality food, which is a mixture of classic European dishes, including veal meatballs, and more global, contemporary offerings, such as the house falafel and burrata. There are also lighter bites, sharing plates and a late-night menu served from 11pm until closing time, featuring comfort foods such as tomato pappardelle pasta and ham omelettes.

Riche ⓦⓦ
Birger Jarlsgatan 4 (08 545 03 560, www. riche.se). T-bana Östermalmstorg. **Open** *7.30am-midnight Mon; 7.30am-1am Tue; 7.30am-2am Wed-Fri; 11am-2am Sat; noon-midnight Sun.* **Map** *p102 O7* ⑬
Contemporary

Riche is one of the most popular places in town for a post-work drink, especially among the media set, and the restaurant is also a safe bet. It serves a mix of traditional Swedish dishes alongside classy contemporary options. Dating back to 1893, Riche takes its inspiration from Parisian brasseries and has a glass-fronted conservatory area, ideal for people-watching.

Lo Scudetto ⓦⓦ
Styrmansgatan 57 (08 640 42 15, www. restaurangloscudetto.se). T-bana Karlaplan or bus 69. **Open** *11am-10pm Mon-Fri; noon-10pm Sat; noon-9pm Sun.* **Map** *p102 Q6* ⑭ *Italian*

A culinary pioneer, this local Italian spot used to be situated on Åsögatan, where it was all about rustic charm. Now located in Östermalm, the place has smartened up its image with white tablecloths and a stylish bar. The food remains marvellously subtle, with the bresaola, ravioli and tiramisu all prepared with a loving and skilful hand. One of the city's few genuinely top-class Italians. Reservations essential.

Sturehof ⓦⓦⓦ
Stureplan 2 (08 440 57 30, www.sturehof. com). T-bana Östermalmstorg. **Open** *11am-2am Mon-Sat; noon-2am Sun.* **Map** *p102 O6* ⑮ *Mediterranean/seafood*

Long opening hours make it possible to get a meal in this classic Stockholm brasserie at almost any time of day or night – a rare thing in this city. The massive dining room is elegant, with white linen tablecloths and uniformed waiters, but the atmosphere stays lively and cheerful. Service is attentive, and the menu follows classic French bistro tradition, with seafood and shellfish a speciality. Among the starters are a few Swedish classics, such as smoked Baltic herring and *toast skagen* (shrimp and other ingredients, on sautéed bread). After dinner, step into the lively **O-baren** (*see p197*).

♥ Sturekatten ⓦ
Riddargatan 4 (08 611 16 12, www. sturekatten.se). T-bana Östermalmstorg. **Open** *9am-7pm Mon-Fri; 9am-6pm Sat; 10am-6pm Sun.* **Map** *p102 O7* ⑯ *Café*

Even if it stops serving fine coffee and cakes, Sturekatten should be delicately preserved forever. With two storeys of lace and antiques, it's like an 18th-century doll's house. The house speciality is apple pie with meringue,

but it also serves delicious *semlor* (whipped cream and almond-paste buns). Though it may sound like a pensioners' pleasure dome, it's actually just as popular with teenagers. During the summer months, there's a pleasant little courtyard terrace. **Other location** Vete-Katten, Kungsgatan 55, Norrmalm (08 20 84 05).

Taverna Brillo ⓦⓦⓦ
Sturegatan 6, (08 519 77 800, www. tavernabrillo.se). T-bana Östermalmstorg. **Open** *11.30am-11pm Mon, Tue, Sun; 11.30am-midnight Wed, Thur; 11.30am-2am Fri, Sat.* **Map** *p102 O6* ⑰ *Italian*

This sprawling venue includes an Italian restaurant, a cocktail bar, a florist, an ice-cream stall and a coffee shop. The food isn't especially adventurous, but it's a safe bet with oodles of atmosphere and late opening hours Wednesday through Saturday. Taverna Brillo is also a popular spot for business breakfasts, with a menu including tasty filled croissants, gluten-free porridge and truffle omelettes.

Bars

Östermalm's Stureplan district is known as a hub for late-night clubs (*see p197*) that draw a glamorous, albeit sometimes bratty crowd, but it's also home to a diverse selection of more laid-back drinking spots.

♥ Ångbåtsbryggan
Strandvägen, berth 18 (08 534 897 04, angbatsbryggan.com). Bus 54, 69 or tram 7. **Open** *11.30am-11pm Mon-Wed; 11.30am-midnight Thur, Fri; 12.30pm-midnight Sat; 12.30pm-11pm Sun.* **Map** *p102 P8* ①

If you're looking for a drinking spot with a view, you can't get much better than Ångbåtsbryggan. It's a jetty bar sandwiched between the luxury yachts that line this stretch of waterfront during summer, from where you can take in the vista of Skeppsholmen and Djurgården islands. Service isn't always speedy, and seats go fast, so get here early if you're planning a scenic sundowner.

Mikkeller *p110*

Bongo Bar

Birger Jarlsgatan 37 (08 23 61 01, bongobar. se/stockholm). T-bana Östermalmstorg or Rådmansgatan or bus 69. Open 4-10pm Tue; 4pm-midnight Wed, Thur; 4pm-2am Fri; 4pm-1am Sat. Map p102 N5 ❷

Located at the back of Bio Zita, an art nouveau cinema dating back to 1913, this compact, sophisticated bar offers a relaxed retreat from the hustle and bustle around Östermalm's main drag. Happy hour runs from 4pm to 6pm, including top-quality discounted cava. There are often DJs at weekends, sometimes themed to tie-in with movie showings. Don't miss the French pop sessions by Benoit Derrier, which crop up sporadically throughout the year.

♥ Hotel Diplomat

Strandvägen 7C (08 459 68 02, www. diplomathotel.com). Bus 54, 69 or tram 7. Open 6.30-10am, 11.30am-10.30pm Mon-Fri; 7.30-11am, 1-10.30pm Sat; 7.30-11am, 1-10pm Sun. Map p102 P7 ❸

Boasting a prime spot on Strandvägen, one of Stockholm's most exclusive streets, Hotel Diplomat's bar lures in suited-and-booted local business types. The decor is bright and airy and, during summer, there's a kerbside seating area overlooking the yachts in Nybroviken harbour. The staff here are attentive and happy to offer advice on the wine and cocktail list.

♥ Mikkeller

Brahegatan 3-5 (073 366 30 49, www. mikkeller.dk/location/mikkeller-stockholm). T-bana Östermalmstorg or bus 54, 69. Open 3-10pm Mon; 3pm-midnight Tue-Thur; noon-1am Fri; 1pm-1am Sat; 1-10pm Sun. Map p102 O6 ❹

Beer enthusiasts will delight in visiting Mikkeller, part of a Danish microbrewery chain that started in Copenhagen in 2006 and has been cropping up in hip neighbourhoods around the world ever since. Östermalm might not seem the most obvious place for the concept in Stockholm, but it's a refreshing contrast to the cocktail and champagne bars that dominate this area. There are more than 20 beers choose from, alongside a selection of Scandinavian open sandwiches.

Story Hotel

Riddargatan 6 (08 545 03 940, www. storyhotels.com/riddargatan). T-bana Östermalmstorg. Open 4-11pm Mon, Tue; 4pm-midnight Wed; 4pm-1am Thur-Sat. Food served until 10pm daily. Map p102 O7 ❺

This is far from your average hotel lobby bar. Past the discreet and purposely scruffy entrance is a spacious Parisian-style lounge framed by raw concrete walls hung with art. During the week, when the bar isn't so crowded and the DJ isn't pumping up the volume, this is a place for real conversations, about art, life and love. Head up the stairs beyond the lobby for a sunny terrace area. Story Hotel attracts a slightly edgier crowd than neighbouring bars.

♥ Tudor Arms

Grevgatan 31 (08 660 27 12, www.tudorarms. com). T-bana Karlaplan, bus 54, 69. Open 11am-11pm Mon-Fri; 1-11pm Sat; 1-7pm Sun. Map p102 Q7 ❻

One of Stockholm's best-loved English pubs, the Tudor Arms celebrated its 50th anniversary in 2019. The pints are on the pricey side compared some of the city's other British- and Irish-style drinking spots, but the venue consequently draws a more mature crowd of local Swedes and English-speaking expats than its rivals. Don't miss the tasty steak and ale pies or a plate of fish and chips if you're hungry.

Shops & services

Östermalm is best for luxury goods and posh delis. **Birger Jarlsgatan** is home to some of the big names of the fashion world. **Sibyllegatan** and **Nybrogatan** are key streets for interior design, while down on **Strandvägen** there are two legendary Swedish design stores: **Svenskt Tenn** (*see p111*) and **Malmstenbutiken**. **Sturegallerian** (www.sturegallerian.se) houses a good range of upmarket stores, including branches of Björn Borg (for underwear, bags and shoes), J Lindeberg and Bang & Olufsen; the renowned **Sturehof** restaurant (*see p109*) is also here.

♥ Androuët

Nybrogatan 6 (08 660 58 33, www.androuet. se). T-bana Östermalmstorg or bus 69. Open 10am-6pm Mon-Fri; 10am-4pm Sat. Map p102 O7 ❶ *Food & drink*

In 1909, Henri Androuët set up his first cheese store in Paris; the Stockholm outlet arrived 98 years later – but it was worth the wait. In this excellent shop you'll find more than 100 different cheeses from all over France. Many are quite obscure, but most are outstanding. **Other location** Götgatan 39, Södermalm (08 641 90 20).

♥ Anna Holtblad

Grev Turegatan 13 (08 545 02 220, www. annaholtblad.com). T-bana Östermalmstorg or bus 69. Open 11am-6pm Mon-Fri; noon-4pm Sat. Map p102 O6 ❷ *Fashion*

💜 Svenskt Tenn

*Strandvägen 5 (08 670 16 00, www. svenskttenn.se). T-bana Östermalmstorg or bus 69, 76 or tram 7. **Open** 10am-6pm Mon-Fri; 10am-4pm Sat. **Map** p102 P7* **⑮** *Interiors*

This Stockholm classic should not be missed. Founded by Estrid Ericson in 1924, Svenskt Tenn is best known for the furniture and, in particular, the textiles created by Austrian immigrant Josef Frank, who worked for the company for 30 years from 1934. Often described as one of the fathers of Swedish modernism, he produced bold and colourful prints that are still the mainstay of the shop's expensive but exquisite products.

Frank moved to Stockholm with his Swedish wife in 1933 to escape rising discrimination against Jews in his home country. Despite previously running a successful company designing home interiors, fabrics and furniture in Vienna, he initially struggled to find work. Fortunately, Svenskt Tenn's owner had long been an admirer of Frank's work and was passionate about creating homes with character, so he gave Frank the lucky break he needed.

Frank's designs are the antithesis of Scandinavian minimalism, featuring tropical fruits, plants and exotic animals, such as elephants and parrots. They are seen as paving the way for more recent ground-breaking Nordic brands, including Finnish design house Marimekko, which specialises in stand-out flower prints, and even IKEA, whose stock includes bright, patterned textiles and furniture.

Svenskt Tenn is also home to a legendary tearoom (08 670 16 00, 11am-5.30pm Mon-Fri, 10am-4pm Sat), decked out in its own designs, on the floor above the store. It serves morning and afternoon tea, alongside decorative cakes, as well as seasonal lunches. Everything is made with organic ingredients. From the tearoom there's a striking view over Nybroviken bay. You usually need to book.

▶ *For the chance to buy more design classics, visit Malmstenbutiken, Modernity and Nordiska Galleriet (for all, see p112).*

Anna Holtblad has been one of Sweden's top designers for the past 25 years. She's best known for her folklore-inspired knitwear and colourful prints. **Other location** Kungstensgatan 20, Vasastan (08 458 93 00).

CQP

Skeppargatan 22 (070 269 08 22 www.c-qp. com). T-bana Östermalmstorg or bus 69 or tram 7. Open 10am-6pm Mon-Fri. Map p102 Q7 ❸ *Fashion*

One of the global brands heralded with transforming the humble trainer into a high-end fashion item, CQP's leather sneakers are designed in Stockholm, handmade in Portugal and renowned for their arch support. The label's flagship store on an Östermalm backstreet is small, serene and staffed by knowledgeable assistants.

Dusty Deco

Brahegatan 21 (08 544 99 195, dustydeco. com). T-bana Stadion, bus 1, 54. Open 11am-6pm Mon-Fri; 11am-3pm Sat. Map p102 O5 ❹ *Vintage interiors*

Featuring vintage furniture, rugs and lighting from Swedish and global heavyweights, this store was founded by Edin Memic Kjellvertz, who previously worked for iconic denim brand Acne Studios. He became obsessed with stockpiling treasures sourced from his travels and started Dusty Deco with his wife Lina when his collection became too big for their apartment.

Hedengrens Bokhandel

Sturegallerian, Stureplan 4 (08 611 51 28, www.hedengrens.se). T-bana Östermalmstorg or bus 69. Open 10am-7pm Mon-Fri; 10am-5pm Sat; noon-5pm Sun. Map p102 O6 ❻ *Books*

Opened in 1897, Hedengrens is one of Stockholm's most famous bookshops. It specialises in novels and the arts, and half the stock is in English. Check out the English translations of Swedish authors such as Selma Lagerlöf, Torgny Lindgren and Astrid Lindgren. The fiction section also includes titles in Spanish, Italian, German, French, Danish and Norwegian.

Kurt Ribbhagen

Birger Jarlsgatan 2 (08 545 07 860, www. kurtribbhagen.com). T-bana Östermalmstorg or bus 54, 69. Open 9am-6pm Mon-Fri. Map p102 O7 ❼ *Antiques*

Kurt Ribbhagen is one of the best antique silver shops in the city and is also handily located next door to the Stockholm branch of renowned Danish silversmith Georg Jensen.

🖤 Malmstenbutiken

Strandvägen 5B (08 23 33 80, www. malmsten.se). T-bana Östermalmstorg or Kungsträdgården or bus 54, 69. Open 10am-6pm Mon-Fri; 10am-4pm Sat; 11am-4pm Sun. Map p102 P7 ❽ *Interiors*

High-quality furniture, textiles and light fittings by legendary Swedish designer Carl Malmsten. The shop, which is now run by his grandson Jerk Malmsten, sells classics from the 1950s and 1960s, as well as rugs and books.

Modernity

Sibyllegatan 6 (08 20 80 25, www. modernity.se). T-bana Östermalmstorg, Kungsträdgården or bus 54, 69. Open noon-5.30pm Mon-Fri; 11am-3pm Sat. Map p102 P6 ❾ *Interiors*

Scotsman Andrew Duncanson specialises in 20th-century Scandinavian design, including furniture, ceramics, glass and jewellery. If you're a fan of Alvar Aalto and Arne Jacobsen, then this place is a must.

Nordiska Galleriet

Nybrogatan 11 (08 442 83 60, www. nordiskagalleriet.se). T-bana Östermalmstorg or bus 69. Open 10am-6pm Mon-Fri; 10am-5pm Sat; 11am-4pm Sun. Map p102 O7 ❿ *Interiors*

Open since 1912, this is a great place to fantasise about your dream Scandi-style apartment. In its large, fashionable home on Nybrogatan, Nordiska Galleriet stocks furniture, lights and gifts from Nordic and international designers. Both past masters (Alvar Aalto, Arne Jacobsen) and big contemporary names (Philippe Starck, Jonas Bohlin) feature. Other Swedish designers include Monica Förster and Maria Nilsdotter. There are also numerous global brands from Denmark's Fritz Hansen to more fledgling talents such as New York-based lighting brand Roll & Hill.

Östermalms Saluhall

Östermalmstorg (www.ostermalmshallen.se). T-bana Östermalmstorg. Open 9.30am-7pm Mon-Fri; 9.30am-5pm Sat. Map p102 P6 ⓫ *Food & drink*

The original food hall served the city's gourmets from the 19th century until 2016, when its grand, red, turreted building closed for renovation. It's due to reopen at the end of 2020. Until then, a temporary construction, situated directly across the street, holds some of the most popular food stalls as well as restaurants, wine bars and cafés, although it lacks the character and ambience of its namesake.

Riddarbageriet

Riddargatan 15 (08 660 33 75, www. riddarbageriet.com). T-bana Östermalmstorg or Kungsträdgården or bus 69. **Open** *7.30am-5pm Mon-Fri; 8am-3pm Sat; 9am-1pm Sun.* **Map** *p102 P7* ⑫ *Food & drink*

Fans of Riddarbageriet believe this place sells the best bread in Stockholm. The cakes are outstanding, but it's Johan Sörberg's sourdough loaves that the locals love the most. There are a handful of small tables inside, and it's one of the few places in town that serves tea in a pot.

♥ Scampi

Nybrogatan 20 (08 665 30 35, www.scampi. se). T-bana Östermalmstorg or bus 69. **Open** *11am-6pm Mon-Fri; 11am-4pm Sat.* **Map** *p102 P7* ⑬ *Accessories*

The name of this Swedish swimwear label may not have an upmarket ring in English, but the colourful bikinis and swimming costumes are top quality (with prices to match), made with long-lasting materials and great attention to detail. There are shapes and sizes to suit a wide range of figures.

Sibyllans Kaffe & Tehandel

Sibyllegatan 35 (08 662 06 63, www. sibyllans.se). T-bana Östermalmstorg. **Open** *10am-6pm Mon-Fri; 10am-4pm Sat.* **Map** *p102 P6* ⑭ *Food & drink*

When the wind comes from the south you can smell the heady fragrance of Sibyllans ten blocks away. This family-run shop dates back to World War I, and the lovely interior hasn't changed much since. There's a vast range of teas from all over the world. Sibyllans' own blend, Sir Williams, is a mix of Chinese green teas.

GÄRDET

Near the intersection of Valhallavägen and Lidingövägen stands Stockholm's historic **Stadion**, built for the 1912 Olympic Games by architect Torben Grut in National Romantic style to resemble the walls surrounding a medieval city; its twin brick towers are a striking landmark. The stadium is surrounded by several higher education institutions.

The southern end of Gärdet is monopolised by the green expanse of **Ladugårdsgärdet**. This parkland is part of the **Ekoparken** (www.ekoparken.org), the world's first National City Park, which also incorporates Djurgården (*see p120*), Hagaparken (*see p99*), Norra Djurgården (*see p115*) and the Fjäderholmarna islands.

Mainly open grassland and woods, with a few scattered buildings, Ladugårdsgärdet stretches for about four kilometres from Valhallavägen to the waters of Lilla Värtan, on the other side of which lies the island of **Lidingö** (*see p170*). Stockholmers come to the park to picnic, jog, ride horses or just get a taste of the countryside. Roughly in the centre is the **Kaknästornet** broadcasting tower, rising up from the forest like a giant concrete spear. On the southern edge of Ladugårdsgärdet is the 'Museum Park', a cluster of three museums: the **Sjöhistoriska Museet**, **Etnografiska Museet** and **Tekniska Museet**. From here, a pedestrian bridge leads south to Djurgården.

Sights & museums

Etnografiska Museet

Djurgårdsbrunnsvägen 34 (010 456 12 00, www.varldskulturmuseerna.se/ etnografiskamuseet). Bus 69. **Open** *11am-5pm Tue, Thur-Sun; 11am-8pm Wed. Check the website for details of guided tours & workshops.* **Admission** *free.* **Map** *p102 W7.*

The dimly lit ground floor of the exotic-looking National Museum of Ethnography features masks, musical instruments and religious objects from seven holy cities (Auroville, Benin, Benares, Jerusalem, Yogyakarta, Beijing and Teotihuacan). Traveller's Trunk is a collection of artefacts brought home by Swedish explorers, the oldest of which were seized by the students of Swedish botanist Carl Linnaeus on their travels with Captain Cook. There's a wide variety of colourful exhibits, beautifully displayed, as well as a small museum shop selling ethnic toys, trinkets and books. Lots of family-orientated workshops are on offer, with activities ranging from recycled sculpture-making to African dance.

Sjöhistoriska Museet

Djurgårdsbrunnsvägen 24 (08 519 54 925, www.sjohistoriska.se). Bus 69. **Open** *10am-5pm Tue-Sun.* **Admission** *free.* **Map** *p102 V7.*

Hundreds of model ships are displayed within the long, curved National Maritime Museum, designed in 1936 by Ragnar Östberg, the architect behind Stockholm's famous Stadshuset (*see p161*). It's an extensive collection – as it should be, considering Sweden's long and dramatic maritime history. Two floors of minutely detailed models are grouped in permanent exhibitions on merchant shipping, battleships and ocean liners. Ship figureheads depicting monsters and bare-breasted women decorate the museum walls, and the upper floor displays two ships' cabins from the 1870s and 1970s. You'll also find a children's room, Blubb, which has an underwater theme.

💜 Tekniska Museet

Museivägen 7 (08 450 56 00, www. tekniskamuseet.se). Bus 69. **Open** *10am-5pm Mon, Tue, Thur-Sun; 10am-8pm Wed. Miniature railway demonstrations 11am, 2pm daily.* **Admission** *150kr; free under-7s. Free with SP (museum only).* **Map** *p102 W7.*

Sprawling across three floors, the Museum of Science & Technology is sure to keep inquisitive minds busy for hours. Although highly pedagogical, it's more like a funhouse than a museum, and a great place for babies, kids and adults alike. Sweden's oldest steam engine, built in 1832, dominates the large Machine Hall, where aeroplanes – including one of Sweden's first commercial aircraft from 1924 – hang from the ceiling above bicycles, engines and cars. As well as celebrating Swedish inventors and engineers, there are also innovative temporary exhibitions featuring the latest technologies.

Restaurants & cafés

Djurgårdsbrunn ⓦⓦ

Djurgårdsbrunnsvägen 68 (08 624 22 00, www.djurgardsbrunn.com). Bus 69. **Open** *Early May-mid Sept 11.30am-4pm, 5-11pm Mon-Fri; 11.30am-4pm, 5.30-11.30pm Sat; 11.30am-4pm, 5.30-11pm Sun. May close for private events; call or check online for details. Closed mid Sept-early May.* **Map** *p102 off map* ⑤ *Traditional Swedish*

At Djurgårdsbrunn you can easily spend hours sitting eating, drinking and enjoying the view across the canal. It serves contemporary Nordic and Mediterranean dishes as well as classic Swedish comfort food, such as meatballs and mashed potatoes. The food and decor make it feel like a lodge in the archipelago or a traditional countryside inn. Either way, it's an easy, pleasant walk from the city centre, and there's plenty of outdoor seating.

Villa Källhagen ⓦⓦ

Djurgårdsbrunnsvägen 10 (08 665 03 00, www.kallhagen.se). Bus 69. **Open** *7-10am, 11.30am-4.30pm, 5-10pm Mon-Fri; 7-10.30am, noon-4.30pm, 5-10pm Sat, Sun.* **Map** *p102 U7* ⑱ *Traditional Swedish*

A dining experience of the first order, where traditional Swedish dishes, with a European twist, are transformed into works of art at this house set in beautiful parkland. In summer you can sit outdoors to eat and then stroll along the water. In autumn and winter there's a fire blazing in the hearth. The popular brunch blends Asian treats with a typical Swedish *smörgåsbord*.

Shops & services

💜 Ejes Chokladfabrik

Erik Dahlbergsgatan 25 (08 664 27 09, www. ejeschoklad.se). T-bana Karlaplan or bus 54. **Open** *10am-6pm Mon-Fri; 10am-3pm Sat.* **Map** *p102 R5* ⑤ *Food & drink*

The mocha nougat and Irish coffee truffles alone are worth the trip to this traditional

Tekniska Museet

Berglanska Trädgården

chocolatier, which was established in
1923. Everything is made by hand without
preservatives. Call to book a tasting.

NORRA DJURGÅRDEN

It's easy to miss out this largely residential
area just north of Östermalm and Gärdet,
but Norra Djurgården shouldn't be
overlooked: it's the location of one of
Stockholm's most beautiful gardens and
an excellent natural history museum. The
Kungliga Tekniska Högskolan (KTH,
www.kth.se), one of Europe's leading
technical and engineering universities,
and **Stockholm University** also have their
campuses here. From the university, you
can explore the Norra Djurgården section
of **Ekoparken** (*see p113*) for hiking, horse
riding or birdwatching, or take a ten-minute
walk west to the shores of **Brunnsviken**,
where you can swim or rent canoes.

Sights & museums

♥ Bergianska Trädgården
*Gustafsborgsvägen 4 (08 16 35 00, www.
bergianska.se). T-bana Universitetet or bus
50, 540.* **Open** *Gardens 24hrs daily. Edvard
Andersons Växthus 11am-4pm Mon-Fri;
11am-5pm Sat, Sun. Victoriahuset May-
Sept 11am-4pm Mon-Fri; 11am-5pm Sat,
Sun. Closed Oct-Apr.* **Admission** *Gardens
free. Victoriahuset 20kr. Edvard Andersons
Växthus 80kr. Free under-15s with an
accompanying adult. Free with SP.*

This botanical garden, a short walk from
Universitetet subway station, is spread
out on a hilly peninsula by the waters of
Brunnsviken lake. The Royal Swedish
Academy of Sciences, which still conducts
research here, moved the garden from
Vasastan to this waterfront area in 1885.
Orchids and vines fill **Victoriahuset**, a
small conservatory (1900); its pond contains
giant water lilies, measuring up to two
and a half metres across. The more recent

Edvard Andersons Växthus, an all-glass
conservatory, contains Mediterranean plants
and trees in its central room, and flora from
Australia, South Africa and California.

Naturhistoriska Riksmuseet
*Frescativägen 40 (08 519 54 000, www.nrm.
se). T-bana Universitetet or bus 50, 540.*
Open *10am-6pm Tue-Sun.* **Admission**
*Museum free. IMAX 80-120kr; 40-60kr
reductions.*

Next to the main Stockholm University
Campus is the National Museum of Natural
History, the largest museum complex in
Sweden, founded in 1739. More than nine
million biological and mineral samples are
stored in this monolithic brick building
designed in 1907 by Axel Anderberg, architect
of the Royal Opera House. Beneath the
black-shingled roof and light-filled cupola
stands an exceptionally well-made tableau
of extinct creatures, prehistoric man and
Swedish wildlife. Visitors enter the dinosaur
exhibit through a dark volcanic room. The
hands-on exhibits about space include a red
Martian landscape and a spaceship's cockpit.
Sweden's only IMAX cinema, the Cosmonova,
is also here, showing movies about the
natural world on its huge screen. There are
several pretty hiking and running trails
nearby, which are popular with students and
academics alike.

Djurgården & Skeppsholmen

If you begin to feel cramped by the narrow streets and tourist crowds of Gamla Stan, head for the green oasis of Djurgården. The island, a short walk from downtown, has many of Stockholm's best museums, including the world-class Vasamuseet, as well as lovely cafés, picnic spots, walking and cycling paths, and the Gröna Lund amusement park. The rest of the island is part of Ekoparken, the National City Park; its acres of undeveloped land are a much-loved retreat from the rest of the city.

Just west of Djurgården, the small island of Skeppsholmen was once an important naval base and shipyard, but is now known for its cultural institutions, many housed in ex-naval buildings, with the highlight being the state art museum, Moderna Museet. The island is a lovely place for an amble, either along the western shore with views of Gamla Stan or along the wooden boardwalk of the eastern shore, where impressive private and historic boats are docked.

❤ **Don't miss**

1 Moderna Museet *p130*
Contemporary art in a historic setting.

2 Rosendals Trädgård *p127*
Organic dishes and a garden idyll.

3 Vasamuseet *p125*
The jaw-dropping 17th-century warship.

4 ABBA The Museum *p121*
Walk in, dance out.

5 Skansen *p122*
Open-air museum about Swedish life.

6 Djurgårdsfärjan *p120*
Fun public ferry.

NORDIC
LIFESTYLE
SINCE 1523

Nordiska Museet *p124*

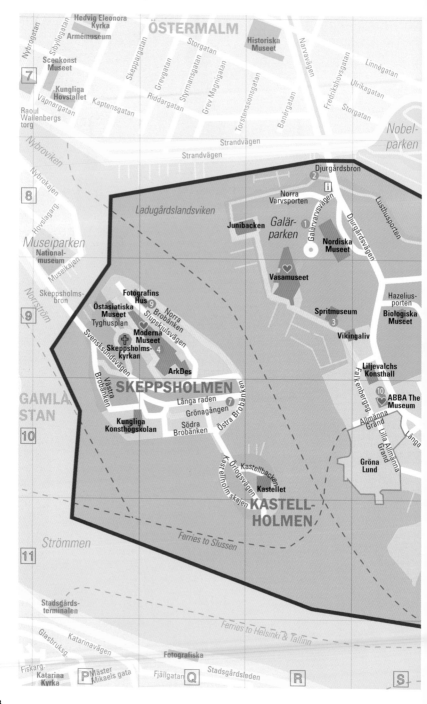

Nybrogatan
Sibyllegatan
Hedvig Eleonora Kyrka
Armémuseum
ÖSTERMALM
Scenkonst Museet
Skeppargatan
Storgatan
Historiska Museet
Narvavägen
Linnégatan
Kungliga Hovstallet
Väpnargatan
Käptensgatan
Grevgatan
Styrmansgatan
Grev Magnigatan
Riddargatan
Torstenssonsgatan
Banérgatan
Fredrikshovsgatan
Ulrikagatan
Storgatan
Raoul Wallenbergs torg

7

Nybroviken
Strandvägen
Strandvägen
Nobelparken

8

Nybrokajen
Hovslagarg.
Djurgårdsbron **2**
Norra Varvsporten
Ladugårdslandsviken
Djurgårdsvägen
Galärvarvsvägen
Lusthusporten
[i]

Museiparken
Nationalmuseum
Museikajen
Junibacken
Galär-parken **1**
Nordiska Museet

9

Norrström
Skeppsholms-bron
Fotografins Hus **9**
Östasiatiska Museet
Tyghusplan
Norra Brobänken
Slupskjulsvägen
Moderna Museet
Skeppsholms-kyrkan **4**
Svensksundsvägen
ArkDes
Vasamuseet
Spritmuseum **3**
Vikingaliv
Hazelius-porten
Biologiska Museet

GAMLA STAN
10
Västra Brobänken
SKEPPSHOLMEN
Långa raden
Grönagången **7**
Östra Brobänken
Kungliga Konsthögskolan
Södra Brobänken
Liljevalchs Konsthall
Falkenbergsg.
ABBA The Museum **10**
Allmänna Gränd
Lilla Allmänna Gränd
Långa

Strömmen
11
Kastellbacken
Orlogsvägen
Kastellet
Kastellholmskajen
Gröna Lund
KASTELL-HOLMEN
Ferries to Slussen

Stadsgårds-terminalen
Ferries to Helsinki & Tallinn

Glasbruksg.
Katarinavägen
Fotografiska
Fiskarg.
Katarina Kyrka
[P] Mäster Mikaels gata
Fjällgatan [Q]
Stadsgårdsleden
[R]
[S]

DJURGÅRDEN & SKEPPSHOLMEN

Restaurants & cafés

1. Cafe Ekorren *p128*
2. Café Petissan *p123*
3. Flickorna Helin *p128*
4. Moderna Museet *p131*
5. Oaxen Krog & Slip *p128*
6. Restaurang Hasselbacken *p128*
7. Restaurang Långa Räden *p131*
8. Restaurang Solliden *p123*
9. Torpedverkstan *p131*
10. Ulla Winbladh *p128*
11. Rosendals Trädgård *p127*

Bars

1. Josefina *p128*
2. Sjöcafeet *p129*
3. Spritmuseum *p129*

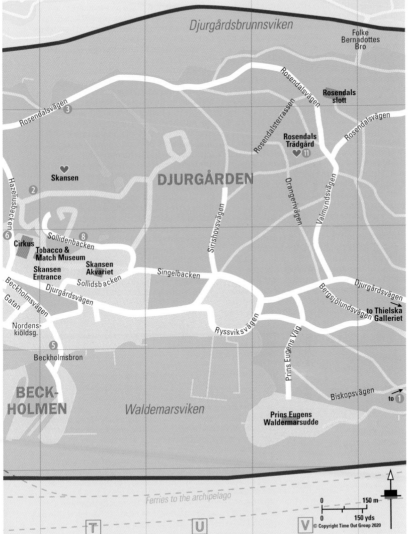

DJURGÅRDEN

Swedish monarchs have owned the island since it was acquired by King Karl Knutsson in 1452. First developed for agriculture, it later became the private hunting grounds of royalty. King Karl XI established a series of manned gates in the 1680s to protect the park from wolves, bears and poverty stricken peasants looking for food. A branch of the royal court continues to administer the island and uses all the rents and fees it collects for Djurgården's preservation.

Crossing to the island from Strandvägen, over Djurgårdsbron – just beyond which is the **Royal Djurgården Visitor Centre** (*see p124* In the know) – you'll see the magnificent **Nordiska Museet** directly in front of you. This city landmark was designed in the style of a Nordic Renaissance palace and holds historical and cultural objects from all over Scandinavia. The path to the right of the bridge leads you to **Junibacken**, a children's theme park organised around the stories of Sweden's beloved Astrid Lindgren.

Further on lies the 'don't miss' **Vasamuseet** (*see p125*), home of the vast *Vasa* warship, which sank just off the island of Beckholmen on her maiden voyage in 1628. Fittingly, the purpose-built museum occupies the site of the former naval dockyard. If you're going to visit just one museum in Stockholm – and there are plenty to choose from – make it this one.

Djurgårdsvägen, the main route into and around the island, passes by the vast Nordiska Museet, the western entrance to Skansen and the quaint, old-fashioned **Biologiska Museet**, devoted to Scandinavian wildlife. Further south, the beautiful **Liljevalchs Konsthall** stands on the corner of Djurgården's most developed area; this is one of the best exhibition spaces in Sweden, with contemporary shows that change every three months. Along the stretch of waterfront towards Vasamuseet, the **Spritmuseum** contains engaging exhibitions as well as a traditional Swedish restaurant and tasting rooms.

Squeals, laughter and live music can be heard coming from the summer-only **Gröna Lund** amusement park, a couple of blocks to the south. Opposite the park is **ABBA The Museum** (*see opposite*), the high-profile attraction that finally opened in 2013 after a decade in the planning. There are several hamburger and pizza places nearby, as well as the 1920s Restaurang Hasselbacken on the hill across the street, next to the **Cirkus** concert/theatre venue (*see p198*).

East of Gröna Lund, **Djurgårdsstaden** is the island's only real residential area. Most of the houses and cottages along this district's narrow streets were built between the mid 1700s and the early 1800s as housing for shipyard workers. About 200 people live here today and the apartments are much sought after. This residential area is often overlooked by tourists, which makes a walk through its well-preserved, historic streets all the more charming. Whipping posts like the one in the district's tiny square, Skampålens Torg, once stood in public places around the city.

Continuing along Djurgårdsvägen, you soon arrive at the entrance to **Skansen** (*see p122*). Stockholm's number one attraction pulls in 1.4 million visitors a year, and is a mix of open-air history museum, amusement park and zoo, covering almost the entire width of Djurgården. It includes the **Skansen Akvariet**, which houses monkeys, crocodiles and bats, but you'll have to pay a separate fee to see this.

The no.7 tram route goes to Ryssviken, from where you can walk south to the

---

❤ Time to eat & drink

Coffee corner
Flickorna Helin *p128*

Lunch with a view
Rosendals Trädgården *p127*, Moderna Museet *p131*

Luxury liquor
Spritmuseum *p129*

Dinner dates
Restaurang Hasselbacken *p128*, Oaxen Krog & Slip *p128*

In the know
Getting around

In summer, tram no.7 is forever packed with tourists on their way to Djurgården, yet the green island can be easily and pleasantly reached on foot, via the Djurgårdsbron bridge, or on the **Djurgårdsfärjan** (a ferry run by Waxholmsbolaget, 08 600 10 00, www.waxholmsbolaget.se, 44kr, or included in period tickets on an SL card). This year-round public ferry service runs between Skeppsbrokajen near Slussen in Gamla Stan and Allmänna Gränd on Djurgården island. It also makes a request stop at Skeppsholmen. It's a fun, cheap, and authentic way of experiencing Stockholm as a collection of islands. If you're heading to the eastern side of Djurgården, take tram no.7 from Norrmalm to Ryssviken (there's no Tunnelbana station on or near Djurgården). Bus no.44 runs along Djurgårdsvägen as far as Skansen. The only ground transport that goes to Skeppsholmen is bus no.65, which runs along the south side of Norrmalm.

♥ ABBA The Museum

Djurgårdsvägen 68 (08 121 32 860, www. abbathemuseum.com). Bus 67, or tram 7, or ferry from Slussen. **Open** *May-Aug 9am-8pm daily. Sept-mid Dec 10am-6pm Mon, Tue, Fri-Sun; 10am-8pm Wed, Thur. Halloween & Christmas 10am-7pm daily.* **Admission** *250kr; 95kr-175kr reductions; free under-7s.* **Map** *p118 S10.*

This museum is, as its name suggests, entirely dedicated to Sweden's most famous pop group, ABBA, who shot to fame in the Eurovision Song Contest in 1974 and went on to top charts worldwide. The band remains one of the country's biggest-selling acts of all time, despite not having released any new material since 1982, and their sound has continued to reach new generations via the stage and film productions of *Mamma Mia!*, a romantic musical written by British playwright Catherine Johnson featuring many of ABBA's biggest hits. The movie's sequel, *Mamma Mia! Here We Go Again*, released in 2018, grossed $394m worldwide.

ABBA The Museum is an interactive attraction, designed around the idea of giving visitors a sense of what it would be like to be the fifth member of the group: you can try on the quartet's colourful satin outfits, enter replica versions of the band's studio and dressing room, and even perform classic tunes on stage.

Some of the museum's more novel touches include the installation of a special telephone for which only ABBA members Björn, Benny, Agnetha and Anni-Frid have the number – if it rings, a visitor will find

In the know
Mamma Mia the Party!

True ABBA fans visiting Stockholm might also want to check out Mamma Mia the Party!, a live cabaret and dining experience at Tyrol, a restaurant that is part of the Gröna Lund theme park (see p122). The show is based around ABBA hits but has a different storyline to the *Mamma Mia!* movies. Tickets can be bought online at mammamiatheparty.com. The luxurious split-level theatre bar at Hotel Rival in Mariatorget, which is owned by band member Benny Andersson, is also a popular spot for ABBA pilgrims.

themselves talking directly to a member of the band – and a piano supposedly linked to Benny's own ivories, which sounds when he rehearses in his studio. There's also a cinema that screens Lasse Hallström's much-loved music videos, and a dancefloor.

The museum opened in 2013, after a decade or so in the planning (it was originally due to be housed in the building that's now home to Fotografiska), and has succeeded in finally providing an ABBA attraction that appeals to both diehard fans and families with children who probably haven't even heard of the pop sensation. If you're hungry, Pop House Hotel, which is part of the same building, serves Mediterranean dishes designed for sharing. There's a museum shop on site too.

DJURGÅRDEN & SKEPPSHOLMEN

palatial mansion of **Prins Eugens Waldemarsudde**, which has amazing views of the water, or walk north for about ten minutes to the café at **Rosendals Trädgård** (*see p127*), a lovely spot for a bite to eat. Nearby is **Rosendals Slott**, the summer retreat of Karl XIV Johan, the French marshal who was elected as Sweden's crown prince in 1810 and later went on to be crowned king.

To explore further east, you'll need to be prepared to walk, cycle or drive. To reach the eastern half of Djurgården by bus, you'll have to plan ahead and take bus no.69 from the northern side of Djurgårdsbron; the bus takes you to the south-eastern tip of the island, where Nordic art is displayed at swanky **Thielska Galleriet** and waterfront cafés at Blockhusudden look out towards the Fjäderholmarna islands. The southern shore of this area of Djurgården is lined with the homes and estates of Stockholm's extremely wealthy.

Most of eastern Djurgården is a designated nature reserve with a marsh, old oak trees and paths for horses, bikes and hikers. The narrow canal, **Djurgårdsbrunnskanalen**, which first opened in 1834, is a pleasant place for a stroll or run, lined with trees and ending with a small footbridge near the sea.

Sights & museums

Gröna Lund

Allmänna Gränd (010 708 91 00, www. gronalund.com). Bus 67, or tram 7, or ferry from Slussen. **Open** *May-late Sept call or check website for days & times. Late June-mid Aug typically 10am-11pm Mon-Thur, Sat; 10am-10pm Sun. Closed late Sept-Apr.* **Admission** *120kr; free under-6s, over-65s & with SP; 399kr 1-day bracelet (all rides).* **Map** *p118 S10.*

Perched on the edge of Djurgården, with great views across the water, Gröna Lund (Green Grove) is Sweden's oldest amusement park. Built in 1883 and owned by the same family ever since, its historic buildings and well-preserved rides retain an old-world charm. You can even travel here by boat, just as fair-goers did over a century ago. Among the older favourites are carousels, bumper cars and Ferris wheels, while the newer fairground thrills come from two rollercoasters intertwined, and the free-fall 'power tower', which is 80m (264ft) high, with four of its seats modified to tilt forward. The Kvasten (Broom) family friendly rollercoaster takes thrill-seekers over the park with their feet dangling in the air at 55km/h (35mph), while the much tamer Tuff-Tuff-Train is a rollercoaster designed for tots. You can buy multi-ride booklets or pay for each ride

❤ Skansen

Djurgårdsslätten 49-51 (08 442 82 00, www. skansen.se). Bus 44, or tram 7, or ferry from Slussen or Nybroplan. **Open** *Jan-Mar, Oct-Dec 10am-3pm Mon-Fri; 10am-4pm Sat, Sun. Apr 10am-4pm daily. May-late June, Sept 10am-6pm daily. Late June-Aug 10am-8pm daily.* **Admission** *60kr-220kr; free under-3s & with SP.* **Map** *p118 T10.*

Founded in 1891 by Artur Hazelius, also responsible for the Nordiska Museet, Skansen is a one-stop cultural tour of Sweden. The 150-plus traditional buildings – homes, shops, churches, barns and workshops – are organised as a miniature Sweden, with buildings from the north of the country at the north, those from the middle in the middle, and so on. Nearly all of the buildings are original and were moved here whole or piece by piece from all over Sweden. Most of the structures, situated along paths lined with elm, oak and maple trees, date from the 18th and 19th centuries. The striking 14th-century Norwegian storage hut that overlooks Djurgårdsbrunnsviken is the oldest; newest is the ironmonger's shop and the co-op grocery store from the 1930s. Most complete is the 1850s quarter, with cobblestoned streets and artisans' workshops, including a baker, glass-blower and potter. Watch them work, then buy the proceeds. Skansen's staff – dressed in

folk costumes – spin wool, tend fires and perform traditional tasks.

Animals from all over Scandinavia, including brown bears, moose and wolves, are kept along the northern cliff in natural-style habitats. There's also a petting zoo with goats, hedgehogs and kittens, and an aquarium/zoo, **Skansen Akvariet**, near the southern entrance, which has a separate entry fee (120kr, 60kr reductions). Alongside a host of tropical fish, the smallest monkeys you've ever seen are on show here. Bright orange tamarins and pygmy marmosets hang from trees behind glass, and you can walk up the steps of a giant treehouse where more than three dozen striped lemurs hop around while chewing on fresh vegetables. The less friendly looking baboons crawl around a steep hill in another exhibit, complete with a crashed jungle jeep hanging from a branch. You can even pet a boa constrictor and a tarantula.

An old-fashioned marketplace sits at the centre of the park, and folk-dancing demonstrations – with foot-stamping and fiddle-playing – take place in summer on the Tingsvallen stage.

Hunger pangs can be satisfied at a variety of places; **Restaurang Solliden** (08 566 37 000, www.skansensrestauranger.se, map p82 T10 ⑧) serves classic Swedish dishes and has a wonderful view of Djurgården

and southern Stockholm. Or there's **Café Petissan** (08 663 47 78, www.cafepetissan. com, map p118, T9 ②), situated in a cosy building dating from the late 17th century. The 19th-century Gubbhyllan building to the left of the main entrance houses an old-fashioned café that serves simple dishes; also here is the **Tobacco & Match Museum** (072 144 01 44, www. snusochtandsticksmuseum.se, included in Skansen general admission) – it was a Swede who invented the safety match.

Skansen is a popular destination on Sweden's national holidays since most of them, including Midsummer and Lucia, are celebrated here in traditional style, and the Christmas market is a massive draw. Every Wednesday from May to September is children's day, when kids will find a host of activities laid on for their amusement, including guided pony rides, horse and carriage rides and a mini-train ride. Also, on summer Tuesdays, be sure to stick around for 'Allsång på Skansen', a sing-along concert on the Solliden stage that's broadcast nationally at 8pm (*see also p184* Singing for Sweden).

▶ *The Skansen shop, located just outside Skansen, sells a lovely range of handcrafted traditional Swedish products, including kitchen and garden tools, pottery, jewellery, clothing and foodstuffs.*

Royal Djurgården Visitor Centre
(Djurgårdsvägen 2, 08 667 77 01,
royaldjurgarden.se) is a tourist information
centre and café located at the entrance to
the island, just off Djurgårdsbron. Pop in
to pick up information about the island's
many attractions, or to buy transport tickets,
Stockholm Passes or tickets for ABBA The
Museum. From the centre's waterside
café **Sjöcaféet** (see p129) you can hire
paddle boats, rowing boats, canoes, kayaks,
bicycles or in-line skates for a practical and
fun way to explore the island and its various
waterways.

separately. The park is baby-friendly, with
pram ramps on all the stairs and a designated
centre for feeding and soothing tots.

There are regular gigs here during
summer; prepare to face long queues if you
arrive during the late afternoon when there's
a big act on. If you're in Stockholm for a
while it's worth buying the Gröna Kortet
(Green Card), which scores you entry to all
concerts for a grand total of 290kr.

Junibacken

*Galärvarvsvägen, Djurgården (08 587 23
000, www.junibacken.se). Bus 67, or tram
7, or ferry from Slussen or Nybroplan.* **Open**
*Mid Aug-Jun 10am-5pm daily. Jul-mid
Aug 10am-6pm daily.* **Admission** *185kr;
155kr reductions; free under-2s & with SP.*
Map *p118 R8.*

A favourite haunt of local kids, Junibacken
is a mini indoor theme park devoted to wild-
child storybook character Pippi Longstocking
and other characters created by Swedish
author Astrid Lindgren. Lindgren, who died
in 2002, was the country's most famous and
beloved children's author, writing some
80 works, including children's and young
adult fiction, detective novels, fairy tales
and TV scripts. She was also a fierce and
outspoken campaigner who fought for,
among other causes, a more child-centred
educational system.

Junibacken is formed around a fairytale
train ride (ask for narration in English) that
crosses miniature fictional landscapes, flies
over rooftops and passes through quaint
Swedish houses (the last train departs 45
minutes before the park closes). On the
upper floor, kids are welcome inside Pippi's
house, Villa Villekulla, where they can dress
up as Pippi, slide down the roof and wreak
general havoc. For those who are unfamiliar
with Lindgren's books, there's a good shop
that carries many of the better-known titles
in translation.

Liljevalchs Konsthall

*Djurgårdsvägen 60 (08 508 31 330, www.
liljevalchs.se). Bus 67, or tram 7, or ferry from
Slussen.* **Open** *Mid May-Aug 10am-5pm Mon-
Fri; 11am-5pm Sat, Sun.* **Admission** *80kr;
free under-18s & with SP.* **Map** *p118 S9.*

This 1916 building, owned by the City of
Stockholm, is a fine example of Swedish
neoclassicism. Originally built from a donation
by the businessman Carl Fredrik Liljevach, it
attracts a wide audience to its 12 exhibition
rooms, where you can view themed and solo
shows (which typically change every three
months) by Swedish and international artists

Nordiska Museet

*Djurgårdsvägen 6-16 (08 519 54 600, www.
nordiskamuseet.se). Bus 67, 69, 76, or tram
7, or ferry from Slussen.* **Open** *June-Aug
9am-6pm daily. Sept-May 10am-5pm Mon,
Tue, Thur-Sun; 10am-8pm Wed.* **Admission**
140kr; free under-18s & with SP. **Map** *p118 R8.*

The Nordic Museum, Sweden's national
museum of cultural history, was the brainchild
of Artur Hazelius, who also created Skansen.
Everything about the place is big: the building
itself, designed by Isak Clason and completed
in 1907, is massive, though only a quarter of
the originally intended size. On entering the
aptly named Great Hall, visitors are greeted
by Carl Milles' colossal pink statue of a seated
Gustav Vasa. (In his forehead is a chunk of
oak from a tree planted by the king himself,
so legend has it.) The museum's collection
of artefacts is immense, although some of
the displays feel stuffy and unimaginative.
Permanent exhibitions include Swedish
traditions, manners and customs; fashion and
folk costumes; recreated table settings from
the 16th to the 20th centuries; and the Sami
people. There are also marvellously detailed
doll's houses and a collection of doom-laden
paintings and photos by Strindberg that do
nothing to dispel his madman image. The
Textile Gallery features 500 textiles dating
from the 1600s onwards.

Lekstugan, the play area aimed at kids
aged five to 12, is always popular. Here, you
can travel back in time to 1895 through the
museum's vivid recreation of life in the
Swedish countryside and try your hand at
different occupations at the farm cottage, the
mill, the stable and the general store.

Prins Eugens Waldemarsudde

*Prins Eugens Väg 6 (08 545 83 700, www.
waldemarsudde.se). Tram 7.* **Open** *11am-5pm
Tue, Wed, Fri-Sun; 11am-8pm Thur.*
Admission *150kr; 130kr reductions; free
under-19s.* **Map** *p118 V11.*

This beautiful waterfront property, comprising
a grand three-storey mansion and an art gallery,
was owned by Prince Eugen from 1899 until

♥ Vasamuseet

Galärvarvsvägen 14 (08 519 54 800, www. vasamuseet.se). Bus 67, 69, 76, or tram 7, or ferry from Slussen. **Open** *Sept-May 10am-5pm Mon, Tue, Thur-Sun; 10am-8pm Wed. June-Aug 8.30am-6pm daily. Check website for guided tour times (price included in entrance fee).* **Admission** *150kr; free under-18s & with SP.* **Map** *p118 R9.*

Entering Scandinavia's most popular museum for the first time is a jaw-dropping experience, as you take in the monstrous size of the 17th-century *Vasa* – the largest (69-metre/226-foot) and best-preserved ship of its kind in the world.

Built in the 1620s, when Sweden was at war with Poland, the *Vasa* had two gun decks and 64 cannons, making it the mightiest ship in the fleet. Unfortunately, though, the gun decks and heavy cannon made the ship top-heavy. During a stability test, in which 30 men ran back and forth across the deck, she nearly toppled over. Still, the king needed his ship and the maiden voyage went ahead. But only a few minutes after the *Vasa* set sail from near present-day Slussen on 10 August 1628, she began to list to one side. The gun ports filled with water and the ship sank after a voyage of only 1,300 metres (just under a mile). Of the 150 people on board, as many as 50 died – the number would have been much higher if the ship had reached Älvsnabben in the archipelago, where 300 soldiers were waiting to board.

The *Vasa* was returned to the surface to royal fanfare in 1961, and was installed in her custom-designed museum in 1991. A project to expand the museum was finished in 2013, allowing for 2,000 visitors at a time, but be warned that queues in summer can still be very long – so try to visit either early or just before closing time.

The reason the *Vasa* was so well preserved at her recovery in 1961 – 95 per cent of the ship is original – is because the Baltic Sea is insufficiently saline to contain the tiny shipworm that destroys wood in saltier seas. Yet her health is still a matter of concern. She was diagnosed with a near fatal disease in 2000, when she became her own worst enemy, producing sulphuric acid that began dissolving her mighty timbers from the inside out. But true to all great drama queens, the *Vasa* beat her affliction.

Upon arrival, head first for the theatre to see a short film about the *Vasa* and her discovery by amateur naval historian Anders Franzén. On your own or with a tour (there are several daily in English), you can walk around the exterior of the warship and view the upper deck and keel from six different levels. The ornate stern is covered with sculptures intended to express the glory of the Swedish king and to frighten enemies. No one's allowed on board, but you can walk through a recreation of one of the gun decks.

In an eerie exhibit down by the keel, the skeletons of ten people who died aboard the *Vasa* are on display, as are reconstructed models of how they would have looked alive. The museum's restaurant has a dockside view, and its gift shop is stocked with everything the *Vasa* enthusiast might need.

In the know
Galärvarvet

Open *Summer 11am-6pm Mon-Fri; 10am-6pm Sat, Sun. Closed winter. Map p118 R9.*

Docked near the Vasamuseet are two ships that are both free to visit. The lightship *Finngrundet* (1903) was anchored in the ice-free part of Sweden's Gulf of Bothnia before lightships were replaced by lighthouses, and has recently been restored. The *St Erik* (1915) was Sweden's first ice-breaker and was used to keep the archipelago channels clear. (They're also known as *Museifartygen* and *Museipiren* respectively.)

DJURGÅRDEN & SKEPPSHOLMEN

his death in 1947. The prince, a well-known Swedish landscape painter and the brother of King Gustav V, moved into the mansion upon its completion in 1904. The house's architect, Ferdinand Boberg, later designed the NK department store. The light, simply decorated rooms on the ground floor are furnished as the prince left them. Temporary art exhibitions, featuring the likes of Anders Zorn, Ernst Josephson, Isaac Grünewald and Carl Larsson, as well as the prince's wonderful landscape paintings, are displayed upstairs and in the gallery next door. The gallery was built in 1913 when Prince Eugen ran out of display space for his collection. The prince designed the classical white flower pots for sale in the gift shop himself.

While the mansion and artworks are impressive, the grounds and views are even more so. Sculptures by Auguste Rodin and Carl Milles adorn the park, which is a great spot to relax in, and a path leads to an 18th-century windmill.

Rosendals slott

*Rosendalsvägen 49 (08 402 61 30, www. kungligaslotten.se). Tram 7 to Bellmansro (then 700m walk, follow signs to Rosendal). **Open** (guided toursonly) June-Aug noon, 1pm, 2pm, 3pm Tue-Sun. Closed Sept-May. **Admission** 100kr; 50kr reductions; free under-7s & with SP. Map p118 V8.*

King Karl XIV Johan's summer retreat, this light-yellow building with grey pillars is designed in the Empire style, its wall paintings and decorative scheme reflecting the king's military background. The cotton fabric around the dining room is pleated to resemble an officer's tent, and the frieze in the Red Salon shows the Norse god Odin's victory over the frost giants. The fable of Eros and Psyche is told on the beautifully painted domed ceiling in the Lantern Room. The palace was designed by Fredrik Blom, who also created the Historiska Museet and Skeppsholm church; it was prefabricated in Norrmalm then shipped out to Djurgården in pieces. Karl Johan always remained a Frenchman at heart: he never ate Swedish food and sometimes forced his less fragrant guests to wash their hands in cologne. The 45-minute tour offered in summer is the only way to see the inside of the palace.

▶ *Just north of the palace, a pedestrian bridge crosses the water to the Museum Park (see p113).*

Spritmuseum

*Djurgårdsvägen 38 (08 121 31 300, www. spritmuseum.se). Bus 67 or tram 7. **Open** 10am-5pm Mon-Wed; 10am-7pm Thur-Sat; noon-5pm Sun. **Admission** 130kr; 60-90kr reductions; free under 15s & with SP. Map p118 R9.*

A dockside museum about spirits might conjure up images of battered naval whisky bottles or rusty distillery pipes, but Spritmuseum is a contemporary, creative venue that reflects on Sweden's relationship with alcohol. There's a permanent exhibition, which includes a painfully accurate hangover simulation, alongside temporary art, design and cartoon collections, often with looser links to drinking. Afterwards, you can head to the tasting room or the restaurant to put Sweden's culture of alcohol consumption into practice.

Thielska Galleriet

*Sjötullsbacken 8 (08 662 58 84, www. thielskagalleriet.se). **Open** noon-5pm Tue, Wed, Fri-Sun; noon-8pm Thur. Check website for guided tour times and dates (price included in entrance fee). **Admission** 130kr; 100kr reductions; free under-18s & with SP. Map p118 off map.*

Wealthy banker and art collector Ernest Thiel built this palatial home on the eastern tip of Djurgården in the early 1900s. The eclectically styled building, with influences from the Italian Renaissance and the Orient, was designed by Ferdinand Boberg, who built Prins Eugens Waldemarsudde at roughly the same time. Thiel lost most of his fortune after World War I, and the state acquired the property in 1924. This museum opened two years later, displaying his collection of turn-of-the-19th-century Nordic art, including works by Carl Larsson, Bruno Liljefors and Edvard Munch (a close friend of Thiel). Although six works, valued at 24 million krona, were stolen in the middle of the night on 20 June 2000 – a crime that remains unsolved – there are still plenty of paintings to see. Thiel's bathroom has been turned into a small café serving cinnamon rolls and meat pies, and the urn containing his ashes lies beneath a statue by Rodin in the park. If you haven't seen enough Scandinavian art at the Nationalmuseum, this gallery should satisfy you.

Vikingaliv

*Djurgårdsvägen 48 (08 400 22 990, vikingaliv.se). Bus 44 or tram 7. **Open** Jan-Sept 10am-6pm daily. Oct-Dec 10am-5pm daily. **Admission** 159kr; 119-139kr reductions; free under-6s. Map p118 R9.*

After years of calls for a museum dedicated to Sweden's famous Viking history, Vikingaliv opened in 2017, promising interactive exhibits designed to offer insights into everyday life during the Iron Age. The end result is less innovative than it might have been and the entrance fee is pricey given the compact nature of the venue; if you do decide to visit, take a guided tour to make the most of the experience. The shop's a great place to pick up Nordic souvenirs.

💜 Rosendals Trädgård

Rosendalsterrassen 12 (08 545 81 270, www. rosendalstradgard.se). Tram 7. **Open** *Apr-Sept 11am-5pm daily. Oct-late Dec, Feb-Mar 11am-4pm daily. Closed late Dec-Jan.* **Map** *p118 V9* ⑪ *European*

There's 'locally sourced' and then there's Rosendals Trädgård, which rustles up daily lunch deals from the fresh vegetables, herbs and flowers plucked directly from its enormous allotments. In the middle of Djurgården island, Rosendals has been producing biodynamic crops for more than three decades, which means it works with natural processes such as composting, using manure and crop rotation.

Guests here get the chance to dine inside a light-filled greenhouse or on the spacious outdoor terrace, surrounded by leafy trees, creepers and flower beds. The kitchen is currently headed up by British chef Billy White, who specialises in hearty flavour-packed European fare. There are typically just two mains to choose from, alongside a vegetarian soup.

Rosendals is also well known for its seasonal desserts and its breads and pastries, which are baked in a wood-burning oven next door. In summer, people devour fruit pie at picnic tables or on the grass under the apple trees; in winter they keep warm with a mug of *glögg* (mulled wine) in

the greenhouses. For kids, there's a small but charming playground built from logs and natural materials. There's also a small shop selling jam, bread and flowers (which you can pick yourself).

Sadly, Rosendals café doesn't offer regular evening meals, shutting up shop at 5pm, but check the website for occasional pop-up supper clubs and cooking classes. Rosendals is a little tricky to find, so be prepared to ask for directions; otherwise just enjoy getting lost in the surrounding woodland.

DJURGÅRDEN & SKEPPSHOLMEN

Restaurants & cafés

In addition to the places listed below, many of Djurgården's museums have good cafés. Worth a visit are **Café Ektorpet**, set outside an 18th-century cottage on a hill overlooking the water, at **Prins Eugens Waldemarsudde** (*see p124*); or one of Skansen's numerous cafés and eateries (*see p123*).

Cafe Ekorren

Biskopsvägen 5 (08 662 01 80, cafeekorren. se). Bus 69 to Blockhusudden (stop at Manilla). **Open** *Summer 11am-6pm Mon-Wed; 10am-8pm Thur-Sat; 10am-6pm Sun (closes at 5pm daily in May). Closed winter.* **Map** *p118 off map* ❶ *café*

This waterfront cafe with sought-after outdoor seating is situated on a relatively remote part of Djurgården, and making the effort to get there is all part of its charm. When you're sipping a coffee or eating an ice-cream here, you'll feel a long way from Stockholm's pulse. Salads, waffles and cinnamon buns are among the menu staples.

❤ Flickorna Helin

Rosendalsvägen 14 (08 664 51 08, www. flickornahelin.se). Tram 7 or bus 67, 74. **Open** *9am-5pm Mon-Sat; 10am-5pm Sun.* **Map** *p118 T8* ❸ *café*

The counter at this charming cafe is always stacked with a mouth-watering selection of cakes, buns, pastries and pies. Alongside strong coffee, juices and smoothies, it also serves a small selection of wines and lagers. While the terrace overlooking the waterfront is a big draw, this is also a great place to warm up and refuel during winter, when the exposed-brick interior is lit up with candles.

❤ Oaxen Krog & Slip

Beckholmsvägen 26 (08 551 53 105, oaxen. com). Tram 7. **Open** *6pm-midnight Tue-Sat.* **Map** *p118 T10* ❺ *Contemporary Scandinavian*

Slap bang on the waterfront, a rebuilt boatshed is home to Oaxen Krog and Oaxen Slip. The melt-in-your-mouth gourmet dishes served at Oaxen Krog won the restaurant two Michelin stars in 2015. Meals here have a strong focus on locally sourced seasonal foods, while the wines are imported from small, carefully selected vineyards. Its sister restaurant Oaxen Slip is a slightly more affordable yet still high-end bistro, with boats hanging from the ceiling in a nod to the venue's nautical roots.

❤ Restaurang Hasselbacken

Hazeliusbacken 20 (08 121 33 302, hasselbacken.com/en/restaurant). Bus 67, or tram 7, or ferry from Slussen. **Open** *6.30-9.30am, 11.30am-1.30pm, 5-10pm Mon-Fri; 7-10am, noon-3pm (brunch) Sat; 7-10am, noon-3pm (brunch) Sun.* **Map** *p118 S10* ❻ *European*

The first restaurant on this site opened in the 1700s, and the hilltop views have made it a favourite with Stockholm's elite ever since. Locals flock here for brunch on weekends and the great value weekday lunch buffet, which offers the chance to enjoy a vast selection of fresh salads, meat and fish cuts, cheeses and sweet treats. A huge sun terrace opens during summer and dog owners are encouraged to bring their charges. Evening meals are a more formal affair, with classic Nordic dishes dominating the a la carte menu. The restaurant and its adjacent hotel have been run by the team behind the neighbouring Pop House Hotel since 2019.

Ulla Winbladh

Rosendalsvägen 8 (08 534 89 701, www. ullawinbladh.se). Tram 7 or bus 67. **Open** *11.30am-10pm Mon; 11.30am-11pm Tue-Fri; 12.30-11pm Sat; 12.30-10pm Sun.* **Map** *p118 S10* ❿ *Traditional Swedish*

Old-fashioned Ulla Winbladh (named after a much-loved friend of Swedish national poet and composer Carl Michael Bellman) scores highly for its wooden interior and spacious outdoor courtyard. The food is a safe bet, although nothing out of the ordinary. Classic meatballs and fried *strömming* (Baltic herring) are among the most-ordered dishes.

Bars

Djurgården's best drinking spots are quite spread out, and its tranquil atmosphere makes it unsuitable for party-goers. If you're visiting for a gig at Gröna Lund, your best bet for a pre-concert pint is to choose one of the bars inside the amusement park.

Josefina

Galärvarvsvägen 10 (08 664 10 04, www. josefina.nu). Tram 7. **Open** *May-mid Sept 11am-1pm daily. Closed Mid Sept-Apr.* **Map** *p118 R8* ❶

Taking inspiration from Miami's moneyed terrace bars, Josefina feels slightly incongruous in this green, calm neighbourhood. Its efforts to ooze style are hit and miss and there's little attention to detail when it comes to service. But Josefina's prime waterfront location means it continues to attract a young aspirational crowd. If you're here during the daytime, the hot dog stand

Spritmuseum

is handy if you're looking for a quick bite in between visiting Djurgården's museums.

Sjöcaféet

Galärvarvsvägen 2 (08 661 44 88, www. sjocafeet.se) Tram 7. **Open** *9am-8pm Mon, Tue, Sun; 9am-9pm Wed-Sat.* **Map** *p118 R8* ②

Situated at Djurgårdsbron (Djurgården bridge), the gateway to Djurgården, Sjöcafeet offers unbeatable views of Strandvägen, which is lined with boats, floating bars and luxury apartments. Chilled rosé, cider and champagne are popular choices here, although there's also a strong selection of lagers and pale ales. The café, as part of the Royal Djurgården Visitor Centre, offers a boat and bike rental service (*see p124* In the know).

♥ Spritmuseum

Djurgårdsvägen 38 (08 121 31 300, www. spritmuseum.se). Bus 67 or tram 7. **Open** *10am-5pm Mon-Wed; 10am-7pm Thur-Sat; noon-5pm Sun.* **Admission** *130kr; 60-90kr reductions; free under-15s & with SP.* **Map** *p118 R9* ③

Tasting trays are the star of the show at Spritmuseum's compact contemporary bar. Take the traditional tray, which offers two *snaps* and a *punsch*, or the Absolut tray, featuring a quadruplet of vodka flavours. Wines, beers and cocktails are also available for those seeking something less strong. The bar is a pleasant spot for a morning coffee too.

If you're looking for something to soak up the alcohol, Spritmuseum also offers vegetarian or meat-and-fish evening tasting menus, compiled by Head Chef Petter Nilsson, who returned from 15 years in Paris to run this fine-dining venue. The decor is achingly sophisticated, weaving together exposed brickwork and industrial chairs, with a marble bar and dark wooden tables.

Shops & services

Djurgården is not a shopping destination. However, **Skansen** (*see p122*) does have a very good shop selling traditional and contemporary Swedish handicrafts, jewellery, condiments and tools. It's open to the general public and situated outside the main entrance. And the Garden Shop at **Rosendals Trädgård** (*see p127*) is also worth a look if you're into rustic tools, French soaps and home-made herbal teas, salts and oils.

SKEPPSHOLMEN

Crossing the narrow bridge from Norrmalm, you'll see the **Östasiatiska Museet** on the hill to your left, housed in a long yellow building designed by Kungliga Slottet architect Nicodemus Tessin the Younger in 1700. The white, Empire-style **Skeppsholmskyrkan** – officially known as Karl Johans Kyrka – stands nearby; designed for the navy by Fredrik Blom, it was completed in 1842 but has now been deconsecrated. The three-masted schooner **Af Chapman**, which is now a youth hostel (*see p233*), is docked to your right. Behind the church stands the **Moderna Museet** (Museum of Modern Art; *see p130*), occupying an earth-toned building designed by Spanish architect Rafael Moneo and completed in 1998; the adjoining **Arkitektur – och Designcentrum** (ArkDes, previously Arkitekturmuseet) is housed in a former naval drill hall. On the south-western corner of Skeppsholmen are **Kungliga Konsthögskolan** (Royal University College of Fine Arts), housed in beautifully restored 18th-century naval barracks, and **Svensk Form**, the headquarters of the Swedish Society of Crafts and Design. A newer addition to the island is the contemporary-styled **Hotel Skeppsholmen** (*see p230*), on the southern side – one of the most chic and calm places to rest your head in Stockholm.

Situated to the south of Skeppsholmen, and connected to it by a bridge, the tiny granite island of **Kastellholmen** is named after a castle built here in the 1660s. The castle was blown up in 1845 after an accident in a cartridge-manufacturing laboratory. A year later, Fredrik Blom designed a new, medieval-style castle (not open to the public) with two red towers, one tall and one squat. The castle's cannons are fired on 6 June, Sweden's national day, as well as on the birthdays of the King, Queen and Crown Princess. Kastellholmen makes for a lovely short stroll, and provides excellent views of Gröna Lund and the sea from its rocky eastern side.

♥ Moderna Museet

Exercisplan 4 (08 520 23 500, www. modernamuseet.se). Bus 65 or ferry from Slussen. **Open** *10am-8pm Tue, Fri; 10am-6pm Wed, Thur; 11am-6pm Sat, Sun.* **Admission** *free.* **Map** *p118 Q9.*

When it opened in 1958, Moderna Museet soon gained a reputation as one of the world's most groundbreaking contemporary art venues. Housed originally in an old, disused naval exercise building, the museum's heyday came in the 1960s and '70s when it introduced Andy Warhol, Jean Tinguely, Robert Rauschenberg, Niki de Saint Phalle and many more to an astonished Swedish audience. The construction of Rafael Moneo's new museum building was completed in 1998, but it closed four years later owing to structural problems, including a mould infestation. The museum reopened in 2004 with a brighter interior, a more open floor plan, an espresso bar and – most importantly – no mould.

Moderna Museet's collection of 20th-century art is small compared to similar European venues, such as London's Tate Modern or Centre Pompidou, however it includes works by plenty of greats including Picasso, Dalí, Pollock and de Chirico.

If you're feeling flush, don't miss the museum's restaurant (*see right*), which has a gorgeous terrace offering stunning views over the Djurgården's green spaces. The cute courtyard café is the place to head for more affordable fare. There's also a well-stocked shop selling posters, books and homewares.

Sights & museums

Arkitektur – och Designcentrum (ArkDes)

Exercisplan 4 (08 520 23 500, www.arkdes. se). Bus 65. **Open** *10am-8pm Tue, Fri; 10am-6pm Wed, Thur; 11am-6pm Sat, Sun.* **Admission** *150kr; 120kr reductions; free under-19s & with SP.* **Map** *p118 Q9.*

The Centre of Architecture and Design, situated in a long hall linked to Moderna Museet (*see left*) has permanent displays (free to access) of famous Swedish buildings and architectural projects, such as Stockholm's Stadshuset (City Hall), the Royal Palace and the five office buildings at Hötorget. It also holds temporary exhibitions that run the full design gamut. Recent shows have focused on futuristic buildings, public spaces and virtual technologies. The annual Young Swedish Design exhibition, typically running between February and March, showcases the most recent developments in Swedish design.

Östasiatiska Museet

Tyghusplan 4 (010 456 12 00, www.varldskulturmuseerna.se/ ostasiatikamuseet). Bus 65. **Open** *11am-8pm Tue; 11am-5pm Wed-Sun.* **Admission** *free.* **Map** *p118 P9.*

The main focus of the Östasiatiska Museet (Museum of Far Eastern Antiquities) is a permanent exhibition on prehistoric China, presenting artefacts from a Chinese village that were unearthed in the 1920s by the museum's founder, Johan Gunnar Andersson. The exhibition, displayed in a dimly lit room echoing with sounds and voices, includes 3,000- to 4,000-year-old tools and pottery, descriptions of burial traditions, and the symbols, as well as patterns, of prehistoric earthenware. The museum also has a large collection of Far Eastern Buddhist sculptures. The shop sells Japanese tea sets, books on Asian art, religions and design, and kimonos.

Restaurants & cafés

❤ Moderna Museet ⓦⓦ

Exercisplan 4 (08 520 23 660, www. modernamuseet.se). Bus 65 or ferry from Slussen. **Open** *11am-45mins before the museum closes Tue-Sun.* **Map** *p118 Q9* ➍ *Contemporary*

Alongside its more traditional museum café, Moderna Museet has a dining room with white-cloth service and excellent food. It's not open in the evening, but at the weekend serves one of the city's best buffet brunches.

There are two sittings, one at 11.30am and the other at 2pm, and reservations are necessary. The food is a modern take on Scandinavian classics and the desserts are particularly glorious. Beverages include the restaurant's own organic wines, plus juices, beers and ciders.

Restaurang Långa Räden ⓦⓦ

Hotel Skeppsholmen, Gröna gången 1 (08 407 23 05, https://hotelskeppsholmen.se/en/ restaurant). Bus 65 or ferry from Slussen. **Open** *7-10am, 11am-10pm Mon-Fri; 7.30-11am, noon-10pm Sat, Sun.* **Map** *p118 Q10* ➐ *Swedish*

Hotel Skeppsholmen's restaurant Långa Räden is open to non-guests and serves well-executed Swedish fare including classic meatballs and mash and its popular shrimp sandwich. Sunday brunch is a big deal here, with a range of filling a la carte dishes on offer, in contrast to the buffets that are more typical in Stockholm. The star of the show is the signature cold salmon on sourdough bread, with rocket salad, egg and hollandaise sauce. The interior here is bright and contemporary, although you'll want to hustle for a table on the terrace in the summer months.

Torpedverkstan ⓦⓦ

Norra Brobänken (08 611 41 00, www. torpedverkstan.se) Bus 65 or ferry from Slussen. **Open** *11.30am-2pm, 5-10pm Mon-Fri, noon-4pm (brunch), 5-10pm Sat; noon-4pm (brunch) Sun.* **Map** *p118 Q9* ➒ *Mexican*

This former shipyard venue specialising in Mexican street food opened to rave reviews in 2018, taking over premises previously occupied by long-running Swedish restaurant Hjerta. The food is excellent, but the place is as much about the setting as the cooking – the outdoor tables overlook the moored boats along Skeppsholmen's shore, and provide the perfect spot from which to see the sun setting over the water. In the colder months, the action moves into the stylish interior. New owner Peter Lax has a music industry background, so look out for occasional live bands and DJ-led brunch events.

Shops & services

There are no standalone shops on Skeppsholmen, but the museum shop at **Moderna Museet** (*see p130*) is worth checking out for art- and design-related posters, books, homewares and knick-knacks.

Södermalm & Around

Södermalm's working-class heritage no longer deters the posh folk from crossing the water locks at Slussen to eat, drink, live and be merry in the city's most colourful district. Cool restaurants, cafés, bars and shops continue to mushroom on the island that's known more simply as 'Söder', while a world-class photography museum, Fotografiska, has cemented its status as a cutting-edge cultural hub. SoFo, in the east, is perhaps the hippest part of the island, but the area around Södra station, on the commuter train line, has also been regenerated, with gritty bars and well-worn office blocks transforming into trendy cafés and co-working spaces in recent years. The process of gentrification is also creeping south to previously ignored suburbs, as Stockholmers seek affordable places to live.

North from Hornstull lies the narrow island of Långholmen (Long Island), almost a mile in length. Thanks largely to the presence of a jail here, Långholmen remained undeveloped for decades and, as a result, is something of a green retreat. Its sandy beaches are favoured summer bathing spots.

❤ Don't miss

1 Monteliusvägen *p149*
Stunning city views from this cliffside boardwalk.

2 SoFo *p137*
Stockholm's hippest neighbourhood.

3 Fotografiska *p139*
One of the world's best photography museums.

4 Långholmsbadet *p153*
City swimming.

5 Hammarby Sjöstad *p155*
Sustainable suburban architecture.

6 Trädgården *p199*
Drink and dance under the stars.

7 Hornstull Market *p51*
Vintage wear and food trucks.

8 Tantolunden *p146*
Allotments and people-watching.

Bellmansgatan, Slussen

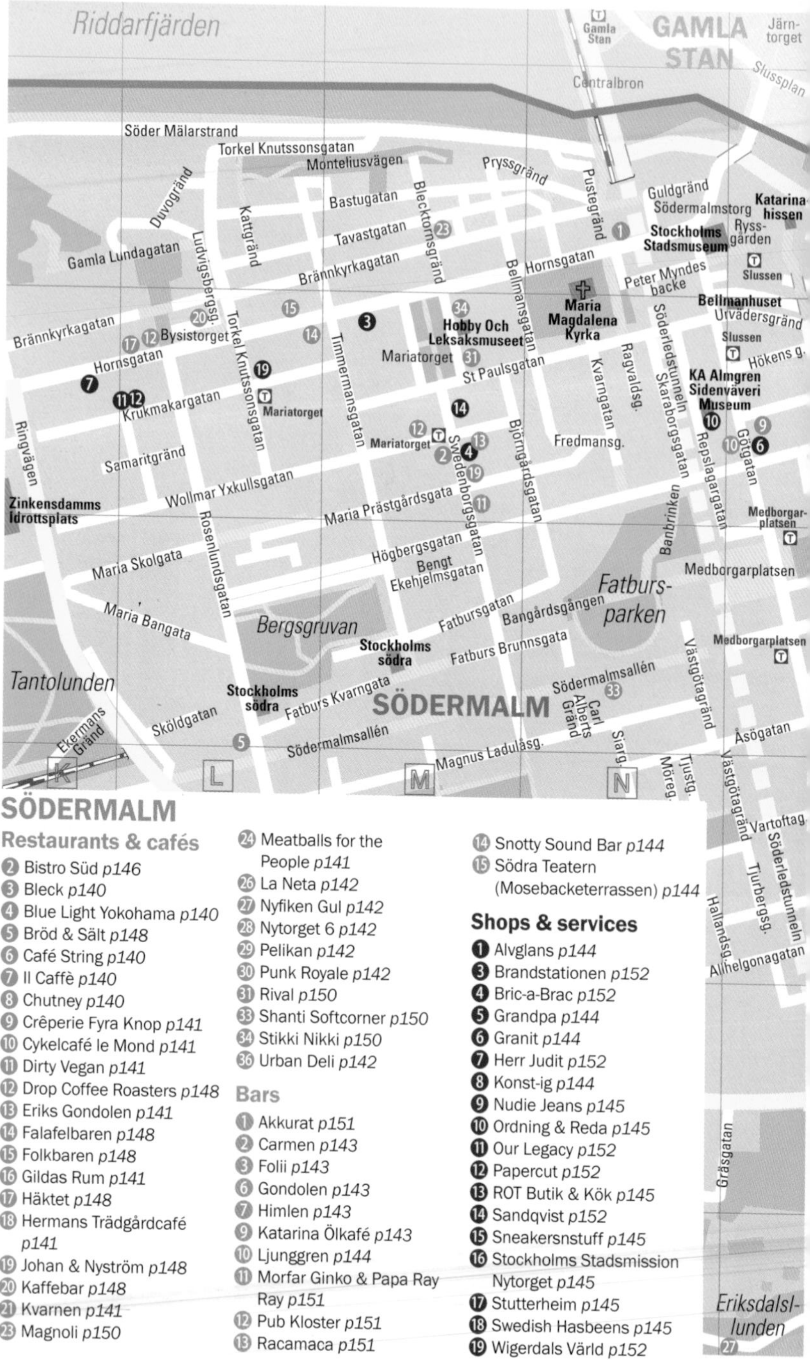

SÖDERMALM

Restaurants & cafés

- ② Bistro Süd p146
- ③ Bleck p140
- ④ Blue Light Yokohama p140
- ⑤ Bröd & Sält p148
- ⑥ Café String p140
- ⑦ Il Caffè p140
- ⑧ Chutney p140
- ⑨ Crêperie Fyra Knop p141
- ⑩ Cykelcafé le Mond p141
- ⑪ Dirty Vegan p141
- ⑫ Drop Coffee Roasters p148
- ⑬ Eriks Gondolen p141
- ⑭ Falafelbaren p148
- ⑮ Folkbaren p148
- ⑯ Gildas Rum p141
- ⑰ Häktet p148
- ⑱ Hermans Trädgårdcafé p141
- ⑲ Johan & Nyström p148
- ⑳ Kaffebar p148
- ㉑ Kvarnen p141
- ㉓ Magnoli p150
- ㉔ Meatballs for the People p141
- ㉖ La Neta p142
- ㉗ Nyfiken Gul p142
- ㉘ Nytorget 6 p142
- ㉙ Pelikan p142
- ㉚ Punk Royale p142
- ㉛ Rival p150
- ㉝ Shanti Softcorner p150
- ㉞ Stikki Nikki p150
- ㊱ Urban Deli p142

Bars

- ① Akkurat p151
- ② Carmen p143
- ③ Folii p143
- ⑥ Gondolen p143
- ⑦ Himlen p143
- ⑨ Katarina Ölkafé p143
- ⑩ Ljunggren p144
- ⑪ Morfar Ginko & Papa Ray Ray p151
- ⑫ Pub Kloster p151
- ⑬ Racamaca p151
- ⑭ Snotty Sound Bar p144
- ⑮ Södra Teatern (Mosebacketerrassen) p144

Shops & services

- ❶ Alvglans p144
- ❸ Brandstationen p152
- ❹ Bric-a-Brac p152
- ❺ Grandpa p144
- ❻ Granit p144
- ❼ Herr Judit p152
- ❽ Konst-ig p144
- ❾ Nudie Jeans p145
- ❿ Ordning & Reda p145
- ⓫ Our Legacy p152
- ⓬ Papercut p152
- ⓭ ROT Butik & Kök p145
- ⓮ Sandqvist p152
- ⓯ Sneakersnstuff p145
- ⓰ Stockholms Stadsmission Nytorget p145
- ⓱ Stutterheim p145
- ⓲ Swedish Hasbeens p145
- ⓳ Wigerdals Värld p152

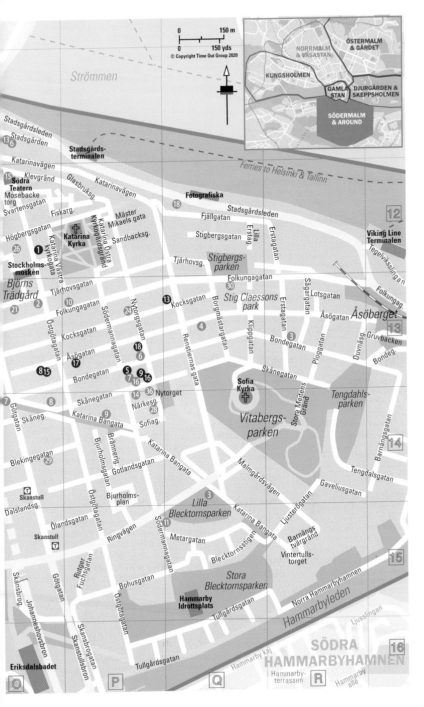

Strömmen

0   150 m
0   150 yds
© Copyright Time Out Group 2020

NORRMALM & VÄSASTAN

ÖSTERMALM & GÄRDET

KUNGSHOLMEN

GAMLA STAN

DJURGÅRDEN & SKEPPSHOLMEN

SÖDERMALM & AROUND

Stadsgårdsleden
Stadsgården
13 6
Katarinavägen
15 Södra Teatern
Mosebacke torg
Klevgränd
Glasbruksg.
Svartensgatan
Högbergsgatan
26
Stockholms-mosken
Björns Trädgård
21 2
Tjärhovsgatan
Folkungagatan
10
Kocksgatan
Östgötagatan
Åsögatan
8 15
Bondegatan
Skåneg.
8
Götgatan
Skåneg.
Katarina Bangata
9
Blekingegatan
29
Skanstull
Dalslandsg.
Skanstull
Ölandsgatan
Ringvägen
Skänsbrog.
Johanneshovsbron
Eriksdalsbadet

Stadsgårds-terminalen
Katarinavägen
Fiskarg.
Glasbruksg.
Katarina Kyrka
Katarina Västra kyrkogata
Mäster Mikaels gata
Katarina Östra Kyrkogårdsgränd
Sandbacksg.
Tjärhovsg.
Södermannagatan
Nytorgsgatan
24
18
6
5 9 16
7 16
14
28
Närkesg.
Sofiag.
Brännerig.
Bjurholmsgatan
Gotlandsgatan
Rutger Fuchsgatan
Bohusgatan
Östgötagatan
Bjurholms-plan
Metargatan
Blecktornsstigen
Hammarby Idrottsplats
Tullgårdsgatan

Fotografiska
18
Stadsgårdsleden
Fjällgatan
Stigbergsgatan
Lilla Erstag.
Stigbergs-parken
Folkungagatan
30
13 Kocksgatan
4
Renstiernas gata
36 Nytorget
Sofia Kyrka
Vitabergs-parken
Lilla Blecktornsparken
3
Katarina Bangata
Stora Blecktornsparken
Tullgårdsgatan

Ferries to Helsinki & Tallinn

12
Viking Line Terminalen
Tegelviksslingan

Erstaggatan
Borgmästargatan
Stig Claessons park
Klippgatan
Bondegatan
Skånegatan
Stora Mejtens Gränd
Malmgårdsvägen

Sågargatan
Erstagatan
Lotsgatan
Åsögatan
Bondegatan
Ploggatan
Tengdahls-parken
Tengdalsgatan
Gaveliusgatan
Ljusterögatan

Åsöberget
Duvnäsg.
Gruvbacken
Bondeg.
13

Barnängsgatan
14

Barnängs tvärgränd
Vintertulls-torget
15

Norra Hammarbyhamnen
Hammarbyleden
Ljussingan
SÖDRA HAMMARBYHAMNEN
Hammarby kaj
Hammarby-terrassen
16
Hammarby allé

EASTERN SÖDERMALM

Slussen (literally 'sluices') takes its name from the locks that regulate water levels on the narrow stretch of water between Gamla Stan and Södermalm. During the 20th century, the locks and bridges developed into a complicated interchange for trains, cars and pedestrians; today, the Slussen Tunnelbana and bus station remain one of the city's busiest transport hubs. Major construction work – for both the new Citybanan railway tunnel and the controversial Future Slussen redevelopment plan – have been under way here since 2014, and the area is likely to remain a building site until at least 2025 (*see p138*). Nevertheless, Slussen is home to one of the island's essential museums, the **Stockholms Stadsmuseum**, where you can learn about the city's history since it was founded back in 1252. The famous black steel **Katarinahissen** lift that towers over it (currently closed for renovation, due to reopen gradually in 2020) can carry visitors 38 metres (125 feet) up from the dock area to the upper reaches of Södermalm for panoramic views of the city and to the **Eriks Gondolen** restaurant. A short walk east along the waterfront from Slussen takes you to the high-profile **Fotografiska** photography museum (*see p139*).

Head directly south of Slussen, meanwhile, and you're faced with a steep climb up the pedestrian section of **Götgatan**, Södermalm's busiest shopping street, which runs down the length of the island. Heading east from this end of Götgatan, walk up Urvädersgränd past the rarely open **Bellmanhuset**, former home of 18th-century balladeer Carl Michael Bellman, to **Mosebacke torg**. This busy cobbled square has been Söder's entertainment centre since the mid 19th century and is bordered by one of Stockholm's most popular nightlife haunts, **Södra Teatern** . The venue offers everything from cutting-edge DJs to live jazz music. South and east is the landmark **Katarina Kyrka**, masterfully restored in the 1990s to its original Baroque splendour; nearby is an area of preserved early 18th-century houses on **Mäster Mikaels Gata**, which was named after the city's first paid executioner.

Once back on Götgatan, continue downhill and you'll reach lively **Medborgarplatsen**, which houses a small galleria, an indoor farmers' market and a cinema complex. This large square has

---

♥ Time to eat & drink

A classy glass
Häktet *p148*, Himlen *p143*, Judit & Bertil *p151*

Barbecue by the water
Nyfiken Gul *p142*

Bargain beers
Carmen *p143*, Pub Kloster *p151*

Cheap dinner date
Crêperie Fyra Knop *p141*

Global flavours on a budget
Falafelbaren *p148*, La Neta *p142*, Shaka Shaka *p150*

Ice-cream dream
Stikki Nikki *p150*

♥ Time to shop

Pre-loved clothing and street eats
Hornstull Market *p51*

Ready-to-heat treats
Meatballs for the People *p141*, ROT Butik & Kök *p145*, Urban Deli *p142*

Scandinavian labels
Grandpa *p144*, Our Legacy *p152*, Sandqvist *p152*

Stylish stationary
Granit *p144*, Ordning & Reda *p145*

Vintage fashion
Beyond Retro *p151*, Herr Judit *p152*, Stockholms Stadsmission Nytorget *p145*

In the know
Getting around

Södermalm is well connected to the city centre via all branches of the red and green subway lines. Slussen is the main transport hub; from here you can catch the red line west towards Hornstull or head south to Skanstull. It's also the starting point for buses heading east to Nacka and Stockholm's archipelago. SoFo, Södermalm's creative district, doesn't have its own subway stop – your best bet is to walk here from Medborgarplatsen or Skanstull on the green line or take bus 3 to Nytorgsgatan or Åsögatan. Bus 4 is another handy route, running between Skanstull and Hornstull. It also stops at Södra station, in the centre of the island, a commuter train stop with connections to Stockholm City station in just four minutes.

💜 SoFo

T-bana Medborgarplatsen or Skanstull, or bus 3. **Map** *p134 P13.*

SoFo is an abbreviation of 'south of Folkungagatan', the busy street that marks the northern perimeter of the neighbourhood. (The area north of here has more recently started to be known as NoHo.) But it's no coincidence that the nickname was designed to sound similar to the Soho/SoHo districts in London and New York. Here, twentysomething media types pack out the independent bars and restaurants, bearded young fathers cycle past on retro city bikes and stylish pensioners eye up the window displays in the many thrift stores.

Most of this area was farmland until the 19th century. A scattering of wooden cottages remains, breaking up the rows of spice-coloured, functionalist apartment buildings that were constructed to accommodate the workers when industrialisation transformed the area into one of the most densely populated parts of the city. It remained unapologetically working class for most of the 20th century.

When gentrification began creeping across Södermalm in the 1990s, SoFo, in the centre of the island, was the first to experience the shift. Vintage bric-a-brac shops found themselves rubbing shoulders with high-end design stores, while traditional inns began fighting for attention with organic coffeeshops and international restaurants and delicatessens. People from across the city were soon flocking here to sample the changes – the area is one of the Swedish capital's most popular spots for eating and drinking. Nytorget – a fountained garden square lined with traditional wooden houses on the western side of SoFo – is something of a focal point, particularly since the opening of the **Urban Deli** restaurant and grocery (*see p142*).

For locals, SoFo's continued popularity does have its downsides. There's been a significant hike in property prices and a growth in illegal subletting, which has pushed out lower-income families and many of the area's more artistic locals. But, for visitors, it's a great place to stroll and window-shop: check out **Grandpa** (*see p144*) and **Sneakersnstuff** (*see p145*) for on-trend fashion; then, refuel at **Meatballs for the People** (*see p141*) or **Il Caffè** (*see p140*).

Grandpa

Meatballs for the People

In the know
Future Slussen

Slussen, one of Stockholm's busiest transport hubs, waited decades for a much-needed facelift, until, after various controversies and feuds about the future of the area, construction finally began in 2014. City planners promise the disruption will be worthwhile. Future Slussen will feature an accessible quayside, new public spaces, pedestrian and cycle routes, and some prominent contemporary architecture. The project's final stages are not expected to be completed until 2025 at the earliest.

undergone a renaissance in recent times, and expansive outdoor seating has been added to the stylish restaurants facing the Medborgarhuset civic hall.

Across the street, the minaret of the city's mosque, **Stockholms Moské**, rises over **Björns Trädgård** park, a welcoming space for all ages that now also features a skate park. South-east from here lies the trendy shopping area dubbed **SoFo** (*see p137*).

At the southern end of Götgatan is a superb swimming complex, **Eriksdalsbadet**, which has Olympic-sized indoor and outdoor pools. The latter are a huge hit in summer. Another of the city's sports arenas, **Globen** (*see p194*), is clearly visible from this part of Södermalm. The huge dome is one of Stockholm's landmark buildings.

Sights & museums
Bellmanhuset
Urvädersgränd 3 (08 767 855 800, www. bellmanhuset.se). T-bana Slussen. **Open** *(guided tours only, in Swedish) 1pm 1st Sun of mth; check website for details.* **Admission** *100kr. No cards.* **Map** *p134 O12.*

This small house just off Götgatan is the former home of legendary Swedish songwriter and poet Carl Michael Bellman (1740-95). During his tenancy, between 1770 and 1774, he wrote much of his *Fredmans Epistlar*, a book of songs about Stockholm's drunks and prostitutes that parodies the letters of the apostle Paul in the New Testament.

▶ *For more on Carl Bellman, visit Stora Henriksvik (see p154).*

Eriksdalsbadet
Hammarby Slussväg 20 (08 508 40 258, www.eriksdalsbadet.se). T-bana Skanstull. **Open** *6am-8pm Mon-Thur; 6am-7pm Fri; 8am-6pm Sat; 8am-7pm Sun. Call or*

visit website to check outdoor pool opening hours. **Admission** *Indoor pool 90kr; 60kr reductions; free under-4s. Outdoor pool 70kr; 20-50kr reductions; free under-4s.* **Map** *p134 O16.*

This is the main arena for Swedish swimming competitions. It also has adventure pools for children and a seasonal outdoor pool (get there early on warm days to avoid the crowds, and bring a padlock for the lockers), plus a spa and gym. The park surrounding the outdoor pool also serves as the site for the annual Popaganda music festival (www. popaganda.se).

KA Almgren Sidenväveri Museum
Repslagargatan 15A (08 642 56 16, www. kasiden.se). T-bana Slussen. **Open** *winter 10am-4pm Mon-Fri; 11am-3pm Sat. Summer 11am-3pm Mon-Sat. Guided tours 1pm Mon, Wed, Sat.* **Admission** *75kr. Free with SC.* **Map** *p134 N12.*

Knut August Almgren stole the technology for this former silk-weaving factory back in the late 1820s. While recovering from tuberculosis in France, he posed as a German-speaking Frenchman and gained access to factories where the innovative Jacquard looms were being used. He took notes, smuggled machinery out of the country and opened a factory in Sweden in 1833. The factory here closed down in 1974 and reopened as a working museum in 1991. It reproduces silk fabrics for stately homes around Scandinavia, including the Royal Palace. The renovated additional floor houses an exhibition on the history of silk weaving in Sweden, along with a collection of silk portraits, landscapes and fabrics. You can watch its 160-year-old looms in action.

Katarina Kyrka
Högbergsgatan 15 (08 743 68 00, www. svenskakyrkan.se/katarina). T-bana Medborgarplatsen or Slussen. **Open** *11am-5pm Mon-Sat; 8.30am-5pm Sun.* **Admission** *free.* **Map** *p134 P12.*

In response to Södermalm's population growth, in the mid 17th century Maria Magdalena parish was split and a new church was commissioned to cater for the excess congregation. Katarina Kyrka, completed in 1695, was designed by Jean de la Vallé in Baroque style with a central plan. A huge fire in 1723 destroyed the church's cupola and half the buildings in the parish. A more recent fire in 1990 burned down all but the walls and side vaults. Architect Ove Hildemark reconstructed the church (based on photos and drawings) using 17th-century building techniques. The church now looks much as it did before, but with a distinctly modern interior.

💙 Fotografiska

Stadsgårdshamnen 22 (08 509 00 500, www.
fotografiska.com). T-bana Slussen. **Open**
9am-11pm Mon-Wed, Sun; 9am-1am Thur-
Sat. **Admission** *165kr; 135kr reductions; free*
under-12s. **Map** *p134 Q12.*

Housed in a huge art nouveau industrial
building built in 1906, the Fotografiska
national museum of photography opened
to great fanfare in May 2010, quickly
becoming one of Scandinavia's – and the
world's – foremost centres for contemporary
photography. With restoration costs to the
former customs house's interior amounting
to around 250 million kroner, the stakes
were high, but the museum has been a great
success, attracting hundreds of thousands
of visitors a year. Fotografiska's success
in Stockholm led to the opening of a sister
venue in London in 2018, and spaces in
Tallinn and New York by the end of 2019.

Rotating temporary exhibitions have
featured works by some of the world's most
respected photographers, including Annie
Leibovitz, Lennart Nilsson, Joel-Peter Witkin,
Marin Schoeller, Bryan Adams and Vee Speers.
As well as showcasing renowned international
names, Fotografiska aims to promote a good
range of Swedish photographers, and to
encourage debate and innovation within
the field through an active programme of
exhibitions, seminars and courses.

Four major exhibitions are held annually,
plus around 20 smaller shows (with an
emphasis on provocative documentary works).
As well as the 2,500 square metres (27,000
square feet) of exhibition space, Fotografiska
also houses a restaurant and café (both with
superb waterside views), events spaces, a
commercial gallery, and an excellent book
and souvenir shop. Note that the Stockholm
Pass is not valid for entry to the museum.

Stockholms Moskén

*Kapellgränd 10 (08 509 10 900, www. islamiskaforbundet.se). T-bana Medborgarplatsen. **Open** 10am-6pm daily. Prayers 5 times daily; see website for details. **Admission** free. **Map** p134 O12.*

The conversion of Katarinastation, a former power station, into Stockholm's first mosque led to heated architectural debates. Prior to its inauguration in 2000, Stockholm's Muslim community had worshipped in cellars and other cramped spaces. The original structure already faced Mecca, but Ferdinand Boberg (the architect behind Rosenbad and NK, *see p93*) was inspired by Andalusian Moorish architecture to decorate the lofty main hall in mosaic brick, with floor-to-ceiling vaulted windows. As long as shoes are removed and women covered up (robes provided), visitors may view the prayer hall and lecture hall. Before you leave, take a look at the massive copper doors facing Östgötagatan, which have been embedded with numerous mundane objects using the process of blast-moulding.

Stockholms Stadsmuseum

*Ryssgården (08 508 31 620, www. stadsmuseum.stockholm.se). T-bana Slussen or bus 2, 3, 53, 71, 76, 96. **Open** noon-6pm Tue-Fri; 10am-4pm Sat, Sun. Tours (in English) July-mid Sept 2pm Tue-Sun, 50kr. **Admission** Free. **Map** p134 N11.*

Nicodemus Tessin the Elder designed this impressive building in the 1670s. After a fire in 1680, the renovations were supervised by his son, Tessin the Younger, architect of the Royal Palace. Recently renovated again, its revamped permanent exhibition charts the growth of the city from medieval times to the present day; temporary exhibitions have focussed on Stockholm's musical and artistic heritage. There are regular tours in English and easy-to-understand Swedish, aimed at helping newcomers to mug up on the history of their adopted city.

Restaurants & cafés

Bleck ⓦⓦ

*Katarina Bangata 68 (08 666 12 34, www.restaurangbleck.se). T-bana Medborgarplatsen. **Open** 11.30am-11pm Mon-Thur, Sun; 11.30am-1am Fri, Sat. **Map** p134 Q14* ❸ *Contemporary*

The Instagrammable menus at this artsy restaurant consist of Courier font food and drink lists typed on to A4 lined paper. Most of the dishes are small plates designed for sharing, such as roasted cauliflower and truffles, and fried chicken with pickled vegetables. The weekend brunch menu

includes savoury waffles, inventive egg-based dishes, milkshakes and hair-of-the-dog cocktails. During the summer there are long, wooden, outdoor benches and grey woollen rugs, to encourage socialising until the early hours.

Blue Light Yokohama ⓦⓦⓦ

*Åsögatan 170 (08 644 68 00, www. bluelightyokohama.com). T-bana Medborgarplatsen or bus 3. **Open** 5-10pm Tue-Sun. **Map** p134 Q13* ❹ *Asian*

This minimalist Japanese restaurant specialising in sushi, soups and tempura is on the pricey side, but the food is incredibly authentic. The Ramen Sunday menu is the best deal, offering a small selection of filling meat and vegetarian broths. It's a popular choice with Japanese expats and locals.

Café String ⓦ

*Nytorgsgatan 38 (08 714 85 14, www.cafestring. com). T-bana Medborgarplatsen. **Open** 9am-8pm Mon, Tue, Thur; 9am-10pm Wed; 9am-7pm Fri-Sun. **Map** p134 P13* ❻ *Café*

Once a furniture shop that served coffee to its customers, String is now a café that also sells furniture. Everything from the deckchair you sit on to the plate you eat off is for sale. String is as fun and hip as its fan base, whose favourite hangover cure is the weekend breakfast buffet. Live music sessions and stand-up comedy are occasionally held here.

Il Caffè ⓦ

*Södermannagatan 23 (08 462 95 00, www. ilcaffe.se). T-bana Medborgarplatsen. **Open** 7am-7pm Mon-Fri; 9am-7pm Sat, Sun. **Map** p134 P13* ❼ *Café*

This industrial space is archetypal of its neighbourhood: it's full of creative locals with their laptops, tucking into excellent toasted sandwiches (with ingredients such as parma ham, bresaola, mozzarella and pesto) and top-notch coffee. Service is refreshingly down-to-earth. **Other locations** Bergsgatan 17, Kungsholmen (08 652 30 04); Långholmsgatan 19, Hornstull; Drottninggatan 85, Norrmalm (08 20 35 05).

Chutney ⓦ

*Katarina Bangata 19 (073 933 79 18, www. chutney.se). T-bana Medborgarplatsen. **Open** 11am-10pm Mon-Fri; noon-10pm Sat; noon-9pm Sun. **Map** p134 O14* ❽ *Vegetarian*

A favourite with the eco crowd, thanks to environmentally conscious art on the walls and vegetarian and vegan food on the plates. Service is friendly, portions are huge and prices are decent. Good for lunch or an early dinner after doing the SoFo shopping rounds.

❤ Crêperie Fyra Knop ⓦ

Svartensgatan 4 (08 640 77 27, www.
creperiefyraknop.se). T-bana Slussen or
Medborgarplatsen. **Open** *5-11pm Mon-Fri;*
noon-11pm Sat, Sun. **Map** *p134 O12* ⑨
French

If you're French and homesick, or looking
for an inexpensive but romantic meal, this
could be the place. The decor in the two dark,
cosy little rooms is kitsch, complete with old
fishing nets and lifebelts. The savoury and
sweet crêpes are delicious, and cheap enough
that you can go drinking in one of the nearby
bars afterwards.

Cykelcafé le Mond ⓦ

Folkungagatan 67 (08 437 48 541, www.
cykelcafe.se). T-bana Medborgarplatsen.
Open *7.30am-5pm Mon, Tue, Thur;*
7am-5pm Wed, Fri; 9am-4pm Sat, Sun. **Map**
p134 P13 ⑩ *Café*

Fresh-fruit açai bowls, toasted sandwiches,
hearty pies and fluffy home-made cakes
are among the varied snacks on offer at this
friendly café with a Brooklyn-style cycling-
themed interior. There's also a large selection
of teas, including a tasty English breakfast
blend. Summertime outdoor pavement
seating makes this a busy spot when the
sun shines.

Dirty Vegan ⓦ

Södermannagatan 53 (www.dirtyvegan.se).
T-bana Skanstull. **Open** *11am-11pm daily.*
Map *p134 P15* ⑪ *Vegan*

Framed around the idea that even clean-
living vegans sometimes crave fried comfort
food, Dirty Vegan's dishes include mushroom
burgers, shawarma-style kebabs made with
soy and wheat protein and dairy-free ice-
cream and peanut butter sandwiches. A
much-hyped venue since its launch in early
2019, it's run by the team behind **Greasy
Spoon** (greasyspoon.se), a popular Anglo-
American brunch chain with branches on
Tjärhovsgatan in Södermalm and Hagagatan
at Odenplan.

Eriks Gondolen ⓦⓦⓦ

Stadsgården 6 (08 641 70 90, www.
eriks.se/gondolen). T-bana Slussen.
Open *11.30am-2.30pm, 5-11pm Mon;*
11.30am-2.30pm, 5pm-1am Tue-Fri;
4pm-1am Sat. **Map** *p134 O11* ⑬ *French/*
Swedish

Entered via the bridge from Mosebacke torg
(if the lift is closed), the Gondolen bar and
restaurant are suspended underneath the
Katarinahissen walkway over Slussen and
look out over Gamla Stan and the water.
Although much of this area is in the midst of
construction work, it's still a great vantage

point from which to get a good view of
the city. The menu offers both French and
Swedish dishes, and lunch deals here are
great value.

Gildas Rum ⓦ

Skånegatan 79 (08 714 77 98). T-bana
Medborgarplatsen or bus 3, 53. **Open**
8.30am-9pm Mon-Fri; 9am-9pm Sat, Sun.
Map *p134 P13* ⑯ *Café*

One of Södermalm's most popular cafés,
Gildas Rum is a hive of activity, full of
freelancer types. A seat outside provides
prime people-watching opportunities, with
Nytorget opposite. The decor is very much
Stockholm new wave, with Scandinavian
clean lines eschewed for a more kitschy,
colourful design. Coffee is top drawer and the
sandwiches are delicious.

Hermans Trädgårdcafé ⓦ

Fjällgatan 23B (08 643 94 80, www.hermans.
se). T-bana Slussen. **Open** *11am-10pm daily.*
Lunch served 11am-3pm daily. **Map** *p134*
Q12 ⑱ *Vegetarian*

This vegetarian café boasts amazing views
over the Stockholm skyline – you can pick out
nearly all the major landmarks, together with
the cruise ships and tourist boats shuttling in
and out of the harbour. The café offers a buffet
menu; you can opt for just a main course or
include one of the delicious fruit pies.

Kvarnen ⓦⓦ

Tjärhovsgatan 4 (08 643 03 80, www.
kvarnen.com). T-bana Medborgarplatsen.
Open *11am-1am Mon, Tue; 11am-3am Wed-*
Fri; noon-3am Sat; noon-1am Sun. **Map**
p134 O13 ㉑ *Swedish*

This traditional Swedish restaurant dates
back to 1908 and is a fail-safe place to treat
yourself to classic Scandinavian dishes,
from meatballs and mash to reindeer stew.
Despite being a large venue, the atmosphere
is cosy, with dark-wood panelling and a long
brass bar in the main dining area. A separate
bar area at the back of the venue has a more
industrial feel. It can get rowdy after 11pm.

❤ Meatballs for the People ⓦ

Nytorgsgatan 30 (08 466 60 99, www.
meatball.se). T-bana Medborgarplatsen.
Open *11am-9pm Mon-Thur, Sun; 11am-11pm*
Fri, Sat. **Map** *p134 P13* ㉔ *Swedish*

This contemporary exposed-brick venue
embodies Södermalm's creative vibe while
serving some of the most affordable and
tasty meatballs in the city. The menu here is
inventive, with chicken and vegan options
alongside moose, veal and ox varieties. It's
often fully booked, but ready-to-heat meals
are also available from the delicatessen area.

♥ La Neta
*Östgötagatan 12B (08 640 40 20, www.laneta.se). T-bana Medborgarplatsen or Slussen. **Open** 11am-9pm Mon-Fri; noon-10pm Sat; noon-4pm Sun. **Map** p134 O12 ㉖ Mexican*

Mexican street food is on trend in Stockholm, and this taquería pulls in the corn-hungry crowds, who devour the fairly authentic selection of soft tacos on offer. The interior, made up of rows of long wooden tables with benches, suits the no-frills cuisine. **Other location** Barnhusgatan 2, Norrmalm (08 411 58 80).

♥ Nyfiken Gul
*Hammarby Slussväg 15 (08 642 52 02, www.nyfikengul.se). T-bana Skanstull. **Open** Apr, Sept 9am-5pm daily. May-Aug 9am-10pm daily. Closed Oct-Apr. **Map** p134 O16 ㉗ Grill*

Located next to the Årstaviken waterfront, this open-air grill is a popular summer spot. Customers can participate in the cooking of their food – which consists of barbecued meat, fish or vegetable wraps, with a healthy dose of sides, sauces, salads and the ubiquitous potatoes. It's usually busy, but the staff work hard to get you a table quickly while you wait at the bar.

▶ *This is a good place to come after a swim in the Olympic-sized open-air pool at nearby Eriksdalsbadet (see p138).*

Nytorget 6
*Nytorget 6 (08 640 96 55, www.nytorget6.com). T-bana Medborgarplatsen. **Open** 7.30am-midnight Mon-Wed; 7.30am-1pm Thur, Fri; 11am-1am Sat, 11am-midnight Sun. **Map** p134 P14 ㉘ Modern European*

There's a smart yet rustic vibe and reasonable prices at Nytorget 6, with an all-day menu and a wide range of dishes that run the gamut from eggs benedict and burgers to Swedish meatballs, pasta dishes and grilled tuna. There are outdoor tables at the front during the summer, and the bar areas are popular with cocktail-lovers.

Pelikan
*Blekingegatan 40 (08 556 09 090, www.pelikan.se). T-bana Skanstull. **Open** 4pm-midnight Mon, Tue; 4pm-1am Wed, Thur; noon-1am Fri-Sun. Kitchen closes 11pm daily. **Map** p134 O14 ㉙ Traditional Swedish*

Not many restaurants feel as genuinely Swedish as this beer hall in Södermalm. Its elegant painted ceilings and wood-panelled walls haven't changed since the days before Söder became trendy, back when restaurants served only *husmanskost* (traditional Swedish home-cooked fare). Classics on offer include

Urban Deli

meatballs with lingonberries and pickled cucumber. Ice-cold schnapps is compulsory.

Punk Royale
*Folkungagatan 128 (08 128 22 411, www.punkroyale.se). Bus 2, 3, 53, 71. **Open** 6pm-midnight Tue-Sat. **Map** p134 Q13 ㉚ Contemporary*

Bizarre, playful, ambitious: three words that sum up Punk Royale and its weird and wonderful tasting-menu experience. You're invited to try a selection of decadent, globally inspired small plates, starting with a scoop of caviar dolloped straight onto your hand, alongside a shot of vodka. The interior provides a striking juxtaposition to the fine-dining menu: the walls are crumbling; a straight-out-of-the-'90s smoke machine fills the room with nostalgic mist, and Lego sets are provided for play between courses. One of the toughest restaurants in Stockholm to book, Punk Royale recently opened an adjacent café, which offers a shorter, more affordable menu alongside decoration that's reminiscent of a Tim Burton movie. You'll either love or hate these venues, and that's the whole point.

♥ Urban Deli
*Nytorget 4 (08 425 50 030, www.urbandeli.org). T-bana Medborgarplatsen. **Open** 8am-11pm Mon, Tue, Sun; 8am-midnight Wed, Thur; 8am-1am Fri, Sat. **Map** p134 P13 ㊱ Contemporary*

This deli-restaurant-café-shop has remained a huge hit since opening a decade ago, offering a New York-style take on the traditional Swedish locale, with concrete floors and industrial fittings. Both the lunch and dinner menus feature a good range of

made a name for himself selecting and serving specialist wines at Fäviken, northern Sweden's most exclusive restaurant. Vinyl records provide the soundtrack, which typically attracts affluent thirty- and fortysomethings looking for a more laid-back atmosphere than the thronging bars and pubs around Nytorget and Medborgarplatsen.

Gondolen

Stadsgården 6 (08 641 70 90, www.eriks.se). T-bana Slussen. Open 11.30am-11pm Mon; 11.30am-1am Tue-Fri; 4pm-1am Sat. Food served until closing. Map p134 O11 6

At the top of the historic Katarinahissen lift (currently closed for renovation), Gondolen is an ideal place for a tall drink. The bar sits under the walkway – it's reached via the restaurant's free lift at Stadsgården 6 – and provides a panoramic view of Djurgården to the east and Riddarfjärden to the west. Drinks are reasonably priced, despite the feeling of international luxury.

♥ Himlen

Götgatan 78 (08 660 60 68, www. restauranghimlen.se). T-bana Medborgarplatsen. Open 11.30am-midnight Mon; 11.30am-1am Tue-Thur; 11.30am-3am Fri; noon-3am Sat. Map p134 O14 7

An unassuming 1960s former office block that's also currently home to student accommodation and a shopping centre is the somewhat improbable location for one of Stockholm's best-loved high-altitude drinking spots. The panoramic views from floor-to-ceiling windows take in the island's most colourful park, Tantolunden, and the green 19th-century spires of Sofia Church. You can also see the sphere of the iconic Ericsson Globen (*see p141*). Himlen's cocktails are fantastic: strong, well-balanced and presented with flair.

Katarina Ölkafé

Katarina Bangata 27 (www.katarinaolkafe. se). T-bana Medborgarplatsen. Open 5-10pm Tue; 5pm-midnight Wed, Thur; 4pm-midnight Sat; noon-10pm Sun. Map p134 P14 9

Cold draft beer on tap is the staple at this New York-inspired venue, although the drinks list also includes a small selection of firm favourites from North American bar and café culture, from Negroni cocktails to home-made hot cocoa served with whipped cream. There's a short but tasty food menu focused around pastrami sandwiches and four styles of mac 'n' cheese. This is a relaxed, though often packed spot on one of the calmer streets in SoFo; arrive early during summer to score one of the outdoor tables.

seafood and make use of the extensive range of Spanish charcuterie and Mediterranean cheeses from the attached grocery. Tables can be hard to get. **Other locations** Sveavägen 44, Norrmalm (08 425 50 020); Hesselmans Torg 12, Sickla (08 425 50 040).

Bars

Södermalm's busiest and most popular spots for a beer are clustered on Götgatan and Medborgarplatsen. But many of the city's more unusual bars are scattered around the SoFo district, south of Folkungagatan.

♥ Carmen

Tjärhovsgatan 14 (08 641 24 12). T-bana Medborgarplatsen. Open 4pm-1am daily. Map p134 O13 2

Nobody drinks at Carmen because of its interior, music or food; this Södermalm institution is famous for offering one of the cheapest drink lists in the city, alongside a laid-back and sociable vibe. It draws a mixed-generation crowd, and the friendly staff always know all the regulars by name. Carmen is also a firm favourite with groups of Anglo-American expats, who flock here to indulge in buying affordable rounds of drinks for one another.

Folii

Erstagatan 21 (www.folii.se). T-bana Medborgarplatsen or bus 2, 53, 66. Open 4pm-1am Wed-Sun. Map p134 R13 3

This compact, classy wine bar is jointly owned by award-winning sommelier Beatrice Becher and Jonas Sandberg, who

Ljunggren

*Götgatan 36 (08 640 75 65, www.
restaurangljunggren.se). T-bana Slussen.*
Open *5pm-midnight Mon, Tue, Sun;
5pm-1am Wed-Sat. Food served until 10pm
Mon, Tue; 11pm Wed-Sat.* **Map** *p134 O12* ⑩

Ljunggren is a cocktail bar and sushi
restaurant that attracts the kind of stylish
crowd of young professionals normally found
in the sleek venues around Östermalm. The
DJs favour hip hop and electronic music,
and the small bar area spills into a trendy,
miniature shopping mall equipped with
an additional bar. The outdoor terrace is
typically open between May and September.

Snotty Sound Bar

*Skånegatan 90 (08 644 39 10). T-bana
Medborgarplatsen or bus 2, 3, 53.* **Open** *Bar
4pm-1am daily.* **Map** *p134 P14* ⑭

Local hipsters and musicians love this tiny
hole-in-the-wall restaurant-bar. The walls are
decorated with images of rock and film stars,
and the bar staff take their music selection
seriously. It trebles in size during the summer
months when a penned outdoor seating area
opens up on the street outside.

Södra Teatern (Mosebacketerrassen)

*Mosebacke torg 1-3 (08 480 04 401,
sodrateatern.com). T-bana Slussen.* **Open**
*11am-11pm Mon-Thur, Sun; 11am-midnight
Fri, Sat.* **Map** *p134 O12* ⑮

A staple of Stockholm's drinking scene,
this buttercup-yellow theatre has been
around since the 1800s and is now home to a
complex of buzzing bars suitable for different
occasions. For the very best views, head up
to the champagne sky bar and terrace on the
seventh floor. During the summer, Södra
Teatern also opens up a giant beer garden,
Mosebacke, with space for 1,000 people.

Shops & services

Micro-mall **Bruno Götgatsbacken** (Götgatan
36, www.brunogotgatsbacken.se), sometimes
called Galleria Bruno, is home to branches of
various mid-range Swedish brands, including
Filippa K, Whyred and Hope. Further south,
at Medborgarplatsen, is mall-like food hall
Söderhallarna, with a great selection of fresh
produce but a rather soulless atmosphere.

Alvglans

*Östgötagatan 19 (070 408 06 35). T-bana
Medborgarplatsen or Slussen.* **Open**
11am-6pm Mon-Fri; 11am-4pm Sat. **Map** *p134
O12* ❶ *Comics*

The Spawn action figures alone are worth
the trip to the comics heaven of Alvglans.

ROT Butik & Kök

The shop stocks bestsellers such as *X-Men*
and *Spiderman*, as well as rare anime movies
and manga.

💗 Grandpa

*Södermannagatan 21 (08 643 60 80, www.
grandpa.se). T-bana Medborgarplatsen or
bus 59, 66.* **Open** *noon-6pm Mon-Sat.* **Map** *p134
P13* ❺ *Fashion*

One of the best fashion stores in SoFo,
Grandpa is particularly strong on
independent menswear labels, stocking items
from British label Folk and Danish brands
Wood Wood and Norse Projects. Womenswear
includes the likes of Minimarket and Swedish
Hasbeens. There's a vintage homewares
shop in the basement, and cool accessories
(sunglasses, candles) displayed throughout.

💗 Granit

*Götgatan 31 (08 642 10 68, www.granit.
com). T-bana Medborgarplatsen or Slussen.*
Open *10am-7pm Mon-Fri; 10am-5pm Sat;
11am-5pm Sun.* **Map** *p134 O12* ❻ *Homewares
& accessories*

Sweden's answer to Muji sells lots of
temptingly simple things at low prices:
storage boxes, unadorned glassware and
crockery, notebooks and photo albums, plus
hundreds of other plain but 'must have'
items. **Other locations** throughout the city.

Konst-ig

*Åsögatan 124 (08 20 45 20, www.konstig.
se). T-bana Medborgarplatsen.* **Open**
*11am-6.30pm Mon-Fri; 11am-5pm Sat; noon-
4pm Sun.* **Map** *p134 O13* ❽ *Books*

Stockholm's leading art bookshop, covering
design, architecture, photography,
fashion and more.

Nudie Jeans

Skånegatan 75 (010 151 57 18, www. nudiejeans.com). T-bana Medborgarplatsen. **Open** *11am-6.30pm Mon-Fri; 11am-5pm Sat; noon-4pm Sun.* **Map** *p134 P13* **9** *Fashion*

Even if you haven't heard of this Swedish label before, chances are you've seen its popular slim-cut jeans with orange stitching and copper buttons. Nudie Jeans promotes sustainability though promising lifetime repairs for its products or giving customers the chance to trade in older pairs if they want to switch to newer versions. **Other location** Jakobsbergsgatan 11, Norrmalm (010 151 57 20).

❤ Ordning & Reda

Götgatan 32 (08 714 96 01, www.ordning-reda.com). T-bana Medborgarplatsen or Slussen. **Open** *10am-7pm Mon-Fri; 11am-5pm Sat; noon-4pm Sun.* **Map** *p134 N12* **10** *Stationery*

A heaven for stationery addicts, Ordning & Reda sells all sorts of fun and brightly coloured notebooks, diaries, photo albums and desktop accessories.

❤ ROT Butik & Kök

Renstiernas gata 20 (08 642 23 50, www. butikrot.se. T-bana Medborgarplatsen, bus 3, 53, 76. **Open** *7.30am-9pm Mon-Fri; 9am-9pm Sat, Sun.* **Map** *p134 Q13* **13** *Food & drink*

A great place to stock up on fresh produce for a picnic or to buy non-perishable store-cupboard favourites, this independent food store is named after the Swedish word for root. It also sells excellent wooden gift boxes of Swedish treats and hosts cookery classes.

Sneakersnstuff

Åsögatan 124 (08 743 03 22, www. sneakersnstuff.com). T-bana Medborgarplatsen. **Open** *11am-6.30pm Mon-Fri; 11am-6pm Sat; noon-5pm Sun.* **Map** *p134 O13* **15** *Accessories*

Focusing on style rather than running, Sneakersnstuff is frequented by trend-conscious twentysomethings, who come here to pick up the latest trainer releases from Nike, New Balance and Vans. Apparel comes courtesy of Norse Projects, Adidas, Carhartt and Danish streetwear label Wood Wood, among others.

❤ Stockholms Stadsmission Nytorget

Skånegatan 75 (08 684 23 450, www.stadsmissionen.se). T-bana Medborgarplatsen. **Open** *10am-7pm Mon-Fri; 11am-5pm Sat; noon-5pm Sun.* **Map** *p134 P13* **16** *Second-hand clothing*

Stockholmers embrace the sharing economy and second-hand boutiques are thriving,

despite a boom in apps and online platforms designed to encourage Swedes to sell off unwanted clothing online. The clothing on sale at this popular thrift store reflects the creativity of this neighbourhood's residents. Profits are donated to local social projects. **Other locations** throughout the city.

Stutterheim

Åsögatan 136 (08 408 10 398, www. stutterheim.com). T-bana Medborgarplatsen. **Open** *11am-6pm Mon-Fri; 11am-4pm Sat; noon-4pm Sun.* **Map** *p134 P13* **17** *Fashion*

The phrase 'there's no bad weather, only bad clothes' is much quoted in Sweden, and this high-end unisex rainwear shop is the perfect place to indulge it. The Swedish fisherman-inspired raincoats are handmade with top-quality rubberised cotton, and the simple cuts and tasteful colours make the prospect of rain more appealing (though the prices may make you squint a little). **Other location** Västerlånggatan 40, Gamla Stan (070 775 55 70).

Swedish Hasbeens

Nytorgsgatan 36A (08 702 01 01, www. swedishhasbeens.com/stores). T-bana Medborgarplatsen, bus 2, 3, 53, 76. **Open** *11am-6pm Mon-Fri; 11am-5pm Sat; noon-5pm Sun.* **Map** *p134 P13* **18** *Shoes*

Clogs, despite usually being associated with the Netherlands, were all the rage in Sweden in the 1970s, and the Swedish Hasbeens brand has encouraged a comeback for these chunky sandals. This flagship store sells bright designs in natural grain leather and a limited selection of boots, belts and bags.

WESTERN SÖDERMALM

The busy thoroughfare of Hornsgatan runs west from Slussen all the way to Hornstull. North of Hornsgatan, there are magnificent views from the **Monteliusvägen** walkway (*see p149*); to the south are **Maria Magdalena Kyrka**, the oldest church on Söder, and **Mariatorget**, an attractive square that is home to the stylish **Rival** hotel complex, which has original art deco features (*see p231*). From Mariatorget you're within easy reach of some prime shopping streets – head for Swedensborgsgatan, Wollmar Yxkullsgatan and, further to the west, Krukmakargatan, if you're into independent boutiques. Hornsgatan itself is also great for vintage stores, with menswear shop **Herr Judit** leading the pack.

From Hornsgatan, the wide street of Ringvägen curves round the southern portion of Södermalm, skirting the island's biggest and best park, **Tantolunden**, which sits near the south-western shore. The park is something of a hipster hangout and is normally packed on sunny summer days. A waterside walkway takes you from the park all the way round the southern side of the island, taking in the lovely Tanto allotment gardens (*see below*) on the way, as well as some popular wild-swimming spots, including a wooden diving pier.

North of Tantolunden, on the other side of Hornsgatan, is the large red-brick church of **Högalidskyrkan**, designed by Ivar Tengbom in the National Romantic style and completed in 1923. Its octagonal twin towers are a striking landmark visible from many parts of the city.

At the very western end of Södermalm is the residential neighbourhood of **Hornstull**, thoroughly enjoying its continuing hipster status. The area's cafés, restaurants and shops count Swedish musicians, rappers and high-profile artists as both owners and customers, while waterside promenade Hornstulls Strand is now home to rock club **Debaser Strand** (*see p198*) with its Mexican-themed restaurant-bar. Also here is the small local **Bio Rio** cinema and bar (*see p190*). Residents of Hornstull are proud of their left-leaning neighbourhood – but there are signs of new-found affluence, most obviously in the subterranean shopping centre next to the Hornstull metro station, which hosts a range of Swedish and international fashion chains. Also, next to the station is the four-storey **Hornhuset** building, housing several restaurants and bars. On the waterfront, locals sell off stylish second-hand clothing and new designs at **Hornstulls Marknad** (Hornstull market; *see p51*), between April and September.

Continue north from here and you'll reach the **Lasse i Parken** café – a charming historic spot for an alfresco lunch or *fika*, which also sometimes hosts live music in the evenings – and then the huge **Västerbron** bridge that connects the island with Kungholmen, offering wonderful views of Långholmen and Gamla Stan en route.

Sights & museums

Maria Magdalena Församling
Bellmansgatan 13 (08 462 29 40, www. svenskakyrkan.se/mariamagdalena). T-bana Slussen. **Open** *11am-5pm Mon-Wed, Fri, Sat; 10am-5pm Sun.* **Admission** *free.* **Map** *p134 N11.*

During his church-destroying spree after the Reformation in 1527, Gustav Vasa tore down the chapel that had stood on this site since the 1300s. His son, Johan III, methodically rebuilt most of the churches in the late 1500s. Construction on this church began in 1580 but was not completed for about 40 years.

It's Söder's oldest church and the first in Stockholm to be built with a central plan rather than a cross plan. Tessin the Elder designed the transept in the late 17th century and his son, the Younger, created the French-inspired stonework of the entrance portal in 1716. The church's rococo interior – with its depiction of Mary Magdalene on the golden pulpit and Carl Fredrik Adelcrantz's elaborate organ screen – was created after a fire in 1759. Several of Sweden's eminent poets are buried here, including beloved troubadour Evert Taube.

♥ Tantolunden
Ringvägen (08 508 12 000). T-bana Zinkensdamm. **Map** *p147 J13.*

Södermalm's largest public park is situated close to the restaurants and cafés of Hornstull, and it is a popular spot in summer for picnicking and bathing at the adjoining beach area. During the winter, it makes for an excellent sledging spot. There's a playground, a beach volleyball court, minigolf and an outdoor gym. Enter via the steps on the corner of Hornsgatan and Liljeholmsbron at the Drakenbergparken end of the park. Stroll up the hill for the Tanto allotment gardens, which were established here over a century ago.

Restaurants & cafés

Bistro Barbro ⓦ ⓦ ⓦ
Hornstulls Strand 13 (08 550 60 266, www. bar-bro.se). T-bana Hornstull or bus 4. **Open** *5-11pm Tue-Thur; 5pm-12.30am Fri, Sat; 5pm-9pm Sun.* **Map** *p147 G13* ❶ *Japanese fusion*

Located just below Liljeholmsbron (hence the name, 'bridge bar'), next to the water, this Japanese-inspired bistro with contemporary decor is part of the new wave of venues that make up gentrified Hornstull. There's an array of fusion-style sharing plates on the menu, taking in everything from fried dumplings, sushi and sashimi to seared tuna with sesame dressing and sirloin steak with udon noodles. The building also houses a cinema-lounge bar, hosting film screenings, film quizzes and live music.

Bistro Süd ⓦ ⓦ ⓦ
Swedenborgsgatan 8A (08 640 41 11, www. bistrosud.se). T-bana Mariatorget. **Open** *5pm-midnight daily. Kitchen closes at 11pm.* **Map** *p134 M12* ❷ *Contemporary*

This is a friendly neighbourhood place for the Mariatorget crowd of well-to-do journalists and artists. The modern European food is straightforward and good, and it's a pleasant place to have a bite to eat and rub shoulders in the crowded but relaxed bar.

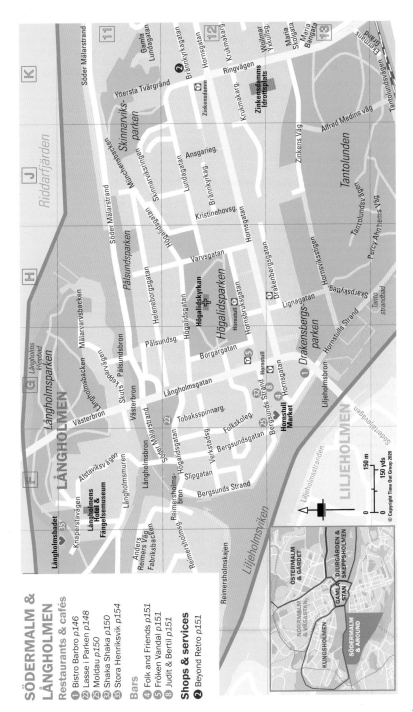

SÖDERMALM & LÅNGHOLMEN

Restaurants & cafés

1. Bistro Barbro p146
24. Lasse i Parken p148
25. Moldau p150
32. Shaka Shaka p150
35. Stora Henriksvik p154

Bars

4. Folk and Friends p151
5. Fröken Vandal p151
8. Judit & Bertil p151

Shops & services

2. Beyond Retro p151

© Copyright Time Out Group 2020

Bröd & Sält ⓦ

Rosenlundsgatan 48D (076 051 61 62, www.
brodsalt.se). T-bana Mariatorget or bus 4.
Open *7am-7pm Mon-Fri; 8am-5pm Sat, Sun.*
Map *p134 L13* ⑤ *Bakery café*

This boutique bakery and coffee chain
serves fresh bread, flavoursome pizza slices
and some of the tastiest cinnamon and
cardamom buns in the capital. This branch is
among those that also has a salad bar. **Other
locations** throughout the city.

Drop Coffee Roasters ⓦ

Wollmar Yxkullsgatan 10 (070 422 95 43,
www.dropcoffee.com). T-bana Mariatorget.
Open *8.30am-6pm Mon-Fri; 10am-6pm Sat,*
Sun. **Map** *p134 M12* ⑫ *Café*

This micro-roastery and café near Mariatorget
is one for true coffee geeks. The baristas take
their trade seriously, making every effort
to ensure that temperature, equipment
and operation are all exactly right, and
favouring manual and filter methods. And
then, of course, there's the coffee itself – the
establishment uses top-quality, fairly traded
and sustainably grown beans, available to
buy. The rustic café is a popular spot for *fika*
and lunch.

❤ Falafelbaren ⓦ

Hornsgatan 39 (072 907 26 37, www.
falafelbaren.se). T-bana Mariatorget. **Open**
11am-7pm Mon-Fri; 11am-4pm Sat. **Map**
p134 L12 ⑭ *Middle Eastern*

There are plenty of budget falafel kiosks
across Stockholm, but it's well worth paying a
couple of extra kronor to taste Falafelbaren's
organic chickpea patties, which are gluten
free and served in home-baked pittas
cooked in a real stone oven. The 'Falafel och
kompisar' (falafel and friends) deal, which
includes fries and a lemonade, is a great
option if you're looking for a budget early-
evening dinner: Falafelbaren closes at 7pm or
when the falafels run out.

Folkbaren ⓦ ⓦ

Hornsgatan 72 (08 658 51 80, www.folkbaren.
se). T-bana Mariatorget. **Open** *11.30pm-1am*
Tue-Fri; noon-1am Sat; 4-10pm Sun. **Map**
p134 L12 ⑮ *Contemporary*

This might be the culinary annexe to the
city's alternative opera scene (*see p204*), but
most of the clientele aren't just in for a pre-
show drink. The restaurant is an attraction
in its own right – there's a bar downstairs, a
cosy lounge with a good menu upstairs, and
a main dining room dishing up ambitious
classic and modern food at reasonable prices,
including *moules frites*, steak tartare and a
house cheeseburger.

❤ Häktet ⓦ ⓦ

Honsgatan 82 (08 84 59 10, www.haktet.
se). T-bana Mariatorget. **Open** *11am-2pm,*
5pm-midnight Mon-Wed; 11am-2pm,
5pm-3am Thur-Fri; 5pm-3am Sat. **Map**
p134 L12 ⑰ *Contemporary*

Medium-sized sharing plates are the trend at
Häktet, an edgy modern restaurant inside a
former 18th-century jail for petty criminals
who couldn't afford to pay their bail. Classic
European flavours with a contemporary twist
are on offer, making the most of seasonal
ingredients. The bar area is usually packed at
weekends, serving craft beers and cocktails to
Södermalm's media set.

Johan & Nyström ⓦ

Swedenborgsgatan 7 (08 530 22 440, www.
johanochnystrom.se). T-bana Mariatorget.
Open *7am-9pm Mon-Fri; 8am-6.30pm Sat,*
Sun. **Map** *p134 M12* ⑲ *Café*

This small boutique coffee store serves all
the hot drinks you'd expect, alongside bags
of beans roasted by hand in small batches
to take home. If you want to extend your
coffee knowledge, there are courses held here
regularly. The indoor space is limited, but this
is a popular spot to enjoy an alfresco espresso
or iced latte during the summer months,
when a larger outdoor area opens up. **Other
locations** throughout the city.

Kaffebar ⓦ

Bysistorget 6 (076 875 29 92). T-bana
Mariatorget. **Open** *7am-6pm Mon-Fri;*
9am-6pm Sat, Sun. **Map** *p134 L12* ⑳ *Café*

This much-loved espresso bar continues to
draw an engaged crowd, who hang at the
outside tables on sunny days. The coffee
is very much the focus here, perfect with a
cinnamon and cardamom bun, but the place
also offers a selection of tasty sandwiches and
fruit juices. Previously named Cafe Mellqvist,
it was a favourite of author Stieg Larsson and
appears in several of his novels.

Lasse i Parken ⓦ ⓦ

Högalidsgatan 56 (08 658 33 95, www.
lasseiparken.se). T-bana Hornstull or bus
4. **Open** *May-Sept 11am-10pm Mon-Sat;*
11am-5pm Sun. Closed Oct-Apr. **Map** *p147*
G12 ㉒ *Swedish*

This charming restaurant-café is set in an
18th-century house with many original
features. The food here is nothing out of the
ordinary, but the comforting meals, such as
grilled char and boiled potatoes or entrecôte
steak with red wine sauce, come in filling
portions. Outside is a large seating area
complete with a stage used for musical and
theatrical performances in the summer, when

💜 Monteliusvägen

*T-bana Mariatorget. **Map** p134 M11.*

Ending the day by watching the sun go down over the shimmering surface of Lake Mälaren is amongst the most magical experiences you can have in Stockholm. One of the best spots for this is Monteliusvägen – a leafy 500-metre (1,640-foot) clifftop walking trail on the northern shore of Södermalm. The trail runs from the north end of Skölgränd to the junction between Kattgränd and Bastugatan; much of it is a purpose-built wooden path, with several terraces and benches along the way, designed to give visitors the chance to linger.

To reach Monteliusvägen, start from Mariatorget subway station and head north to the leafy square of **Mariatorget**. Be sure to stop to admire the central fountain, which depicts the Norse god Thor slaying a sea serpent. If the sun's shining, you might want to grab an ice-cream at **Stikki Nikki** (*see p150*). Cross Hornsgatan and continue north up Bleckstorngränd. If the steep hill gets too much, pause for a pit-stop at **Magnolia Café** (*see p150*), conveniently placed next to the steps up to Tavastgatan. Continue up to Bastugatan and then (ignoring the route to Monteliusvägen in front of you), turn right and continue until you see another small path to Monteliusvägen on your left. Follow the path for a short distance to be greeted by a panoramic view of Riddarfjärden, the Old Town and Riddarholmen with their characterful spires laid out before you;

In the know
Skinnarviksberget

An alternative viewpoint on Södermalm is **Skinnarviksberget**, a rocky hilltop most easily accessed from a footpath off Yttersta tvärgränd, just behind Zinkensdamm station. It's more of a scramble to get up here, so it's not suitable for small children or those with weaker knees, but the panorama is just as good.

you'll also see Stadshuset and the tree-lined boulevard of Norr Mälarstrand.

The walkway continues west around the cliff. About a third of the way along, there's access to **Ivar Los Park**, a popular weekend play space for local families and a romantic date spot for couples. Enjoy a picnic here in summer, or a take a hip flask to warm you on a clear winter's night. Directly below Monteliusvägen you'll see **Söder Mälarstrand**; this quayside road isn't as bustling or picturesque as Kungsholmen's Norr Mälarstrand, but it still offers great views and is home to a number of boat bars and floating hostels. Monteliusvägen itself finishes with an uphill climb to Kattgränd. From here make a detour onto Bastugatan to reach **Lilla Skinnarviksgränd** on your left. This tiny side street has a cluster of 17th- and 18th-century wooden houses, dwarfed by the 19th-century architecture all around them. From Bastugatan, the long slope of Timmermansgatan will bring you back down to Mariatorget T-bana station.

SÖDERMALM & AROUND

a barbecue area serving meat and halloumi burgers opens up. As this is a popular place at weekends, it can take time to queue up and get your refreshments; however, it's such a lovely location that it's worth it.

Magnolia ⓌⓌ

Blecktornsgränd 9 (076 397 97 77, www. magnoliastockholm.se). T-bana Mariatorget. Open 11.30am-11pm Mon-Thur; 11.30am-1am Fri; noon-1am Sat; noon-11pm Sun. Map p134 M11 ㉓ Café-bar

This artsy venue is situated halfway up the steps from Hornsgatan to Monteliusvägen. It's worth the climb for the delicious food and excellent coffee and cava, as well as the colourful atmosphere provided by the in-house florist. Frequent exhibition openings and wine-tasting events create a sociable vibe in the evenings, when you can enjoy a range of *pintxos*.

Moldau ⓌⓌ

Bergsunds Strand 33 (08 84 75 48). T-bana Hornstull. Open 5-11pm Tue-Sat. Map p147 G12 ㉕ Austrian

This Austrian *schnitzel* eatery, housed in an unassuming building at the western tip of Söder, has been around for years, but has recently regained popularity with the twenty- and thirtysomethings of Hornstull who love it for its unpretentious dishes and affordable prices. The Alpine-style interior gives it a rustic atmosphere, while the *schnitzel* menu includes six meat and two vegetarian options.

Rival ⓌⓌⓌ

Mariatorget 3 (08 545 78 900, www.rival. se). T-bana Mariatorget. Open 5-11pm Mon-Thur; 4-11pm Fri-Sun. Map p134 M12 ㉛ Contemporary

Benny of ABBA fame is part-owner of this food and hotel emporium, which has all the components for a complete date under one roof: dinner, movie, late-night cocktail and, if you get lucky, a stay in one of the boutique hotel rooms. The food menu is mainly run-of-the-mill Swedish staples, with dishes such as *toast skagen* (shrimp salad on toast), meatballs and *svampfyllda kroppkakor* (mushroom-filled potato dumplings served with lingonberries). For a review of the hotel, *see p231*.

♥ Shaka Shaka Ⓦ

Bergsunds Strand 51 (08 710 56 38, www. shakashaka.se). T-bana Hornstull or bus 54. Open 11am-8pm Mon-Fri; 11.30am-6pm Sat; 11.30am-4pm Sun. Map p147 G12 ㉜ Hawaiian

Stockholm has experienced a boom in Hawaiian poke bowl joints in recent years, and this tiny restaurant-cafe deserves its

reputation as one of the best. The generous and affordable portions always taste fresh and are available both to eat in and take away. Despite not being open late, the music here is on the loud side, so don't come here for conversation. **Other location** Ringvägen 123, Skanstull (08 408 11 169).

Shanti Softcorner ⓌⓌ

Södermalmsallén 34 (08 643 97 00, www. shanti.se). T-bana Medborgarplatsen. Open 11am-11pm Mon-Fri; 1-11pm Sat, Sun. Map p134 N13 ㉝ Indian

Stockholm's Indian restaurants have a reputation for dulling their flavours to suit the Swedish palette, but the menus at the small Shanti chain packs a punch, with authentic spicy dishes and stylish interiors to boot. The Shanti Softcorner branch, in a quiet neighbourhood surrounded by offices and apartment blocks, aims to channel New York vibes. There are several other branches of Shanti on Södermalm, including Shanti Gossip (Skånegatan 71, SoFo), which specialises in Bengali street food. All serve the chain's own-brand ale and lager.

♥ Stikki Nikki Ⓦ

Mariatorget 1C (www.stikkinikki.com). T-bana Mariatorget. Open 11am-9pm daily. Map p134 M12 ㉞ Ice-cream

From peanut butter to passion fruit, the Stikki Nikki brand (owned by an American expatriate) has tried and tested hundreds of organic gelato flavours since launching as a tiny kiosk in central Stockholm in 2008. This

Stikki Nikki

branch in Mariatorget is 100% vegan. **Other locations** throughout the city.

Bars

Akkurat

Hornsgatan 18 (08 644 00 15, www.akkurat. se). T-bana Slussen. **Open** *3pm-midnight Mon, Tue, Sun; 3pm-1am Wed-Sat. Food served until closing.* **Map** *p134 N11* ❶

Beer lovers frustrated by Stockholm's lack of good ale should head straight to Akkurat. Don't be put off by the run-of-the-mill pub interior, this bar offers no fewer than 28 varieties of beer on tap, from fermented Belgian lambics to British cask-conditioned ale. There are 600 varieties of bottled beer and 400 whiskies too.

Folk and Friends

Hornsgatan 180 (070 494 59 48, www.folk. beer). T-bana Hornstull or bus 54. **Open** *4-9pm Tue; 4-10pm Wed, Thur; 4-11pm Fri, Sat; noon-6pm Sun. Food served until closing.* **Map** *p147 G13* ❹

This dog-friendly bar serves low-alcohol craft beer (known as *folköl* in Swedish) and encourages guests to linger thanks to its stack of board games and tasty, homely pies. There are also treats on sale for canine visitors, including 'snuffle dog beer' and 'snuffle dog fries'. **Other location** Norr Mälarstrand 32, Kungsholmen.

Fröken Vandal

Hornsbruksgatan 24-26 (www.instagram. com/froken_vandal). T-bana Hornstull. **Open** *11.30am-midnight Mon; 11.30am-1pm Tue-Thur; 11.30am-3am Fri; 5pm-3am Sat; 5pm-midnight Sun. Food served until closing.* **Map** *p147 G12* ❺

Founded by veteran Swedish rapper Petter, this unique wine bar and restaurant has hip hop coming through the speakers and street art on the walls. Popular from the moment it opened its doors in 2018, it attracts a creative clientele. There's filling food on offer too, such as spaghetti or salmon with roasted vegetables. The latest menu is posted regularly on Instagram.

❤ Judit & Bertil

Bergsunds Strand 38 (08 669 31 31, www. juditbertil.se). T-bana Hornstull or bus 4. **Open** *5pm-midnight Mon, Tue, Sun; 5pm-1am Wed-Sat. Food served until closing.* **Map** *p147 G13* ❽

This Hornstull favourite is named after, and dedicated to, a couple who lived nearby in the 1930s and were related to one of the owners. The downstairs is dominated by a beautiful blue-tiled bar, and up a spiral staircase there's

a parlour-style lounge. The furniture is comfy and the vibe homely and welcoming.

Morfar Ginko & Papa Ray Ray

Swedenborgsgatan 13 (08 641 13 40, www. morfarginko.se). T-bana Mariatorget. **Open** *4pm-1am Mon-Thur; 3pm-1am Fri-Sun. Food served until 10pm Mon-Thur, Sun; until 11pm Fri, Sat.* **Map** *p134 M12* ⓫

Morfar Ginko is a two-room industrial-style bar that attracts a relaxed but edgy crowd. In the summer, punters sup beers at the outside tables or in the back courtyard (complete with ping pong) until around 11pm, at which point the terrace closes and the place becomes more of a cocktail-fuelled DJ bar. Pappa Ray Ray is the bar next door, run by the same owners and offering well-priced cava and tapas.

❤ Pub Kloster

Hornsgatan 84 (08 669 23 06, www. pubkloster.se). T-bana Zinkensdamm or Mariatorget. **Open** *1pm-1am Mon, Tue; 1pm-3am Wed-Fri; 11am-3am Sat; 11am-1am Sun. Food served until closing.* **Map** *p134 L12* ⓬

Kloster's deliberately peeling walls are covered in bold street art and black-and-white photographs. Its long bar tables and high stools are designed to encourage the city's sometimes-shy residents to mingle, a goal that's definitely aided by the cheap alcohol prices. Kloster is a popular place to watch Swedish and international football matches.

Racamaca

Wollmar Yxkullsgatan 5B (www.racamaca. se). **Open** *5-10pm Mon-Thur; 4-11pm Fri; 5-11pm Sat. Food served until closing.* **Map** *p134 M12* ⓭

Run by an enthusiastic gang of thirtysomething friends, Racamaca is a walk-in-only bar and tapas restaurant that's so packed with energy it's never a chore to wait for a table. There's a small but well-selected choice of wines and beers, although the vibe here will probably get you in the mood for a glass of cava, even if you've nothing in particular to celebrate. Open since 2016, Racamaca doubled in size in 2019.

Shops & services

For details of Hornstull Market, *see p51*.

❤ Beyond Retro

Brännkyrkagatan 82 (08 559 13 643, www. beyondretro.com). T-bana Zinkensdamm. **Open** *11am-7pm Mon-Fri; 11am-5pm Sat; noon-4pm Sun.* **Map** *p147 K12* ❷ *Vintage fashion*

From vintage prom dresses and bowler hats to retro sweatshirts and sneakers, Beyond Retro's 450 sq m (4,845sq ft) headquarters is a treasure trove for second-hand fans. The label is a Swedish-British collaboration that claims to save 600,000 garments a year from landfills.

Brandstationen

Hornsgatan 64 (08 658 30 10, www.herrjudit. se/brandstationen). T-bana Zinkensdamm or Mariatorget. Open 11am-6pm Mon-Fri; 11am-5pm Sat; noon-4pm Sun. Map p134 M12 ❸ *Vintage homewares*

This antiques shop, run by vintage menswear store Herr Judit (*see p152*), plays to contemporary tastes, with a cherry-picked selection of retro maps, globes, 20th-century furniture and lighting. There's also a cabinet full of costume jewellery. Prices are fairly high, but browsing's a pleasure.

Bric-a-Brac

Swedenborgsgatan 5A (08 643 75 00, www. bric-a-brac.se). T-bana Mariatorget. Open 11am-7pm Mon-Fri; 11am-4pm Sat; noon-4pm Sun. Map p134 M12 ❹ *Fashion*

This boutique stocks a well-selected range of mid- to high-end Scandinavian and European labels, including Ally Capellino, Ganni and Marimekko, for men and women. Look out for the seasonal sales, when there are often huge discounts.

♥ Herr Judit

Hornsgatan 65 (08 658 30 37, www.herrjudit. se). T-bana Zinkensdamm or Mariatorget. Open 11am-6pm Mon-Fri; 11am-5pm Sat; noon-4pm Sun. Map p134 K12 ❼ *Vintage*

This high-end vintage menswear shop is a great source of good-quality blazers and jackets by the likes of Edwin, Acne and Burberry, as well as collectable vintage watches, classic leather satchels and designer luggage. Vintage homewares shop Brandstationen (*see above*), situated a ten-minute walk away, is run by the same team. **Other location** Sibyllegatan 29, Östermalm.

♥ Our Legacy

Krukmakargatan 24-26 (08 668 20 60, www. ourlegacy.se). T-bana Zinkensdamm. Open 11am-6.30pm Mon-Fri; 11am-5pm Sat; noon-4pm Sun. Map p134 L12 ⓫ *Fashion*

This contemporary Swedish menswear label, the brainchild of Christopher Nying and Jockum Hallin, is all about high-quality wardrobe staples – simply cut plain shirts, T-shirts, sweaters and jackets dominate. **Other location** Jakobsbergsgatan 11, Norrmalm.

Papercut

Krukmakargatan 24-26 (08 13 35 74, www. papercutshop.se). T-bana Zinkensdamm. Open 11am-6.30pm Mon-Fri; 11am-5pm Sat; noon-4pm Sun. Map p134 L12 ⓬ *Books*

Papercut, in the same building as menswear label Our Legacy (*see above*), stocks an impressive range of international art magazines, coffee-table books and arthouse DVDs.

♥ Sandqvist

Swedenborgsgatan 3 (076 221 04 75, www. sandqvist.com). T-bana Mariatorget. Open 11am-6.30pm Mon-Fri; 11am-5pm Sat; noon-4pm Sun. Map p134 M12 ⓮ *Luggage*

Head here for messenger bags, laptop cases, leather satchels, rucksacks, weekend bags and wallets, all made from quality leather and/or canvas, in a range of tasteful tones. This Swedish brand has grown rapidly over the past few years, and its bags are now seen on the back of many a stylish Stockholmer. **Other location** Jakobsbergsgatan 9, Norrmalm.

Wigerdals Värld

Krukmakargatan 14 (08 31 64 04, www. wigerdals.com). T-bana Mariatorget or bus 4, 66, 74, 94. Open noon-6pm Mon-Fri; 11am-3pm Sat. Map p134 L12 ⓳ *Homewares*

Wigerdals Värld is a delightful little vintage shop selling a well-edited range of 20th-century homewares, furniture and knick-knacks.

LÅNGHOLMEN

Off the north-west tip of Söder, near Hornstull, lies the long, narrow island of Långholmen (Long Island). For 250 years (1724-1975) this beautiful green island, almost a mile long, was home to a prison, which meant that it remained largely undeveloped. As a result, it is now something of a green retreat, complete with tree-shaded paths, allotment gardens, cliffs dotted with nest-like nooks and two sandy beaches perfect for swimming. Today, the remaining part of the prison is run as the **Långholmen Hotel**, a very pleasant budget hotel/hostel (*see p233*), with a café, conference centre and museum (**Långholmens Fängelsemusuem**). You can walk to the island across Långholmsbron (which provides closest access to the former prison from Hornstull), or via Pålsundsbron to the east. To access the middle of the island directly, walk across the enormous Västerbron bridge (worth crossing to take in the view of the city) and then take the ramp or stairs down.

💜 Långholmsbadet

Bus 4, 54, 77, then 10min walk.
Map *p147 E11.*

Stockholmers are proud of the fact that, thanks to a successful purification treatment in the 1960s, you can take a safe, free-of-charge dip in almost any of the waters around the city centre – despite the often-chilly conditions. At this latitude, summer is more a state of mind than a certain temperature.

Långholmsbadet on Långholmen island is one of the city's most popular swimming spots. It has its own beach surrounded by inviting green spaces and a large rocky area that gets crowded during weekends and holidays, so arrive early. Due to its proximity to trendy Hornstull, Långholmsbadet offers your best chance of spotting a Swedish indie rock star in a bathing suit. There are cold-water open-air showers on the lawn and a cute café, **Stora Henriksvik** (*see p154*), nearby, although many bathers choose to bring their own picnic.

Other scenic swimming locations in the area include **Långholms klippbad** (map p147 G10), a tiny, sandy cove on the eastern side of Långholmen; **Tanto strandbad** (map p147 H14), a man-made beach in Tantolunden park, and **Fredhällsbadet** on Kungsholmen (*see p160*). In the southern suburbs, you'll find **Örnsbergsbadet** by the cliffs and marina near Hägerstenshamnen, and **Trekantsbadet** a short walk from Liljeholmen subway stop. Alternatively, for those who require a certain water temperature, or who aren't thrilled at the prospect of swimming with live fish, there's **Eriksdalsbadet** (*see p138*) in Skanstull, an Olympic-size pool that was built for the 1962 European Aquatics Championships and remains a popular summer destination.

Boats moored between Långholmen and Södermalm

A walking/cycling path leads from the south of the island to the cliffs and beach in the north. The lovely **Stora Henriksvik**, a 17th-century house with a delightful café and garden, lies behind **Långholmsbadet** (*see p153*), one of the most popular beaches in the city. To the west of the former prison stands **Carlshälls gård**, the previous residence of the prison warden, now a conference centre and restaurant. Curving back round to the south, take in the grace of the lovingly cared-for wooden sailboats lining the picture-perfect canal.

Sights & museums

Långholmens Fängelsemuseum
Långholmsmuren 20 (08 720 85 00, www. langholmen.com). Bus 4, 54, 77, then 10min walk. **Open** *11am-4pm daily.* **Admission** *25kr; 10kr reductions; free for hotel & hostel guests. Guided tours (July, Aug) 2pm Sun; 65kr.* **Map** *p147 F11.*

This small museum describes the history of the Swedish penal system and gives a flavour of life inside Kronohäktet prison before it was turned into visitor accommodation. You can visit a typical cell used between 1845 and 1930, read about Sweden's last executioner, Anders Gustaf Dalman, and see a scale model of the guillotine imported from France and used only once, in 1910. Visitors can view an assortment of prison paraphernalia, including the sinister hoods worn to hide an accused person's identity until sentenced (used until 1935). Book in advance if you want a tour in English.

Restaurants & cafés

Stora Henriksvik ⓦ
Långholmsmuren 21 (070 024 44 17, www. storahenriksvik.se). Bus 4, 54, 77, then 10min walk. **Open** *Apr-Sept 11am-5pm daily. Closed Oct-Mar.* **Map** *p147 F11* ㉟ *Café*

The oldest part of this attractive two-storey house was built in the late 17th century as the toll office for boats travelling into Stockholm. The Bellmanmuseet (Bellman Museum) that was until recently on the ground floor – devoted to celebrated troubadour/songwriter Carl Michael Bellman – is now just a small exhibition, but the pleasant café remains, offering own-made pastries, good coffee and simple dishes. The café is popular with bathers who use the beach in front of the house (*see p153*).

SOUTH OF SÖDERMALM

The area known by locals as *Söder om Söder* (south of Södermalm) has experienced a surge in cultural and gastronomic activity in recent years, meaning there are now several suburbs that are worth a visit on a longer stay in Stockholm.

Liljeholmen, just one subway stop south from Hornstull, is home to **Färgfabriken** (Lövholmsbrinken 1, 08 645 07 07, www. fargfabriken.se), Stockholm's Centre for Contemporary Art and Architecture, which occupies an important position on the Stockholm art scene and aims to promote unusual projects which might otherwise be ignored. Founded in 1995, it is housed in an old factory, with one main exhibition space, plus three smaller rooms, and there are outdoor music and food events in the summer (*see p201*).

Further along both branches of the red T-bana line, the neighbouring suburbs of Midsommarkransen, Aspudden, Telefonplan and Hägerstensåsen have become magnets for creative types priced out of Södermalm. **Midsommarkransen** has the most to offer, boasting several trendy interior stores such as the contemporary **2 Little Spoons** (Vattenledningsvägen 42, 072 190 89 21), along with one of Stockholm's last surviving single-screen cinemas, **Biograf Tellus** (*see p191*). Nearby **Scandwich** (Vattenledningsvägen 44, 073 531 33 93, www.scandwich.se) sells some of the most hyped open sandwiches in the city.

A short walk away, **Telefonplan** (which takes its name from its proximity to Ericsson's former headquarters) is best known for **Landet** (*see p201*), a bar, restaurant and indie gig venue. There's also the always-packed **A.B.Café** (Valborgsmässovägen 34, 08 18 31 38), a partner of the award-winning **Drop Coffee** (*see p148*) in Södermalm.

Southern Stockholm is also home to Sweden's first eco suburb, **Hammarby Sjöstad** (*see p155*), which is accessible by boat from Södermalm or by tram from Liljeholmen.

💙 Hammarby Sjöstad

Train (Tvärbanan) to Sickla Udde or bus 74.

Futuristic apartment blocks, family-friendly parks and a reed-fringed shoreline characterise the waterfront suburb of Hammarby Sjöstad, just south-east of Södermalm. This former industrial wasteland has won numerous awards for sustainability, thanks to the way it handles energy and waste, as well as its efforts to encourage residents to adopt eco-friendly habits. For visitors, it provides an insight into Scandinavian green living as well as making for a great outing, thanks to its cycle paths and its wooden sundecks, which are perfect for soaking up the views of southern Södermalm on a summer's day.

Hammarby Sjöstad was the first development project in Stockholm in which city planners, real estate agents and state-funded agencies (including water, environmental health and traffic) worked together in one office. Construction began in the late 1990s, when hundreds of apartments were built using raw materials designed to optimise heat retention during Sweden's harsh winters. Other green innovations include the exclusive use of renewable sources, including solar panels and biogas, for power, and the sourcing of water from rain and snow melt. Locals sort their rubbish into categories and throw it into outdoor chutes that lead to a central underground waste storage point. The latest wave of building work has focused on bringing more businesses to the area by transforming former factories into offices and co-working spaces for green-thinking companies. In 2019, digital creative business school **Hyper Island** moved here from Midsommarkransen.

Residents and visitors to Hammarby Sjöstad are discouraged from commuting by car. Instead, the suburb is accessible on foot or by bike over the Skanstullsbron bridge near Skanstull subway station and has numerous wide walkways and cycle lanes. It can also be reached on a shiny, purpose-built light railway (Tvärbanan 22), or by using the regular commuter boats that cross from Barnängsbryggan (for timetables, see www.ressel.se).

Hammarby Sjöstad's developers have incorporated plenty of space for restaurants and cafés into their master plan, thus enticing Stockholmers to the neighbourhood from across the city. Microbrewery and gastropub **Nya Carnegie Bryggeriet** (Ljusslingan 15-17, 08 510 65 082, www.nyacarnegiebryggeriet. se) enjoys an especially plum spot on the waterfront and holds regular live music events; **Rusty Rascals** (Hammarby Allé 59, 08 660 56 00, www.rustyrascals.com) is a popular barber shop and smoothie bar, while **Namaskaar** (Lugnets Allé 67, 08 640 06 19, www.namaskaar.se) serves authentic Indian curry.

Kungsholmen

The majestic Stadshuset (City Hall), an architectural gem visible from far and wide, faces visitors as they cross Stadshusbron from Norrmalm, and the city's famous landmark tends to leave the rest of Kungsholmen in its shadow. It's most famous for hosting the 1,300 or so guests who are lucky enough to be invited along to the annual Nobel Prize banquet, held on 10 December after the prizes have been awarded at Konserthuset.

Beyond Stadshuset, this largely residential island has a sprinkling of tranquil parks, hip bars and decent neighbourhood restaurants, alongside some of the city's most popular swimming spots. The island is within a whisker of a Swedish mile (6.2 miles/ten kilometres) in circumference, and its waterside walkways are popular with joggers seeking a run with a view.

❤ **Don't miss**

1 Stadshuset *p161*
The majestic City Hall is Stockholm's most prominent landmark.

2 Rålambshovsparken *p160*
This waterside park is a hive of activity in summer.

3 Fredhällsbadet *p160*
A swimming spot surrounded by cliffs.

Stadshuset

EXPLORING KUNGSHOLMEN

During the 1640s, craftsmen, labourers and factory owners were lured to Kungsholmen, then mostly fields, by the promise of a ten-year tax break. The island soon became home to all of the noxious, fire-prone and dangerous businesses that nobody else wanted. Unsurprisingly, given the conditions, many residents became ill, and Sweden's first hospital, the Serafimerlasarettet, was built here in the 1750s. During the Industrial Revolution, conditions hit an all-time low – its diseased, starving inhabitants earned Kungsholmen the nickname 'Starvation Island'. The factories finally left the island in the early 1900s to be replaced by government agencies, offices and apartment buildings.

The quickest way to get to the unmissable **Stadshuset** (City Hall) is to walk across Stadshusbron bridge from Norrmalm – though navigating the roads and railway lines leading from Central Station can be a bit confusing. Stadshuset is on your left – it's gigantic – and the former Serafimerlasarettet hospital is on your right. Continue on down Hantverkargatan and you'll reach **Kungsholms**

Kyrka (Kaplansbacken 1), a 17th-century church with a Greek cross plan and a park-like cemetery. Two blocks further on, a right on to **Scheelegatan** puts you on one of Kungsholmen's major thoroughfares, packed with restaurants and bars.

Further down Scheelegatan, at the corner of Bergsgatan, squats the city's gigantic, majestic **Rådhuset** (courthouse) (Scheelegatan 7), designed by Carl Westman (1866-1936), a leading architect of the National Romantic School. Completed in 1915, it was designed to look like 16th-century Vadstena Castle in southern Sweden, but also has art nouveau touches. There are no guided tours, but you can take a look around the public areas, including the lovely cloister-like garden.

Continuing west on Bergsgatan, you arrive at **Kronobergsparken** (Parkgatan 6), a pleasant hillside park with Stockholm's oldest Jewish cemetery in its north-west corner. **Fridhemsplan**, in the centre of the island, is known for its string of unglamourous dive bars, although it boasts a few gems, including a lively branch of the Scottish craft brewery chain **BrewDog**.

Kungsholmen's shops tend to offer a fairly bland retail diet, but the bright and

♥ Time to eat & drink

Lazy lunches
Lily's Burger *p163*, Petite France *p164*

Meat feasts
AG Restaurang *p160*, Boteco Da Silvania *p162*

Sundowners
Mälarpaviljongen *p164*, Solstugan *p164*

Tea breaks
Haga Tårtcompani & Bageri *p162*

♥ Time to shop

Outdoor living
Naturkompaniet *p165*

Timeless fashion
59 Vintage Store *p165*

In the know
Getting around

Kungsholmen is easily accessible by subway, with all northbound branches of the green line connecting its busiest neighbourhoods, Fridhemsplan and Kristineberg, as well as the more residential Thorildsplan. Blue line subways also stop at Fridhemsplan and Rådhuset. Bus routes 1 and 4 are the core overground bus routes; the former connects Kungsholmen to Hötorget in the city centre and Östermalm's nightlife hub, Stureplan, while the latter travels north from Fridhemsplan to Vasastan before heading along Vallhällavägen, which connects the outskirts of Östermalm and Gärdet, and south past Marieberg towards Hornstull and Gullmarsplan. Kungsholmen's circular coastal path lends itself to walking.

KUNGSHOLMEN
Restaurants & cafés

1. AG Restaurang *p160*
2. Bagel Deli *p162*
3. Bageriet Bulleboden *p162*
4. Boteco Da Silvania *p162*
5. Haga Tårtcompani & Bageri *p162*
6. Hong Kong *p163*
7. Lily's Burger *p163*
8. Lux Dag för Dag *p163*
9. Mäster Anders *p163*
10. Meno Male *p163*
11. Petite France *p164*
12. Roppongi *p164*
13. Spisa Hos Helena *p164*

Bars

1. AG Bar *p164*
2. BrewDog *p164*
3. Mälarpaviljongen *p164*
4. Orangeriet *p164*
5. Solstugan *p164*
6. Theodora *p165*

Shops & services

1. 59 Vintage Store *p165*
2. HuGo *p165*
3. Naturkompaniet *p165*
4. Taylors and Jones *p165*
5. Västermalmsgallerian *p165*

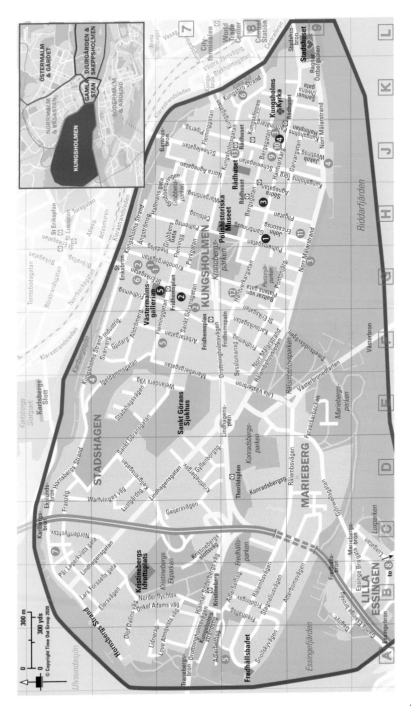

KUNGSHOLMEN

Rådhuset p158

airy **Västermalmsgallerian** shopping mall, on the corner of St Eriksgatan and Fleminggatan has a decent array of Sweden's favourite fashion labels, as well as branches of popular homeware stores Granit and Designtorget. The best independent boutiques are on Hantverkargatan, including **59 Vintage Store** and a tasty British delicatessen, **Taylors and Jones**.

The huge yet elegant double-spanned **Västerbron** bridge (1935) connects Kungsholmen with Södermalm across the expanse of Lake Mälaren. It's always busy with traffic, but you'll get a spectacular view of Stockholm from the centre of the bridge.

Marieberg, the area on Kungsholmen just to the north of Västerbron, once contained military installations and a porcelain factory, but is now the city's newspaper district. Two of the four Stockholm dailies – *Dagens Nyheter* and *Expressen* – have offices here. The *Expressen* building, designed by Paul Hedqvist, is prominent, soaring to 82 metres (270 feet). Mariebergsbron bridge connects this district to neighbouring island Stora Essingen. Further north, the suburb **Kristineberg** has enjoyed a revamp in recent years, with new glass-fronted restaurants and bars and wooden sunbathing decks on the waterfront.

The flat green lawns of **Rålambshovsparken** were created in 1935, at the same time as Västerbron; the park is popular with runners, picnickers and hipsters. There's also a skatepark and an outdoor gym. Walking and cycling paths line the northern and southern shores of Kungsholmen. For

a beautiful view across the water, stroll from the Stadshuset along tree-lined **Norr Mälarstran**. Vintage boats and yachts moor here, and there are a couple of well-placed cafés en route. The grand apartment blocks along this stretch were built in the early 20th century when the factories had finally departed; look out for no.76, which was designed by Ragnar Östberg, architect of Stadshuset.

Sights & museums

♥ Fredhällsbadet
*Kungsholms strandstig 602 (www. fredhallsbadklubb.se). T-bana Kristineberg. **Open** June-Aug 9am-7pm daily. Closed Sept-May. **Admission** free. **Map** p159 A8.*

Experienced swimmers will enjoy this popular bathing spot at the base of Kungsholmen's cliffs, in the Fredhäll district. The water is deep here and often chilly. There is no beach, just a sun deck that is rammed on sunny days.

Hornsbergs strand
*Northern tip of Kungsholmen. T-bana Stadshagen or Kristineberg, bus 65. **Map** p159 A6.*

While Hornsbergs strand literally translates as Hornsberg's beach, there isn't any sand along this waterfront promenade. However the route is dotted with jetties that you can jump off and there are well-groomed patches of parkland and wooden sun terraces to relax on. A small pavilion hosts salsa and *bachata* events during high season.

♥ Rålambshovsparken
*Smedsuddsvägen 6, west of Västerbron bridge. T-bana Thorildsplan or Fridhelmsplan. **Open** daily. **Admission** free. **Map** p159 E9.*

This well-used lakeside park comes alive in summer when a popular boules bar opens, and the outdoor gym, skate park and children's playground are at their busiest. The plentiful trails around the park are popular with joggers. An amphitheatre on the eastern side, which was built in the 1950s, is used for open-air concerts, theatre and children's shows. There is also a small sandy beach just along the shore at Smedsuddsbadet.

Restaurants & cafés

♥ AG Restaurang ⓦⓦⓦ
*2nd floor, Kronobergsgatan 37 (08 410 68 100, www.restaurangag.se). T-bana Fridhemsplan or bus 1, 54, 65. **Open** 11.30am-2pm Mon-Fri; 5pm-1am Mon-Sat. **Map** p159 G6 ① Contemporary*

💙 Stadshuset

*Hantverkargatan 1 (08 508 29 058, https://
international.stockholm.se/the-city-hall).
T-bana Rådhuset or T-Centralen, or bus 53.*
Open *Guided tours only. Sept-May 10am,
11am, noon, 1pm, 2pm, 3pm daily. June-
Aug every half hour 9am-4pm. No prior
booking. Tower May-Sept 9.10am-3.50pm
daily; 9.10am-5.10pm June-Aug.* **Admission**
*Guided tour Nov-Mar 90kr; 40kr-80kr
reductions; Apr-Oct 120kr; 40-100kr
reductions. Tower 60kr; free under-6s and
with SC.* **Map** *p159 L9.*

The City Hall (1923), Stockholm's most
prominent landmark, stands imposingly
on the northern shore of the bay of
Riddarfjärden. A massive red-brick building,
it was designed by Ragnar Östberg (1866-
1945) in the National Romantic style, with
two inner courtyards and a 106-metre (348-
foot) tower. It's most famous for hosting
the annual Nobel Prize banquet, an event
held in the Blue Hall on 10 December each
year. The Blue Hall – which is designed to
look like an Italian Renaissance piazza –
was meant to be painted blue, but Östberg
liked the way the sun hit the red bricks
and changed his mind; the hall is also the
home of an immense organ, with more than
10,000 pipes and 138 stops.

In the astonishing Golden Hall upstairs,
scenes from Swedish history are depicted
on the walls in 18 million gold leaf mosaic
pieces. The artist, Einar Forseth (1892-1988),
covered the northern wall with a mosaic
known as the 'Queen of Lake Mälaren',
representing Stockholm being honoured
from all sides. The beamed ceiling of the
Council Chamber, where the city council
meets every other Monday, resembles
the open roof of a Viking longhouse; the
furniture was designed by Carl Malmsten.

The opulent Oval Room, which is part of
the guided tour, is a popular place for Swedish
nuptials. Such is the demand, it's a speedy
marriage merry-go-round as couples tie the
knot in a no-frills 40-second ceremony. The
extended version is three minutes.

You can only go inside Stadshuset with
a guided tour, and to ascend the tower – a
worthwhile climb of the winding red-brick
slopes then wooden stairs to emerge to a
fantastic view over Gamla Stan – you need
to book a slot from the ticket office on the
day of your visit. Three gold crowns – the
Tre Kronor, Sweden's heraldic symbol –
top the tower. At the edge of the outdoor
terrace below the tower, by the waters of
Riddarfjärden, are two statues by famous
Swedish sculptor Carl Eldh (1873-1954):
the female *Dansen* (Dance) and the
male *Sången* (Song).

For refreshments, a cafeteria-style
restaurant, **Ragnars Skafferi**, serves up
classic Swedish dishes at lunchtime, while
the **Stadshuskällaren** cellar restaurant is
run by the same team that puts together the
menu for the Nobel banquet.

KUNGSHOLMEN

This is a place for meat lovers – the first things you see upon entering the industrial-style space are large fridges filled with chunks of cured produce. Head chef Johan Jureskog, something of a celebrity in Stockholm, is known as a keen follower of nose-to-tail eating. The menu also includes classics from the French and Swedish kitchens, with full flavours to the fore. The tapas bar is a good spot for some appetisers before being seated.

Bagel Deli ⓦ

*St Göransgatan 67 (08 716 11 40, bageldeli. se). T-bana Fridhemsplan or bus 1, 3, 4, 40, 49, 62. **Open** 7am-8pm Mon-Thur; 7am-7pm Fri; 9am-6pm Sat, Sun. **Map** p159 G7* ❷ *Sandwiches & salads*

This bagel joint wouldn't look out of place in New York. They're keen on cream cheese here, but there's a feast of other fillings on the menu. Beyond bagels, the salads are stomach-stuffing, there's always something typically Swedish and seasonal on the menu, and the lattes and freshly baked cakes are top quality.

Bageriet Bulleboden ⓦ

*Parmmätargatan 7 (08 653 05 42, www. bulleboden.se). T-bana Rådhuset or bus 3, 62. **Open** 7.30am-5pm Tue-Fri; 10am-4pm Sat. **Map** p159 J8* ❸ *Café*

A gorgeous little café conveniently situated right beside the subway exit at Rådhust. The entrance is a slightly perilous set of steps down into a cosy little cavern. Boasting some of the best carrot cake in Stockholm, this is the perfect place to hole up on a winter's day.

💜 Boteco Da Silvania ⓦⓦ

*Kungsholms strand 173 (08 650 81 28, botecodasilvania.se), T-bana Stadshagen or bus 65. **Open** 4.30-10pm Wed-Sat. **Map** p159 E5* ❹ *Brazilian*

Diners are crammed into every space in this compact yet vibrant Brazilian restaurant. The decor is bright, with yellow walls covered in South American trinkets and green- and-white checked tablecloths. Tapas-style plates designed for sharing are the main food fare. Fruity caipirinha cocktails are the house drink.

💜 Haga Tårtcompani & Bageri ⓦ

*Fleminggatan 107 (08 19 34 34, www. hagabageri.se). T-bana Fridhemsplan or bus 54, **Open** 7am-6pm Mon-Fri; 7.30am-4pm Sat. **Map** p159 F7* ❺ *Bakery café*

Head to Haga for freshly baked bread and sweet buns to eat in or take away. If you're sticking around for a cup of tea or coffee, make a beeline for the window seats, where you can watch the world go by while propped up by fluffy cushions with bold prints. This

AG Restaurang p160

Västerbron p160

is where the locals come for large decorative tarts and sponges for birthdays and anniversaries.

Hong Kong ⓦ

Kungsbro strand 23 (08 653 77 20, www. restauranghongkong.com). T-bana Rådhuset or bus 54, 65. **Open** *10am-10pm Mon-Fri; 1-10pm Sat, Sun.* **Map** *p159 K8* ❻ *Asian*

This is one of only a few places in Stockholm serving authentic Chinese food. Owner Sonny Li delivers spicy Cantonese and Sichuanese dishes from the giant gas stove. Apart from the stir-fry dishes, there's an ambitious array of steam-cooked choices. The speciality is Peking duck – Chinese business folk (and the King, no less) all come here for the red-glazed bird, which must be ordered two days in advance.

❤ Lily's Burger ⓦ

Hornsbergs strand 47 (08 656 90 06, lilysburger.com). T-bana Stadshagen or bus 65. **Open** *11am-9.30pm Mon-Fri; noon-9.30pm Sat, Sun.* **Map** *p159 C5* ❼ *American*

An American-inspired diner, Lily's is home to crowd-pleasing gourmet burgers and thick tasty milkshakes. Part of a small chain part-owned by Swedish actor Joel Kinnaman, this restaurant is one of the best places to grab a bite close to the waterfront at Hornsbergs strand. **Other location** Södermannagatan 27, Södermalm.

Lux Dag för Dag ⓦⓦ

Primusgatan 116, Lilla Essingen (08 619 01 90, www.luxdagfordag.se/en). T-bana Thorildsplan or bus 1, 56. **Open** *11.30am-2pm, 5-11pm Tue-Fri; noon-4pm, 6pm-11pm Sat.* **Map** *p159 B10* ❽ *Contemporary Scandinavian*

There are few reasons for tourists to visit Lilla Essingen island, a short bus ride from Kungsholmen, but Lux Dag för Dag is one of them. Owned by celebrity chef Henrik Norström, its focus is on the freshest ingredients and a creative, daily-changing menu. At the back of the imposing red-brick former factory building is the restaurant's 'Lux Walk Through' mini-market area (11.30am-7pm Tue-Fri), where you can buy fruit and vegetables, dishes from the menu, meat and fish, flowers, cakes and takeaway coffee.

Mäster Anders ⓦⓦ

Pipersgatan 1 (08 654 20 01, www. masteranders.se). T-bana Rådhuset or bus 54. **Open** *11.30am-3pm, 5pm-midnight Mon-Thur; 11.30am-midnight Fri; 5pm-midnight Sat.* **Map** *p159 J8* ❾ *Brasserie/Grill*

With traditional decor (black-and-white floor tiles, big mirrors, round tables and globe hanging lights) and well-executed dishes, Mäster Anders is very much the classic brasserie. As good for a quick bite as it is for a full dinner, it takes its inspiration from Paris and New York. Highlights are the seafood and chargrilled dishes.

Meno Male ⓦ

Hantverkargatan 14 (08 14 14 10, menomale. se). T-bana Rådhuset or bus 3, 53, 54. **Open** *11am-10pm Mon-Fri; noon-10pm Sat, Sun.* **Map** *p159 J8* ❿ *Italian*

Pizza dominates the menu at this friendly no-frills Italian restaurant. Always packed at peak times, Meno Male's great-value lunch deals are on offer between 11am and 3pm, making this an ideal option if you can avoid the midday rush. Gluten-free bases are available, although they are baked in the same oven, so might not suit those

with severe allergies. **Other locations**
Roslagsgatan 15, Vasastan; Sibyllegatan 47,
Östermalm.

♥ Petite France ⓦ
*John Ericssonsgatan 6 (08 618 28 00,
petitefrance.se). T-bana Rådhuset or bus
3, 54, 65. **Open** 7am-6pm Mon; 7am-10pm
Tue-Sat; 7am-5pm Sun. **Map** p159 H9* ⑪
Bakery café

This bakery café is known for its
mouthwatering array of both French and
Swedish breads, buns and cakes, but it also
offers classic bistro dishes including croque
monsieur or madame, quiche lorraine and
omelettes. The outdoor courtyard area closest
to the main entrance is an afternoon suntrap.

Roppongi ⓦⓦ
*Hantverkargatan 76 (08 650 17 72, www.
roppongi.se). T-bana Fridhemsplan or bus
3, 50, 54, 65. **Open** 11am-9pm Mon, Tue;
11am-10pm Wed-Fri; 5-10pm Sat; 5-9pm Sun.
Map p159 G8* ⑫ *Japanese*

Roppongi serves some of the best sushi in this
part of town, plus decent tempura and *gyoza*.
It's always crowded, especially the few tables
outside in the summer, but you can always
order takeaway sushi and walk down to the
water at nearby Rålambshovsparken.

Spisa Hos Helena ⓦⓦ
*Scheelegatan 18 (08 654 49 26, www.
spisahoshelena.se). T-bana Rådhuset
or bus 53, 54, 65. **Open** 11am-2.30pm,
4pm-midnight Mon-Fri; 4pm-midnight
Sat; 4-10pm Sun. **Map** p159 J8* ⑬
Contemporary European

A home from home for many locals, serving
straightforward, delicious, meat-focused
modern European cuisine. *Toast skagen*
(shrimp toast) is on the list of starters, while
mains feature the likes of grilled rack of lamb
with fresh herbs, served with rocket and feta
salad, and grilled entrecôte with spinach and
fennel salad.

Bars

AG Bar
*2nd floor, Kronobergsgatan 37 (08 410 68 100,
www.restaurangag.se). T-bana Fridhemsplan
or bus 1, 54, 65. **Open** 11.30am-2pm Mon-Fri;
5pm-1am Mon-Sat. **Map** p159 G6* ①

AG doesn't have its own street entrance.
Instead, patrons must pass through the door
of a dimly lit office building and climb down
two flights of stairs to enter. Inside, the look
is exceedingly cool – tiled white walls offset
by brown Chippendale couches and dark
designer furniture. The clientele is a mix of

trendy creative types and designer suits. The
gin cocktails here pack a punch.

BrewDog
*St Eriksgatan 56 (08 650 21 10, www.
brewdog.com/bars/global/kungsholmen).
T-bana St Eriksplan or bus 3, 54, 65. **Open**
4-11pm Mon; 4pm-midnight Tue-Thur;
4pm-1am Fri; 2pm-1am Sat. **Map** p159 G6* ②

This industrial-style bar specialises in own-
brand craft beer produced by the Scottish
brand BrewDog, which selected Stockholm
as its first city outside the UK in which to set
up shop. That was in 2013, and since then
this venue in Kungsholmen and its brother
bar in Södermalm have continued to offer
hoppy, happening alternatives to the Swedish
capital's more traditional pubs. **Other
location** Ringvägen 149B, Södermalm (08
30 72 17).

♥ Mälarpaviljongen
*Norr Mälarstrand 64 (08 650 87 01, www.
malarpaviljongen.se). T-bana Frihemsplan
or bus 3, 54, 65. **Open** Apr-June, Sept-Oct
11am-midnight daily. July, Aug 11am-1am
daily (weather permitting). Food served until
11pm daily. **Map** p159 G9* ③

This jetty bar is packed with blooming
plants and flowers, string lights popping
with primary colours and an unpretentious
gay-friendly crowd. Floating on the water
next to one of the city's most stunning
tree-lined footpaths, Norr Mälarstrand,
Mälarpaviljongen also boasts incredible
views towards Södermalm (look out for
the iconic red-brick former brewery,
Munchenbryggeriet).

Orangeriet
*Norr Mälarstrand, Kajplats 464 (08 684
23 875, http://trattorian.se/restauranger/
orangeriet). T-bana Rådhuset or bus 3, 53,
54. **Open** 11am-11pm Mon-Thur; 11am-1am
Fri; 11.30am-1am Sat; 11.30am-10pm Sun.
Map p159 J9* ④

Boasting a country-chic vibe and situated
right on the waterfront, this bar and brasserie
is a popular spot with well-heeled locals in
their thirties and forties. The wines here are
good quality, and Italian antipasti such as
cold cuts and fried artichokes are on hand
if you're feeling peckish. A small fake beach
with deckchairs usually opens here during
the summer.

♥ Solstugan
*Snoilskyvägen 37 (08 656 20 80 solstugan.
com). T-bana Kristineberg or bus 65. **Open**
11am-10/11pm daily. **Map** p159 A8* ⑤

This chilled-out bar and café sits atop the
cliffs of Fredhäll, a short tree-lined walk from

Kristineberg subway stop. Mismatched woven cushions and tablecloths give Solstugan a bohemian feel, while the view takes in the rows of shiny boats and yachts docked at Kristineberg's boat club. Check online for live music events during the summer.

Theodora
Sankt Eriksgatan 53B (08 651 43 60). T-bana St Eriksplan or bus 1, 54, 65. Open 1pm-3am daily. Map p159 G6 6

Fridhemsplan has a reputation for dive bars and Theodora is a neighbourhood institution. Nobody comes here for the bland, dated interior, but it's popular with both students and thrifty locals looking for a cheap after-work drink. Theodora has a surprisingly large selection of lagers, wines and spirits, and is open until 3am every day of the week.

Shops & services

♥ 59 Vintage Store
Hantverkargatan 59 (08 428 63 845, 59vintagestore.se). T-bana Fridhemsplan or bus 3, 50, 54. Open 11am-6pm Tue-Fri; 1-4pm Sat. Map p159 H8 1 *Fashion*

Selling vintage clothing from the 1920s onwards, 59 Vintage Store has a reputation for stocking high-end global brands from Dior to Hermes, as well as Nordic labels such as Marimekko and Katja of Sweden. Check the store's Instagram for some of the latest offerings.

HuGo
St Eriksgatan 39 (08 652 49 90, www.hugo-sthlm.com). T-bana Fridhemsplan or bus 54, 65. Open 10.30am-7pm Mon-Fri; 11am-4pm Sat; noon-4pm Sun. Map p159 G7 2 *Fashion*

Fashion-conscious men who don't worry about paying a little extra to look a little extra can get everything from underwear to suits at HuGo. Staff hand-pick a few garments from international labels every season, so this is the place to find something exclusive. Popular Swedish designer label Tiger is also sold here.

♥ Naturkompaniet
Hantverkargatan 38-40, (08 651 35 00, www. naturkompaniet.se/butiker/stockholm-hantverkargatan).T-bana Rådhuset or bus 3, 53, 54, 65. Open 10am-6pm Mon-Fri; 10am-3pm Sat. Map p159 H8 3 *Outdoors*

There's a decent selection of adventure clothing and equipment crammed into this small branch of one of Sweden's best-loved outdoor brands. Swedish label Fjällräven is among the most popular labels sold here, the brand behind the iconic, brightly coloured

Kånken backpacks with a 1970s cut that you'll see kids, students and commuters alike sporting across the city.

Taylors and Jones
Hantverkargatan 12 (08 651 29 10, taylorsandjones.com). T-bana Rådhuset or bus 3, 53, 54, 65. Open 10am-6pm Mon-Fri; 10am-2pm Sat. Map p159 J8 4 *Food*

Handmade sausages are the stars of the show at this tiny neighbourhood butcher, run by two British friends – David Taylor and Gareth Jones – since 2007. The store also stocks other British comfort foods, including baked beans and Scottish shortbread. If you can't make it here, look out for Taylors and Jones products in larger supermarkets.

Västermalmsgallerian
St Eriksgatan/Fleminggatan (www. vastermalmsgallerian.se). T-bana Fridhemsplan or bus 1, 3, 54, 65. Open 10am-7pm Mon-Fri; 10am-5pm Sat; 11am-5pm Sun. Map p159 G7 5 *Mall*

This pleasant mall includes an ICA Supermarket (open until 10pm daily), Björn Borg, FACE Stockholm, Granit, Designtorget and many others. There's a Joe and the Juice smoothie bar in the entrance that's busy all day long.

Day Trips

Lovely though Stockholm is, it would be a great shame not to head out of the city during your visit. There are some fantastic places within easy reach, many of them perfect for day trips. Stockholm's archipelago is perhaps the biggest draw: a scattering of islands to the east of the city, promising fresh air, summer bathing and a few surprises.

The region's rich history means that the area to the west of Stockholm is stuffed with castles and palaces, the grandest being the royal family's home of Drottningholm – an hour's trip by boat from the city centre. A little further afield is Mariefred, a stunning historic town with a castle on the south shore of Lake Mälaren. North of Stockholm, meanwhile, lies the former Viking stronghold of Sigtuna, one of the oldest towns in Sweden and, beyond that, charming and historic Uppsala. Situated at the northern tip of Lake Mälaren, the city is dominated by its university and grand cathedral.

❤ **Don't miss**

1 Stockholm archipelago *p174*
Take a boat trip to at least one of the islands during your visit.

2 Hellasgården *p171*
Sauna in a nature reserve.

▶ *For some recommended accommodation options outside Stockholm, see p233 Out of Town Retreats.*

DAY TRIPS

Gripsholms Slott *p170*

DROTTNINGHOLM

The grand palatial estate of Drottningholm – the permanent residence of the Swedish royal family since 1981 – attracts more than 100,000 visitors annually. Located just ten kilometres to the west of central Stockholm, on the sparsely populated island of Lovön, it's an essential excursion from the city. The very well-preserved grounds incorporate 300-year-old trees, which frame the statues and fountains of the French garden behind the palace. There's also some excellent 17th- and 18th-century architecture, including a still-functioning theatre from 1766 and the exotic Kina Slott at the western end of the estate. The site was added to UNESCO's World Heritage List back in 1991.

Constructed at the very height of Sweden's power in Europe during the mid 17th century, **Drottningholms Slott** (08 402 61 00, www.kungligaslotten.se, closed Jan-June) was built to impress – and impress it certainly does. Wealthy dowager Queen Hedvig Eleonora financed the initial phase of the palace's construction, which lasted from 1662 to 1686. The royal architect Nicodemus Tessin the Elder modelled the waterfront residence on the Palace of Versailles. Don't-miss highlights include the monumental staircase, the Ehrenstrahl drawing room and Hedvig Eleonora's state bedchamber.

The palace's second period of growth began after Lovisa Ulrika married Crown Prince Adolf Fredrik in 1744. She was a great lover of the arts and it was at her commission that architect Carl Fredrik Adelcrantz constructed **Drottningholms Slottsteater** (08 556 93 100, www.dtm.se, closed Jan, Feb). With its original stage sets and hand-driven machinery in place, this is one of the world's oldest working theatres: concerts, ballets and operas are still held here in the summer.

Behind the palace is the long, rectangular **French Baroque Garden**, laid out in five stages separated by lateral paths. Its bronze statues are copies of early 17th-century works by the Dutch sculptor Adriaen de Vries. In 2001, the originals – spoils of war from Denmark's Fredriksborg Palace and from Prague – were moved across the street to the **Museum de Vries** (08 402 61 00, closed Sept-mid May), the former royal stable, where they are arranged in the same pattern as those in the garden.

North of the Baroque Garden is the beautiful, lake-studded **English Park**, so named because it followed the English style of naturalistic landscaping that was fashionable at the time. It was added by Gustav III after he took over the palace in 1777.

Kina Slott (08 402 62 70, closed Oct-Apr) stands near the end of the garden down a tree-lined avenue. As a surprise for Lovisa Ulrika's 33rd birthday in 1753, Adolf Fredrik had a Chinese-inspired wooden pavilion built here. Ten years later it was replaced by this rococo pleasure palace, also designed by CF Adelcrantz. The palace, which was extensively renovated between 1989 and 1996, sports its original red colour with yellow trim and light-green roofs; tours are available.

Across from Kina Slott is the small **Confidencen** pavilion. When the royal family wanted to dine in complete privacy, they sat in the top room and servants hoisted up a fully set table from below. Down the road behind the palace is the former studio of the 20th-century Swedish artist **Evert Lundquist** (073 396 64 95, www. evertlundquistsateljemuseum.se, closed Sept-Apr, free entry).

Restaurants & cafés

Just metres from the waterfront and right by the pier where tour boats dock, **Karamellan** (Drottningholms Slott, 178 93 Drottningholm, 08 759 00 35, www.drottningholm.org, closed Mon, Tue Jan-Apr, ⓦ) is housed in a historic building dating back to 1880. The restaurant and café specialise in classic Swedish home-cooked food, but there's also good coffee, pastries, sandwiches, beer and wine. A short walk over the bridge from Drottningholm to Kärsön island, **Brostugan** (Brostugans väg 1, 08 759 03 01, www.brostugan.se, ⓦ) serves great-value warm dishes, including Swedish meatballs and *gulasch* soup as well as salads, sandwiches and plenty of baked sweet treats. It's popular during summer – but, thanks to its 280 outdoor seats, you shouldn't have to jostle to find a table.

> **In the know**
> **Getting to Drottningholm**
>
> By **public transport**, the most direct route is the T-bana to Brommaplan, then bus nos.176, 177 or 311. Between May and early September you can travel by **steamboat** from Stadshuskajen near Stadshuset on Kungsholmen to Drottningholm (www. stromma.se, 230kr return); the journey takes one hour, though various cruise packages are also available. If you're travelling by **car**, take Drottningholmsvägen west from Kungsholmen towards Vällingby, then at Brommaplan follow signs to Drottningholm; it's a 15-minute drive. There is also a **cycle** path from Stadshuset in Stockholm to Drottningholm; the ride takes about 50 minutes.

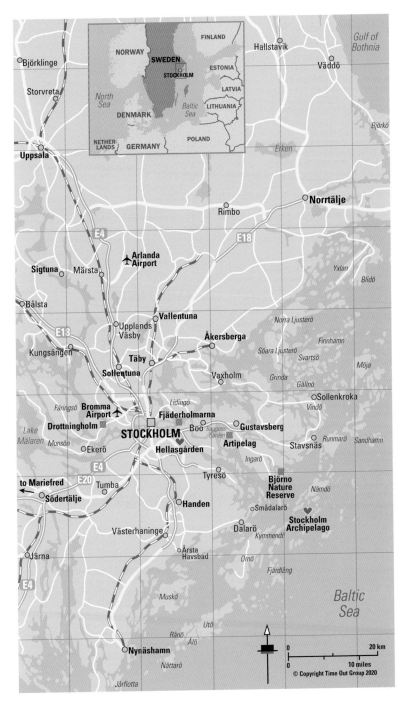

LIDINGÖ

Lidingö, a largely residential island north-east of the city centre, is a playground for the city's wealthiest inhabitants: some live in luxury villas and apartments along the coastline; others visit to play golf at the oldest course in Sweden (www.lidingogk.se) or to go horse-riding. There's plenty on offer for active visitors too: cycling and jogging paths criss-cross the island, becoming Nordic ski trails in winter. There are even two downhill ski slopes at 70-metre (230-foot) **Ekholmsnäsbacken** (www.ekholmsnasbacken.se), just south of the Hustegafjärden inlet, with skis, poles and helmets available for hire from 250kr for half a day (200kr for children). In summer, you can swim at **Fågelöuddebadet** on Lidingö's north-east coast, or at **Breviksbadet** (www.breviksbadet.se) a man-made pool in the south.

The main sightseeing attraction is **Millesgården** (Herserudsvägen 32, 08 446 75 90, www.millesgarden.se), the former home and studio of sculptor Carl Milles, which he donated to the state in 1936. His bronze statues stand alongside works by other artists on wide stone terraces, and the hilltop setting provides a dramatic backdrop of sky, land and water. The house is decorated with paintings and antiques purchased by Milles on his travels and forms the largest private collection of Greek and Roman statues in Sweden. Lidingö is also the birthplace of Raoul Wallenberg, the World War II diplomat who disappeared mysteriously in 1945 while in Soviet custody. Sculptures around the island have been erected in his honour.

In the know
Getting to Lidingö

Lidingö is easily accessible by **tram** or **bus** from Ropsten, the last stop on the red Norsborg–Ropsten T-bana line. The Lidingöbanan tram passes along the south-eastern side of the island to Gåshaga jetty, while bus nos.204 and 214 slice through the island towards Tennisbanor. Commuter **boats** running between Nybrokajen and Nacka or between Frihamnen and Nacka Strand stop off at Lidingö, as do some Waxholmsbolaget services from Nybrokajen and Strömkajen. If you're travelling by **car**, take the E20 east out of Stockholm, which passes through Hjorthagen and then over Lidingöbron (Lidingö bridge). Lidingö is a fantastic space to reach or explore by **bike**. It takes about 40 minutes to cycle there from central Stockholm, with cycle lanes for much of the route.

Restaurants & cafés

In the Millesgården sculpture park, **Millesgården Lanthandel** (08 446 75 93, www.millesgardenlanthandel.se, closed evnings in summer, ⏺) is a courtyard restaurant and café, packed with green plants and blossoming flowers. It serves daily lunch specials and good-value traditional evening meals with a focus on Swedish and European cuisine. All hot dishes are available in half portions for children. The cakes and desserts are divine. For something different, head to **450 Gradi** (Periskopvägen 19, 08 766 64 60, www.450gradi.se, closed Mon, ⏺), a stylish yet affordable dockside restaurant where pizzas are the stars of the show. Wine pairings are offered for every dish: think Henriot champagne with goat's cheese pizza or chianti Classico Poggio Scalette to complement the Parma ham and mozzarella option.

MARIEFRED

A small town on the south shore of Lake Mälaren, Mariefred is best known for **Gripsholms Slott** (Gripsholm, Mariefred, 0159 101 94, www.kungligaslotten.se/english/royal-palaces-and-sites/gripsholm-castle.html), one of Sweden's most imposing Renaissance castles, erected by King Gustav Vasa in 1537 on the site of an earlier 14th-century castle. The castle is situated on a small peninsula opposite downtown Mariefred, a short walk from the centre. As you approach the main gate, don't miss the runestones along the path, brought to Gripsholm from their original locations nearby. Highlights inside the castle include the Swedish national portrait collection, along with Duke Karl's chamber from the 16th century and Gustav III's theatre from the 1700s.

The town itself is charming, with many well-preserved 18th- and 19th-century buildings, as well as a variety of shops and cafés. It's a relaxing place to spend a day, particularly during the summer, when the streets bustle with life and restaurants spill out on to the sidewalks and pier. South-west of town is Mariefred's distinctive yellow railway station, **Läggesta**, which has an exhibition on railway history. From May to September you can take a historic steam train ride on the **Östra Södermanlands Järnväg** (www.oslj.nu) from here to Taxinge-Näsby. Engines and cars from the late 19th and early 20th centuries travel the route.

❤ Hellasgården

*Ältavägen 101, Nacka (08 716 39 61, www.
hellasgarden.se/en). Bus 401.* **Open**
10am-9pm Mon-Fri; 10am-6pm Sat, Sun.
Admission *70kr; 40kr under-15s. Aroma
sauna (from 5pm Mon, Wed) 110kr.*

Embrace the Nordic ritual of sweating out
your stresses in a sauna, by making the
15-minute bus journey from Slussen in the
city centre to Hellasgården, a recreation area
inside Nacka Nature Reserve. Here you'll
find separate male and female saunas and,
yes, it is compulsory to strip off completely
in both. Outside, there's a jetty from which
you can jump (or for the less brave, gingerly
ease yourself) into the waters of Lake
Källtorp to cool off. Locals make the leap
year-round, with a hole drilled into the
ice once it freezes over. Entrance is cheap,
and you can rent towels and padlocks for
the changing-room lockers if you don't
have your own. The sauna is mixed all
day on Monday, and on Wednesday and
Friday evenings, with popular scented

'aroma' steam sessions on Monday
and Wednesday from 5pm.

It's worth combining a trip to the sauna
with one of the easy hiking trails around
the lake. Check the giant map at the main
entrance for inspiration and bring a picnic
on sunny days. Otherwise, there are several
eating options if you need to refuel. Next to
the sauna reception, you'll find **Sjöcaféet**
(same hours as the sauna), a small, no-frills
café. Closer to the park entrance is **Hellas
Storstugan** (Ältavägen 101, 08 666 12 34,
www.hellasstorstugan.se), a farmhouse-
style wooden restaurant with simple
yet top-quality fare, usually including
soup, salad, meat and fish options, plus a
short children's menu.

While Hellasgården makes for an easy
half-day or evening visit, there's also the
option to stay the night in one of the *stugor* –
affordable small wooden huts with space for
up to four people – giving you the chance to
wake up in the forest and be the first to take
a morning dip; see the website for details.

DAY TRIPS

In the know
Getting to Mariefred

There are hourly **trains** from Stockholm Central Station to Läggesta (40 minutes), from where you can switch to a bus (nos.302, 304, 642), which will take you into the town centre in ten minutes. By **car**, take the E20 south-west out of Stockholm and turn off towards Mariefred at the junction by Läggesta railway station.

Restaurants & cafés

Situated between Gripsholm Castle and Mariefred's town centre, **Slottspaviljongen** (Gripsholm Lottenlund, 0159 100 23, www. slottspaviljongen.se, noon-9pm daily, ⓦⓦ) scores points for its huge terrace overlooking Lake Mälaren. During the summer there are regular barbecue nights. The main evening menu has a Swedish focus, with plenty of fresh fish alongside meatballs and salads. Elsewhere, **Två Goda Ting** (Storgatan 6, 0159 132 50, www.tvagodating. com, 10am-6pm Mon-Fri; 10am-5pm Sat, Sun, ⓦ) is an Instagrammable café and shop that specialises in 'two delicious things', namely coffee and chocolate. But it also sells tea, liquorice and assorted ice-creams during the summer.

SIGTUNA

Founded around 980 by King Erik Segersäll, this small town by Lake Mälaren was the most important trading centre in Sweden during Viking times. Later, Sigtuna became the focus of activity for Christian missionaries, but the town fell into ruin following King Gustav Vasa's Reformation in the 16th century, when he demolished many churches and monasteries. Virtually all that is left from the

In the know
Getting to Sigtuna

The commuter **train** from Stockholm City to Märsta (www.sl.se) takes 40 minutes (72kr-80kr depending on whether you buy it in advance or on the train). From Märsta, take bus no.570 or 575 to Sigtuna bus station, near the centre. The whole trip should take one hour. If you're travelling by **car**, head north on the E4 for about 30km (18 miles), then exit on the 263 and follow signs to Sigtuna. Drive about ten kilometres west until you come to a roundabout, where you turn towards Sigtuna Centrum. The journey takes about 50 minutes.

town's period of greatness are the remains of three 12th-century granite churches (from an original seven) bordering the town centre, and a collection of artefacts in the **Sigtuna Museum**. The museum is built on the site of a former king's residence and has an excellent exhibition on the Vikings.

Many of the buildings date back to the 18th and 19th centuries, including the **Rådhus** (Stora Torget, closed Sept-May, free), in the central square, which was built in 1744 and is the smallest town hall in Sweden. The Sigtuna Museum also manages the **Lundströmska Gården** (Stora Gatan 39, closed Sept-May, free with museum entry), a middle-class house where a merchant lived with his family. Stop by the tourist office, **Destination Sigtuna** (Stora Gatan 33, 08 594 80 650, www.destinationsigtuna.se), to book a tour of the town. Off the main street, you can take a stroll through the church ruins and cemeteries of **St Lars**, **St Per** and **St Olof**. The church of **St Maria**, which looks quite new compared to the others, was actually built by the Dominicans in the 13th century. Summer is the ideal time to visit Sigtuna, as you can rent canoes and bicycles or grab an ice-cream by the water; much of the town closes down during winter, although frozen Lake Mälaren is a breathtaking sight.

Restaurants & cafés

A wooden dock leads to **Båthuset Krog & Bar** (Hamngatan 2, 08 592 56 780, www. bathuset.com, closed Mon, ⓦⓦ), a floating restaurant and bar on the lake. It serves portions of fresh mussels and cod, as well as seasonal meat and vegetarian dishes. There's a carefully curated drinks list, with a focus on wine and beer labels that emphasise sustainability. For another waterfront view, visit the terrace at **Restaurang 1909** (Stora Nygatan 3, 08 592 50 100, www. sigtunastadshotell.se/en/restaurant, closed Sun, closed July, ⓦⓦⓦ). It's part of Sigtuna Stadshotell, which markets itself as Sweden's smallest five-star accommodation. The menu focuses on traditional, seasonal Swedish cuisine, but it's also a charming location for afternoon tea. There's an on-site bakery and a well-stocked wine cellar.

UPPSALA

The historic city of Uppsala is the site of the oldest university in Scandinavia – dating back to 1477. It's a bustling, charming city, situated at the northern tip of Lake Mälaren, about 70 kilometres (40 miles) north of Stockholm, with ancient landmarks, plenty of cafés and parks and some

30,000 students. The buildings of Uppsala University are scattered throughout the city.

The city's magnificent **Domkyrkan** (Domkyrkoplan 2, 018 430 36 30, www. uppsaladomkyrka.se), Scandinavia's largest cathedral, stands on a ridge to the west of the downtown area. It's a red-brick Gothic structure built on a cross plan and completed in 1435. The building is as tall as it is long, with two western towers rising up to a neck-craning 118.7 metres (389 feet). Inside, there's an enormous vaulted ceiling, a floor covered with gravestones and Sweden's largest Baroque pulpit.

Across from the cathedral stands the **Gustavianum** (Akademigatan 3, 018 471 75 71, www.gustavianum.uu.se), formerly the university's main building, now a museum. Beneath its dome are exhibits on the history of science, an old anatomical theatre, some Nordic, classical and Egyptian antiquities, and the curiosities of the Augsburg Art Cabinet.

Up the hill from the cathedral stands the huge, earth-red **Uppsala Slott** (018 54 48 11, www.uppsalaslott.com), built as a fortress by Gustav Vasa in the late 1540s. His sons later added to the building, although much of it was destroyed in the city fire of 1702. It houses an art gallery and the county governor's residence, Vasaborgen, but is not as spectacular as you might expect. The castle's freestanding bell tower, Gunillaklockan, has become a symbol of Uppsala; it strikes at 6am and 9pm.

The small Fyrisån river separates the castle and cathedral from the centre of town. One block to the east of the river is a pedestrian shopping street and the busy main square of **Stora Torget**. **Linnéträdgården**

(Svarbäcksgatan 27, 018 471 28 38, www. linnaeus.uu.se, closed Oct-Apr), the former home and garden of the famous botanist Carl Linnaeus (whose face adorns the Swedish 100kr note), is located one block north of pedestrianised Gågatan. This was the university's first botanical garden and was restored by Linnaeus (1707-78), also known as Carl von Linné, in 1741 soon after he took up a professorship at the university. One of the world's most famous scientists, Linnaeus developed a method of classifying and naming plants and animals that was adopted by scientists around the world and is still in use today. He lived in the small house on the corner of the property, now the **Linnémuseet**, which has a permanent exhibition on his life and work. The university's current grand **Botaniska Trädgården** (Villavägen 8, 018 471 28 38, www.botan.uu.se) lies west of the castle and includes a tropical greenhouse, Baroque formal garden and 11,000 plant species.

Gamla Uppsala (Old Uppsala; Disavägen, 018 23 93 12, www.raa.se/gamlauppsala), two kilometres to the north of Uppsala, is the site of the original settlement. The **Gamla Uppsala Museum** (Disavägen 15, 018 23 93 01) has exhibits about Viking history and myths.

Restaurants & cafés

Domtrappkällaren (St Eriksgränd 15, 018 13 09 55, www.domtrappkallaren.se, 😊😊) is a 13th-century vault near the cathedral steps that serves excellent Swedish and French cuisine. Another historic spot is **Ofvandahls Hovkonditori** (Sysslomansgatan 5, 018 13 42 04, www.ofvandahls.se, 😊), which was founded in the 19th century and is one of Uppsala's most famous cafés. Come here to enjoy a slice of cake or a bun; there's a good selection of teas and coffees too. **Hambergs Fisk** (Fyristorg 8, 018 71 21 50, www.hambergs.se, closed Sun, Mon and in high summer, 😊😊) is a homely restaurant and delicatessen that has been popular for more than 20 years; it specialises in seafood. **Fröjas Sal Vegetarisk Restaurang** (Bäverns Gränd 24, 018 10 13 10, www. frojassal.se, closed Sat, Sun, 😊) is a modern vegetarian café that serves a daily hot lunch buffet, salads and pies.

💜 Stockholm Archipelago

Artipelag

While Stockholm's city skyline is jaw-droppingly beautiful, the crown jewels of the wider region are the islands that make up its dazzling archipelago. Spilling out into the Baltic Sea, you'll find 30,000 islands, ranging from chic tourist spots boasting boutique hotels and sandy beaches, to deserted rocky outposts sprouting pine trees.

Navigating the area can feel overwhelming – there's less information online in English than you'd expect, perhaps a hint that Swedes want to keep this beautiful spot to themselves. But that doesn't mean you have to resort to a package tour in order to visit. Buses from Slussen station connect to the main commuter boat lines (yes, some Swedes are lucky enough to actually live in the archipelago), or you can catch slightly pricier direct ferries to popular destinations run by **Waxholmsbolaget** (www.waxholmsbolaget.se) and **Strömma** (www.stromma.com); book online or take your chances at the docks at Nybrokajen or Strömkajen. Head straight to the top deck as soon as you get on any ferry to ensure you snag an outdoor seat, and aim to catch the second crossing of the day in high season for a less sardine-like journey.

There are countless destinations in the archipelago to choose from, but here's our run-down of some of the highlights for visitors on a short trip.

Artipelag

Not many people associate the Stockholm archipelago with contemporary art and architecture; indeed, the islands are really a place to escape urban life. But, since 2012, visitors have been able to mix culture and nature at **Artipelag** (08 570 13 000, www.artipelag.se, closed Sept-Apr), an exhibition space housed in a wonderfully innovative coastal building on Baggensfjärden, in the municipality of Värmdö.

Reached from Stockholm by bus or boat, Artipelag is the manifested vision of BabyBjörn founder Björn Jakobson, an art lover and lifetime visitor to the archipelago. He wanted to blend modern art with the Scandinavian love of nature by creating a ground-breaking exhibition space in a stunning waterside setting. There's an overriding sense of space here that's both calming and stimulating: the site covers

In the know
Visiting the archipelago

The archipelago is best visited from mid June to mid August – during the rest of the year many of the hotels, restaurants and other facilities are closed, and ferries are more limited. If you're planning to stay over, always book ahead to ensure there will be accommodation available.

During the summer months the archipelago often gets more sunshine than the mainland, but it's still a good idea to pack a raincoat and sweater. Sunscreen and mosquito repellent are also recommended. Take provisions, and both cards and cash, as shops are not always open and cashpoints are scarce.

22 hectares (54 acres) and incorporates 1,800 square metres (19,000 square feet) of exhibition space, a concert hall, two high-quality restaurants and a design shop. Far-reaching sea views and fresh Nordic air can be enjoyed through large windows or from the minimalist rooftop terrace.

That Artipelag doesn't have a permanent art collection is perhaps its only drawback. The temporary art exhibitions are an ambitious but not always successful mix of contemporary and classical pieces, loosely held together by the organisation's aim to 'explore the borderland between fine art, crafts and design'.

A dedicated bus service runs from Vasagatan 24 in Stockholm directly to Artipelag (journey time 25mins, 50kr return) or you can take SL bus no.474 from Slussen to Gustavsbergs Centrum and then bus 468 to Hålludden. Artipelag can also be reached via a scenic 90-minute boat trip from Nybrokajen (Norrmalm); book through Strömma (*see left*).

Björno Nature Reserve

Björnonaturereservat, on the island of Ingarö, is a popular weekend retreat with Stockholmers, who catch the bus here from Slussen (nos.428 and 429, journey time 60-90mins). The mossy forest hiking trails are a magnet year-round, and, during summer, many come to Björno to sunbathe on the rocky cliffs, or to swim at the fine sandy beach at **Torpesand Strandbad**. There's very little in the way of civilisation in this area: come prepared with your own packed lunch and chilled water.

Fjäderholmarna

Just a 20-minute boat ride from downtown Stockholm, a trip to the Feather Islands is perhaps the easiest way to get a taste of the archipelago, especially if you're tight on time. About a dozen people live on the main island of **Stora Fjäderholmen** and on **Ängsholmen**, while the smaller islands of **Libertas** and **Rövarns Holme** provide sanctuary for birds and are only accessible by private boat. Ferries drop visitors off on the northern shore of Stora Fjärderholmen. There are plenty of rocky outposts where you can picnic or swim, alongside a selection of artisan stores selling Scandinavian art, design and souvenirs. If you want to buy lunch, check out **Fjäderholmarnars krog** (08 718 33 55, www.fjaderholmarnaskrog. se, 🐱🐱) or **Rökeriet** (08 716 50 88, www. rokeriet-fjaderholmarna.se, 🐱🐱), two popular restaurants near the harbour.

Boats to Fjäderholmarna depart from Nybrokajen between May and September (journey time 30mins, 155kr, 78kr reductions, free under-6s).

Artipelag

🖤 Stockholm Archipelago (cont.)

Grinda

This tranquil green island is two hours by ferry from central Stockholm (services are run by **Waxholmsbolaget**; reduced services in winter, 95kr, 69kr reductions) and **Strömma** (Apr-Aug 140kr, 70kr reductions). It offers a range of hiking trails through pine forests, several bathing areas and plenty of places to picnic. Children will enjoy a visit to **Grinda Gård**, a farm where they can make friends with chickens, goats, cows and sheep. Grinda's main restaurant, **Wärdshuset** ⓦ is a cosy traditional inn, with a log fire during winter, that serves seasonal Swedish dishes, such as seafood stew, smoked pork and meatballs. If you want to stay longer than a day, there's are hotel rooms, a hostel, wooden cottages and camping facilities. For further details of dining, accommodation and the island in general, see www.grinda.se.

Sandhamn (Sandön)

Sandhamn, on the outermost edge of the Stockholm archipelago, was a port used by customs agents and ships' pilots in the late 17th century. It gradually evolved into a permanent settlement, and today it's a gathering spot for Sweden's moneyed sailing and yachting community. About 120 people currently live on the island year-round, but in the summer the population swells with seasonal residents and short-term visitors, and a party atmosphere takes over. To escape the hustle, head away from the village into the pine-covered interior. There are beaches at **Fläskberget**, to the west of the village, and at **Skärkarlshamn** to the east, but you should really take the 20-minute walk through the forest to the beautiful sandy beach at **Trouville** in the south. For further exploration, kayaks and bikes can be hired (call 07 034 74 339). The boutique **Sandhamn Seglarhotell** (www.sandhamn.com) is one of the best spots to enjoy a drink in the sunshine or a stylish night's sleep.

Sandhamn is an hour by passenger ferry from Stavsnäs, which is reached in an hour by direct bus (no.434 or 433) from Slussen in Stockholm. From April to August, Stromma boats also run directly from Strandvägen in the city centre to Sandhamn (journey time 2hrs). Stromma also runs a summer excursion boat from Nybroviken that follows a slower route through the scenic Strömma Canal (8hr return day trip, 385kr, 192.50kr reductions). For more information, check out www.destinationsandhamn.se.

Utö

The southern part of Stockholm's archipelago is often neglected by foreign visitors. But Utö, one of its largest islands (alongside neighbouring Rånö and Nåttarö) is easily accessed and attracts plenty of local visitors as a result. The main harbour and tourist centre is **Gruvbryggan**, reached

by boat from Årsta Brygga, a short bus ride from Västerhaninge station, which is on the commuter train line from central Stockholm. You can also catch a boat from the pretty fishing town of Nynäshamn (also on the train line) to Ålö, a smaller island to the south that is connected to Utö by road.

Cycling is a popular draw for visitors to Utö; you can hire bikes on the island or bring your own (cycles are allowed on commuter trains outside of peak hours). Utö is also ideal for swimming; some of the best beaches can be found on the southern shore, although families should head for **Barnesbad**, a child-friendly beach 1.5 kilometres north of Gruvbryggan harbour. Alternatively, hire a kayak or rowing boat to explore the coast. There are several guesthouses if you want to take your time and stay the night. For more information visit www.uto.se.

Vaxholm

Located about 17 kilometres (11 miles) north-east of Stockholm, the island of Vaxholm began as a defensive outpost during the 16th century and received its town charter in 1647. During the 19th century it developed into a popular weekend and summer getaway for Stockholmers. Today, it is by far the most populated and easily accessible island in the archipelago. In summer, roughly a million visitors come to enjoy Vaxholm's waterfront restaurants, handicraft shops and art galleries.

Vaxholm

Vaxholm is connected to the mainland by highway 274 and served by bus no.670, which you can pick up from the Tekniska högskolan subway stop in Stockholm. Alternatively, passenger ferries run by Waxholmsbolaget and Strömma dock at Vaxholm's historic downtown, located on the island's south-east corner. The town has a lively, beach-side feel and hosts frequent outdoor events in the summer, including a steamboat festival, **Skärgårdsbåtens Dag** (*see p183*), on the second Wednesday in June. It's an enchanting place to walk around; the small streets are lined with pastel-coloured houses, most of which date from the turn of the 20th century. There are also shops selling homewares, baked goods, sweets, clothing, groceries and other items. The city's old **Rådhuset** (Town Hall) is home to the tourist office (08 541 31 480, www.vaxholm.se), where you can get hold of island maps, fishing licences and an events schedule; the cobbled square outside has stalls selling handicrafts in summer. West of Hamngatan, the main street, is **Vaxholm Kyrka**, designed in the 1760s, which hosts concerts in the summer. Follow Trädgårdsgatan north-east from here to reach **Vaxholms Hembygdsgårds Café** (Trädgårdsgatan 19, 08 541 31 980, 11am-5pm daily, ☕), an idyllic waterfront garden café serving cakes and Nordic open sandwiches. Offshore to the east of town is Vaxholm's imposing island citadel, whose origins date back to the 16th century. Several additions were made to the fortress during the 19th century and today it contains the **Vaxholms Fästnings Museum** (08 120 04 870, www.vaxholmsfastning.se, closed mid Sept-mid May & midsummer, 80kr, free with SP). The museum is easily reached by a two-minute boat trip from Vaxholm wharf.

Utö

Experience

Nötknäpparen, Kungliga Operan *p205*

Events

From summer fun to winter cheer

Swedes hold hard to tradition, so the calendar is dotted with popular, quintessentially Swedish events, such as the bonfire-packed Valborgsmässoafton (Walpurgis Night) and the candle-lit Luciadagen (Lucia Day), both of which are great opportunities for visitors to dabble in Swedish culture. It's not all about age-old customs, though. There are plenty of annual events with a more contemporary and diverse flavour, from the Stockholm Film Festival to live-music marathon Popaganda, plus an increasing number of innovative start-up and tech events. Sporting competitions are also a major part of Stockholm life: if you're feeling fit, you might want to enter the Midnattsloppet or even the appropriately named extreme obstacle contest, Tough Viking.

▶ *For a sense of seasonal Stockholm and advice on when to visit, see p28 When to Visit.*

♥ Best events

Gather *p184*
Music festival meets political forum.

Kulturnatt *p182*
A cornucopia of cultural offerings.

Midnattsloppet *p184*
Thousands take part in a midnight run around Södermalm.

Popaganda *p184*
Alternative fest for Scandi music-lovers.

Stockholm International Film Festival *p185*
A showcase for Nordic and international cinematic talent.

Stockholm Pride Week *p183*
The largest LGBTQ event in Scandinavia.

Spring

Påsk (Easter)
Date Mar/Apr.

The painting and eating of boiled eggs is a hallowed tradition at the Easter *smörgåsbord*, along with salmon and pickled herring prepared in endlessly creative ways. On Maundy Thursday or Easter Saturday, young girls dress up and paint themselves as Easter witches, and then go around begging sweets from generous neighbours, handing over home-made Easter cards in exchange.

Supermarket
Sickla Front, Uddvägen 7, Sickla (www. supermarketartfair.com). Bus 401, 403, 422. ***Tickets*** *120 kr.* ***Date*** *early Apr.*

Also known as Stockholm Independent Art Fair, this local artist-run initiative

was established in 2006 and has grown into an increasingly international event. Installations, talks and performances run over four days. Expect the unexpected.

♥ Kulturnatt
Throughout the city (https://kulturnatt stockholm.se). ***Date*** *Mid Apr.*

Free dance, music, art, fashion and literature events take place across Stockholm on a single night in April. Offerings in recent years have included live gospel performances, feminist walking tours and Danceoke (group dancing to music videos) inside the Nordic Museum (*see p124*). The extensive programme can be overwhelming, so check online and plan ahead before you set off on your cultural safari.

Valborgsmässoafton
Throughout the city. ***Date*** *30 Apr.*

Though they once protected Swedes from witches, the bonfires of Walpurgis Night now mark the end of winter and the coming of spring. Walpurgis Night is celebrated all over Sweden, but for visitors to Stockholm the place to be is either the open-air Skansen museum (*see p122*), where fireworks add extra sparkle to the evening's festivities, or Evert Taubes Terras on Riddarholmen.

Första Maj
Throughout the city. ***Date*** *1 May.*

If you happen to be in Stockholm on May Day, you might run into marchers waving banners in Sergels torg and other large squares throughout the city. The first of May has been celebrated in various ways since 1890. It's a lot more low-key these days but is still an important event for left-wing Stockholmers. Due to the cold weather, there's no maypole dancing – that's saved for Midsummer Eve (*see p183*).

Ö till Ö
Sandhamn to Utö (https://otilloswim run.com/races/uto). ***Date*** *May.*

The world's original Swimrun race involves teams swimming ten kilometres between 24 islands in the Stockholm archipelago and then running over them, with a total trail distance of 65km. There are various spectator spots and pop-up restaurants along the way. For further details, see the website.

Stockholm Marathon
From Östermalms Idrottsplats to Stockholms Stadion, Lidingövägen, Östermalm (https:// www.stockholmmarathon.se/). T-bana Stadion. ***Date*** *end May/early June.* ***Map*** *p102 Q3 & P3.*

Few cities can match the breathtaking beauty of this marathon route, which takes runners along waterside routes including Strandvägen, Norr

Kulturnatt

Mälarstrand and around Djurgården. If you want to glimpse the winner at the finish line, position yourself at Stockholms Stadion. For details of how to take part, see the website.

Summer
Parkteatern
Parks throughout the city (www. stadsteatern.stockholm.se). Date June-Aug.

There's been free outdoor theatre in Stockholm's parks since 1942, and many performances can be enjoyed by non-Swedish speakers, such as circus shows, concerts and dance. Look out for workshops on everything from steel drums to klezmer to Swedish folk dance.

Nationaldag
Date 6 June.

Sweden's National Day celebrates both Gustav Vasa's election as King of Sweden on 6 June 1523 and the adoption of a new constitution on the same date in 1809. For a glimpse of the royal family in their traditional blue-and-yellow folk costumes, visit the open-air Skansen museum (*see p122*), where, since 1916, the King of Sweden has presented flags on this day to representatives of various organisations and charities.

Smaka på Stockholm
Kungsträdgården, Norrmalm (www. smakapastockholm.se/in-english/). T-bana Kungsträdgården. Date early June. Map p80 O8.

A mecca for foodies, the Taste of Stockholm festival draws around 350,000 visitors to Stockholm's central Kungsträdgården park each year. From pop-up stalls run by some of Sweden's top chefs to food truck entrepreneurs testing out new concepts,

---

there's plenty to choose from, and you're guaranteed to go home with a very full belly.

Stockholm Early Music Festival
Tyska Brinken 13, Gamla Stan (www.semf. se). T-bana Gamla Stan. Tickets 1980kr. Map p65 N10. Date early June.

This four-day event attracts an impressive roster of established and new artistic talent from Sweden and Europe performing a programme of music from the Middle Ages, Renaissance and Baroque periods.

Skärgårdsbåtens Dag
Strömkajen, Norrmalm (08-662 89 02, www.skargardstrafikanten.se). T-bana Kungsträdgården. Tickets 150kr-200kr. Map p80 O8. Date 2nd Wed in June.

Archipelago Boat Day offers the chance to travel aboard one of Stockholm's old-fashioned steamboats as part of a parade of vessels that makes its way from Strömkajen to Vaxholm (*see p177*) in the early evening. For those who don't catch a ride, good places to view the boats are Strömkajen, Skeppsholmen, Kastellholmen and Fåfängen. The boats arriving in Vaxholm are greeted by live music and an outdoor market; visitors have a couple of hours to explore Vaxholm before returning to Stockholm.

Midsommarafton
Date Fri closest to 24 June.

The longest day of the year has been revered in Scandinavia since the days of pagan ritual. On Midsummer's Eve, modern Swedes flock to their summer cottages or set sail for quiet coves in the archipelago to commemorate this fertility feast. But if you're in Stockholm, Skansen open air museum (*see p122*) is the best place to experience the festivities (www.skansen.se/sv/midsommar). Here you can see people in traditional dress dancing around the flower-decorated maypole. It's said that if an unmarried girl picks seven different flower types and puts them under her pillow on Midsummer Eve, she will dream of her future husband.

♥ Stockholm Pride Week
Östermalms Idrottsplats, Fiskartorpsvägen 2, Östermalm & around the city (www. stockholmpride.org). Tickets 600kr (online in advance). Date late July/early Aug.

Since its birth in 1998, Stockholm Pride Week has grown into the biggest gay Pride celebration in Scandinavia. The focus of activity is Pride Park, which hosts food and drink stalls from the city's gay cafés and bars, plus a stage for pop concerts. There's also a huge parade through the city. For more information, *see p195*, and for a full programme of events, see the website.

In the know
Crayfish feast

If you're in Stockholm in August, an absolute don't miss is one of the city's legendary crayfish parties. A late summer phenomenon that marks the closing of the season, the crayfish are eaten outdoors in a setting traditionally decorated with colourful paper lanterns. Paper hats are also worn. The crayfish are served cold, with dill, and eaten with the fingers, accompanied by vast quantities of beer and schnapps, which adds to the sense of camaraderie. Although crayfish have been eaten in Sweden since the 16th century, the parties were the preserve of the upper classes until the 20th century, when the festivities were taken on by the hoi polloi.

💙 Midnattsloppet
From Zinkensdamms Idrottsplatts, Ringvägen to Hornsgatan, Södermalm (077 184 08 40, www.midnattsloppet.com). **Tickets** *325kr-425kr.* **Date** *mid Aug.*

This popular night-time race could only be possible in the land of the midnight sun. More than 40,000 runners of all ages navigate a 10km or 5km course around the island of Södermalm. But it's much more than a race: thousands of spectators get in on the act with cheering, music and partying. To catch the starting gun, position yourself at Ringvägen, just south of the Zinkensdamm athletics field, and then wait for the first runners to cross the finish line at Hornsgatan, not far from the starting point. For details of how to take part, see the website.

💙 Popaganda
Skanstull Eriksdalsbadet, Södermalm (www.popaganda.se). Transport T-bana Skanstull or bus 4. **Tickets** *see website for festival passes.* **Map** *p134 O16.* **Date** *late Aug.*

One of Stockholm's most established alternative music festivals, Popaganda has welcomed Swedish music darlings such as Tove Lo and First Aid Kit in recent years, alongside acclaimed international artists including Parcels and Two Door Cinema Club. There are typically two stages and multiple food trucks erected next to the Eriksdalsbadet outdoor swimming pools.

Tough Viking
Djurgården (toughviking.se). Bus 67 or tram 7. **Tickets** *795kr.* **Map** *p118.* **Date** *late Aug.*

Scandinavia's leading obstacle race takes place in various Stockholm locations several times a year. The August course on the island of Djurgården gives participants the chance to flex their muscles and get very wet and muddy against a beautiful backdrop of forest and water. The obstacles are designed in conjunction with the Swedish elite maritime special forces unit, Kustjägarna.

Autumn
Sthlm Tech Fest
Stockholm Waterfront Congress Centre, Nils Ericsons Plan 4, Norrmalm (www.sthlmtech. com). T-bana T-Centralen. **Tickets** *free (sign up online in advance).* **Date** *early Sept.* **Map** *p80 L8.*

One of the largest tech events in Europe, Sthlm Tech Fest is the pinnacle of Stockholm Tech Week, designed to show off the Swedish capital's vibrant start-up ecosystem and to inspire future tech entrepreneurs with talks by visiting international guests. In previous years, high-profile speakers have included Spotify co-founder Daniel Ek and gaming giant King's co-founder and CTO Thomas Hartwig. Numerous side events from hackathons to job fairs also pull in the crowds.

💙 Gather
Expohuset, Järnvägsgatan 31, Nacka (www.gatherfestival.com). Sickla rail. **Tickets** *2850kr-5650kr.* **Date** *mid Sept.*

Inaugurated in 2017, Gather combines live music gigs and DJ sets with thought-provoking talks and presentations, designed to make the audience question society and its future. Much less corporate and pretentious than most conferences in the Nordics, it draws a smart, creative crowd with an interest in tech, science and innovation as well as public policy and culture. It's run by one of the founders of Trädgården open-air club (see p199).

Lidingöloppet
Around Lidingö (08 765 26 15, www. lidingoloppet.se). T-bana Ropsten or bus 203, 204, 212. **Tickets** *450kr-895kr* **Date** *Sat, Sun in late Sept.*

The world's biggest cross-country race has become a tradition for Swedes. The first Lidingöloppet was held in 1965; these days, thousands of runners from some 30 different countries pass the finish line on Grönsta Gärde. For details of how to enter, see the website.

Stockholm Jazz Festival
Various venues (https://stockholmjazz.se). **Tickets** *vary.* **Date** *mid Oct.*

Gather

The Stockholm Jazz Festival is one of Sweden's premier live music festivals with more than 100 concerts taking place across 10 days. It's prestigious enough to pull in some big international artists.

Stockholm Open
Kungliga Tennishallen, Lidingövägen 75, Norra Djurgården (073 312 55 76, www. stockholmopen.se). T-bana Gärdet. **Tickets** *100kr-780kr.* **Date** *mid Oct.* **Map** *p102 S2.*

In 1969, veteran tennis star Sven Davidson received a letter from American colleagues asking him to arrange a competition in Sweden with tennis pros and amateurs from all over the world. The event now attracts around 40,000 spectators each year.

💙 Stockholm International Film Festival
Various venues (08 677 50 00, www. stockholmfilmfestival.se). **Tickets** *vary.* **Date** *early Nov.*

The ten-day Stockholm Film Festival aims to launch young filmmakers and broaden the forum for innovative high-quality films in Scandinavia. It may not be Cannes, but it can still attract some big names: past guests have included Quentin Tarantino, the Coen brothers and Danish director Lars von Trier.

Winter

Skansen Christmas Market
Djurgårdsslätten 49-51, Djurgården (08 442 80 00, www.skansen.se/en/christmas-market). Bus 67 or tram 7, or ferry from Slussen or Nybroplan. **Date** *early-end Dec.* **Map** *p118 T9.*

Skansen's Christmas market is held at weekends throughout December until Christmas Eve (the only day Skansen is closed). Look out for Swedish craft products, traditional Christmas ornaments made of straw, hand-dipped candles and Christmas foods such as smoked sausage, eel and salmon. This is also a good place to try out *glögg* (Swedish mulled wine), which also comes in non-alcoholic versions.

Luciadagen
Date *13 Dec.*

Among the best-known of Sweden's festivals, St Lucia is celebrated in the heart of the winter darkness. The Lutheran Swedes adopted the Sicilian St Lucia because of her connection with *lux*, the Latin for light. All over Sweden, a procession of singers, dressed in white, full-length chemises with red ribbons around their waists, are led by a woman dressed as Lucia, with a crown of lit candles on her head.

Jul (Christmas)
Date *24-26 Dec.*

The main celebration is held on Christmas Eve at home, although restaurants all over the city offer the traditional, overflowing *Julbord* or *smörgåsbord* for most of December. A traditional *Julbord* (Christmas table) is typically eaten in three stages. You start with herring and salmon, then move on to the meats (meatballs, sausages and ham), accompanied by Jansson's Temptation – an anchovy, potato and cream casserole. You polish it all off with a sweet berry-filled pastry. Christmas Day itself is usually a quiet day.

Nyårsafton (New Year's Eve)
Date *31 Dec.*

The New Year's Eve celebration in Sweden is a public and raucous contrast to the quiet and private Christmas festivities that have gone before. Visitors can join the crowds at Skansen (*see p122*), where New Year's Eve has been celebrated every year since 1895 by a well-known Swede reading Tennyson's 'Ring Out, Wild Bells' at the stroke of midnight. Throughout the city, crowds fill the streets, feasting on seafood at various restaurants and moving from one club or bar to another.

Stockholm Design Week
Stockholmsmässan, Mässvägen 1, Älvsjö, & venues throughout the city (www.stockholm designweek.com). T-bana Älvsjö. **Date** *early Feb.*

All of Sweden's top creatives are in town for this world-class design event, which centres around the Stockholm Furniture and Light Fair held at the Stockholmsmässan trade centre, south-west of Södermalm. Shops, showrooms, museums and galleries put on special events and parties throughout the week, with both industry figures and the general public attending.

Film

Cinema pioneers, Hollywood émigrés and small-screen successes

Sweden has a long and varied filmmaking history and a passion for the silver screen. Which makes it all the more sad that several Stockholm arthouse treasures – including Biblioteksgatan's Röda Kvarn (now a restaurant and delicatessen, Eataly) and Nybrogatan's Astoria – have been forced to close their doors over the past decade, partly as a result of the recent monopoly by production/distribution house and cinema operator SF (Svensk Filmindustri). Fortunately, a few gems still remain, most notably Biografteatern Rio and Zita Folkets Bio.

In the sphere of film production, things look brighter. The number of films made per year have been increasing, although new funding initiatives have meant that much of the work has moved to production centres outside Stockholm – especially Film i Väst outside Gothenburg, now Scandinavia's major regional film organisation.

Sweden is increasingly making its mark on Hollywood too, thanks to the likes of director Ruben Östlund (*The Square, Force Majeure*), composer Ludwig Göransson, who wrote the score for the 2018 Marvel movie *Black Panther,* and actors Alicia Vikander (*The Danish Girl, Tomb Raider*) and Alexander Skarsgård (*The Legend of Tarzan, The Hummingbird Project, Zoolander*).

Ingmar Bergman and Victor Sjöström

Bio Rio *p190*

Sweden's cinema history

In the 1920s, Sweden was among the world's leading filmmaking nations. Directors such as Victor Sjöström and Mauritz Stiller made an impact with films that are still regarded as classics of early cinema. Several of these were based on books by Selma Lagerlöf (Nobel Laureate, 1909), including *The Phantom Carriage* (1921) and *The Treasure of Arne* (1919) by Sjöström, and *The Story of Gösta Berling* (1924) by Stiller (the film that catapulted Greta Garbo to fame). These films broke new ground by shooting on location, using nature as a key element, at a time when most films were still shot in studios.

This golden age of Swedish film was brief though, as some of the industry's biggest stars were lured abroad: Sjöström, Stiller and Garbo all emigrated to Hollywood. The 1930s and '40s were characterised by rather provincial burlesque comedies, and it wasn't until the early '50s that Swedish film again attracted the world's attention when Alf Sjöberg's version of Strindberg's play *Miss Julie* (1951) and Arne Mattsson's *One Summer of Happiness* (1952) stunned audiences in Venice and Berlin. At Cannes in 1956, Ingmar Bergman won international fame with *Smiles of a Summer Night*, and he remained in the spotlight throughout his filmmaking career (*see p191* Ingmar Bergman). But, with the exception of Bergman, Swedish

In the know
Greta Garbo

Born, raised and buried in Stockholm, Swedish actress Greta Garbo (1905-1990) remains one of the city's best-loved movie stars. Her acting career began with a short advertising commercial in the department store where she worked as a teenager (now the Haymarket Hotel in Norrmalm, *see p230*). After winning a scholarship to Dramaten (the Royal Dramatic Theatre's Acting School), she was spotted by famed Swedish director Mauritz Stiller and selected for the lead role in *The Saga of Gösta Berling* (1924). She went on to have success with a wide range of Hollywood movies including *Anna Christie* (1930), *Anna Karenina* (1935) and *Camille* (1936). Greta Garbo retired from the movies after World War Two and moved to New York, where she died aged 84. Her body was flown back to Sweden and buried in Stockholm's Skogskyrkogaarden woodland cemetery, 15 minutes' drive south of the city centre.

Greta Garbo and Mauritz Stiller

Small Screen, Big Impact

Swedish TV shows attract a global audience

Sweden has enjoyed global success with numerous television productions in recent years, largely – but not exclusively – within the Nordic noir genre: crime fiction typically told from the standpoint of police protagonists. *The Bridge*, which focused on the investigations of Swedish detective Saga Norén and her Danish co-workers, has made the most impact. Running for four seasons between 2011 and 2018, it has been shown in more than 100 countries. A joint production between Swedish publish television network SVT and Danish broadcaster DR, it is mainly set around the Øresund Bridge between Malmo and Copenhagen, although its creator Hans Rosenfeldt and several of the actors, including Sofia Helin who plays Saga, are based in Stockholm.

Other notable Nordic noir series include *Wallander* (2008-2016), about a detective living in the rural coastal town of Ystad; *Jordskott* (2015-2017), a thriller about a missing boy, and *Midnight Sun* (2016) a Swedish-French production about the murder of a French national in the far north of Sweden.

The mystery of who carried out a high school shooting was the plot of Sweden's first made-for-Netflix series *Quicksand* (called *Störst av allt* in Swedish), which quickly became a success following its release in 2019. Based on a novel by Swedish writer Malin Persson Giolito, it's set in Djursholm, one of Stockholm's richest suburbs.

But Swedish television isn't all doom-and-gloom. Before starring in hit US-Canadian romantic comedy series *You, Me, Her*, actor Greg Poehler wrote and starred in Stockholm-based sitcom *Welcome to Sweden* (2014-2015), loosely based on his own experiences of following his Swedish girlfriend back to her home country after meeting in New York. And Sweden's answer to Downton Abbey, *Vår tid är nu*, pulled in more than a tenth of the country's population when it debuted in 2017. The heart-warming (although sometimes bleak) post-war drama has been shown in several other European countries and on Amazon Prime with the title *The Restaurant*.

film wasn't especially fertile until the late 1960s, when government funding helped a new generation of talent to emerge. Directors such as Jan Troell, Bo Widerberg and Viglot Sjöman became big names in an increasingly politicised era of filmmaking.

In the 1980s, Stockholm-born Lasse Hallström drew the attention of the film world with his 1987 hit *My Life as a Dog*, which earned two Oscar nominations and a Golden Globe for best foreign-language film. Like so many foreign-language filmmakers before and after him – including Victor Sjöström and Lucas Moodysson – Hallström answered Hollywood's siren call and worked with US studios on *What's Eating Gilbert Grape*, *The Shipping News*, *Chocolat* and *Salmon Fishing in the Yemen*, proving that Swedish filmmakers are more than able to adapt to the very different rules of US cinema.

An exciting new era in Swedish filmmaking began with Lukas Moodysson's excellent *Fucking Åmål* (also known as *Show Me Love*; 1998), in which he challenged the norm by making a film with a serious teenage protagonist. Moreover, Moodysson showed that such filmmaking was possible on quite a small budget. He went on to make several critically acclaimed films, including *Together* (2000) and *We are the Best* (2013). During this period immigrant filmmakers Reza Parsa

and Josef Fares also gained international recognition, with *Before the Storm* (2000) and *Jalla! Jalla!* (2000) respectively.

Acclaimed Swedish writer Stieg Larsson's Millennium series was successfully adapted for the big screen. Swedish-language versions of the trilogy, directed by Niels Arden Oplev and Daniel Alfredsson, were largely well received after their release in 2009. In 2011, an English-language version of the first book, *The Girl with the Dragon Tattoo*, was popular with global reviewers and earned actress Rooney Mara an Oscar nomination. A spin-off novel by David Lagercrantz, *The Girl in the Spider's Web*, featuring many of Larsson's original characters, was transformed into a

In the know
Blue movies

Sweden has the largely undeserved reputation as the birthplace of pornographic film, thanks to movies including *Do You Believe in Angels?* (1961), *Dear John* (1964) and *I Am Curious: Yellow* (1967). These films were seen as extremely daring in their time, but by today's standards they are far from pornographic. Paradoxically, along with being the first makers of 'porn', Swedes have the oldest system of film censorship in the world, established in 1911.

Zita Folkets Bio

big-budget production filmed in Stockholm and Berlin in 2018. British actress Clare Foy was widely praised for her performance as the lead character Lisbeth Salander, although the movie itself got mixed reviews.

Other notable figures in the Swedish film industry today include Amanda Kernell, who won the Europa Cinemas Label Award and the Fedeora Award for Best Debut Director in 2016 for her coming-of-age drama about a teenage girl from a Sami community in northern Sweden, *Sami Blood*. Hannes Holm was nominated for an Oscar for Best Foreign Language Film at the Academy Awards in 2017 for his film adaptation of Swedish author Fredrik Bergman's bestselling novel *A Man called Ove*, and Ruben Östlund was on the shortlist the following year for *The Square*, his quirky dark comedy set in the art world, but also missed out on the award. Oscar fame for Sweden finally came in 2019, when Ludwig Göransson, who wrote the soundtrack to the Marvel superhero movie *Black Panther* won the Academy Award for Best Original Score.

Cinemas

Bio Rio
Hornstulls Strand, Södermalm (08 669 95 00, www.biorio.se). T-bana Hornstull or bus 4. **Map** *p147 G13.*

Biografteatern Rio, formerly Kvartersbion, looks similar to how it did in the 1940s, although both the cinema and its café have been extensively refurbished in recent years. It shows an eclectic range of indie and arthouse films.

Capitol
Sankt Eriksgatan 82, Vasastan (08 511 65 781, www.capitolbio.se). T-bana Sankt Eriksplan. **Map** *p80 H5.*

Open since 2018, this neighbourhood cinema in Vasastan was crowdfunded by local residents and investors. It's inside a building used as a cinema between 1926 and 1985, before falling into disrepair. Much work has been put into reviving its 1920s roots and flair. There are green velvet chairs and small drinks tables between every seat. It screens a selection of new releases but is best known for showing musicals and classic films.

Cosmonova IMAX
Naturhistoriska Riksmuseet, Frescativägen 40, Norra Djurgården (08 519 54 000, www. nrm.se/cosmonova). T-bana Universitetet. No under-2s admitted unless otherwise stated; check website for details.

This IMAX cinema is a paradise for families. Films shown on its 11m-tall (36ft) dome-shaped screen are usually nature-based and worth seeing. Screenings are in Swedish only, so don't forget to buy an earphone for translation with your tickets.

Filmhuset
Borgvägen 1-5, Gärdet (08 665 11 00, www. filminstitutet.se). T-bana Karlaplan or bus 69, 76. **Map** *p102 T5.*

Filmhuset houses several screens and is home to the Swedish Film Institute, which works to preserve and promote Sweden's film heritage at home and abroad.

Filmstaden Sergel
Hötorget, Norrmalm (08 562 60 000, www. filmstaden.se). T-bana Hötorget or bus 1. **Map** *p80 M7.*

With no fewer than 14 screens to choose from, this cinema is the place to go for a bustling multiplex atmosphere.

Rigoletto
Kungsgatan 16, Norrmalm (08 562 60 000, www.filmstaden.se). T-bana Hötorget or Östermalmstorg, or bus 1, 54, 69. **Map** *p80 N6.*

Rigoletto's red neon lighting sign, dating back to 1939, makes it one of Stockholm's most

In the know
Times and tickets

Cinemas open one hour before the first screening (usually around 11am or 5pm). Most films are shown in their original language with Swedish subtitles, although children's films are usually dubbed. Tickets usually cost between 100kr and 200kr. Listings and information can be found in the daily papers, online or, for SF cinemas, using the SF app. Some smaller independent cinemas still have listings leaflets in their foyers.

Ingmar Bergman

Still the most prolific Swedish filmmaker of all time

Ingmar Bergman began his creative life in the theatre, following the Scandinavian traditions of Ibsen and Stockholm's own August Strindberg. But Sweden's other great dramatist was always destined for the cinema. Bergman recalled 'listening' to the light falling through a window of his grandmother's house in Uppsala, and lovingly described the rickety film projector that he was given at the age of ten as 'my first conjuring set'.

The would-be conjurer grew up in the privileged district of Östermalm, the son of a pastor. A childhood spent amid the angels and devils of his father's sermons provided Bergman with a tangible sense of the spiritual 'to revolt against' and a fascination with morality and mortality that would remain a theme throughout his career. Perhaps the director's most recognisable image is that of the medieval knight playing chess with Death in The Seventh Seal (1956), iconic long before being parodied, first by Woody Allen and, later, in Bill and Ted's Bogus Journey.

Many of Bergman's early films take place in a medieval world defined by the uneasy co-existence of paganism and religion, culminating in The Virgin Spring, which won the Academy Award for Best Foreign Language Film in 1961. From then on, Bergman's thematic eye shifted from the allegorical past and ventured internally; films like Through a Glass Darkly and Persona examine human faith and sexuality with an unflinching psychological honesty that has informed cinema ever since.

Though never a box-office draw in his homeland, Bergman famously despised Hollywood, calling it a 'ruthlessly efficient sausage machine'. Indeed, it was only his self-imposed exile from Sweden in 1976 over charges of tax evasion that saw him leave his beloved country (somewhat ironically he features on the 200kr notes). Bergman returned in 1982 to direct Fanny och Alexander – which he said at the time would be his last film. He kept that promise for 20 years, then made Saraband (2003), a follow-up to his internationally successful TV series Scenes from a Marriage. He spent the last years of his life in Fårö, remaining active in the theatre until his death in 2007.

Visitors to Stockholm and Bergman newcomers should watch Wild Strawberries (1957). One of his more accessible films, it's a comedic love letter to the director's own teenage years spent in the archipelago.

---

iconic cinemas. It shows blockbusters and some arthouse films. Just next door is Bistro Rigoletto serving good-quality grub.

Skandia
*Drottninggatan 82, Norrmalm (08 562 60 000, www.filmstaden.se). T-bana Hötorget or bus 1, 54, 69. **Map** p80 M6.*

This eccentric cinema opened in 1923. Most of the interior, designed by architect Gunnar Asplund, is still intact. It shows mainstream fare.

Sture
*Birger Jarlsgatan 41A, Östermalm (08 562 60 000, www.filmstaden.se). T-bana Östermalmstorg or bus 54, 69. **Map** p102 N5.*

This three-screen cinema shows arthouse films, as well as more commercial fare. The curtain in Cinema One was made by Ernst Billgren, one of Sweden's most famous contemporary artists.

Tellus
Vattenledningsvägen 46, Midsommarkransen (08 645 75 51, http://tellusbio.nu). T-bana Midsommarkransen.

One of Stockholm's last surviving single-screen cinemas, Biograf Tellus has been showing movies since 1920. The cinema building also includes a retro café serving homemade baked goodies, wine and beer, which you can also take into theatre with you.

Victoria
*Götgatan 67, Södermalm (08 562 60 000, www.filmstaden.se), T-bana Medborgarplatsen. **Map** p134 O13.*

This cosy six-screen cinema is a welcome retreat from the thronging Götgatan thoroughfare in Södermalm. It focuses on arthouse movies and has an excellent café that's also open for breakfast.

Zita Folkets Bio
*Birger Jarlsgatan 37, Östermalm (08 23 20 20, www.zita.se). T-bana Östermalmstorg or bus 54, 69. **Map** p102 N5.*

One of the only cinemas in town with a bar and restaurant, Zita screens films from all over the world, including documentaries and short films. There are DJs at weekends; sometimes themed to tie-in with movie showings.

Nightlife

Long summer parties and warm winter hideaways

Thanks to Sweden's rather byzantine laws and regulations, venues with a dancefloor require a dance licence; in order to get a dance licence, they must have an alcohol licence, and in order to get an alcohol licence, they have to serve food. As a result, small and intimate music bars still rule the city's nightlife. That said, a few larger venues, with big-name DJs, lavish visuals and proper dancefloors, have established themselves in the city.

Stockholm's live music scene, meanwhile, is better than you might expect given its out-of-the-way location in northern Europe; the city is often a tour stop for visiting bands from the UK and US. Then, of course, there are all the home-grown stars. Ever since ABBA emerged in the 1970s, Sweden has been a dominant force in pop and dance music, with current talents such as Zara Larsson, Icona Pop, Mike Perry and Tove Lo joining globally renowned Swedish music icons from Roxette and Robyn to Swedish House Mafia and the late Avicii, who died in 2018.

Swedes with immigrant backgrounds have also made a huge impact at home and abroad in recent years, from Swedish-Argentinian indie folk singer José González to R'n'B queen Cherrie.

Slakthuset *p201*

♥ Best nights out

Debaser Strand *p198*
From intimate indie-rock gigs to '90s-themed raves.

Landet *p201*
Mix with Midsommarkransen's media crowd.

Riche *p197*
Östermalm's flash-pack hangout.

Slakthuset *p201*
Rave in the former meatpacking district.

Södra Teatern *p201*
A stunning space for international acts.

Stockholm Under Stjärnorna *p197*
Cocktails and DJs on a giant roof terrace.

Trädgården *p199*
Outdoor partying beneath an iconic bridge.

Debaser Strand

In the know
Förfest

The high price of alcohol, an integral part of the city's nightlife, means that people tend to go out pretty late at the weekend, after first having a *förfest* (pre-party) at someone's house. If you're invited to one and want to bring a bottle, remember that the state monopoly alcohol stores (*Systembolaget*) close at 3pm on Saturdays and are closed altogether on Sundays. During the week, Swedes tend to go out much earlier; happy hour typically starts at 4pm and many locals sit down to eat at 6pm. On sunny summer days, outdoor terraces are packed from lunchtime.

CLUBS & MUSIC VENUES

Stockholm's nightlife is concentrated in the inner city, split between Stureplan, the hub of the town's VIP world of limos and high heels, and Södermalm, the creative district where former working-class inhabitants have been replaced by designers, DJs and musicians. Here, many of the live music venues also double up as late-night clubs. Norrmalm has some popular hangouts too, including the hotel bars around the newly revamped Brunkebergstorg area (*see p85*), which regularly invite Nordic and international DJs to play.

Vasastan and Kungsholmen have fewer options, although there are a couple of crowd-pleasing neighbourhood late-night bars if you feel like dancing to guilty pleasures. Nightlife in Gamla Stan combines tourist hangouts, small-stage pubs and gay venues. Gröna Lund theme park (*see p198*) on Djurgården island hosts live music events throughout the summer, as well as popular salsa nights.

Check social media for pop-up clubs at artsy venues such as **Fotografiska** (*see p198*), **Färgfabriken** (*see p201*) and **Münchenbryggeriet** (*see p200*). Two very popular nights with locals are *Out of Office* (www.oooaw.com), a monthly commercial club night, and *Natten* (@nattenstockholm on Facebook), a semi-regular power ballads event, which lures in even the most ice-cool of Stockholmers.

Large-scale venues
Friends Arena
Råsta Strandväg 1, 169 56 Solna (077 170 70 70, www.friendsarena.se). T-bana Solna centrum or bus 502, 505. Box office 10am-1pm Mon-Fri & 2hs before events. Tickets prices vary.

With a capacity for 75,000 people, Friends Arena is the largest venue in the city: a giant illuminated setting for the biggest Swedish and international live music stars when they come to town, as well as major sporting events. Coldplay, Guns n' Roses and Eminem are among the acts to have performed here since it opened in 2012.

Globen
Globentorget 2, Johanneshov (information 08 600 91 00, box office 077 131 00 00, www.stockholmlive.com/en/our-arenas/ericsson-globe). T-bana Globen. Box office 9am-6pm Mon-Fri; 10am-2pm Sat, Sun. Admission varies.

Like it or not (and many don't), you can't deny that Globen – still the world's largest

LGBTQ Stockholm

Out and about in the Swedish capital

NIGHTLIFE

In comparison with other European capitals, Stockholm's gay scene can seem underwhelming. There's no gay neighbourhood and few specific bars. One reason for this lack of exuberance is that Stockholm is a thoroughly enlightened city by global standards. Although there are venues that attract a loyal LGBTQ following, they tend not to be exclusive: basically, if a bar or café or club is any good, everyone wants to go there regardless of their sexual orientation or gender identity. LGBTQ visitors may want to make a note of out-and-proud clubs, such as **Club Backdoor** (see p201), **Patricia** (see p200), **Sidetrack** (see p201) and **SLM** (see p201), but they shouldn't feel restricted to these venues.

The trick with Stockholm is not to judge it on what it lacks, but to appreciate that what it offers is unique and wonderful. When the weather is good, the city can be magical. Standing on the deck of *Patricia* and watching the sun set (or rise); having a fancy cocktail at **Mälarpaviljongen** (see p164), or going for a post-club swim in the centre of town (see p149 Top 20) – these are the sorts of experiences that only Stockholm can deliver, and they're open to everyone.

While the LGBTQ scene is understated for much of the year, it really lets its hair down for **Stockholm Pride** (www.stockholmpride.org; see p183) in late July or early August. This is the largest Pride event in Scandinavia and is an excuse to celebrate the city's open, inclusive nature. The focus is Pride Park, a ticketed festival with a concert stage and food stalls set up by some of the city's cafés and bars. There's also a huge parade through the city, with floats representing groups ranging from gay fetish clubs to charities, universities and even the Swedish army and police. For a full programme of events and tickets, see the website. For practical information for LGBTQ visitors, see p241.

spherical building – is one of Stockholm's most recognisable structures. It's also an arena for everything from sports events to gala parties and, of course, big-name concerts and events (Beyoncé performed in 2018 and Michelle Obama brought her book tour here in 2019). The atmosphere in the large stadium can be lacking, but Globe City does house smaller, more personal venues, such as Annexet.

Gamla Stan

Secret Garden
Kornhamnstorg 59 (08 599 01 959, www.secretgardensthlm.se). T-bana Gamla Stan. Open 11am-3am Mon-Fri; noon-3am Sat, Sun. Admission 100kr-150kr. Map p65 O10.

This compact late-night bar and restaurant is a popular LGBTQ hangout, with a long drinks list and affordable prices. There are usually DJs from Wednesday to Sunday. Karaoke nights were launched on Mondays in early 2019 and have remained a hit ever since. During the weekends it expands to include two dancefloors, with an additional basement area opened on the busiest nights.

Stampen
Stora Gråmunkegränd 7 (08 20 57 93, www.stampen.se). T-bana Gamla Stan. Open 5pm-1am Tue-Fri, Sun; 2pm-1am Sat. Admission free-160kr. Map p65 N10.

Once a pawn shop, tiny Stampen is Stockholm's best-known jazz pub. It might have passed its heyday, but interesting live acts still appear every night, playing swing, dixie, trad jazz, blues, rockabilly and country. The crowd is more mature (and touristy) these days.

Norrmalm & Vasastan

Berns
Berzelii Park (08 566 32 200, www.berns.se). T-bana Kungsträdgården or bus 2, 54, 55, 67, 69. Open varies; see website for details. Map p80 O7.

Located in the landmark Berns Hotel, one of the longest-running entertainment hubs in the city, this sprawling late-night venue has several spaces where you can drink or dance the night away. **Stora Salongen**, a huge wooden-panelled room, hosts major international artists, with live acts ranging from US folk band the Lumineers to veteran German house DJ Paul Kalkbrenner in recent years. Local DJs mix on **Terrasen**, a terrace area overlooking the statues and flowerbeds of Berzelii Park. Downstairs in the basement, **Neu** is an electro club, with a more underground feel and impressive lasers (it is closed during the summer).

Café Opera
Kungliga Operan, Karl XIIs Torg (08 676 58 07, www.cafeopera.se). T-bana

Kungsträdgården or bus 2, 54, 65, 69. **Open** 10pm-3am daily. **Admission** 150kr. Minimum age 23. **Map** p80 N8.

Café Opera, which first opened in 1980, has a long reputation as a nightlife landmark. There's a mixed crowd here, from businessmen with ties round their foreheads and girls in tiny dresses to media folk, celebrities and even the odd royal bumbling about. VIP tables take up much of the space. The interior is grand, with chandeliers and ornate pillars. Note that the entry queue can become unbearable in the small hours, so try to arrive before midnight.

Cliff Barnes

Norrtullsgatan 45 (08 31 80 70, www. cliff. se). T-bana Odenplan or bus 2, 40, 65. **Open** 5-10pm Tue; 5-11pm Wed, Thur; 3pm-1am Fri; 5pm-1am Sat. **Admission** free. **Map** p80 K3.

On the outskirts of Vasastan, in what was once a home for widows, Cliff Barnes is a down-to-earth party bar-restaurant. The worn wooden floors, high ceilings and large vaulted windows make it ideal for enthusiastic beer drinking and loud conversation. At 11pm on Fridays and Saturdays, the lights are turned down and the music (popular classics from the 1960s to today) is turned up. Cliff Barnes takes its name from JR's unlucky arch-rival in the '80s US TV show Dallas.

F12 Terrassen

Fredsgatan 12, (08 505 24 400). T-bana T-centralen or bus 65. **Open** late May-early Sept 10pm-3am Mon-Thur; 10pm-5am Fri, Sat; midnight-5am Sun. Closed mid Sept-mid May. **Admission** 75kr before 11pm, 125kr after 11pm Mon-Thur; 100kr before 11pm, 200kr after 11pm Sat; 120kr Sun. Minimum age 21. **Map** p80 M8.

Renovated in 2019, this summer-only terrace bar, with a huge iconic staircase, has a plum location, moments from Stockholm central station and the old town. Its managers have focused on bringing in quality DJs and live acts in recent years, across a range of genres from electro to hip hop.

Fasching

Kungsgatan 63 (08 20 00 66, www.fasching. se). T-bana T-centralen or Hötorget. **Open** 6pm-midnight Mon-Thur, Sun; 6pm-4am Fri, Sat (check website for concert times). **Admission** 100kr-450kr. Minimum age 20 (18 for concerts). **Map** p80 L7.

There are gigs and jam sessions at this legendary jazz hangout six nights a week, but it's the late-night weekend club nights that really lift the roof. Club Soul, which has been running for more than 25 years, is a clubbing

institution that packs the dancefloor with the best in funk, northern soul and disco.

Glenn Miller Café

Brunnsgatan 21 (076 882 45 49, www. glennmillercafe.se). T-bana Hötorget or Östermalmstorg. **Open** 6pm-midnight or 1am Wed-Sun. **Admission** free (reserve in advance to get a table). **Map** p80 N6.

This simple, cosy jazz pub has live music several nights a week. The intimate space is often packed with a mix of older fans and thirtysomethings who are mates with the band. If you love jazz and aren't claustrophobic, this is a great choice.

Nalen

Regeringsgatan 74 (08 505 29 200, www.nalen.com). T-bana Hötorget or Östermalmstorg. **Open** varies; see website for details. **Admission** varies. **Map** p80 N6.

Built in 1888, Nalen was famous as a jazz mecca from the 1930s until the end of the '60s, when a church took over and got rid of all that sinful noise. Thoroughly renovated, Nalen now caters for all kinds of live music, from jazz and folk to pop and hip hop, and hosts occasional club nights.

Solidaritet

Lästmakargatan 3 (08 678 10 50, www. solidaritet.eu). T-bana Östermalmstorg. **Open** 11pm-5am Wed; 1-5am Thur; 11pm-5am Fri, Sat. **Admission** varies; check website for details. Minimum age 18 Wed; 21 Thur; 22 Fri, Sat. **Map** p80 N6.

Don't let the name fool you. Solidaritet (Solidarity) is the quintessential Stureplan bar/club with a long queue, steep cover charge, sleek Miami Vice-inspired interior and plenty of reserved tables. The venue has

Stockholm Under Stjärnorna

two spacious levels and four bars, with DJs playing electronic and house music. Dress smartly and arrive before 11pm to avoid the queue.

♥ Stockholm Under Stjärnorna
Brunkebergstorg 2-4 (www. sthlmunderstjarnorna.com). T-bana T-centralen. **Open** *3-11pm Mon-Wed; 3pm-midnight Thur; 3pm-1am Fri; 1pm-1am Sat; 1-10pm Sun.* **Admission** *free.* **Map** *p80 N8.*

'Stockholm beneath the stars' is a huge rooftop bar that boasts one of the best views in the capital, overlooking the royal palace. Although it's only open until 1am, there's a party vibe on Friday and Saturday nights, with live DJs and a smart crowd sipping cocktails as they dance. There are heated areas for cooler nights or when the sun goes down. Access is via street-level lifts in an office block next to Hobo Hotel, although Stockholm Under Sjärnorna is actually part of the group that owns the At Six Hotel, further up the street. Take the elevator to the top floor and cross over the walkway.

Tranan Bar
Karlbergsvägen 14 (08 527 28 100, www. tranan.se). T-bana Odenplan or bus 2, 4, 40, 65, 96. **Open** *11.30am-11pm Mon-Wed; 11.30am-midnight Thur, Fri; noon-11pm Sat, Sun.* **Map** *p80 K4.*

The basement bar beneath classic Swedish restaurant **Tranan** (*see p97*) is open late every night of the week. There are DJs at weekends and sporadic live music by an eclectic mix of performers: Tom Waits, A Tribe Called Quest and Craig David have all put on a show here.

Vasateatern
Vasagatan 19 (08 512 52 000, www. scandichotels.se/hotell/sverige/stockholm/ scandic-grand-central/vasateatern). T-bana T-centralen or bus 1. **Open** *varies.* **Admission** *varies.* **Map** *p80 L7.*

This private theatre, next to the Scandic Grand Central Hotel, transforms into an intimate semi-regular gig venue for local and global artists. Dating back to 1886, it reopened in 2016 after extensive renovations, yet still retains many charming period details, including decorated columns and glittering chandeliers.

Östermalm

East
Stureplan 13 (08 611 49 59, www.east.se). T-bana Östermalmstorg. **Open** *11.30am-3am Mon-Fri; noon-3am Sat; 5pm-3am Sun.* **Admission** *free. No cash.* **Map** *p102 O6.*

A sushi restaurant by day, East turns into a hip hop and soul hangout by night. Two bars serve beer and cocktails, while a DJ plays to a diverse crowd. In summer, East has an outdoor bar-terrace area that offers a great chance to people-watch in the area around Stureplan.

Hell's Kitchen
Sturegatan 4 (08 545 07 601, www. stureplansgruppen.se/nattliv/hells-kitchen). T-bana Östermalmstorg. **Open** *11pm-5am Thur-Sat. Minimum age 23.* **Map** *p102 O6.*

This bar is a bit of a novelty for Stureplan, as it's not just for posh boys and pretty girls, but also for music aficionados in their 30s who just don't want to go to bed (after 3am). The philosophy is 'rampant maximalism', hence the individual waitress service at every table.

Obaren
Stureplan 2 (08 440 57 30, www.obaren.se). T-bana Östermalmstorg. **Open** *8pm-2am daily.* **Admission** *free.* **Map** *p102 O6.*

Walking past the older restaurant crowd sitting down for a classy dinner at the exclusive Sturehof restaurant (*see p109*) can feel awkward, but it adds to the thrill when you step into the dark rock, hip hop and soul den hidden at the back. Obaren has a bar and dancefloor bounded by bleacher-like seats, but the place is small and can get overcrowded. Check the website for regular free live gigs.

♥ Riche
Birger Jarlsgatan 4 (08 545 03 560, www. riche.se). T-bana Östermalmstorg. **Open** *7.30am-midnight Mon; 7.30am-1am Tue; 7.30am-2am Wed-Fri; 11am-2am Sat; noon-midnight Sun.* **Admission** *free* **Map** *p102 O7.*

A favourite with Stockholm's business, media and advertising professionals, Riche is more atmospheric than most Stureplan bars. Twenty- and thirtysomethings hang out in the smaller bar (Lilla Baren) with loud DJs and spontaneous dancing. The larger bar-dining area features an older crowd who remember when Riche was the coolest place in town in the 1980s. The two queues get bad around 11pm at weekends.

Sturecompagniet
Sturegatan 4 (08 545 07 600, www. sturecompagniet.se). T-bana Östermalmstorg. **Open** *10pm-3am Thur-Sat. Admission varies. Minimum age 23.* **Map** *p102 O6.*

This beautiful three-storey, five-dancefloor party palace, with an elaborate interior of marble, roses and purple, is where the rich and famous play at the weekend. It can make for a great (if rather expensive) night out if you get in, but the bouncers are selective about who makes it through the doors.

Djurgården

Cirkus

Djurgårdsslätten 43-45 (box office 08 660 10 20, www.cirkus.se). Bus 67 or tram 7 or ferry from Slussen. **Open** *varies; see website for details.* **Admission** *varies.* **Map** *p118 S10.*

Cirkus is a live music venue housed in a cylindrical wooden structure that was built in 1892 for circus troupes. There's seating for 1,700, plus a bar and restaurant. It's an awe-inspiring place and attracts some big names, but concerts can lack atmosphere due to it being an all-seated venue. Comedy acts and shows also perform here.

Gröna Lund

Allmänna Gränd (010 708 91 00, www.gronalund.com). Bus 67 or tram 7 or ferry from Slussen. **Open** *shows 8pm. Park opening times vary. Check website for details.* **Admission** *tickets 290kr (access to all concerts throughout the summer).* **Map** *p118 S10.*

Sweden's oldest amusement park hosts regular gigs during summer, from emerging Swedish artists to global superstars: Elton John, Lionel Richie, Sting, the Cardigans and Lennie Kravitz have all performed here over the past few years. Prepare to face long queues when there's a big act. For more on the amusement park, *see p122.*

Pop House

Djurgårdsvägen 68 (08 502 54 140, https://pophouse.se). Bus 67 or tram 7 or ferry 82. **Open** *varies; see website for details.* **Admission** *free.* **Map** *p118 S10.*

Housed in the same building as ABBA The Museum and run by the same team, the Pop House Hotel (*see p231*) capitalises on its musical connections with regular live gigs that are popular with both guests and locals. These take place in its rustic conservatory area, Glashuset, where you can dance between the giant indoor pot plants. Although there's plenty of cheesy Europop, especially in the run-up to the Eurovision Song Contest or during Stockholm Pride week, the venue showcases a wide range of Sweden-based artists and singer-songwriters.

Södermalm

♥ Debaser Strand

Hornstulls Strand 9 (08 462 98 60, www.debaser.se). T-bana Hornstull or bus 54. **Open** *times vary.* **Admission** *varies.* **Map** *p147 G13.*

Named after a Pixies song, Debaser quickly became one of the leading live rock venues in the city when it opened in an old distillery in Slussen in 2002. The venue moved to the site of the former Strand club in Hornstull in late 2013 and has retained the industrial feel, with dark walls and red accents. Bands play here seven nights a week, and there's DJ action on club nights. The Debaser-run Mexican restaurant Calexico's is next door, alongside Bar Brooklyn.

Fotografiska

Stadsgårdshamnen 22 (08 509 00 500, www.fotografiska.com/sto/upplev/mat-dryck/studiolive). T-bana Slussen. **Open** *Terrace 11am-10pm daily. See website for upcoming dates.* **Admission** *included in museum entry price 165kr.* **Map** *p134 Q12.*

Stockholm's huge photography museum is a must-see (*see p139*), but what many visitors don't know is that Fotografiska also puts on regular live music events (called Studio Live), which move to its terrace during the summer months. There are also occasional club nights.

Glashuset WY13

Hellstens Glashus, Wollmar Yxkullsgatan 13 (08 460 07 900, hellstensglashus.se). T-bana Mariatorget. **Open** *Live music late Aug-late May usually 8pm Wed.* **Admission** *free.* **Map** *p134 M12.*

Designed to channel Manhattan vibes, with its exposed brick walls and leather sofas, this is an intimate live music venue inside Hellstens Glashus hotel. Open since 2017, it welcomes up-and-coming local and international artists. Bigger names also occasionally perform smaller gigs here to experiment with new material or simply to feel more closely connected to their fans.

Kafé 44

Tjärhovsgatan 46 (08 644 53 12, www.kafe44.org). T-bana Medborgarplatsen. **Open** *varies; see website for details. Closed July.* **Admission** *40kr-100kr. No cards.* **Map** *p134 P12.*

This hangout for Södermalm's anarchists hosts punk and rock concerts, as well as an alternative, righteous brand of hip hop. There's no minimum age limit and no alcohol is served, but with the sort of bands that play here, you won't need a drink to get a kick. Music nights (usually Tuesdays and Thursdays) aren't normally held during the summer months; visit the Facebook page for updates.

Kvarnen

Tjärhovsgatan 4, (08 643 03 80, www.kvarnen.com). T-bana Medborgarplatsen. **Open** *11am-1am Mon, Tue; 11am-3am Wed-Fri, noon-3am Sat; noon-1am Sun.* **Map** *p134 O13 .*

💙 Trädgården

*Hammarby Slüssvag 2 (08 644 20 23, www.
tradgarden.com). T-bana Skanstull.* **Open**
*May-Sept 8pm-3am Tue; 5pm-3am Wed-Fri;
2pm-3am Sat; 3pm-1am Sun.* **Admission**
free-170kr. Minimum age 21. **Map** *p134 P16.*

No trip to Stockholm between May and
September is complete without a visit to the
mother of outdoor party spaces, Trädgården.
Sprawling beneath a giant concrete bridge,
the capital's largest open-air club is home
to a massive courtyard dance area, a burger
shack, table tennis, a pizza joint and a jigsaw
of smaller terraces and bars that burst into
life with DJs and live bands during peak
season. When the evening sun is shining at
Trädgården, Stockholmers rip out of their
stereotype as a closed and shy bunch and
become gregarious extroverts. Book ahead
for the popular Daytime Sessions, which
draw respected EDM, garage and house DJs.

Open since 2003, much of this venue's
spirit is thanks to its charismatic founders,
Jakob Grandin and Johan Wiklund. Grandin
has since gone on to launch the successful
annual Gather Festival *(see p184)*, which,
since 2017, has combined live music gigs
and DJs with global speakers designed
to make guests question society and its
future. Another of Trädgården's alumni

In the know
Under Bron

During the colder seasons, Trädgården
scales down to a two-floor techno and
electro club called Under Bron (Under the
Bridge). This has a much more underground
feel, and the crowd itself seems cooler and
more reserved than during the summer
months. Wrap up warm and prepare for a
long queue.

is Australian-born former front-of-house
manager Kristian Hell, who became the first
'lifestyle concierge' at Downtown Camper by
Scandic Hotel *(see p231)* in 2017. He is also
the founder of Ssideline City Run Club, one
of the most dynamic sporting communities
in the city, which organises cheering events
and legendary parties connected to some of
the city's biggest races.

While Trädgården remains a Stockholm
institution, it has faced tough competition
in recent years, jostling for attention with
newer outdoor spaces such as **Stockholm
Under Sjärnorna** *(see p197)* and **Urban
Deli Takpark** *(see p142)*, as well as classic
terrace venues such as **Södra Teatern** *(see
p201)* and the revamped **F12** *(see p196)*.

NIGHTLIFE

Originally a beer hall, Kvarnen (Windmill) has evolved into one of the most popular late-night pubs on Söder; it even features in Stieg Larsson's bestseller *The Girl with the Dragon Tattoo*. The lofty main room, filled with rows of tables and loud chatter, retains the look and feel of a beer hall. It is flanked by two more recent additions: a smaller, more industrial bar in what used to be a kitchen, and a basement bar, where the music is cranked up at weekends. For details of the restaurant, *see p141*.

Laika

Långholmsgatan 15B (08 525 20 260, www. hornhuset.se). T-bana Hornstull. **Open** *5pm-1am Tue-Thur, Sat; 4pm-1am Fri.* **Map** *p147 G12.*

This low-lit industrial venue, with a focus on live acts and DJs, is situated on the second floor of the glass-fronted Hornhuset complex in Hornstull (the rest of the venue is made up of restaurants). You can rest your legs in the shabby-chic lounge corner by the bar where there are vintage chairs and sofas.

Morfar Ginko

Swedenborgsgatan 13 (08 641 13 40, www. morfarginko.se). T-bana Mariatorget. **Open** *4pm-1am Mon-Thur; 3pm-1am Fri-Sun.* **Admission** *free.* **Map** *p134 M12.*

Glowing neon signs, exposed silver pipes and walls lined with scuffed white tiles set the tone for this industrial-chic bar. DJs are a frequent addition at weekends, playing to the crowd from a mini loft above the back bar. Morfar Ginko is popular with Stockholm's LGBTQ crowd and sometimes hosts lesbian events and festivals.

Munchenbryggeriet

Munchenbryggeriet, Torkel Knutssonsgatan 2 (08 658 20 00, www.munchenbryggeriet. se). T-bana Mariatorget. **Open** *times vary; see website for details.* **Admission** *varies.* **Map** *p134 L11.*

This long-running concert hall and arts space inside a converted red-brick brewery is one of the best places to catch a gig in Stockholm. It's a popular venue with electro-acoustic and indie acts who've outgrown Södermalm's smaller venues, but still want to perform in a space with plenty of atmosphere.

Nada Bar

Åsögatan 140 (08 644 70 20). T-bana Medborgarplatsen or bus 2, 3, 53, 76. **Open** *5pm-1am Mon-Sat.* **Map** *p134 P13.*

With regular DJs specialising in old school R'n'B, hip hop and a sprinkling of UK garage classics, Nada is a petite, cosy, low-lit bar that transforms into a compact dancefloor at weekends. It typically attracts a fun-loving unpretentious crowd of twenty- and thirtysomethings.

Patricia

Söder Mälarstrand, Berth 19 (08 743 05 70, www.patriciastockholm.se). T-bana Mariatorget. **Open** *6pm-midnight Thur; 6pm-5am Fri-Sun.* **Admission** *120kr after 9pm; 150kr after midnight.* **Map** *p134 L11.*

The *Patricia* was built in Middlesbrough in the UK and once served a stint as the royal yacht of Queen Elizabeth, the Queen Mother, but now it's established as one of the crown jewels of gay life in Stockholm. Every Sunday for the past 15 or so years, Stockholm's LBGTQ crowd have gathered here to eat, drink and

Södra Teatern

dance on this three-level party boat, now moored at Söder Mälarstrand. It mostly attracts a slightly more mature crowd than the city's other gay venues.

Sidetrack

*Wollmar Yxkullsgatan 7 (08 641 16 88, www. sidetrack.nu). T-bana Mariatorget. **Open** 6pm-1am Wed-Sat. **Map** p134 M12.*

Primarily a late-night basement bar, this is one of Stockholm's longest-running gay drinking and eating spots. Calm during the week, it gets very lively at weekends. It's a popular place for a pre-drink.

SLM

*Wollmar Yxkullsgatan 18 (08 643 31 00, www.slmstockholm.se). T-bana Mariatorget. **Open** 7pm-midnight Wed; 10pm-2am Fri; 10pm-3am Sat. **Admission** Non-members 50kr after 11pm Sat. **Map** p134 M12.*

Scandinavian Leather Men (SLM) is a men-only basement fetish bar that brings a little corner of Berlin to Stockholm. A heavy door and flight of stairs lead down to a labyrinth of darkrooms, bars and a dancefloor. See the website for more information.

♥ Södra Teatern

*Mosebacketorg 1-3 (08 480 04 400, www. sodrateatern.com). T-bana Slussen. **Open** box office 2hrs before performance. **Admission** varies. **Map** p134 O12.*

This cultural complex has always got something interesting going on. Built in 1859, the main auditorium, **Stora Scenen** (capacity 400), has red velvet chairs and puts on pop, electronic, jazz and folk concerts. Otherwise there's world music, plus poetry readings and spoken word. Indie, house and hip hop nights are hosted in the bar and club area, and there are DJs on the outdoor terraces in summer.

South of Södermalm

Club Backdoor

*Arenavägen 75, Johanneshov (www. facebook.com/clubbackdoor). T-bana Globen or bus 4, 94. **Open** 11pm-5am Tue, Thur-Sat. **Admission** free but some events ticketed.*

The most popular Friday night hangout for Stockholm's LGBTQ community, Club Backdoor describes itself as the best and gayest club north of Ibiza. It focuses on electronic music, although it also has a smaller pop/house stage. There are occasional drag queen shows here and plenty of strobe lights.

Färgfabriken

*Lövholmsbrinken 1, Liljeholmen (08 645 07 07, www.fargfabriken.se). T-bana Liljeholmen. **Open** times vary; see website for details. **Admission** 70kr; 60kr reductions; free under-18s. **Map** pull-out map E13.*

The Centre for Contemporary Art and Architecture, housed in an old factory in the southern suburb of Liljeholmen (across the bridge from Hornstull), occupies an important position on the Stockholm art scene. But it's more than just a gallery, as the arts space turns into a glowing electro club, concert hall and/or party venue on specific weekends.

♥ Landet

*LM Ericssons väg 27, Hägersten (08 410 19 320, www.landet.nu). T-bana Telefonplan or bus 147. **Open** 4pm-11pm Mon, Tue; 4pm-midnight Wed, Thur; 4pm-1am Fri, Sat.*

In the vibrant suburb of Midsommarkransen, students and media folk flock to Landet ('countryside'), a laid-back restaurant and bar. There are regular gigs from local bands (usually Wed-Sat).

♥ Slakthuset

*Slakthusgatan 6, Johanneshov (www. slakthuset.nu). T-bana Globen. **Open** 10pm-3am Fri, Sat. **Admission** varies. Minimum age 21.*

This mega-club is a far cry from the Stureplan glitz. It's far out, in the meatpacking district south of Södermalm. There are still traces of its former incarnation as a slaughterhouse in the form of rusty meat hooks and refrigerators. These raw and gritty details from the past are mixed up with heavy velvet drapes and designer furniture. The programme focuses on electronic club nights, with some live music thrown into the mix. It has a popular outdoor terrace, open during the summer months.

Kungsholmen

Lemon

*Scheelegatan 8 (08 650 17 78, www. lemonbar.se). T-bana Rådhuset. **Open** 5pm-1am Tue; 5pm-3am Wed-Sat. **Admission** free. **Map** p159 J8.*

A no-frills bar with an underground dancefloor, Lemon is a popular venue with Stockholmers who don't take themselves too seriously. Here, you'll find plenty of locals doing shots and letting loose to commercial club tracks.

Performing Arts

Classical music and contemporary dance take centre stage on the Stockholm cultural scene

Stockholm has far more ensembles and performing arts venues than most cities of a similar size, boasting two full-strength symphony orchestras that can compete with the best in Europe, two permanent opera houses, three major theatres and a healthy chamber music scene. Such riches are partly down to the fact that the old Swedish social democratic cultural policy prevails when it comes to the arts, with the state subsidising many cultural institutions.

Whereas local theatre tends to be rather staid and mostly of local interest (unless you have a strong grasp of Swedish), the Stockholm dance scene is considerably more international in outlook. Innovative modern dance, led by Dansens Hus, is particularly vibrant, and dance theatre is also big in the city.

Kulturhuset Stadsteatern *p205*

❤ Best cultural venues

Dansens Hus *p207*
The apex of the city's contemporary dance scene.

Konserthuset *p204*
A fitting home for the Royal Stockholm Philharmonic Orchestra.

Kulturhuset Stadsteatern *p84, p205*
Theatre, art, lectures and more.

Kungliga Operan *p205*
Opera and ballet in a neo-Baroque landmark.

CLASSICAL MUSIC & OPERA

The music and opera calendar is seasonal, running from August to June, with concerts held primarily on weekdays. In the summer, the focus moves to the outdoor theatres and parks around town. One exception is the **Stockholm Konserthuset**, which stays open in July. Two other important dates are the five-day **Stockholm Early Music Festival** (www.semf.se; *see p183*) in June, and the **Baltic Sea Festival** in late August (*see right*). The monthly English-language tourist magazine *Totally Stockholm* (www.totallystockholm.se) has some concerts in its listings; you'll also find information in the culture section of daily newspaper *Dagens Nyheter* (www.dn.se/kalendariet). You can buy tickets by phone or online from most venues. For major venues and listings, try **Ticnet** (077 170 70 70, www.ticnet.se).

Venues & ensembles

Berwaldhallen

Dag Hammarskjölds väg 3, Östermalm (box office 08 784 18 00, www.berwaldhallen.se). Bus 4, 69, 76. **Box office** *noon-6pm Mon-Fri & 2hrs before show. By phone 9am-6pm Mon-Fri; 10am-3pm Sat; 2hrs before show.* **Tickets** *vary.* **Map** *p102 S7.*

The Berwaldhallen was built in 1979 for the **Sveriges Radio Symfoniorkester** (Swedish Radio Symphony Orchestra) and the **Radiokören** (Radio Choir). The acclaimed modernist hall, surrounded by parkland, is mainly underground. The Symfoniorkester, established in 1967, enjoyed a particularly successful period under the direction of Finn Esa-Pekka Salonen during the second half of the 1980s. The orchestra has a more contemporary touch than other Swedish orchestras, commissioning a significant

amount of new music from home-grown and international composers. The Radiokören, in turn, is considered to be one of the best choirs in the world. The Berwaldhallen is the main venue for the **Baltic Sea Festival** in late August, which uses classical music as a platform to promote sustainability and environmental awareness in the Baltic region.

Folkoperan

Hornsgatan 72, Södermalm (box office 08 616 07 50, www.folkoperan.se). T-bana Mariatorget. **Box office** *by phone 9am-6pm Mon-Fri; 10am-2pm Sat. Card only.* **Tickets** *vary.* **Map** *p134 L12.*

Folkoperan has been a healthy rival to Kungliga Operan (*see p205*) since its founding in 1976. Its modern stagings of classic operas sung in Swedish, its unconventional and often controversial productions and the intimacy of the auditorium are among Folkoperan's distinctive features. The main season runs from September to May, when there are performances most nights of the week. The bar and restaurant are popular with a trendy young crowd.

Hedvig Eleonora Church

Storgatan 7, Östermalm (08 545 67 570, www.hedvigeleonora.se). T-bana Östermalmstorg. **Concerts** *Sept-May 12.15pm Wed.* **Admission** *free.* **Map** *p102 P6.*

This church is known for its free 30-minute lunchtime performances, which it has been putting on since the 1950s. There are ticketed evening concerts too, including by the Stockholm Sinfonietta, which has worked with a host of venerable names, including conductors Sixten Ehrling and Okko Kamu, and soloists such as Catalan soprano Montserrat Caballé and Swedish cellist Frans Helmerson. The repertoire stretches all the way from Baroque to contemporary. For more on the church, *see p104*.

❤ Konserthuset

Hötorget 8, Norrmalm (box office 08 50 66 77 88, www.konserthuset.se). T-bana Hötorget. **Box office** *11am-6pm Mon-Fri (mid June-mid Aug 11am-5pm); 11am-3pm Sat; 2hrs before show.* **Tickets** *vary.* **Map** *p80 M7.*

Konserthuset has been the home of the **Kungliga Filharmonikerna** (Royal Stockholm Philharmonic Orchestra) since its inauguration in 1926, and Sakari Oramo has been principal conductor since 2008. Architect Ivar Tengbom wanted to 'raise a musical temple not far from the Arctic Circle', and the bright blue structure is one of the foremost examples of early 20th-century Swedish neoclassical design. The 1,800-seat Main Hall is used for major concerts, while the beautiful Grünewald Hall (capacity

460), decorated by painter Isaac Grünewald, handles smaller chamber music concerts. Konserthuset's repertoire is based solidly in the classical and romantic periods, but it also hosts the renowned and well-established **Stockholm International Composer Festival** each autumn, focusing on living composers.

💜 Kungliga Operan

Gustav Adolfs Torg 2, Norrmalm (box office 791 44 00, www.operan.se). T-bana Kungsträdgården or bus 2, 53, 55, 57, 62, 65, 76. **Box office** *noon-6pm Wed-Sat; 2hrs before show.* **Tickets** *vary; half-price under-26s & students.* **Map** *p80 N8.*

When it opened in 1782, the Royal Opera House was considered the height of modern design. Just 100 years later it was demolished to make way for the current opera house, which was inaugurated by King Oscar II in 1898. While the building's exterior is neo-Renaissance in style, its interior has a Baroque design. The most lavish room is the first-floor Golden Foyer (Guldfoajén), with murals by Carl Larsson, gold stucco walls and ceiling, and crystal chandeliers.

Contemporary art exhibitions are displayed here when the opera house is dark during the summer months.

The **Royal Opera** has sent a string of great singers on to the international stage – among them Jenny Lind, Jussi Björling, Birgit Nilsson and Elisabeth Söderström; the most talented leave the country at a young age and rarely return to the Kungliga. It's also home to the **Swedish Royal Ballet** (*see p207*). Note that the opera house is dark between June and the end of August, but there are guided tours throughout the year in Swedish and English (for details, call the main box office). For information on the opera house's restaurants, *see pp87-88*.

Riddarhuset

Riddarhustorget 10, Gamla Stan (www.riddarhuset.se). T-bana Gamla Stan or bus 3, 53. **Box office** *1hr before concert.* **Tickets** *free.* **Map** *p65 N9.*

Hosting classical concerts and lectures since 1731, Riddarhuset welcomes choirs and musical ensembles from across Sweden. It holds a popular concert on Sweden's national day (6 June) each year.

THEATRE

Kungliga Dramatiska Teatern, or Dramaten, is Sweden's national theatre, established in 1788. Over the years it has hosted a large number of superb actors and directors (most famously, Ingmar Bergman). The city's other key theatre, **Stockholms Stadsteatern**, located in the Kulturhuset, also has numerous stages and has a wider repertoire than Dramaten.

The largest commercial theatre, showing large-scale musicals and comedies (in Swedish), is **Oscarsteatern** (Kungsgatan 63, 08 20 50 00, www.oscarsteatern.se). Other commercial theatres include **Göta Lejon** (Götgatan 55, 08 505 29 00, www.gotalejon. se), **Maximteatern** (Karlaplan 4, 08 30 11 00, www.maximteatern.com), **Intiman** (Odengatan 81, 08 30 12 50, www.intiman.nu) and **China Teatern** (Berzelii Park 9, 08 562 892 00, www.chinateatern.se). **Cirkus** (*see p198*) also presents large-scale shows. **Södra Teatern** (*see p201*) is mainly a music venue, but occasionally puts on good theatre shows.

Major venues

💜 Kulturhuset Stadsteatern

Sergels torg, Norrmalm (box office 08 506 20 200, www.kulturhusetstadsteatern. se). T-bana T-centralen. **Box office** *11am-7pm Mon-Fri; 11am-5pm Sat, Sun.* **Tickets** *vary.* **Map** *p80 M7.*

Kungliga Operan

Reopening after refurbishment in autumn 2020, the Stockholm City Theatre at the House of Culture has sought to push boundaries in recent years with experimental drama and spoken-word events focused around themes ranging from the Me Too movement to gay activism. It is also the home to the popular **Marionetteatern** puppet theatre and organises the annual **Parkteatern** festival, when home-grown and international theatre and dance takes place in parks all over the city (*see p183*). Be aware that some listings on Kulturhuset Stadsteatern's website are for smaller venues around the city. For more on Kulturhuset, *see p84*.

Kungliga Dramatiska Teatern

Nybroplan, Östermalm (box office 08 667 06 80, www.dramaten.se). T-bana Östermalmstorg or Kungsträdgården, or bus 54, 69. **Box office** *noon-7pm Tue-Sat; noon-4pm Sun (summer times vary).* **Tickets** *150kr-450kr.* **Map** *p102 O7.*

The lavish Royal Dramatic Theatre (known as Dramaten) was built between 1902 and 1908 in Jugendstil style, with a white marble façade and gilded bronzework. The glorious interior features paintings and sculptures by Sweden's most famous artists: Theodor Lundberg created the golden statues of Poetry and Drama at the front; Carl Milles was responsible for the large sculptural group below the raised central section of the façade, and Carl Larsson painted the foyer ceiling. The theatre's architect, Fredrik Liljekvist, wanted to create a grand and imposing structure, and added the domed attic to give the building more prominence. It worked – the theatre is one of Stockholm's most striking landmarks, particularly when the setting sun hits the golden lampposts and statues. The auditorium is equally stunning.

Dramaten has several stages for its productions, which range from traditional plays to more modern offerings. Ingmar Bergman was the driving force at the theatre from the early 1960s, directing a colossal number of productions here, and the place also played host to a pre-Hollywood Greta Garbo. The main stage mounts plenty of Shakespeare and Strindberg, mixed with avant-garde dramatic works. A guided tour (in English at 4pm Tue-Sat) covers the main stage, smaller stages and rehearsal rooms. For a wonderful view over Nybroviken, visit the outdoor café.

Dramaten's other stage, **Elverket** (Linnégatan 69, Östermalm, *map p102 Q6*) – a converted power station – has a younger profile, producing modern drama, often with dance or Nouveau Cirque elements.

▶ *For more on Ingmar Bergman, see p191.*

Smaller venues & fringe groups

Since the 1970s, several experimental theatre groups working with new forms and expressions have sprung up, performing in smaller venues around the city. Of these, **Teater Galeasen** and **Moment** are two prominent groups that seldom disappoint. Stockholm is also home to English-language theatre company **SEST** (Stockholm English Speaking Theatre www.sestcompany. com), which performs Shakespeare plays at outdoor venues, such as Djurgården's Parkteatern and Drottningholm Palace in summer. **International Theater Stockholm** (www.internationaltheater. se) specialises in improvised comedy productions in English, which offer humorous insights into living, working and dating in Sweden.

Dockteatern Tittut

Lundagatan 33, Södermalm (box office 08 720 75 99, www.dockteaterntittut.se). T-bana Zinkensdamm. **Box office** *15mins before show.* **Tickets** *120kr.* **Map** *p147 J12.*

This puppet theatre in Södermalm has been making high-quality shows for children (aged from two) for more than 25 years, combining puppet and shadow play. Performances are during the daytime.

Fylkingen

Münchenbryggeriet, Torkel Knutssonsgatan 2, Södermalm (08 84 54 43, www.fylkingen. se). T-bana Mariatorget. **Box office** *varies.* **Tickets** *vary.* **Map** *p134 L11.*

Founded way back in 1933, Fylkingen is the place to be if you're into new music and intermedia art. It's always been committed to new and experimental forms: 'happenings' that combined musical theatre and text-sound compositions were prominent during the 1960s. In recent years, it has staged an increasing number of ambitious art and dance performances. Fylkingen holds several festivals each year; check the website for details of forthcoming events.

Orionteatern

Katarina Bangata 77, Södermalm (www. orionteatern.se, www.tickster.se). T-bana Skanstull or bus 3, 76. **Box office** *1hr before show. Closed midsummer-mid Aug.* **Tickets** *vary.* **Map** *p134 R15.*

The Orion Theatre, Stockholm's largest avant-garde company, was formed in 1983, and has since collaborated with the likes of Peking Opera from Shanghai and Complicité from London. The building, once a factory, makes an effective theatre space.

Playhouse Teater

Drottninggatan 71A, Norrmalm (08 654 40 30, www.playhouseteater. se). T-bana Hötorget or T-centralen. Tickets vary. Map p80 L6.

Sweden's only 'off-Broadway' theatre (meaning it's between the size of a main theatre and a fringe one) mainly shows plays from New York – both classics and award-winning new productions – translated into Swedish.

Strindbergs Intima Teater

Barnhusgatan 20, Norrmalm (www. strindbergsintimateater.se). T-bana Hötorget or T-centralen. Box office 30mins before performance. Tickets vary. Map p80 L6.

Founded by August Strindberg back in 1907, this small theatre used to show the dramatist's plays exclusively. Nowadays the programme, co-ordinated by Strindbergsmuseet, is more varied and includes guest performances and theatre for children.

Teater Galeasen

Slupskjulsvägen 30-32, Skeppsholmen (box office 08 611 00 30, www.galeasen. se). Bus 65. Box office tickets from website. Tickets vary. Map p118 Q9.

In the 1980s and early 1990s this was the hip spot for theatregoers. Nowadays, actors from that generation are household names. But Galeasen continues to be a breeding ground for young actors and directors, and the work on show here is still high quality.

Teater Pero

Sveavägen 114, Vasastaden (box office 08 612 99 00, www.pero.se). T-bana Rådmansgatan or bus 2, 4, 6, 50, 57, 61, 67, 72, 515. Box office 1hr before performance. Closed summer. Map p80 L4.

Teater Pero has a strong tradition of mime and has been producing shows for children and adults for more than 20 years.

DANCE

Ballet and classic performances by the **Kungliga Baletten** (Royal Ballet) are staged at the **Kungliga Operan** (*see p205*). The dancers are outstanding and, though the repertoire is largely traditional, there is occasionally some modern work on show. Beyond this, Stockholm has a strong and varied dance scene, reflecting its increasingly diverse population. **Moderna Dansteatern**, in Skeppsholmen, has been the home base for many freelance dancers and choreographers for more than 20 years, while **Dansens Hus** (House of Dance), which

opened in 1991, hosts visiting companies from around the world. In recent years it has welcomed the likes of Senegalese dancer and choreographer Germaine Acogny and Reykjavík-based award-winning troupe Dance For Me.

The Swedish capital has some impressive amateur youth and adult dance schools that regularly showcase their work. These include **Base23** (also known as Stockholm Dance Academy; www.base23.se), which teaches genres from street dance to musical theatre, and **Layali Orientaliska Dansakademi** (www.orientaliskdans.se), which specialises in Arabic dance. To watch some of the city's best hobby lindy hop, charleston and jazz dancers in action, head to **Chicago Swing Dance Studio** in Södermalm (www. chicago75.se). Stockholm also has a huge salsa and *bachata* scene, so look out for international stars visiting throughout the year, giving both performances and workshops (see www.stockholmsalsadance. com for information). For dance listings, check the Swedish-language magazine *Danstidningen* (www.danstidningen.se) or the culture section of daily newspaper *Dagens Nyheter* (www.dn.se/kalendariet).

Venues

♥ Dansens Hus

Barnhusgatan 12-14, Norrmalm (box office 08 508 99 090, www.dansenshus. se). T-bana Hötorget or T-Centralen. Box office 4-6pm Tue-Fri; 2hrs before show Sat, Sun. Closed Midsummer-mid Sept. Tickets vary. Map p80 L6.

The two-stage House of Dance is the major venue for Swedish dance, with around 35 performances a year. This is where you'll find the renowned **Cullberg Ballet** (www. cullberg baletten.se) when it's in town. The guest list might also include Anna Teresa de Keersmaeker's Rosas company, Nederlands Dans Theater and Akram Khan. Swedish dance group Bounce! has also been a huge success here, with its funny, street dance-inspired shows drawing large audiences.

Moderna Dansteatern (MDT)

Slupskjulsvägen 30, Skeppsholmen (www.mdtsthlm.se). Bus 65. Box office 045 561 97 00, www2.nortic.se/dagny/ organizer/546. Tickets 180kr; 90kr reductions. Map p118 Q9.

Sharing the space with Teater Galeasen, the small Modern Dance Theatre was founded by Margaretha Åsberg, the grande dame of Swedish dance, and single-handedly provides a space for postmodern and avant-garde dance in Stockholm. Performance art has also found a refuge here.

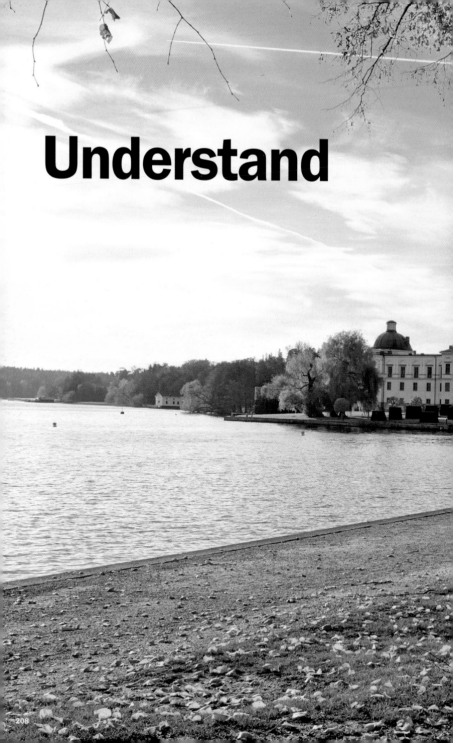

Understand

Drottningholms Slott *p215*

History

Blond ambition

Compared with many European capitals, Stockholm is a relative newcomer. While human activity in the region around Lake Mälaren dates back thousands of years, the city itself wasn't founded until the 13th century, when Birger Jarl came to power, following 300 years of Viking culture. The population of the island now known as Gamla Stan steadily grew, but it took until the 14th and 15th centuries for Stockholm to be recognised as Sweden's political and economic centre. It was during these centuries that the city started to expand, with the mainland area of Norrmalm and the large island of Södermalm forming new urban areas. Construction was, from here, unstoppable. The Royal Palace and Opera House were constructed in the 17th century, cementing Stockholm's place as one of Europe's cultural centres, while sea trading in the centuries that followed led to further growth and the city's increasing importance in the region.

Bolinders factory, 1900 *p217*

First tracks

The earliest evidence of human habitation in Sweden is of nomadic reindeer hunters from continental Europe, who seem to have followed the receding glaciers north into Scandinavia at the end of the last Ice Age in approximately 11,000 BC. By about 7500 BC, Mesolithic hunter-gatherers had migrated to the coastal areas of central and northern Sweden. Between 4000 and 2800 BC, villages dotted the southern half of the country and people eked out a living as farmers. Sweden's inhabitants began establishing trading links with the wider world during the Bronze Age (1500 to 500 BC). They had access to large supplies of fur and amber, which they traded for raw metals, weapons and decorative objects.

Between AD 550 and 1000 two main rival groups emerged – the Svear, who were based in the Lake Mälaren region, and the Götar, who controlled a swathe of territory to the west and south. The geographical terms Svealand and Götaland are still in use today, and Sverige, Sweden's modern name in Swedish, comes from Svea rike – the Svea kingdom.

While often violent, the Vikings of Sweden were somewhat more business-minded than those of Denmark and Norway

Viking spirit

The Viking culture emerged in various parts of Scandinavia in the early ninth century. The word 'Viking' is thought to come from the *viks* (Old Norse for 'inlets') in which they harboured their long ships. By the mid ninth century, these extremely capable mariners had reached both the Black and Caspian Seas, where they launched attacks on Byzantium and north-east Iran. While often violent, the Vikings of Sweden were somewhat more business-minded than those of Denmark and Norway, and they successfully developed lucrative trading contacts with Byzantium.

Taken as a group, the Vikings effectively dominated the political and economic life of Europe until the mid 11th century. Remnants of their civilisation have been uncovered at a number of sites not far from Stockholm's city limits, most notably at Birka, a town founded in about AD 700

that was Sweden's leading trading centre in the early tenth century. Gamla Uppsala is even older than Birka, with some of its royal graves dating back to the sixth century. The **Historiska Museet** (*see p106*) has an excellent exhibition introducing visitors to a wealth of information and artefacts that cast light on Viking culture.

The Swedes were among the last Europeans to abandon paganism. In spite of the efforts of a number of crusading monks and priests, and the baptism of King Olof Skötkonung in 1008 (and all his successors after him), many Swedes stubbornly remained true to the old Norse gods until the end of the 11th century. By the middle of the 12th century, the Church had finally gained a foothold and Sweden's first archbishopric was established in Uppsala. The first Swedish archbishop, appointed in 1164, was an English monk called Stephen. King Erik Jedvardsson (1156-60), who had led a crusade to christianise the Finns, was chosen to become Sweden's patron saint. He is commemorated in place names such as St Eriksplan and St Eriksgatan; his remains are entombed at **Uppsala Cathedral** (*see p173*).

Birth of a city

The foundation of Stockholm is intimately connected to the power struggles between the monarchy and the nobility that characterised Swedish history after the collapse of Viking culture. The physical city and its name can be traced to 13th-century ruler Birger Jarl.

Birger Jarl came to power in 1229, after the then king, Erik Erikssen, had been deposed. He is remembered for two main accomplishments: the long and turbulent process he initiated to centralise political power in Sweden, and the founding of the city of Stockholm. In 1247-51, he made great progress towards achieving his first goal by using German money and soldiers to successfully defeat a rebellion led by noblemen in the area around Lake Mälaren. Shortly after this victory he offered good trading terms to German merchants, especially those from Lübeck, which led to Sweden's long-lasting ties to the Hanseatic League.

The 13th-century Swedish kingdom consisted of the area around Lake Mälaren, the Stockholm and Åland archipelagos, and the Gulf of Finland all the way to Viborg (now part of Russia). Low sea levels meant that the passage from the Baltic Sea into Lake Mälaren was restricted to a narrow channel now known as Norrström. This passage became a vital trade route and a key defensive position, and in 1252 Birger Jarl constructed a mighty fortress on the site:

the **Tre Kronor** (on the site of the present Kungliga Slottet, *see p67*). It would grow to become the city of Stockholm.

In that same year, Birger Jarl wrote two letters in which the name 'Stockholm' is mentioned for the first time. The origin of the name is unclear, but it may be derived from the fact that logs (*stockar*) were used to build up the small island (*holme*) upon which the fortress was built.

The settlement at Tre Kronor soon became one of Sweden's most important economic centres. Ships from Lübeck and other Hanseatic towns traded enthusiastically with the expatriate Germans who were setting up copper and iron-ore mines in Sweden, while products from the interior of the country (fur, grain and iron) were traded with merchants from across northern Europe.

Birger Jarl's son Magnus took power in 1275. A renewed repression of the country's unruly nobles concentrated power in his hands, and the various edicts and rulings with which he limited the power of the nobility are credited with forestalling the development of feudalism in Sweden. After his death in 1290, power shifted briefly back to the nobility before Magnus's son Birger assumed the throne in 1302, but his rule was blighted by a power struggle with his brothers, who demanded that he divide the kingdom between them. In 1317, he had them arrested, thrown in prison and starved to death. The horrified nobility deposed him, forcing him to flee the country.

Magnus, the child of a Swedish duke and, at the age of three, already king of Norway, was to be his successor. Upon reaching adulthood Magnus assumed the throne and set about making changes to the Swedish social order. He abolished *träldom*, a form of slavery, in 1335, and established Sweden's first national legal code in 1350. His dual kingdom was huge – after the signing of the treaty of Novgorod in 1323 Finland had officially become part of the Swedish realm – but the majority of his subjects lived in abject poverty. During the mid 14th century the kingdom was hit by the bubonic plague, and approximately a third of the population was killed.

By the mid 1300s, King Magnus was in serious trouble. Long-running disputes about the then Danish provinces of Skåne and Blekinge resulted in devastating Danish attacks on Swedish targets. In the 1360s, the nobility lost all patience with Magnus and enlisted the help of Duke Albrecht of Mecklenburg (1364-88) to unseat him. Albrecht and his forces quickly conquered Stockholm and the nobles carved up the country for themselves.

Nordic alliance

Upon the death in 1386 of Bo Jonsson Grip – chief of Sweden's ruling nobles – the nobility turned to Margaret, daughter of Danish King Valdemar and wife of Magnus's son King Håkon of Norway. She had been a regent for her son Olaf in both Denmark and Norway since the deaths of her father and husband. Though Olof died in 1387, she retained her hold on power in the three kingdoms. In 1389, she was proclaimed ruler of Sweden and in return she confirmed all the privileges of the Swedish nobility. When they asked her to choose a king she nominated 14-year-old Erik VII of Pomerania. As he was already king of

Cenotaph of Birger Jarl, Stadshuset p161

Norway and Denmark, Scandinavia now had just one ruler. However, Margaret was the real power behind the throne and remained so until her death in 1412.

In 1397, she formalised a Nordic alliance called the Kalmar Union to limit the commercial and political influence of the Hanseatic League. By the start of the 15th century the Union encompassed Norway, Sweden, Finland, Iceland and Greenland, making it the largest kingdom in Europe. The Union was threatened many times over the next 125 years by Swedish rebellion against Danish forces.

Christopher of Bavaria ruled the Union from 1439 to 1448. Upon his death, the noble families of Norway, Sweden and Denmark could not agree on a single candidate to fill the kingship. Sweden's nationalists, led by the Sture family, seized this opportunity to attempt to free Sweden from the Union. This led to vicious fighting with Sweden's unionist faction, which was led by the Oxenstierna family. Finally, in 1470, the nationalists had the upper hand and Sten Sture the Elder (1471-97, 1501-3) was appointed the 'Guardian of the Realm'. A year later the Battle of Brunkeberg broke out in what is now the centre of Stockholm, resulting in the decimation of the unionist forces. The statue of *St George and the Dragon* in **Storkyrkan** (*see p71*) was donated by Sture to commemorate the victory.

Stockholm bloodbath

Aside from his crucial military victories, Sten Sture the Elder is remembered for the many technological, cultural and educational steps forward that Sweden made under his leadership. He established Sweden's first university in Uppsala in 1477, and in 1483 Sweden's first printing press was set up. Decorative arts became more sophisticated, as shown by the many fine German- and Dutch-style paintings that adorn Swedish churches of this period. Stockholm continued to grow throughout the 15th century, and by the early 16th century the city had between 6,000 and 7,000 inhabitants, most of them living in present-day Gamla Stan. Though these numbers made Stockholm Sweden's largest town, by continental standards it was tiny. In 1500, Lübeck had 25,000 inhabitants and Paris more than 100,000.

From the start, the population of Stockholm was a mix of people from different parts of Sweden and other areas of Europe. The largest 'foreign' contingent – between ten and 20 per cent of the population – was made up of Finns, largely a result of Finland's status, since the mid 12th century, as a Swedish province. The

Germans comprised a smaller, but much more powerful, proportion; since the city had been founded with Hanseatic support, wealthy German merchants had been living in Stockholm from its beginnings. Dutch, Scottish, French, English, Italian, Danish, Russian and Polish merchants and traders also became increasingly significant in Stockholm during the 15th century.

By the late 15th century, most Swedes thought the Kalmar Union was a thing of the past, but the alliance was still popular in Denmark and Sweden's rulers had to deal with numerous Danish attacks. When Christian II assumed the Danish throne in 1513, the unionist movement rejoiced, thinking it had now finally found a leader who would be able to crush the Swedish nationalists.

Sure enough, Christian attacked Sweden and killed the then ruler, Sten Sture the Younger (1512-20). After Sture's death, Christian gathered leading members of the Swedish nobility together at Tre Kronor castle under the guise of granting them amnesty for their opposition to the union. After three days of feasting and celebrating, he locked the doors to the castle and arrested his guests.

Around 90 men were sentenced to death and taken to Stortorget, outside the castle, where they were killed one by one. The event came to be known as the Stockholm Bloodbath, and it earned Christian II the name Christian the Tyrant. After the killings, Sture's followers were ruthlessly persecuted. This proved counter-productive, as it provoked widespread opposition to Danish rule and finally resulted in the complete breakdown of the union in 1521-23. Sweden then became a totally independent country under the leadership of Gustav Eriksson, who was crowned King Gustav Vasa (1523-60).

Age of empire

During Gustav Vasa's long reign Sweden was changed in two fundamental ways: it was unified under a strong hereditary monarch, and it became a Protestant country. Gustav Vasa was never a particularly religious man, and his Reformation had more to do with politics and economics than theology. Lacking the wealth he required to fulfil his ambitions, he confiscated Church property, reassigned it to the Crown, and began a propaganda campaign that stressed the negative role the Church's leadership had played in the past – in particular, Archbishop Gustav Trolle's support for Christian the Tyrant. These measures resulted in the eventual adoption of the Lutheran faith as the state religion.

The Reformation led to the state-sanctioned destruction of scores of Swedish monasteries, convents and churches, their riches going to an increasingly wealthy and powerful king. Gustav Vasa even had plans to tear down Storkyrkan because he felt it was situated too close to the royal residence at Tre Kronor castle, thereby complicating its defence. But public opinion was strongly opposed to the destruction of Stockholm's spiritual heart, so the king relented and decided only to make minor alterations. (Gustav Vasa's son Johan was more interested in both architecture and religion than his father, and in the 1580s he had a number of Stockholm's demolished churches rebuilt.)

His larder full and his domestic goals largely accomplished, Gustav Vasa launched a campaign to weaken Russia, Poland and Denmark and thereby make Sweden the dominant Baltic power, beginning with a modestly successful war against Russia in 1555-57. After his death in 1560, his sons, King Erik XIV, King Johan III and King Karl IX, took up the mission. Gustav Vasa is seen as the monarch who was most responsible for turning Sweden into a nation. He created a modern army, navy and civil service, and the intellectual figures he brought to his court connected Sweden with the Renaissance in the arts and sciences.

In 1570-95, Sweden fought another war against Russia, with some success. But Denmark was harder to beat – in spite of the break-up of the Kalmar Union, it had remained the most powerful country in the region, as Sweden learned to its cost in the expensive wars of 1563-70 and 1611-13. It was not until the Thirty Years War, which began in Germany in 1618, that the tide finally turned decisively in Sweden's favour in its rivalry with the Danes. After suffering a devastating defeat at the hands of the Swedes in the Battle of Lutter-am-Barenburg in 1626, Denmark was forced to pull out of the war. In 1630, Sweden officially entered the war on the side of the Protestants. The resulting peace treaty of 1648 gave Sweden new provinces in northern Germany, and by 1658 a severely weakened Denmark had been forced to surrender parts of Norway plus all Danish provinces east of Öresund. As a result, by the end of the 17th century Sweden had become the most powerful nation in northern Europe.

Gustav II Adolf and his chancellor, Axel Oxenstierna, were eager to develop Stockholm and make it the political and administrative centre of the growing Swedish empire. They strengthened Stockholm's position as a centre of foreign trade, founded Sweden's Supreme Court in the city and reorganised the national assembly into four estates: nobility, clergy, burghers and farmers. The medieval wall was torn down so that the city could expand to the north and south, and the old wooden buildings that dominated Södermalm and Norrmalm were replaced by straight streets lined with stone buildings.

The 17th century was a golden age in Swedish history, in military, cultural, economic and social terms

After Gustav II Adolf's death his young daughter, Christina, became queen, with Oxenstierna as regent until 1644. In 1654, Christina converted to Catholicism, renounced the throne and moved to Rome, where she lived out her life building up one of the finest art and book collections in Europe. She left the throne to Karl X Gustav (1654-60), who is remembered best for his invasion and defeat of Denmark in 1657, creating the largest Swedish empire ever. He was succeeded by his son, Karl XI (1660-97), who in 1682 pronounced himself to be Sweden's first absolute monarch, answerable only to God.

Stockholm's population grew rapidly during Sweden's age of empire; by the 1670s the city had between 50,000 and 55,000 citizens. Literacy rates were rising, grammar schools were established and creativity flourished under the likes of George Stiernhielm (1598-1672), the father of modern Swedish poetry. Architecturally, this was the age of the Tessins, who completed the fabulous **Drottningholms Slott** in 1686 (*see p168*). It was a golden age in Swedish history, in military, cultural, economic and social terms.

Karl XI

Tre Kronor, 1661

Rise of the aristocracy

It was during the reign of Karl XII (1697-1718) – who assumed the throne at the tender age of 15 – that Sweden lost her empire. Between 1700 and 1721, Sweden fought the Great Northern War against a number of opponents, notably the defensive alliance of Saxony-Poland, Russia and Denmark. The young king fought valiantly against the odds to hold on to all of Sweden's far-flung possessions but suffered a terrible loss to Russia's Peter the Great at the Battle of Poltava in 1709. His bravery in battle is still revered in Sweden's far-right circles to this day. He was finally killed in Norway by a sniper's bullet in 1718. Since he had no heir, the period after Karl's death was marked by a weakening of the monarchy and the rise of the aristocracy.

In 1719, the role of the monarch was reduced to that of nominal head of state, and with the government dominated by cabals of squabbling noblemen, the economy was left to stagnate, and political and social reforms were slow in coming.

By the end of the Great Northern War in 1721, Sweden had lost parts of Pomerania in Germany, as well as its strongholds in modern-day Estonia, Latvia, north-west Russia and Finland. Disastrous attempts were made to reconquer some of these territories by fighting wars with Russia in 1741-43 and 1788-90. Participation in the Seven Years War (1756-63) resulted in the loss of Swedish territory to Prussia. Sweden was no longer the great power it had been.

This was also a trying time for the citizens of Stockholm – on top of coping with their country's political and military difficulties, their city was ravaged by fire and disease. In 1697, it was devastated by a fire that

destroyed Tre Kronor, the royal palace and pride of Stockholm. In 1710, plague swept through, killing about a third of the population.

Later in the century Stockholm suffered three more devastating fires, which resulted in a municipal ban on wood as a material for new houses. Over the course of the 18th century the population stayed static at about 70,000 inhabitants. Unsanitary conditions, overcrowding, cold and disease all contributed to the fact that Stockholm's death rate was among the highest of all European cities.

But there was a brighter side. In the decades leading up to 1754, Stockholm buzzed with the building of the new **Kungliga Slottet** (*see p67*) to replace Tre Kronor. The construction work was a huge stimulus for the city's artisans, and for Stockholm's economy overall. There was an influx of skilled workers from overseas and new industries began to grow up in Stockholm. The city's foreign trade was also developing rapidly – not only with Europe but also with the Far East and the Americas.

Many of Stockholm's burghers used their increasing wealth to build larger houses, especially along Skeppsbron in Gamla Stan. New residential neighbourhoods sprang up on Södermalm and Norrmalm, and many of the houses on Gamla Stan were renovated.

Scientific progress

The 18th century was also an age of scientific and intellectual advance in Stockholm, and throughout Sweden. Key figures included the famous botanist Carl von Linné (aka Linnaeus, 1707-78); Anders Celsius (1701-44), inventor of the centigrade temperature scale; and mystical philosopher

Emanuel Swedenborg (1688-1772). Sweden's best-loved poet, Carl Michael Bellman (1740-95), did much to encourage Swedish nationalism. Religious life became less strictly constrained; Jews were allowed to settle in Sweden in 1744, and in 1781 Catholics were permitted to establish a church in Stockholm for the first time since the Reformation.

The monarchy regained some of its old power under Gustav III (1771-92). Seeing that the Riksdag (Parliament) was divided, the king seized the opportunity to force through a new constitution that would make the nobility share power with the Crown. Gustav III was initially popular with his subjects because he built hospitals, allowed freedom of worship and lessened economic controls. He was also a man of culture who imported French opera, theatre and literature to Sweden, and in 1782 he founded Stockholm's first opera house. During his reign, several newspapers were established, and political and cultural debate flourished. The nobility were not so happy with his tyrannical behaviour, however, especially after the start of the French Revolution. In 1792, Gustav III was shot by an assassin at a masked ball at the Kungliga Operan; he died two weeks later.

In 1805, Gustav III's successor, Gustav IV Adolf (1792-1809), was drawn into the Napoleonic Wars on the British side. This resulted in a number of gains and losses; most significantly, Sweden lost Finland to Russia and gained Norway from Denmark. All this upheaval resulted in political changes, notably the constitution of 1809, which established a system whereby a liberal monarchy would be responsible to an elected Riksdag.

The union with Norway was established in 1814 and formalised in the 1815 Act of Union. The settlement took account of the Norwegian desire for self-government, declaring Norway a separate nation from Sweden. However, King Karl XIII (1748-1818) was now sovereign over Norway. The tension between the Swedish desire to strengthen the union, and the Norwegian wish for further autonomy, was set to increase over the century that followed.

Following the death of Karl XIII in 1818, one of Napoleon's generals, Jean-Baptiste Bernadotte, was invited to assume the Swedish throne. He accepted and took the name Karl XIV Johan (1818-44). In spite of the fact that he spoke no Swedish and had never visited Scandinavia prior to accepting the kingship, Sweden prospered under his rule.

His successor, Oscar I (1844-59), gave women inheritance rights equal to those of their brothers in 1845, passed an Education Act (1842) and a Poor Care law (1855), and reformed the restrictive craftsmen's guilds. The reign of his son, Karl XV (1859-72), is remembered for the reformation of the Riksdag in 1866 – the old four estates were replaced with a dual-chamber representative parliament. This act marked the beginning of the end for the monarch's role in politics, essentially reducing the role to a figurehead.

Industrial revolution

Industrialisation arrived late to Sweden, and the mechanisation of what little industry did exist (mining, forestry and the like) was half-hearted – hardly what you would call a revolution. Meanwhile, the rural population had grown steadily through the first half of the 19th century. There was neither enough land, nor jobs in the cities, to support everyone. A severe famine during 1867-68 tipped the scales, and over one million Swedes emigrated to North America between 1860 and 1910 – a traumatic event for a country whose population in 1860 was only four million.

In the 1860s, Sweden's first railway lines finally opened reliable communications between Stockholm and the country's southern regions; by 1871 the railway to the north was complete. The railways were a boon for nascent industry. High-quality, efficiently made steel and safety matches (a Swedish invention) were to become the two most notable Swedish manufactured products. By the late 19th century, a number of large industries had been established in Stockholm, including a shoe factory on Södermalm and a huge Bolinders factory on Kungsholmen producing steam engines, cast-iron stoves and other household items. In 1876, Lars Magnus Ericsson opened his Ericsson telephone company in Stockholm, and soon the city had more phones per capita than any other city in Europe.

By 1900, one in four Swedes lived in a city, and industrialisation was finally in full swing. Stockholm's factories attracted workers from all over the country, causing the population to grow from 100,000 in 1856 to 300,000 in 1900. Conditions in many factories were appalling, and unions emerged to fight for the rights of workers. The unions formed a confederation in 1898 but found it difficult to make progress under harsh laws on picketing.

Living conditions in the city were nearly as bad as working conditions. In response to Stockholm's growing housing crisis, the city planners – led by Claes Albert Lindhagen – put forward a proposal in 1866 to build wide boulevards and esplanades similar to those in Paris, which would create some green space within the city as well as allowing traffic to move freely. The plan resulted in the construction of some of the city's key arteries, such as Birger Jarlsgatan, Ringvägen, Karlavägen and Strandvägen. In just one decade, the 1880s, Stockholm's population increased by 46 per cent – more buildings were constructed in the 1880s than during the previous 70 years; neighbourhoods such as Östermalm, Vasastaden, Kungsholmen, Hornstull and Skanstull were created.

The late 19th century also saw the arrival of Stockholm's first continental-style hotels, cafés, restaurants, shopping galleries and department stores, to serve the city's upper classes, and the beginnings of a tourist industry. The arts and academies also prospered. Swedish dramatist August Strindberg achieved critical success across Europe, and folk historian Artur Hazelius founded the **Nordiska Museet** (*see p124*) and open-air **Skansen** museum (*see p122*). The Academy of Stockholm (now the University of Stockholm) was founded in 1878, and in 1896 Alfred Nobel donated his fortune to fund the Nobel Prizes (*see p74*).

Social democracy to the fore

In 1905, the union between Sweden and Norway finally dissolved. Norway took full control of its own affairs, and the Swedish state assumed its current shape.

At the outbreak of World War I Sweden declared itself neutral, in spite of its German sympathies. The British demanded that Sweden enforce a blockade against Germany. When Sweden refused to co-operate, the British blacklisted Swedish goods and interfered with Swedish commercial shipping, going so far as to seize ships' cargoes. The economy suffered dramatically and inflation shot through the roof. The British tactics led to rationing, as well as severe food shortages. Demonstrations broke out in 1917-18, partly inspired by the Russian Revolution. The demonstrators focused on food shortages and demands for democratic reforms, particularly the extension of voting rights to women.

The privations of the war helped social democracy make its breakthrough. By the end of the war, the Social Democrat Party had been active for some time – its first member had been elected to the Riksdag in 1902 – though it remained marginal. After the Russian Revolution, it presented a less extreme alternative to communism in Sweden and gained popularity. In 1920, Hjalmar Branting became Sweden's first Social Democrat prime minister, and reforms quickly followed: women were

awarded the vote; the state-controlled alcohol-selling system was established; and the working day was limited to eight hours.

The Social Democrats' dominance of political affairs began in earnest in the 1930s. From 1932, the party enjoyed an unbroken 40 years in power. This made it possible to take the first steps towards building the notion of a People's Home (Folkhemmet), in which higher taxes would finance a decent standard of living for all. The first components of the welfare system were unemployment benefits, paid holidays, family allowances and increased old-age pensions.

During World War II, the main goal for the Swedish government was to avoid Sweden being dragged into the conflict

At the outbreak of World War II there was little sympathy in Sweden for the Germans – unlike in 1914. Sweden declared neutrality but was in a difficult position. Germany was allied with Finland against the Soviet Union, and the relationship between Sweden and Finland was traditionally close – with Russia the age-old enemy. But when the Soviets invaded Finland in 1939, Sweden was only drawn in to a certain

Stockholm riots, 1917

degree, providing weapons, volunteers and refuge to the Finns, but refusing to send regular troops. Sweden's position became even more uncomfortable in 1940, when Germany invaded Denmark and Norway, thus isolating Sweden and compelling it to supply the Nazis with iron ore and to allow them to transport their troops across Swedish territory and in Swedish waters. In 1942, the Swedish navy fought an undeclared war against Soviet submarines.

On the other hand, allied airmen were rescued in Sweden and often sent back to Britain, and Danish and Norwegian armed resistance groups were organised on Swedish soil in 1942-43. Jewish lives were also saved, notably by Swedish businessman Raoul Wallenberg, who managed to prevent about 100,000 Hungarian Jews from being deported by the SS. After the Soviet conquest of Budapest in January 1945, Wallenberg was arrested as a suspected spy and disappeared. For years, rumours flew about whether or not he had died in a Moscow prison in 1947; Soviet documents unearthed in 1989 indicated this was what had most likely happened.

The main goal for the Swedish government during the war was not to maintain strict neutrality but rather to avoid Sweden being dragged into the conflict – this was accomplished at high diplomatic and moral cost.

At the start of the Cold War, in 1948-49, Sweden tried to form a defensive alliance with Denmark and Norway, but the plans failed partly because the other two countries wanted close links with the western allies. When the Danes and Norwegians became members of NATO in 1949, Sweden remained outside, ostensibly to prevent Finland becoming isolated in the face of the Soviet Union. In recent years it has emerged that Sweden was, in fact, in secret co-operation with NATO from as far back as the early 1950s.

Changing skyline

After the end of World War II, a large-scale transformation of Stockholm's city centre began, despite the fact that Stockholm was one of the few European capitals to survive the war unscathed. Once the rebuilding process on the Continent was in full swing, with American-style skyscrapers rising from the ashes of all the bombed-out cities, Sweden felt left out. The city government began to tear down many of its decaying old buildings and construct anew. As more and more people moved to Stockholm in the post-war period (the capital's population more than doubled in the 20th century), the city once again developed a severe housing

Dag Hammarskjöld

crisis. Stockholm's underground system, called the Tunnelbana, was inaugurated in 1950 and new suburbs were built along it, to the south and north-west.

Under the leadership of Tage Erlander (1946-69), the Social Democrats introduced models for industrial bargaining and full employment that were successful in boosting the economy. At the same time, the country created a national health service and a disability benefits system, improved the quality of its schools and instituted free university education. Sweden established itself as a leading industrial country and was proud of its 'Third Way', a blending of corporate capitalism with a cradle-to-grave social safety net for all.

In 1953, Swedish diplomat Dag Hammarskjöld was appointed secretary-general of the United Nations. A controversial figure who tried to use his position to broker peace in the conflicts of the period, he became a thorn in the side of the superpowers. He died in 1961 in a mysterious plane crash over northern Rhodesia while on a mission to try to solve the Congo crisis. News of his death caused profound sadness across Sweden, as he personified the Swedes' perception of themselves as the world's conscience.

Sweden's booming post-war economy produced a demand for labour that the national workforce could not meet. From about 1950, Sweden began to import skilled labour, primarily from the Nordic countries but also from Italy, Greece and Yugoslavia. This immigration continued unrestricted until the mid 1960s, reaching its peak in 1969-70, when more than 75,000 immigrants were entering Sweden each year. Thereafter numbers fell significantly, although Sweden continued to welcome political refugees from around the globe. By the mid 1990s, 11 per cent of Sweden's population were foreign-born.

In the 1970s, international economic pressures began to put the squeeze on Sweden's social goals, and it was under Olof Palme's leadership (1982-86) that the Third Way began to falter. Palme spent a lot of time and energy building up Sweden's international image, while Sweden's high-tax economy was sliding into stagnation. When an unknown assailant murdered Palme on a Stockholm street in 1986, it created a national trauma.

The end of the Cold War in the late 1980s led to a serious re-evaluation of Sweden's position in international politics. The early 1990s saw the Social Democrats replaced by a centre-right coalition. This coincided with an economic crisis; long-term economic stagnation and budgetary problems led to a huge devaluation of the krona. A programme of austerity measures was then implemented, but it wasn't enough. Sweden suffered its worst recession since the 1930s and unemployment soared to a record 14 per cent. In 1994, the Social Democrats were returned to power. With its economy and confidence severely shaken, Sweden voted (by a very narrow margin) to join the European Union, its membership taking effect on 1 January 1995.

Since then, the economy has improved considerably, with both unemployment and inflation falling greatly, particularly during the IT boom of the 1990s. The bursting of the IT bubble seemed to threaten this renewed prosperity, but the industry picked itself up, growing steadily over the past decade.

Sweden's relationship with the EU remained controversial, with many on the left fearing that closer co-operation with other European countries threatened to undermine the tenets of the welfare state. These arguments were given a good airing in the referendum in 2003 on the euro. Despite support for membership from almost all the major parties, voters chose to stay outside the single currency zone. After the vote, Prime Minister Göran Persson declared that Sweden would not hold another referendum on the issue for at least ten years.

The 2003 referendum came two days after the murder of Anna Lindh, the popular foreign minister, in a Stockholm department store. A young Swede of Serbian origin, Mijailo Mijailovic, was convicted of her killing. A motive was never established, but Mijailovic was later ruled to have been suffering from a mental illness at the time of the attack.

The killing came as a huge shock to Swedes, and to the Social Democrat Party. It was to be the first of a number of blows to Prime Minister Göran Persson that would culminate in his defeat in the 2006 general election.

Tsunami tragedy

A tragedy of much greater proportions befell Sweden on 26 December 2004, when 543 Swedes were killed in the Asian tsunami. With most ministers and civil servants at home for Christmas, it took a whole day for the government to realise that thousands of Swedes were holidaying in the area. The episode dented the government's reputation, and the next two years were dominated by inquiries into the handling of Sweden's response to the disaster.

The opposition found themselves in a good position to capitalise on the Social Democrats' discomfort. The four centre-right parties – the Moderate Party, the Liberal People's Party, the Centre Party and the Christian Democrats – agreed to campaign on a joint manifesto. Calling themselves the Alliance for Sweden, they went on to win the election in September 2006, promising modest tax cuts and reductions to some benefits. The aim, they said, was to reduce Sweden's hidden unemployment, which by some measures was between 15 and 20 per cent.

Moderate leader Fredrik Reinfeldt was the first non-Social Democrat prime minister for 12 years. He was also a rarity from a longer-term perspective, since the Social Democrats had ruled Sweden for 67 of the previous 76 years. Reinfeldt was the youngest prime minister for 80 years, and his cabinet included the first Swedish minister of African descent and the first gay minister (same sex marriage was legalised in Sweden in 2009). Although the tax cuts and benefit reforms were small, Reinfeldt also put into action plans to privatise state industries such as Vin&Sprit, maker of Absolut Vodka, which was bought by Pernod Ricard in 2008.

Floral tribute following truck attack, 2017

Crown Princess Victoria, Prince Daniel and Princess Estelle

The left strikes back

Reinfeldt was re-elected in 2010, after a closely fought campaign. However, the Alliance for Sweden fell short of an overall majority by two seats, forcing it to form a minority coalition government. It was in this election that the far-right, anti-immigration Sweden Democrats Party first gained ground, winning 20 parliamentary seats – the first seats it had ever won. A December 2010 suicide bombing in Stockholm, the first terrorist attack in the Nordic countries to be linked to Islamic terrorism, is thought to have fuelled far-right, anti-immigration sentiment further, after two people were injured.

Riots erupted in the Stockholm immigrant suburb of Husby in 2013, following the fatal shooting of an elderly Portuguese expat by local police. Some 150 vehicles were set on fire during the seven-day riots, which spread to several other suburbs and unleashed a vast amount of discontent.

The increased concern over Sweden's high unemployment, mounting inequality and declining welfare state led to the comeback of the Social Democrats, under Stefan Löfven, in the September 2014 general election, when the party won 43.7 per cent of seats – enough to end the centre-right Alliance's rule by forming a coalition with the Greens. However, the Sweden Democrats won 13 per cent of seats, making it the country's third biggest party.

Immigration remained a divisive political issue as the European migrant crisis unfolded. In 2015, Sweden took in around 160,000 asylum seekers, more than any other EU country relative to its population size. Stockholm experienced a second terror attack linked to Islamic extremism in April 2017, when an Uzbek man who had been denied residency in Sweden and expressed sympathy for the so-called Islamic State (IS), drove a truck through a pedestrian area killing four people.

Support for the Sweden Democrats continued to creep up, while the larger mainstream parties tumbled in the polls. In elections in September 2018, the nationalists made less of an impact than the establishment had feared, scoring 17.5 per cent of the vote and remaining in third place. But their growth, alongside rising support for the ex-Communist Left Party, meant that neither the ruling centre-left nor the opposition centre-right bloc was able to form a majority coalition. Following four months of political deadlock, Stefan Löfven struck a deal to stay on as prime minister, leading another Social Democrat-Green minority coalition government, by agreeing to implement a list of policies favoured by two smaller centre-right parties, the Centre Party and the Liberals.

A royal affair

A spell of royal weddings and births in the last decade have helped to lighten the public mood. Sweden's Crown Princess Victoria walked down the aisle with Daniel Westling, her former personal trainer, in June 2010 and, in 2012, gave birth to Princess Estelle, who became second in line to the Swedish throne. Victoria's second child, Prince Oscar, was born in 2016. Victoria's younger sister, Princess Madeleine, married British-American investment banker Christopher O'Neill in June 2013 and has since had two children, Princess Leonore and Prince Nicolas. Victoria and Madeleine's brother, Prince Carl-Philip, tied the knot with Sofia Hellqvist, a former reality television star in June 2015 and the pair went on to have two sons, Prince Alexander and Prince Gabriel.

Design

Never forget the three Fs: form, function and flat-packing

In the world of furniture, glassware, industrial and fashion design, Swedes have carved out a profitable niche, creating products that are functional and effortlessly stylish. The result is big business around the world, with Swedish design flying off the shelves from Tallinn to Tokyo. IKEA, the biggest exporter of the Swedish functionalist concept, still furnishes the majority of Swedish homes, but this cheap-and-cheerful exponent is balanced by the boutiques of Östermalm and fashionable SoFo, where you'll find achingly simple furniture, homewares and fashion at achingly high prices. Sleek and functional is still the order of the day in most Stockholm studios, but a new generation of designers is less bound to the philosophy that underpins the minimalist tradition. Today, designers of glassware, furniture, wallpaper and industrial products are looking abroad to the rest of Europe, the Middle East, Africa and Asia for inspiration.

Lathörnet, Carl Larsson *p224*

Development

Though modern Swedish design dates back roughly 100 years, its aesthetic roots can be traced further still. The highly influential Gustavian style, which came about during the reign of King Gustav III in the 18th century, marked a move away from elaborate Baroque to a more classical, restrained elegance characterised by white wood and simple curves. Then, in the late 1800s, the Swedish elite was exposed to German art nouveau, a new style that changed the way well-to-do Swedes thought about their homes. It marked a further shift towards organic forms and sinewy curves, inspired by nature, and led to even plainer and more ergonomic furniture and household accessories.

The paintings of late 19th-century artist **Carl Larsson** (1853-1919) played a significant role in the development of Swedish interior design. In 1899, he created a widely reproduced series of watercolours called *Ett Hem* ('A Home'), featuring the simple furniture and pale-coloured textiles created by his wife Karin, who was inspired by local design traditions, the English Arts and Crafts movement and art nouveau trends on the Continent. In Larsson's paintings, it is easy to recognise the rural wooden floors and rectangular woven rag rugs that are still common in Swedish homes. The striped patterns on the simple white-painted chairs are also strikingly similar to those sold today by Swedish interior decorating monolith IKEA.

In an essay entitled 'Skönhet för Alla' ('Beauty for All'; 1899), which was inspired by the Larssons' aesthetics, Swedish social critic **Ellen Key** defined the democratic ideals embodied in the Larssons' rustic home: 'Not until nothing ugly can be bought, when the beautiful is as cheap as the ugly, only then can beauty for all become a reality.' These democratic principles, as well as those expressed by **Gregor Paulsson** in 1919 in his book *More Beautiful Things for Everyday Use*, still inform much of Swedish society and influence new design.

Many of the classics of Swedish design came out during the creatively fertile 1930s, as modernism blossomed throughout northern Europe. The movement made its breakthrough in Sweden at the Stockholm Exhibition in 1930, organised by influential Swedish architect **Gunnar Asplund** (1885-1940), and the Swedish offshoot came to be known as functionalism. Some speculate that Sweden was especially receptive to the gospel of functionalism – and later to minimalist severity – because of sober Swedish Lutheranism, as well as a national penchant for social engineering.

The fresh air, natural light and access to greenery extolled by Asplund's functionalism quickly became the defining characteristics of Swedish home design and urban planning. During the next two decades, as news of the practical and beautiful designs coming out of the Nordic region spread to other parts of Europe, as well as to North America, the reputation of Scandinavian style became firmly established.

Design icons

The demigods of Swedish furniture design – Carl Malmsten and Bruno Mathsson – both flourished during the dynamic pre-war period. **Carl Malmsten** (1888-1972) sought forms that some described as 'rural rococo', and he aspired to a craft-oriented and functional approach to furniture design. The company/shop that he founded 60 years ago – Malmstenbutiken (*see p112*) – is still in the same family. His counterpart, **Bruno Mathsson** (1907-88), is famous for his groundbreaking work with bentwood. Mathsson's light and simple modernistic designs can be seen in Stockholm at Studio B3's permanent showroom (Barnhusgatan 3, Norrmalm, 08 21 42 31, www. scandinaviandesign.com/b3).

A third giant of the pre-war design era was modernist architect and designer **Josef Frank** (1885-1967), an Austrian exile in Sweden, who created elegant furniture and vibrant floral textiles. Frank was so ahead of his time that his brilliant patterns look as though they were created yesterday, and they remain very popular. Check them out at Svenskt Tenn (*see p111*), a much-loved design shop in Östermalm.

In the 1950s, the Brooklyn Museum's exhibition 'Design in Scandinavia' toured North America. In the years that followed, Scandinavian design, with its clean lines, high-level functionality and accessibility, became the most internationally influential design movement of the era. The latter half of the 20th century inevitably brought some variance from the founding facets of Scandinavian design, as designers started to experiment in response to the changing times. In the 1960s, an 'anti-functional' movement saw Swedish designers, in particular, looking to their Italian counterparts for inspiration. Free from the rules of functionalism, they began to produce chairs, lamps and sofas in all sizes, shapes and colours, and in a variety of new and unusual materials, notably plastic.

During the economic boom of the 1980s, the rise of eclecticism and postmodernism saw designers such as **Jonas Bohlin** (born 1953; www.jonasbohlin.com) and **Mats**

Studio B3

style. The result is a local design scene that, while loyal in many ways to its minimalist heritage, is daring to think outside the monochrome box.

These days, a fresh generation of creators, inspired by everything from Baroque furniture to Japanese cartoons, is bringing a playful twist to the Swedish aesthetic. **Fredrik Färg** and his French-born business partner **Emma Marga Blanche** have made waves with their experimentation with textiles (www.fargblanche.com), while **Anna Holmquist** and **Chandra Ahlsell** from the studio Folkform (www.folkform.se) have won accolades for creating high-end designs from cheap materials, including fake marble, fake fur and chipboard. Sustainability and innovation have also emerged as core trends, with designers such as **David Ericsson** (davidericsson.se) focused on creating recyclable furniture.

Established and up-and-coming designers are showcased at Stockholm Design Week (www.stockholmdesignweek.com) in February every year, which centres around the Stockholm Furniture & Light Fair (www.stockholm furniturelightfair.se).

Swedish fashion, meanwhile, continues to go from strength to strength, with big-name labels such as Acne, Filippa K and WhyRed leading the way and allowing for the emergence of a new wave of successful fashion designers, including **Ann-Sofie Back** (annsofieback.com), and **Ann Ringstrand** and **Stefan Söderberg**, the duo behind fashion-forward Swedish label Hope (www.hope-sthlm.com).

Theselius (born 1956) creating 'work of art' furniture in limited editions for sale to collectors. Bohlin's breakthrough came in 1980 with 'Concrete', a chair made out of, yes, concrete. A kind of neo-functionalist minimalism had taken over by the 1990s. Suddenly every bar and restaurant in Stockholm, it seemed, was painted white, with unobtrusive furniture and almost no decoration on the walls or tables. This Scandinavian ultra-simplicity quickly spread to the rest of the world, in no small part owing to the praise it earned from international style magazines such as *Wallpaper**.

Fresh faces

It is more than a decade since the *International Herald Tribune* declared that Swedish design was 'minimalist no more', but this assertion hasn't really been borne out in the intervening years: Swedish designers such as **Thomas Bernstrand** (www.bernstrand.com), **Anna von Schewen** (www.annavonschewen.se) and Jonas Bohlin remain keen disciples of the clean lines and functionalism that have long characterised the country's fashion, furniture and industrial design. However, a new generation of creative talent is breaking out of the mould, creating in the process a more opulent, witty Swedish

On display

A good place to get a sense of Swedish design is the **Nationalmuseum** (*see p84*), which features an impressive collection of applied art, design and industrial design from the 16th century to the present day. The museum reopened in October 2018 after a huge five-year refurbishment project by architects Gert Wingårdh and Erik Wikerstål.

Also worth a visit is Sweden's national centre for architecture and design, **ArkDes** (*see p131*) on the island of Skeppsholmen. The museum and study centre hosts small rotating exhibitions on urbanism, architecture and product design. Nearby, the **Moderna Museet** (*see p130*) is home to the world's largest collection of Nordic fine art, photography, drawings and prints; you can glimpse what wealthy Swedes have hung on their walls through the years and then buy posters and a selection of homeware products in the popular gift store.

▶ *For suggestions on where to buy Swedish design pieces in Stockholm, see p48 Shopping.*

Plan

Pryssgrand, Södermalm

Accommodation

Stockholm is a pricey place to rest your head, but its accommodation options have been expanding rapidly in recent years, with budget spots such as Generator and Skanstulls Hostel joining an impressive list of world-class design hotels.

For sheer style, At Six, the Lydmar and Ett Hem lead the pack. However, standards tend to be high across the board, reflecting Sweden's reputation for thoughtful interior design (*see p222*). Wherever you stay, staff will almost certainly speak excellent English.

Lydmar Hotel *p230*

Many of the most popular accommodation options are in Östermalm and Norrmalm, although hotels and hostels close to Södermalm's nightlife can also get booked up quickly. For a more sedate stay, away from the hubbub, it's worth checking out rooms on the green islands of Djurgården and Skeppsholmen; or try even further afield (*see p233* Out-of-Town Retreats) for a taste of the Swedish countryside.

Prices and reservations

Stockholm is a business hub so hotel rates can drop by as much as half at weekends. This means you can often enjoy deluxe surroundings for much less than you might expect. Always ask about packages and special deals; you may have to book two nights to get a discounted rate, for example. Rates in July, when most Swedes take the month off, are often cheaper too.

Most hotels and hostels are listed on popular booking sites such as Booking.com, Expedia and Hostelworld. The tourist office produces a free hotel brochure and runs a reservations service in conjunction with **Nordic Travel**: book online with its comprehensive accommodation search-and-book facility (stockholm.visit.com) or by phone (08 409 06 400).

> **In the know**
> **Price categories**
>
> Our price categories are based on a hotel's standard prices (not including seasonal offers or discounts) for one night's bed and breakfast in a double room with en suite shower/bath. Rates can vary wildly according to season or room category within a single property, so these prices should only be used as a rough guide.
>
> **Luxury**   above 2,000kr
> **Expensive** 1,300kr-2,000kr
> **Moderate** 800kr-1,300kr
> **Budget**   up to 800kr

Apartments and Short-Term Lets

Suite dreams

One of the most authentic ways to experience Stockholm is by renting a private home. The global heavyweight **Airbnb** (www.airbnb. com) operates in Sweden, although it is up to each housing association to decide whether or not to allow listings on the site. Many properties are also posted on **Homeaway** (www.homeaway.com). Guesthouses and apartments can also be booked via agencies such as **Stockholm Guesthouse** (www. stockholmguesthouse.com) and **CoStockholm** (www.costockholm.com).

Finding longer-term accommodation is a major challenge in the Swedish capital, where there is a serious shortage of affordable rental options. However, many Swedes go on holiday for at least a month during the summer, so you might get lucky by searching local websites such as **Blocket** (www.blocket.se, Sweden's version of Craigslist or Gumtree) or housing rental platform **Qasa** (https://qasa.se). There is also a fairly strong **Couchsurfing** community (www.couchsurfing.com) in Stockholm, offering spare bedrooms or couches for free.

Luxury

Other luxury options include the **Radisson Blu Strand Hotel** (Nybrokajen 9, Norrmalm, 08 506 64 000, www.radissonblu.com/ strandhotel-stockholm), which has views of the harbour, and the flagship **Nobis Hotel** (Norrmalmstorg 2-4, Norrmalm, 08 614 10 00, www.nobishotel.se), with its ultra-stylish aesthetic and glamorous **Gold Bar** (*see p90*).

At Six

Brunkebergstorg 6, Norrmalm, 111 51 (08 578 82 800, www.hotelatsix. com). T-bana T-Centralen. **Rooms** *343.* **Map** *p80 N8.*

This design and art hotel, open since 2017, turns heads with its bold marble entrance staircase and draws in the punters with its multiple drinking and dining options. Situated in Brunkebergstorg square (*see p85*), one of Stockholm's recently revived urban districts, its ground-floor wine bar and coffeehouse, **Blanche & Hierta**, is one of the area's more relaxed venues, with long wooden benches designed for socialising and co-working, and outdoor seating during the summer. The intimate **Hosoi** room, which hosts regular DJ sessions, live podcasts and debates, is also worth checking out on a dark winter afternoon, thanks to top-of-the-range wood-framed speakers, leather armchairs, shelves stacked with LPs and a small bar. The guest rooms combine velvet furnishings with stone, leather and wood accents. There is also

a popular fitness and wellness centre. For details of the hotel's main cocktail bar, *see p89*.

Berns Hotel

Näckströmsgatan 8, Norrmalm, 111 47 (08 566 32 200, www.berns. se). T-bana Kungsträdgården or Östermalmstorg, or bus 54, 65, 69. **Rooms** *82.* **Map** *p80 O7.*

Part of the 19th-century Berns complex (which includes **Berns Asiatiska** restaurant, *see p87*, and numerous nightlife venues, *see p195*), this boutique hotel has a fantastic location near Kungsträdgården, the shops of Hamngatan and the boats of Nybroviken. Top-floor rooms have big windows overlooking Berzelii Park. If you really want to push the boat out, consider the Clock Suite, situated behind the distinctive Berns clock, with a private sauna.

Ett Hem

Sköldungagatan 2, Östermalm, 114 27 (08 20 05 90, www.etthem. se). T-bana Stadion or train to Stockholm Östra station. **Rooms** *12.* **Map** *p102 N3.*

One of Stockholm's most appealing boutique hotels is set in an Arts and Crafts townhouse on the outskirts of Östermalm. Ett Hem, meaning 'a home', is the vision of owner Jeanette Mix, who wanted to create a space defined by luxurious comfort. A dream team of designers has created spectacularly soothing rooms featuring bespoke furniture, high-end Scandinavian

materials (oak, sheepskin, stone and brass) and chalky white tones. Suites raise the bar even further, with four-poster beds and marble bathrooms, while the library area has vintage Kaare Klint leather chairs and parquet floors. Top-quality food, made from seasonal ingredients, is served up daily in the homely kitchen area, designed for conversation. There's also a courtyard garden. You'll want to move in.

Grand Hôtel

Södra Blasieholmshamnen 8, Norrmalm, 103 27 (08 679 35 00, www.grandhotel.se). T-bana Kungsträdgården. **Rooms** *278.* **Map** *p80 O8.*

The location of the Grand Hôtel could hardly be more perfect – or more symbolic. Built in 1874, it stands by the harbour, with splendid views of the Royal Palace. Unlike so many classic hotels that simply let themselves go in old age, the Grand has kept up with the times: though the decor is traditional, materials and amenities are top notch, and while the cheapest rooms are far from spacious, the suites have real wow factor. There's Michelin-starred food on offer in the **Mathias Dahlgren** restaurants (*see p88*), and the revamped **Cadier Bar** is deservedly popular for its dark wood and leather interior, its prime location and supreme service. If quality and class are top of your list, and money is no object, then this is the place to be.

Hotel Skeppsholmen

Haymarket by Scandic

Hötorget 13-15, Norrmalm 111 57 (08 517 26 700, www. scandichotels.se). T-bana Hötorget or bus 1, 55. **Rooms** *401.* **Map** *p80 M7.*

Once a department store where Swedish actress Greta Garbo worked, Haymarket channels the 1920s in its buzzing lobby bar and tearoom on the ground floor. The guest rooms here are spread over eight floors and come complete with art deco-inspired furniture, black-and-white photos and velvet trimmings. Haymarket is situated in a busy part of the city, right next to a market and close to several popular nightspots, so be prepared for plenty of activity in the vicinity, especially at weekends. The hotel bistro, **Gretas** (*see p88*), is worth visiting even if you're not staying the night.

Hotel Diplomat

Strandvägen 7C, Östermalm, 114 56 (08 459 68 00, www. diplomathotel.com). T-bana Östermalmstorg, bus 54, 67, 69 or tram 7. **Rooms** *130.* **Map** *p102 P7.*

Hotel Diplomat is one of Stockholm's best-preserved art nouveau buildings, and its glamorous Strandvägen site affords some stunning waterfront views. This family-run establishment oozes old-fashioned charm, with its antique cage lift, spiral staircase and intricate lattice windows. But its history is combined with a modern Scandinavian vibe, which means the bedrooms are light, airy and decorated in a neutral palette. There's a restaurant and bar on the ground floor (*see p110*); it is usually a serene place to enjoy afternoon tea, but it gets much livelier in the early evening, when it transforms into a popular after-work hangout for well-heeled locals. The staff here are known for paying close attention to every detail.

Hotel Skeppsholmen

Gröna gången 1, Skeppsholmen, 111 49 (08 407 23 00, www. hotelskeppsholmen.se). Bus 65. **Rooms** *81.* **Map** *p118 Q10.*

On the tiny cultural island of Skeppsholmen, this hotel is a calm oasis, just minutes from the city centre. Located in a former navy barracks that dates back to 1699, the hotel has garnered international acclaim for its contemporary interior, superb restaurant and welcoming, distinctly Swedish vibe. Rooms are inspiring and soothing at the same time, featuring unique Boffi basins, stylish furniture, Scandinavian wool blankets and views of the island and the surrounding water. Don't miss brunch in the hotel restaurant (*see p131*).

Lydmar Hotel

Södra Blasieholmshamnen 2, Norrmalm, 103 24 (08 22 31 60, www.lydmar.com). T-bana Kungsträdgården. **Rooms** *46.* **Map** *p80 P8.*

No two rooms are the same in this decadent luxury hotel, which offers a boutique feel with unobstructed waterfront views overlooking the Baroque Royal Palace. The building formerly housed the archives of the Swedish National Museum, dating back to 1829. It's only fitting that its exquisitely decorated rooms, lobbies and hallways serve as a showcase for rotating art and photography exhibitions. Never stuffy or overdone, the guest rooms feature period fireplaces, Nespresso machines and surround sound. Suites come with separate living room areas, a working desk and a guest bathroom; many offer harbour views. The second-floor outdoor terrace is a place to see and be seen on a warm summer's evening, when live DJs and bands perform at least once a week.

Expensive

Clarion Hotel Sign

Östra Järnvägsgatan 35, Norrmalm, 111 20 (08 676 98 00, www.clarionsign.com). T-bana T-Centralen or Hötorget. **Rooms** *558.* **Map** *p80 L7.*

The Clarion Sign is one of Stockholm's largest hotels. Located right next to Central Station, it has more than 500 rooms across 11 floors, a spa, an outdoor pool and a healthy dose of Scandinavian attitude. There are furnishings by Arne Jacobsen, Norway Says, Poul Kjærholm and Alvar Aalto. The Selma Cityspa is on the roof, alongside a heated outdoor pool with fabulous city views.

Downtown Camper by Scandic

Brunkebergstorg 9, Norrmalm, 111 51 (08 517 26 300, www.scandichotels.se). T-bana T-centralen. **Rooms** *494.* **Map** *p80 N8.*

For those with active lifestyles, Scandic's Downtown Camper is the perfect spot. Not only is it located conveniently close to major attractions, the waterfront and Stockholm Central Station, but the hotel provides daily activities for guests, including running, walks, workshops, movie nights and DJs. There's also an in-house gym, pool, spa and yoga classes. Plus, you'll find a selection of skateboards, kayaks and bikes in the foyer that you can hire out. There are plenty of great places to eat in the area around the hotel, but if you're exhausted after all the exercise, head for the house grill restaurant, **Campfire**, which serves up designer comfort food, and then enjoy a nightcap at **Nest** (*see p90*).

Hobo Hotel

Brunkebergstorg 4, Norrmalm, 111 51 (08 578 82 700, www.hobo.se). T-bana T-centralen. **Rooms** *201.* **Map** *p80 N8.*

As you might have guessed from the name, Hobo Hotel doesn't play by the rulebook. On the brutalist square of Brunkebergstorg is a slick and modern hotel whose rooms are designed around the theme of adventure travel. Each comes with a board of pegs loaded with useful things for visitors: not only maps and local info, but also bags and umbrellas. There are speakers through which you can stream your own music, and the occasional decorative cactus. Pay a bit more for the bigger rooms on the top floors and you get your own panoramic view of central Stockholm. Check the website for details of gigs and exhibitions held at the hotel, and don't miss a meal or drink at **Tak** (*see p89*), located just next door.

Hotel Rival

Mariatorget 3, Södermalm, 118 91 (08 545 78 900, www.rival.se). T-bana Mariatorget. **Rooms** *99.* **Map** *p134 M12.*

Part-owned by Benny from ABBA, Rival was created by combining the best parts of the 1930s hotel that once stood here with more contemporary touches. The old cocktail bar and plush red-velvet cinema are art deco treasures. The small rooms are comfortable and stylish, while the large rooms have great views over Södermalm's rooftops. The next-door Rival café (*see p150*) is a great spot to enjoy a Swedish bun and a coffee. This is a really good bet if you want to be in the heart of Södermalm.

Miss Clara by Nobis

Sveavägen 48, Vasastan, 111 34 (08 440 67 00, www.missclarahotel.com). T-bana Hötorget. **Rooms** *92.* **Map** *p80 M6.*

This Nobis group hotel (which also runs Nobis Hotel and Hotel Skeppsholmen) opened in 2014, in an art nouveau building that once housed the Ateneum girls' school. Original features, such as the beautiful staircase railings, have been left intact, while signature Nobis touches – design-focused lighting and premium Scandinavian textiles – can be found throughout the hotel. Rooms are large, light and supremely stylish and comfortable, with parquet floors, a neutral colour scheme and deluxe bathrooms.

Nordic Light Hotel

Vasaplan 7, Norrmalm, 111 20 (08 505 63 200, www.nordiclighthotel.com). T-bana T-Centralen or bus 1, 53, 65, 69. **Rooms** *175.* **Map** *p80 L7.*

The Nordic Light is stylish in a very Scandinavian way: white walls, wooden floors, absurdly comfortable beds and hearty breakfasts. Sophisticated lighting effects are employed throughout, with pretty patterns projected on to the walls of the 175 bedrooms and a chandelier that slowly changes colour in the airy bar-restaurant. The hotel's location near the Arlanda Express means it's only 20 minutes from hotel check-out to airport check-in.

Pop House Hotel

Djurgårdsvägen 68, Djurgården, 115 21 (08 502 54 140, https://pophouse.se/en). Bus 67 or tram 7. **Rooms** *49.* **Map** *p118 S10.*

ABBA obsessives who have travelled to Stockholm partly

Miss Clara by Nobis

to visit ABBA The Museum (see p121) might want to go the whole hog and stay in the heart of the action, at the museum's official hotel, located in the same wooden-fronted building. The brightly coloured guest rooms are filled with light, thanks to panoramic sliding windows. There's a decent restaurant serving Swedish and American main courses, as well as smaller sharing plates, and an airy conservatory bar and café. Check the website for semi-regular free live gigs. Only a five-minute tram ride from downtown, the hotel is also close to popular attractions such as Gröna Lund (see p198) amusement park and open-air museum Skansen (see p122).

Moderate

Good chain options include **Connect City** and **Connect Stockholm** (http://connecthotels. se), the **Story Hotels** in Sundbyberg and Riddarholmen (https://storyhotels.com) and the charming **Best Western Hotel Bentleys** (Drottninggatan 77, Norrmalm, 08 14 13 95, www. bentleys.se).

Ersta Konferens & Hotell

*Erstagatan 1K, Södermalm, 116 91 (08 714 63 41, www.erstadiakoni. se/sv/konferenshotell). Bus 2, 53, 66, 76. **Rooms** 22. **Map** p134 R12.*

This 22-room hotel is a quiet oasis on the north-east shore of Södermalm, where tour buses stop off for one of Stockholm's most phenomenal views over the city. Constructed for the Deacons' Society in 1850, the building is in a square amid beautifully landscaped gardens and across from Ersta Café. There are small guest kitchens on each floor, and when the weather's good you can eat your Fairtrade breakfast in the garden.

Hotel Hellstens Malmgård

*Brännkyrkagatan 110, Södermalm, 117 26 (08 46 50 58 00, http://hellstensmalmgard.se). T-bana Zinkensdamm or bus 4, 66. **Rooms** 49. **Map** p147 J12.*

Housed in a beautiful mansion with a cobbled yard, located towards the Hornstull end of Södermalm, Hellstens Malmgård has as much character as its original sister hotel, with vintage Gustavian-style furniture, four-poster beds and colourful textiles; 18th-century porcelain stoves can be found in 12 of the rooms.

Hotell Anno 1647

*Mariagränd 3, Södermalm, 116 46 (08 442 16 80, www.anno1647.se). T-bana Slussen. **Rooms** 21. **Map** p134 N11.*

As its name suggests, this is an old building dating back to the 17th century, and the interior tries earnestly to stay in sync with the historic exterior. The 21 rooms range from singles and small doubles to superior rooms, meaning there's a bed for all tastes and budgets, and the traditional decor makes up for the lack of facilities in the more basic rooms. Besides, the location is terrific: it's hidden down a cul-de-sac just off Södermalm's most fashionable shopping street, Götgatan, and the cobbled alleys of the Old Town are just minutes away.

Queen's Hotel

*Drottninggatan 71A, Norrmalm, 111 36 (08 24 94 60, www. queenshotel.se). T-bana Hötorget or bus 1, 55. **Rooms** 59. **Map** p80 L6.*

On the main pedestrian street in the heart of the shopping district, this hotel is a good bet if you like hustle, bustle and a convenient location. Family owned, it has 59 clean, plain but stylish-enough rooms with private bathrooms. Most of the doubles can accommodate an extra bed or sofa bed.

Scandic No.53

*Kungsgatan 53, Norrmalm, 111 22 (08 517 36 50, www.scandichotels. com). T-bana Hötorget. **Rooms** 274. **Map** p80 L7.*

This innovative Scandinavian mini-chain has hit on a winning formula that appeals to a wide range of visitors keen to stay in a central location without breaking the bank. Rooms are smaller than the norm, but well designed, with pleasant decor, basic digital mod cons, under-bed storage and blackout curtains. The spacious communal area is the highlight, with a buzzy vibe, a courtyard bar and a restaurant. This is also great spot if you need to get some work done, with desk lamps and plenty of plugs.

Budget

City Backpackers Inn

*Upplandsgatan 2, Norrmalm, 111 23 (08 20 69 20, www. citybackpackers.org). T-bana T-Centralen or Hötorget. **Beds** 144. **Map** p80 L6.*

Set in a 19th-century building just off Norra Bantorget square, this large hostel is ten minutes' walk from Central Station, close to Hötorget and the shopping district. Dorm rooms sleep from four to 12. Alternatively, there are private en suite rooms or six-person apartments with private kitchen and bathroom. Facilities include a comfy lounge with a TV, books and games, kitchen, laundry, free internet access and a sauna.

Generator Hostel

*Torsgatan 10, Norrmalm, 111 23 (08 505 32 370, staygenerator. com/destinations/stockholm). T-bana T-Centralen. **Beds** 796. **Map** p80 K6.*

This flashpacker hostel is a hit with solo travellers, groups of friends and families. There's an industrial-style lobby bar and a large events space that hosts film nights, DJ events, talks and conferences. By Stockholm standards it's not as close to subway connections as other budget accommodation options, but it's only a ten- to-15-minute walk to Stockholm Central Station and there are regular buses.

In the know
Beds & bedding

Swedes pay special attention to the quality of beds and bedding; note that double beds tend to come with two single duvets rather than one double.

Out-of-Town Retreats

Leave the city behind

While Stockholm has a relaxed pace and plenty more green spaces than your average European city, if you're really seeking to unwind, there is a decent selection of spa hotels and countryside lodges within easy reach of the Swedish capital.

North of the city, the medieval town of Sigtuna (see p172) is close to Arlanda Airport, so it's a perfect place to start or end a Swedish trip. In the town centre, the **Sigtuna Stads Hotel** (www.sigtunastadshotell.se) looks fairly ordinary from the outside, but it has impeccably stylish and utterly seductive interiors. It's all very Scandinavian, with modern furniture, polished wooden floors and pale walls. Outside town, the **Sigtunahojden** (https://sigtunahojden.se) is a woodland spa hotel offering a wide range of organic massage options and skincare treatments.

In Nacka, a 30-minute boat ride east of central Stockholm, Sweden's only Japanese spa **Yasuragi** (www.yasuragi.se) is the place to ease those travel-weary muscles with a traditional Japanese bath, a swim or a soak

in an outdoor jacuzzi overlooking the sea. Refresh yourself at the fruit and juice buffet, try a session of qi gong or Zen meditation – or take your kids to sushi school. Most of the 191 sparsely furnished rooms and suites have water views. **Hotel J** (www.hotelj.com), also in Nacka but slightly closer to central Stockholm, is another beautifully situated choice on the coast. It has a nautical feel, fusing New England vibes with the Scandinavian seaside. Many of the bedrooms have private balconies. Restaurant J on the quayside has excellent views.

The **Steam Hotel** (www.steamhotel.se) in Västerås, an 80-minute drive west of the Swedish capital, has become a popular weekend retreat for locals since opening in 2017. It's housed in a defunct former power plant and boasts a luxury 800-metre-square (8,611-square-foot) spa heated by a steam turbine salvaged during the building's refurbishment. There's also a rooftop pool overlooking Lake Mälaren.

Hotel Tre Små Rum

Högbergsgatan 81, Södermalm, 118 54 (08 641 23 71, www. tresmarum.se). T-bana Mariatorget or. **Rooms** *7.* **Map** *p134 M13.*

This tiny, likeable hotel in Söder had three small rooms (hence the name) when it opened in 1993 but now there are seven (six doubles and one single), sharing three shower rooms. Clean and simple, it's ideal for budget travellers who plan to spend most of their time out and about. It's just a few minutes' walk from Mariatorget T-bana station.

Långholmen Hotel & Youth Hostel

Långholmsmuren 20, Långholmen, 102 72 (08 720 85 00, www.langholmen.com). T-bana Hornstull or bus 4, 54, 94. **Hostel beds** *26.* **Hotel rooms** *103.* **Map** *p147 F11.*

A 19th-century former prison has been converted into a hotel and hostel on this small, green island south of Kungsholmen. Although you'll be sleeping in the former cells, these are arranged around a light-filled central atrium to create a pleasing atmosphere.

There's a prison museum on site (*see p152*). One of Stockholm's most arresting places to stay.

Skanstull's Hostel

Ringvägen 135, Södermalm, 116 61 (08 643 02 04, www.skanstulls. se). T-bana Skanstull. **Rooms** *10.* **Map** *p134 P15.*

One of the best budget options in Södermalm, this quirky hostel stands out thanks to brightly coloured rooms with bold wallpaper prints and a homely vibe. There's kitchen-diner area where you can mingle with other guests as well as a library. SoFo's nightlife is a ten-minute walk away.

STF Hostel af Chapman & Skeppsholmen

Flaggmansvägen 8, Skeppsholmen, 111 49 (08 463 22 66, www.svenskaturistforeningen. se/boende/stf-stockholmaf-chapman-skeppsholmen-vandrarhem-huset). Bus 65. **Beds** *282.* **Map** *p118 P9.*

You can't miss this youth hostel – the huge white boat, which dates from 1949, is one of Skeppsholmen's most recognisable landmarks and

has been a hostel since 1972. Cabins are small but cosy, simply arranged with beds and a sink. There are two single cabins available; the rest are shared (six beds). You'll need to book well ahead to secure a place on deck in the summer months; if it's fully booked, note that there are additional rooms available in an adjacent 19th-century building, which has standard hostel facilities, shared internet access, and a TV room with a pool table.

Zinkensdamm Vandrarhem & Hotell

Zinkens väg 20, Södermalm, 117 41 (hotel 08 616 81 10, hostel 08 616 81 00, www.zinkensdamm.com). T-bana Hornstull or Zinkensdamm. **Rooms** *70.* **Map** *p147 J13.*

This youth hostel and family-friendly hotel is tucked away in peaceful Tantolunden park, a few minutes from busy Hornsgatan. Nearby are lots of *koloniträdgårdar* – allotment gardens with charming wooden houses where Stockholmers cultivate a bit of countryside in the city. The yellow wooden hostel has a large courtyard and a small pub where guests congregate.

Getting Around

ARRIVING & LEAVING

By air

Four airports serve Stockholm: Arlanda, Bromma, Skavsta and Västerås.

Arlanda Airport *010 109 10 00, www.arlanda.se.*
Stockholm's main airport, the largest in Scandinavia, is 42km (27 miles) north of the city centre and serves more than 16 million passengers a year. International flights arrive and depart from terminals 2 and 5. Domestic flights arrive and depart from terminals 3 and 4.

It's a light, well-designed place, with good facilities. For currency exchange, there's Forex (terminals 2 and 5), X-Change (terminal 5) and SEB exchange (terminal 5), as well as Handelsbanken and SEB banks in the Sky City shopping and eating area (which connects terminal 5 with 3 and 4). There are ATMs at terminals 2, 4, 5 and Sky City. There's a pharmacy (open 7am-8pm Mon-Fri, 9.30am-5pm Sat, 9.30am-8pm Sun) in Sky City. All terminals have cafés and bars, but head to Sky City for more serious eating.

The fastest way to get into Stockholm is on the bright yellow **Arlanda Express** train service (www.arlandaexpress.com), which arrives at its own terminal next to Central Station. Trains depart 4-6 times an hour, from Arlanda 5.05am-1.05am daily, and from Central Station 4.35am-12.35am daily. Journey time is 18mins; single fare is 295kr (195kr earlybird, 165kr under-25s, free under-18s with each full-price passenger). Buy tickets from the yellow automatic ticket booths at Arlanda or Central Station, or on

the train (for 100kr extra). The booths take all major credit cards.

Alternatively, **Flygbussarna** airport buses (077 151 52 52, www.flygbussarna.se) leave about every 10mins from all terminals to Cityterminalen (the main bus station next to Central Station, *see p80*). Buses run from Arlanda 5am-1am daily (between 1am and 5am buses meet connecting flights, leaving half an hour after arrival), and from Cityterminalen 3.45am-10pm daily. The journey takes around 45mins. A single fare is 99kr (89kr under-17s).

There are also plenty of **taxis** at the airport – many offer fixed prices and these vary from company to company, but make sure you ask the driver first since many taxi firms set their own prices. Reliable firms include Taxi Stockholm (15 00 00, www.taxistockholm.se) and Taxi Kurir (30 00 00, www.taxikurir.se); note that they can be most easily identified by looking at the phone numbers on the sides of the cars.

Bromma Airport *010 109 40 00, www.swedavia.com/bromma.*

Stockholm's city airport, Bromma, is 8km (5 miles) west of the city centre. Its location makes it popular, but only 11 airlines operate from it.

You can get into the city centre on **Flygbussarna** airport buses (*see above*). Buses run from Bromma 7.15am-10pm Mon-Fri, 9.35am-4.20pm Sat, 12.20-10pm Sun; and to Bromma 5.20am-8.20pm Mon-Fri, 7.30am-3.30pm Sat, 11.15am-8.15pm Sun. Single fare is 75kr and the journey takes about 20mins to Cityterminalen. Taking a **taxi** into town will cost you around 250kr.

Skavsta Airport *0155 28 04 00, www.skavsta.se.*
Skavsta serves Stockholm, even though it's 100km (62 miles) to the south. It's the airport of choice for budget airlines. Airport facilities include a Forex exchange bureau, restaurant, café, bar, playground and tax-free shops. **Flygbussarna** airport buses (*see left*; single 139kr) take 80mins to reach the centre of Stockholm. Buses leave Skavsta 20mins after each arriving flight, and Cityterminalen about 3hrs before a departing flight. If you can't find

Carbon Off-setting

Direct emissions from aviation account for more than 2% of global greenhouse gas emissions. A return economy flight from London to Arlanda airport, calculated as roughly 2900 kilometres (1800 miles), produces 500-600kg of CO_2. If flying is your only option, then consider off-setting this carbon. Organisations such as www.atmosfair.de, climatecare.org and www.goldstandard.org enable you to calculate the emissions associated with your flight and then pay to offset these by investing in sustainable development and environmental projects around the world. Some airlines also offer the chance to buy carbon offsets directly when booking a flight; always check that these are high-quality certified carbon-offsetting programmes before you commit.

a **taxi** at the airport, you can order one, but the trip to Stockholm will set you back about 1,425kr.

Västerås Airport *021 80 56 00, http://vasterasairport.se*
Ryanair flies into Västerås, located 110km (68 miles) north-west of Stockholm. Facilities include a small café (open 6am-6pm daily), bar, tax-free shop and car hire. The **airport bus** (single 139kr, journey 75mins) leaves 20mins after an arriving flight for Cityterminalen in Stockholm; it returns about 2hrs before departing flights. There are **trains** every hour to the city (but you'll have to take a bus or taxi to the station first). A **taxi** to Stockholm will cost around 1,450kr.

By train

The major rail operator in Sweden is SJ (www.sj.se). Domestic and international trains arrive and depart from Stockholm's Central Station on the western edge of Norrmalm. Arlanda Express trains to and from Stockholm's airport also terminate at bespoke platforms here. Just below the station is T-Centralen, the main station on the Tunnelbana underground network; taxis are available outside. Commuter trains depart from Stockholm City, which is part of the same complex.

It is possible to travel to Stockholm by rail from the UK in two days, via Brussels, Cologne, Hamburg and Copenhagen. This route includes taking a 'train ferry' between Germany and Denmark and crossing the magnificent Öresund Bridge between Denmark and Sweden. For more details, see seat61.com.

SJ *SJ Central Station, Vasagatan, Norrmalm (077 175 75 75). T-bana T-Centralen or bus 1, 3, 53, 56, 59, 65, 91. Open 7am-8pm Mon-Fri; 8am-6pm Sat; 8am-8pm Sun. Map p80 L8.*
To book tickets from abroad, call +46 771 75 75 75 (open 8am-5pm Mon-Fri) or visit www.sj.se and print your e-ticket (or collect at any SJ ticket machine with a credit or debit card).

By bus

Most long-distance coaches stop at Cityterminalen, Stockholm's main bus station, next to Central Station. T-Centralen is an escalator ride away, and there are always taxis outside. **Eurolines Scandinavia** (08 30 24 25, timetable from abroad +46 31 100 240, www.eurolines.eu) operates coach services to more than 500 European cities.

Swebus Express *Cityterminalen, Klarabergsgatan, Norrmalm (077 121 82 18, www.swebusexpress.se). T-bana T-Centralen or bus 1, 3, 53, 56, 59, 65, 91. Open Telephone enquiries 8am-8pm Mon-Fri; 9am-5pm Sat, Sun. Map p80 L7.*
One of the larger Swedish bus companies, Swebus Express covers Sweden's major cities, along with Oslo and Copenhagen. Tickets can be purchased online and by phone up to 1hr before departure and at Cityterminalen until departure.

By car

Stockholm's main road link with western Europe is via the Öresund toll bridge between Copenhagen in Denmark and Malmö in Sweden. It is crossed by more than 19,500 cars daily; the toll is €43 return. It's 615km (382 miles) from Malmö to Stockholm. Alternatively, there's a 3hr ferry from Frederikshavn in Denmark to Göteborg, from where it's 475km (295 miles) to Stockholm. The E18 runs 530km (328 miles) from Oslo in Norway to Stockholm. Driving in Sweden is relatively safe – roads are in great condition and there are no other tolls.

By sea

If you arrive by sea, you've most likely come from Finland or Estonia. The main companies operating ferries to/from Stockholm are:

Birka Cruises *Stadsgårdsterminalen, Södermalm (08 702 72 00, www. birka.se). T-bana Slussen or bus 2, 3, 43, 53, 55, 59, 71, 76, 96. Open*
phone enquiries 9am-9pm daily. *Map p134 P11.*
Daily cruises in summer to Gotland, Finland, Tallinn, Riga and Poland. The boat terminal, Stadsgårdskajen, is right next to Slussen.

Tallink Silja Line *Sea and Sky Travel, Hamnpirsvägen 10 (08 22 21 40, www.tallinksilja.se). T-bana Ropsten and then bus 76. Open 8am-7pm Mon-Fri; 9am-4pm Sat, Sun. Map p102 U2.*
Tallink Silja Line operates ferries to/from Helsinki, Turku, Riga and Tallinn. Boats dock at the new Värtahamnen terminal just north-east of the city centre. The terminal has parking, luggage lockers, an ATM, a kiosk and a café. There are taxis at the terminal, or there's a dedicated bus service to Cityterminalen (single 60kr). Signs show you how to walk the 5-10mins to the nearest T-bana station, Gärdet (and from Gärdet to the terminal).

Viking Line *Cityterminalen, Klarabergsviadukten 72, Norrmalm (08 452 40 00, www. vikingline.se). T-bana T-Centralen or bus 1, 3, 53, 56, 59, 65, 91. Open 8am-6pm Mon-Fri, Sat; 11am-6pm Sun. Map p80 L7.*
Ferries to/from Finland, and from Helsinki to Tallinn. Boats dock at Vikingterminalen on Södermalm (*map p134 S12*). The terminal has parking and luggage lockers. There are taxis at the terminal, but many prefer to walk the 10mins to Slussen. Viking Line has its own bus link to Stadsgården and Cityterminalen (return 110kr).

PUBLIC TRANSPORT

The **Tunnelbana** (abbreviated to T-bana) metro system is the quickest, cheapest and most convenient way to get around the city. The efficient, comprehensive bus network operates around the clock and covers areas not reached by the metro or the commuter trains. Both the T-bana and city buses are run by **Storstockholms Lokaltrafik**, or **SL**.

SL Center *Central Station, Norrmalm (08 600 10 00, www. sl.se). T-bana T-Centralen or bus 1, 3, 53, 56, 59, 65, 91.* **Open** *7am-9pm daily.* **Map** *p80 L8.*
This information centre can answer any questions you might have about public transport. It's located on the floor below the main concourse at Central Station. You can pick up maps and timetables here. **Other locations** Sergels torg, Fridhemsplan and Tekniska Högskolan (7am-6.30pm Mon-Fri; 10am-5pm Sat).

Fares & tickets

Tickets for travel within Stockholm can be purchased in the T-bana but not on buses, although some bus stations have ticket machines. Single tickets cost 45kr and are valid for 1hr 15mins from when the trip starts. However, it's cheaper and easier to buy a blue **SL Access card** (similar to London's Oyster card), available from Pressbyrån kiosks and SL Centers, and valid on all public transport in Stockholm. These initially cost 20kr, and tickets or credit (*reskassa*) are then loaded on to them electronically. You place the card on top of the card reader at automatic barriers. A single journey on an SL Access card costs 32kr. A 24hr travelcard uploaded to an SL Access card costs 130kr; a 72hr pass is 260kr; a 7-day unlimited travel pass is 335kr.

Tunnelbana

The three metro lines are identified by colour – red, green or blue – on maps and station signs. All three lines intersect at T-Centralen. At interchanges, lines are indicated by the names of the stations at the end of the line, so you should know in which direction you're heading when changing between lines. The T-bana runs 5am-1am Mon-Thur, Sun; 24hrs Fri, Sat.

Buses

Most bus routes operate from 5am to midnight daily. You board at the front and get off through the middle or rear doors. Single tickets cannot be bought on board. If you have an SL Access card, you should touch in by the driver's seat, whether you have a travel pass or pre-paid credit. Paper tickets or tickets bought using the SL app should be shown to the driver.

Most **night buses** run from midnight until 5am, when the regular buses take over. The main stations are Slussen, T-Centralen, Odenplan, Fridhemsplan and Gullmarsplan.

Ferries

Many ferry companies operate on Stockholm's waterways. Some routes are used daily by people commuting to work and are part of the SL network, while others are designed for sightseeing or excursions into the archipelago. SL travel passes are not valid on the archipelago ferries.

Cinderella Båtarna *12 00 40 45, www.stromma.se/skargard.* Ferries to Vaxholm, Grinda, Santahamina, Möja and more, operated by Stromma Skargard. Boats depart from Nybrokajen on Strandvägen. Buy tickets on board.

Djurgårdsfärjan Year-round ferry service operated by Waxholmsbolaget (*see below*) within Stockholm harbour. It runs between Slussen and Djurgården (stopping at Allmänna Gränd, next to Gröna Lund), Skeppsholmen and Nybroplan. From May to August, it also stops at the Vasamuseet. Buy tickets in ticket booths before boarding; single 44kr. SL travel passes are valid.

Strömma *08-12 00 40 00, www.stromma.com* Departs from Stadshusbron (next to Stadhuset) to Drottningholm and Birka, and from Strandvägen to Fjäderholmarna, Vaxholm and Sandhamn. Tickets can be purchased online and for some tours on board (cash only) or in the ticket booths by the departure points – check the website for details.

Waxholmsbolaget *08 600 10 00, www.waxholmsbolaget.se* These ferries cover the whole archipelago, from Arholma in the north to Landsort in the south. Boats depart from Strömkajen outside the Grand Hôtel, opposite the Royal Palace. Buy tickets on board.

Local trains

For trips into the suburbs and surrounding towns, there are **commuter trains** run by SL. The same tickets may be used on these trains as on the T-bana. Stockholm City is a station for commuter rail services that opened in summer 2018. It can be accessed at various points from street level and via tunnel and escalator links from inside T-Centralen. Trains will take you as far north as Bålsta and Kungsängen, and as far south as Södertälje, Nynäshamn and Gnesta. The **Citybanan** (Stockholm City Line) is a new commuter railway tunnel that runs beneath central Stockholm for 6 km (3.7 miles). Its two key stations are T-Centralen and Odenplan.

TAXIS

Taxis can be ordered by phone, online or hailed on the street, and there are taxi ranks near railway and bus stations. Taxi services offered in private, unmarked cars are illegal in Sweden and should be avoided. Fares (starting at around 30kr) are quite steep; current rates and supplements should be displayed inside each cab. Uber taxis are cheaper and widely available.

Taxi companies

The firms listed below take bookings 24hrs a day.

Flygtaxi (airport taxis) *08 120 92 000, www.flygtaxi.se*

Taxi Kurir *08 30 00 00, www.taxikurir.se*

Taxi Stockholm *08 15 00 00, www.taxistockholm.se*

Top Cab *08 33 33 33, www.topcab.com*

DRIVING

Driving in Stockholm can be a hassle. There's a lot of traffic, free parking is difficult to find, and fuel is expensive. There is also a congestion charge for Swedish-registered vehicles in central Stockholm (6.30am-6.29pm Mon-Fri, 11kr-35kr, maximum 105kr per day). Eco-vehicles and foreign-registered cars are exempt, and rental agencies incorporate the charge into their fees upfront.

However, if you plan to explore more of the country, then a car may be an asset. It's wise to familiarise yourself with the dos and don'ts of Swedish road travel; visit the Swedish road administration (www.trafikverket.se) for the lowdown on the driving laws.

Breakdown services

Motormännens Riksförbund
Fridhemsgatan 30, Kungsholmen (02 021 11 11, www.msverige.se). T-bana Fridhemsplan or bus 1, 3, 4, 77, 94. **Open** *noon-5pm daily.* **Map** *p159 F7.*
The Swedish equivalent of the British AA, with reciprocal arrangements with most European motoring organisations.

Parking

Parking is not easy in the city centre. If you've parked illegally or not paid the right fee, you'll get

a hefty fine. *Parkering Förbjuden* means 'parking prohibited'. Car parks (*parkering*), indicated by a white 'P' on a blue sign, charge 85kr-120kr/hr Mon-Fri.

Vehicle rental

To rent a car in Sweden, you must be at least 18 years old (age may vary by car category) and you must have held your licence for 2 years. Drivers who plan to rent a car under the age of 25 may incur a young driver surcharge.

Avis *Klarabergsviadukten 92, Norrmalm (010 494 80 50, www.avis.se). T-bana T-Centralen or bus 3, 52, 56, 62, 65.* **Open** *7am-6pm Mon-Fri; 8am-1pm Sat; 3pm-8pm Sun.* **Map** *p159 K9.*
Other locations *Arlanda Airport (010 494 80 10); Bromma Airport (010 49 48 080).*

Europcar *Östra Järnvägsgatan 27, Norrmalm (08 21 06 50, customer service 08 12 07 48 49, www.europcar.se). T-bana T-Centralen or bus 3, 53, 56, 62, 65.* **Open** *6am-10pm Mon-Fri; 8am-10pm Sat; noon-8pm Sun.* **Map** *p80 L7.* **Other locations** *Arlanda Airport (08 555 98 400); Bromma Airport (08 80 08 07).*

Hertz *Mäster Samuelsgatan 71, Norrmalm (08 454 62 50, www.hertz.se). T-bana T-Centralen or bus 3, 53, 59, 62, 65.* **Open** *6am-11pm daily.* **Map** *p80 L7.* **Other locations** *Arlanda Airport*

(08 590 90 500); Bromma Airport (08 629 27 50).

CYCLING

Stockholm is very bike-friendly: not too big or busy, and with plenty of bike lanes. Its popular public cycle-share scheme, **Stockholm City Bikes** (www.citybikes.se) has around 100 stands across the city centre. The cost of rental can be loaded on to an SL travel card on the website (*see left*) or in person at branches of Pressbyrån, 7-Eleven and SL Centers. Hiring a bike for the first time can be confusing – note that the rental card needs to be placed on the card reader located at the end of the stand. Since summer 2019, app-based electric scooter-sharing schemes from **Voi** (www.voiscooters.com) and **Lime** (www.li.me) have also become increasingly popular.

If you're visiting off-season, or simply prefer to keep the same bike with you for the whole day, then good rental places include **Visit Djurgården** (*see p124*), **Rent a Bike** (Strandvägen Kajplats 18, www.rentabike.se) and **Gamla Stans Cykel** (Lilla Nygatan 10, Gamla Stan, 08 411 16 70, www.gamlastanscykel.se).

WALKING

Stockholm is compact, and walking is often the best way to get around. For details of guided walks, *see p61*.

Resources A-Z

Travel Advice

For up-to-date information on travel to a specific country – including the latest on safety and security, health issues, local laws and customs – contact your home country government's department of foreign affairs. Most have websites with useful advice for would-be travellers.

AUSTRALIA
www.smartraveller.gov.au

CANADA
www.voyage.gc.ca

NEW ZEALAND
www.safetravel.govt.nz

REPUBLIC OF IRELAND
foreignaffairs.gov.ie

UK
www.fco.gov.uk/travel

USA
www.state.gov/travel

ACCIDENT & EMERGENCY

To contact the police, ambulance or fire service in an emergency, call 112 (free of charge). For central police stations, *see p243* Police. The following hospitals have 24-hour emergency rooms; for other hospitals, *see p240* Health.

Danderyds sjukhus
Mörbygårdsvägen, 182 88 Danderyd (08 655 50 00, www. ds.se). T-bana Danderyds sjukhus.

St Görans Sjukhus
Sanktgöransgatan 1, Kungsholmen (08 587 01 000, www.stgoran.se). T-bana Fridhemsplan or bus 49. **Map** *p159 E7.*

Södersjukhuset *Sjukhusbacken 10, Södermalm (08 616 10 00, www.sodersjukhuset.se). Bus 3, 4, 55, 74, 94.* **Map** *p134 L14.*

ADDRESSES

In Sweden, addresses are written with the building number after the street name. As in the UK, but not the US, the first floor is the floor *above* street level. The floor at street level is *bottenvåning*, often abbreviated to 'BV'.

AGE RESTRICTIONS

The legal drinking age for bars and restaurants is 18, but you must be 20 years old to buy alcohol at the state-owned monopolistic off-licence **Systembolaget**. Many clubs also set their own age restrictions – customers typically need to be 20, 21, 23 or over to enter them.

You can smoke and drive at 18. At 15, teens become *byxmyndig*, which, loosely translated, means they are 'in charge of their pants'. In other words, they can legally have sex.

ATTITUDE & ETIQUETTE

Swedes are reserved by global standards and small talk is typically kept to a minimum, especially in public spaces such as stores or on trains and buses. However, locals are usually happy to offer help if they are asked, and typically speak good English. Timekeeping is important in Swedish culture: assume public transport will run on time, and if you receive an invitation to an event or a party, arrive promptly. Swedes typically take their shoes off at home and in some offices (especially during the snowy winter), and guests are expected to follow suit. In social and business settings, Swedes typically greet people they don't know with a handshake (usually introducing themselves to everyone in the room). They hug family, friends and acquaintances that they've met before.

CLIMATE

Stockholm has four distinct seasons. December to February is the coldest period, with temperatures dropping below zero and a strong chance of snow. Spring (March to May) is the driest time of the year, although the weather can be fickle. Snow could still make an appearance, or days might be gloomy and chilly. Summer temperatures (June to August) typically peak at around 20C, dropping to around 10C or lower in September and October. November is a very dark month in Stockholm: the sun sets at around 3pm. For more on the climate in Stockholm, *see p240* Local Weather; for more on seasonal Stockholm, *see p28* When to Visit.

CONSUMER

Many Swedish stores offer *öppet köp*, which means you can return an item within either 14 or 28 days of buying it, even if there is no defect. The time limit is usually noted on your receipt. If you buy something and a fault occurs within six months of your purchase, you are entitled to complain and if the company can't fix the item they are required to offer a refund. Sweden's National Board for Consumer Disputes (ARN; www. arn.se) assesses more serious cases. For information on sales tax, *see p243.*

CUSTOMS

The import of firearms, narcotics, animals and medicines is strictly regulated; check the Swedish customs website, www.tullverket. se, for details. You must be at least 18 years old to bring tobacco products into Sweden, and 20 to bring in alcohol. Visitors from the EU can bring in alcohol and tobacco for private use without incurring customs duty; again, check www.tullverket.se for details of what constitutes private and commercial use.

If you are arriving into Sweden by commercial airline or ferry from a non-EU country, you can bring goods with you (not alcohol or tobacco) up to a maximum value of 4300kr (€430) without paying any duty or tax; if you travel by other means, the limit is 3000kr (€300).

DISABLED VISITORS

It is not usually a problem for disabled visitors to get around the city; facilities are good compared to much of Europe, and recent legislation means that all public buildings must be accessible to the disabled and visually impaired.

The streets are in good condition and have wide pavements, and kerbs have ramps for wheelchairs. Wheelchair-adapted toilets are common, and many hotels even have allergy-free rooms. The public transport system is quite wheelchair-accessible, especially the T-bana, which has plenty of elevators, and most buses can 'kneel' at bus stops – although wide gaps between trains and platforms remain a common complaint.

Most taxis are large enough to take wheelchairs, but check before you order a cab. Try **Taxi Stockholm** (08 15 00 00).

De Handikappades Riksförbund *Storforsplan 44, 123 21 Farsta (08 685 80 00, www. dhr.se). T-bana Farsta.* **Open** *10am-noon Mon, Wed, 1-3pm Tue.* Information on facilities for the mobility-impaired. The website has an English version with tips about accessible hotels, restaurants, cinemas, museums and theatres.

DRUGS

Drugs, including cannabis, are nowhere near as widely accepted in Sweden as in some parts of Europe. Possession of any controlled drug, including medicine for which you do not have a prescription, is illegal, and you can be heavily fined for the very smallest amounts.

ELECTRICITY

Sweden, along with most of Europe, has 220-volt AC, 50Hz current and uses two-pin continental plugs. The 220V current works fine with British-bought 240V products with a simple plug adaptor (available at airports or department stores). With US 110V equipment you will need to use a current transformer.

EMBASSIES & CONSULATES

Many foreign embassies are clustered in Diplomatstaden, near Ladugårdsgärdet in Östermalm. For details of all foreign embassies in Sweden and Swedish embassies abroad, see embassy.goabroad.com.

Australian Embassy *Klarabergsviadukten 63, Norrmalm (08 613 29 00, https://sweden.embassy.gov. au). T-bana T-Centralen.* **Open** *8.30am-4.30pm Mon-Fri.* **Map** *p80 L8.*

British Embassy *Skarpögatan 6-8, Östermalm (08 671 30 00, www.ukinsweden.fco.gov.uk). Bus 69.* **Open** *Visas by appt only, book online. Consulate & information 9am- 5pm Mon-Fri.* **Map** *p102 U7.*

Canadian Embassy *Tegelbacken 4, 7th Floor, Norrmalm (08 453 30 00, www.sweden.gc.ca). T-bana T-Centralen.* **Open** *8.30am-5pm Mon-Fri.* **Map** *p80 M8.*

Irish Embassy *Hovslagargatan 5, Norrmalm (08 545 04 040, www.embassyofireland.se). T-bana Kungsträdgården or bus 65.* **Open** *10am-noon, 2.30-4pm Mon-Fri.* **Map** *p80 P8.*

New Zealand Embassy *Skarpögatan 6, Östermalm (08 400 17 270, www.mfat.govt.nz). Bus 69.* **Open** *by appt only.* **Map** *p102 U7.*

US Embassy *Dag Hammarskjöldsväg 31, Östermalm (08 783 53 00, www.stockholm. usembassy.gov). Bus 56, 69, 76.* **Open** *8am-4.30pm Mon-Fri.* **Map** *p102 T7.*

HEALTH

Most healthcare across Sweden is financed by social insurance, which means all citizens have access to subsidised services. Dental care, including emergency treatment, is not fully subsidised and is relatively expensive. Basic, non-urgent medical care is handled by local health centres (called *vårdcentral*). Urgent, but not life-threatening conditions

Local Weather

Average monthly temperatures and rainfall in Stockholm

	High (°C/°F)	Low (°C/°F)	Rainfall (mm/in)
January	0 / 32	-5 / 23	39 / 1.5
February	0 / 32	-5 / 23	27 / 1.1
March	3 / 37	-3 / 27	26 / 1
April	8 / 46	1 / 34	30 / 1.2
May	15 / 59	6 / 43	30 / 1.2
June	21 / 70	11 / 52	45 / 1.8
July	22 / 72	13 / 55	72 / 2.8
August	20 / 68	13 / 55	66 / 2.6
September	15 / 59	9 / 48	55 / 2.2
October	10 / 50	5 / 41	50 / 2
November	4 / 39	0 / 32	53 / 2.1
December	1 / 34	-3 / 27	46 / 1.8

are treated at small emergency units (called *närakut*). Emergency hospital clinics (called *akutmottagning*) handle serious accidents or sudden illness.

EU nationals should obtain a **European Health Insurance Card (EHIC)** before travelling, which facilitates medical care under the Swedish national health service at the standard, subsidised fee paid by Swedes. Citizens of non-EU countries will usually have to pay for treatment. Visitors of all nationalities are strongly advised to arrange comprehensive health insurance prior to their trip.

For advice on minor illnesses or prescription drugs, call the 24-hour **Healthcare Information Service** (1177, www.1177.se); stay on the line when the automatic answering service kicks in and you will be connected to a nurse. For hospital emergency departments, *see p239* Accident & emergency.

Dentists

Afta Akuttandvård *Sergels torg 12, Norrmalm (08 409 04 060, www.akuttandvard.se). T-bana T-Centralen or bus 1, 56, 59.* **Open** *Drop-in patients 8am-5pm Mon-Fri.* **Map** *p80 M7.*

City Akuten Tand *Olof Palmes Gata 13A, Norrmalm (01 060 10 201, www.cityakuten.se). T-bana Hötorget or bus 1, 56, 59.* **Open** *8am-7pm Mon-Fri; 10am-4pm Sat, Sun.* **Map** *p80 M6.*

Doctors

These clinics offer daily drop-in services for urgent but non-emergency problems, either throughout the day or at specific time slots.

City Akuten Vårdcentral *Apelbergsgatan 48, Norrmalm (08 128 55 600, www.ptj.se). T-bana Hötorget.* **Open** *8am-8pm daily.* **Map** *p80 M6.*

Rösenlunds Vårdcentral *Tideliusgatan 12, 4 tr, Sodermalm (08 616 94 00, www.vcr.se). Train Stockholm Södra or bus 3, 4.* **Open** *8am-5pm daily.* **Map** *p134 M14.*

Opticians

Synsam *Sergelarkaden 12, Norrmalm (08 21 20 44, www.synsam.se). T-bana T-Centralen.* **Open** *10am-7pm Mon-Fri; 10am-6pm Sat; 11am-5pm Sun.* **Map** *p80 M7.* Scandinavia's largest group of opticians has around a dozen branches in Stockholm.

Pharmacies

Pharmacies (*apotek*), identified by a green and white sign, can be found all over the city. Most are open 10am-6pm Mon-Fri with varied weekend opening hours.

Apoteket C W Scheele *Klarabergsgatan 64, Norrmalm (077 145 04 50, www.apoteket.se). T-bana T-Centralen.* **Open** *24hrs daily.* **Map** *p80 L8.*

STDs, HIV/AIDS

There are a range of drop-in clinics offering free testing for sexually transmitted infections.

SMSH *Barnhusgatan 20, Norrmalm (08 123 40 500, www.slso.sll.se/vard-hos-oss/ sexuell-halsa). Transport.* **Open** *4-7pm Mon; noon-2pm Wed; 10.30am-12.30pm Fri; or by appt at other times.* **Map** *p80 L6.* STD testing, contraception counselling and sexual counselling for those aged 23 and older.

ID

Swedes are required to have national identity cards, but many use a driving licence as ID. It is a good idea to carry some form of identification when you go to bars and clubs if you're under 25 or look like you could be. A form of ID will also be needed if you want to pay the lower price sometimes offered at museums for people under 25 or over 65, as well as when buying alcohol in Systembolaget stores.

INSURANCE

All foreign visitors are advised to take out private travel insurance to cover a wide range of eventualities from injury to theft. Non-EU citizens should always ensure that their insurance cover includes medical costs (including repatriation, if necessary), luggage, personal belongings and any activities that they wish to pursue while abroad.

LANGUAGE

Swedish is Sweden's primary official language, although there are also five national minority languages: Finnish, the Finnish dialect of the Torneå Valley, Sami (spoken by Sweden's indigenous population who live largely in the north of the country), Romani and Yiddish. Swedes are among the best in the world at speaking English as a second language. Increasingly, hotels, bars and stores employ foreign staff who serve customers in English.

LEGAL HELP

If you get into legal difficulties, contact your embassy (*see p240*), which will have a list of English-speaking lawyers.

LGBT

Two men or two women checking in to a Stockholm hotel together won't cause so much as a raised eyebrow. There are, however, a number of hotels that actively court gay visitors and are members of **Stockholm LGBT** (www.stockholmlgbt.com), a network of businesses that work to maintain the city's reputation for openness, tolerance and inclusivity. Its website has listings and articles aimed at LGBTQ visitors. For further information, consult the **QX** website, www.qx.se, which has a guide to the city in English. For details of the LGBT nightlife scene, *see p195.*

RFSU *Saltmätargatan 20, Norrmalm (08 501 62 900, www.rfsu.se). T-bana Rådmansgatan.* **Open** *Phone enquiries 1-3 pm Mon; 2-4pm Wed; 10am-noon Fri* **Map** *p80 L5.* The main office for the National Association for Sexual Equality works for an open, positive view of sex and relationship issues and provides support to Sweden's gay, lesbian and trans community as well as straight residents.

LIBRARIES

Stockholm's libraries are open to anyone for reference, but if you want to take a book out, you will need ID and an address in Sweden (a hotel address will not do). For a list of public libraries in Stockholm, contact **Stadsbiblioteket** (08 508 31 900, www.biblioteket.stockholm.se).

LOST/STOLEN PROPERTY

Both of Stockholm's two main public transport companies have lost-and-found centres. There are also lost luggage offices at all of the city's airports.

SJ *Kungsgatan 79, Kungsholmen (08 578 84 800). T-bana T-Centralen or bus 1, 3, 53, 56, 59, 65, 91.* **Open** *10am-6pm Mon-Fri.* **Map** *p159 J8.* For objects lost on long-distance trains.

SL *Klara Östra Kyrkogata 6, Norrmalm (08 600 10 00). T-bana T-Centralen or bus 3, 47, 53, 56, 59, 62, 65.* **Open** *11am-7pm Mon; 11am-6pm Tue-Fri; 10am-4pm Sat.* **Map** *p80 M8.* For objects lost on the Tunnelbana, city buses and commuter trains.

MEDIA

International newspapers & magazines

Press Stop (Götgatan 31) and **Papercut** (*see p152*), both in Södermalm, are great for English-language arts magazines and journals. Copies of major foreign magazines and newspapers, especially English-language ones, can be found in larger branches of **Pressbyrån** (www.pressbyran. se), including at Stockholm Central Station and Arlanda Airport.

National & local news

The two main daily papers are **Dagens Nyheter** (www.dn.se), and the more right-leaning **Svenska Dagbladet** (www. svd.se). **Aftonbladet** (www. aftonbladet.se) and **Expressen** (www.expressen.se) are popular tabloids with the latest scandals and gossip. **Nöjesguiden** (available monthly in print and online at www.nojesguiden.

se) features stories about the Stockholm cultural scene and events listings (in Swedish). For Swedish news in English, **Radio Sweden** lists brief summaries on its website (www.sverigesradio. se). **The Local** (online only; www.thelocal.se) provides a round-up of Swedish-related news in English, alongside advice for newcomers and some travel and culture features. **Totally Stockholm** (monthly in print and online at www. totallystockholm.se) provides entertainment news and listings in English.

Radio

Mix Megapol *www.radioplay.se/ mixmegapol* Contemporary pop and dance music.

NRJ *105.1 MHz, www.radioplay. se/nrj* The latest hits.

Radio Sweden *89.6 MHz, https://sverigesradio.se/ radiosweden* Check online for English programming during evenings and weekends.

Sveriges Radio P1 *https:// sverigesradio.se/p1* Talk shows, debates and documentaries (in Swedish).

Sveriges Radio P2 *96.2 MHz, https://sverigesradio.se/ p2* Classical music, jazz and opera.

Sveriges Radio P3 *https:// sverigesradio.se/p3* New music, news and documentaries aimed at under-30s.

Sveriges Radio P4 Stockholm *https://sverigesradio.se/ Stockholm* Pop and rock music and local news.

Television

The state channels of **SVT 1** and **SVT 2** were the first to broadcast in Sweden and still earn the highest ratings. Their commercial-free programmes are varied enough to appeal to all ages. Deregulation during the mid 1980s ended the state's television broadcasting monopoly and allowed for the creation of several private channels. The most successful of these is the terrestrial **TV4**,

with news, soap operas, sitcoms and game shows. Similar programming can be found on **TV3** and **Kanal 5**, both of which are broadcast from abroad and – much to the chagrin of the government – do not always adhere to Swedish broadcasting regulations. Foreign-made programmes and films are shown in their original language with Swedish subtitles. For more on TV in Sweden, *see p186.*

Internet & WiFi

Free public WiFi networks are widespread in Stockholm, so you should have no trouble getting online. A good tip is to log on at Pressbyrån convenience stores, which are located at or nearby most underground stations around the city. Tech-savvy Sweden is expected to start offering the next generation of mobile broadband, 5G, in 2020.

MONEY

The Swedish *krona* ('crown'; plural *kronor*, abbreviated to kr or SEK) is divided into 100 *öre*. It comes in coins of 1kr, 5kr and 10kr, and notes of 20kr, 50kr, 100kr, 200kr, 500kr and 1,000kr.

Stockholm is expensive by most standards, although not that different to London or Paris these days. Expect to pay 48kr-84kr (roughly £4-£7) for a beer and to pay a bit more than you're used to for 'budget' food (*see p40* Price categories). Taxis (including Uber) are more expensive than elsewhere. For accommodation prices, *see p228* Price categories.

Sweden has one of the most cashless economies on the planet; you can pay by card almost anywhere and many shops, bars and hotels demand it. Major credit and debit cards, including contactless cards, are widely accepted. The Swedish mobile payment app Swish is widespread among locals; Applepay is also accepted by some businesses. If you do choose to get money out, there are two types of ATM: **Bankomat** (the joint system of the business banks) and **Uttag** (which belongs to Swedbank). You'll find ATMs at some shopping centres and department stores as well as banks.

Banks & bureaux de change

Banks are usually open 9am-3pm Mon-Fri, and some stay open until 6pm at least once a week. All banks are closed at weekends and on public holidays, as well as the day before a public holiday. Banks will advance cash against a credit card, but prefer you to use an ATM. A growing number of banks in Sweden have stopped handling cash altogether, so if you need to change money its best to do this at exchange offices at Central Station or Arlanda Airport.

Forex *Centralstation, Norrmalm (010 211 16 04, www.forex.se). T-bana T-Centralen.* **Open** *7am-9pm Mon-Fri; 9am-8pm Sat, Sun.* **Map** *p80 L8. Also at Arlanda Airport in Terminal 2, Terminal 5 & Sky City (08 593 62 271).*

Money transfers

Local banks don't do money transfers unless you're a customer of the bank. **Forex** *(see above)*, **Western Union** (www.westernunion.com) and **MoneyGram** (www. moneygram.com) are your best bets for money transfers to and from Sweden; all have several branches around Stockholm – see the websites for details.

Tax

The sales tax for most commodities is 25%. There is a 12% sales tax on food and hotel bills, and 6% sales tax on books, movie and concert tickets, and transport (taxis, flights, trains). The sales tax is always listed separately on the bill but is included in the displayed price. Non-EU residents can reclaim tax on purchases above 200kr in shops displaying a 'Tax-Free Shopping' sticker. All you have to do is ask for a tax-free receipt (*kvitto*) when paying for an item. When you leave the EU, show your purchases, receipts and passport to customs officials and have your Global Refund cheques stamped. The refund

can be collected from any Global Blue office or credited to your own bank account. Call **Global Blue** (00800 32 111 111, www. globalblue.com).

OPENING HOURS

Normal opening hours for shops are 10am-6pm Mon-Fri, 10am-5pm Sat, 11am-5pm Sun. Some smaller shops close earlier on Sat and do not open on Sun. All shops used to be closed on public holidays, but this is changing more and more. Many grocery stores are now open 365 days per year.

Restaurant opening hours vary greatly. They are usually open by 11am if they serve lunch; otherwise they'll open at some point in the afternoon (usually 4pm or 5pm). Closing time is around midnight unless the restaurant has a bar, in which case it may stay open until 1am or even later. Note that many restaurants close in July.

Office hours are generally 8.30am-5pm Mon-Fri. For bank opening hours, *see left* Banks & bureaux de change.

POLICE

The police are not that common a sight in Stockholm but can always be spotted at concerts or any special events. They speak English and are friendly and helpful. If you're the victim of a crime, call the police on 112, or dial 114 14 in non-emergency situations.

Police HQ *Kungsholmsgatan 43, Kungsholmen (114 14). T-bana Rådhuset or bus 1, 40, 56, 91.* **Map** *p159 H7.* This is the main police station; it's also the place where people suspected of committing a crime are kept until trial. Sub-station is at Torkel Knutssonsgatan 20, Södermalm.

POSTAL SERVICES

Sweden no longer has post offices, but there are service points at supermarkets and convenience stores around the city from where you can send and pick up parcels. For a list of service points check www. postnord.se, which has an

information section in English. You can also buy stamps at tobacco kiosks, 7-Elevens and the tourist office.

PUBLIC HOLIDAYS

On public holidays, virtually all shops, banks and offices, and many restaurants and bars, are closed.

New Year's Day Nyårsdagen *1 Jan*
Epiphany Trettondedag Jul *6 Jan*
Good Friday Långfredagen
Easter Sunday Påskdagen
Easter Monday Annandag Påsk
May Day Första Maj *1 May*
Ascension Day Krist Himmelfärds Dag
National Day Nationaldagen *6 June*
Midsummer Eve Midsommarafton *Fri 19-25 June*
Midsummer Day Midsommardagen *Sat 20-26 June*
All Saints' Day Alla Helgons Dag *1 Nov*
Christmas Eve Julafton *24 Dec*
Christmas Day Juldagen *25 Dec*
Boxing Day Annandag Jul *26 Dec*
New Year's Eve Nyårsafton *31 Dec*

RELIGION

Most Swedes are nominally members of the Church of Sweden, which is Evangelical Lutheran, but less than 10% of the population attends church regularly. Many other Christian sects are represented in Stockholm, and significant numbers of Muslims and Jews live in or near the city.

SAFETY & SECURITY

Stockholm is largely considered a very safe city, so the chances of a visitor being the victim of a crime are small. Still, pickpocketing does occur in crowded places and, although muggings are rare, it's wise to take the usual precautions: don't openly flaunt money or jewellery, keep a close eye on your surroundings and be careful in dark and/or isolated areas, such as parks, late at night. Terror crimes are rare in Sweden, although five people died in April 2017 when a hijacked truck ploughed into pedestrians in central Stockholm. Instances of gang-related crime, including shootings and explosions, have been reported with increasing frequency in some outer Stockholm suburbs.

SMOKING

Sweden passed a law on 1 June 2005 that banned smoking in bars and restaurants. A second law, passed in 2018 and active from July 2019, extended the ban to include a wider range of public places, including playgrounds, train station platforms and outdoor cafes and restaurants.

STUDY

Many students come from abroad to study in Sweden.

Universities & colleges

Berghs School of Communication *Sveavägen 34, Norrmalm (08 587 55 000, www. berghs.se). T-bana Hötorget.* **Map** *p80 M6.* Offers programmes in journalism, media, advertising and PR.

Handelshögskolan *Bertil Ohlins Gata 4, Norrmalm (08 736 90 00, www.hhs.se). T-bana Rådmansgatan.* **Map** *p80 L5.* Stockholm's School of Economics, the city's main business school, was founded in 1909.

Hyper Island *Trikåfabriken, Virkesvägen 2, Hammarby Sjöstad (08 744 30 50, www.hyperisland. com). Tram 22.* This global digital business school was founded in southern Sweden but has its second branch in Stockholm in the suburb of Hammarby Sjöstad.

Konstfack *LM Erikssonsväg 14, Telefonplan, 126 27 Hägersten (08 450 41 00, www.konstfack. se). T-bana Telefonplan.* The University College of Arts, Crafts and Design.

Kungliga Tekniska Högskolan *Brinellvägen 8, Norra Djurgården (08 790 60 00, www.kth.se). T-bana Tekniska Högskolan or train Stockholms Östra.* **Map** *p118 N/O2/3.* The Institute of

Technology is around 200 years old. It provides one third of Sweden's technical research and has established exchanges all over the world.

Stockholms Universitet *Norra Djurgården (switchboard 08 16 20 00, student services 08 16 28 45, www.su.se). T-bana Universitetet.* Stockholm University campus lies north of the city centre and caters for about 34,000 undergraduate students and 1,700 postgraduate students.

TELEPHONES

International & local dialling codes

To call Stockholm from abroad, dial 00, then 46 for Sweden, then 8 for Stockholm, then the number. Stockholm phone numbers vary in the number of digits they contain. The area code for Stockholm (including the archipelago) is 08. All phone numbers in this guide are given as dialled from a mobile phone or from outside Stockholm. Swedish mobile phone numbers begin with 07. Numbers beginning 020 are always toll-free lines.

To make an international call from Stockholm, dial 00 and then the country code, followed by the area code (omitting the initial 0, if there is one) and the number. The international code for the UK is 44; it's 1 for the US and Canada; 353 for the Irish Republic; 61 for Australia; and 64 for New Zealand.

Mobile phones

Sweden is on the worldwide GSM network, so compatible mobile phones should work fine. Since Sweden is in the EU, making calls, texting or surfing the web using sim cards from other EU countries will not incur additional roaming charges. Pre-paid Swedish sim cards can be bought at Pressbyrån convenience stores or at branches of the major telecoms operators: Telia, Telinor, Tele2 and 3. Tech-savvy Sweden is expected to start offering the next generation of mobile broadband, 5G, in 2020.

TIME

Stockholm is one hour ahead of GMT, six hours ahead of US Eastern Standard Time and nine hours ahead of Pacific Standard Time. The clocks go forward one hour for Swedish summer time, which runs from late March to late October, with the same changeover days as the UK.

TIPPING

There are no fixed rules about tipping in Sweden because the service charge is almost always included. In restaurants, some people leave 5 %-10% extra, depending on how satisfied they are. Rounding up the bill is usually sufficient when you pay a bartender or a taxi driver. *See also p41.*

TOILETS

Public toilets (*toalett*; small, green booths) are usually found near or in parks. They usually cost 10kr to use and are kept clean. Many only accept card or Swish (the Swedish mobile app) payments. There are public toilets at Central Station including a disabled toilet that has a shower and a breastfeeding room (5am-midnight daily, 10kr).

TOURIST INFORMATION

Stockholm Visitor Centre *Kulturhuset Stadsteatern, Sergels torg 3, Norrmalm (50 82 85 08, www.visitstockholm.com). T-bana T-Centralen or bus 1, 3, 53, 56, 59, 65, 91.* **Open** *9am-6pm Mon-Fri (May-Aug until 7pm); 9am-4pm Sat (Jul-mid Aug until 6pm); 10am-4pm Sun. Closed 24, 25 Dec & 1 Jan.* **Map** *p80 N7.* This is the main tourist office in Stockholm, with huge amounts of useful information, plus free books and maps. You can also buy the Stockholm Pass (in person or online), and theatre and concert tickets. The hotel booking centre can find and book hotels in all price brackets. Free WiFi is available.

VISAS & IMMIGRATION

Sweden is one of the European Union countries covered by the

Schengen agreement, meaning many shared visa regulations and reduced border controls. (The Schengen zone takes in the entire EU, with the exception of the UK and Ireland, and also extends to Norway and Iceland.) To travel to Schengen countries, British and Irish citizens need full passports, while other EU nationals usually only need to carry their national identity card, although it's always wise to carry a passport as some airlines require them.

Passports, but not visas, are needed by US, Canadian, Australian and New Zealand citizens for stays of up to three months. Citizens of South Africa and many other countries do need visas, obtainable from Swedish consulates and embassies abroad (or in other Schengen countries that you're planning to visit). Visa requirements can change, so always check the latest information with your country's Swedish embassy (see embassy. goabroad.com).

WEIGHTS & MEASURES

Sweden uses the metric system. Decimal points are indicated by commas, while thousands are defined by full stops. Throughout this guide, we have listed measurements in both metric and imperial.

WOMEN

Great measures have been taken in Sweden to guarantee equal opportunities for men and women. There is state-subsidised childcare and a generous parental leave system, available to both parents. Swedish women still earn less than men, though, partly because of the professions they choose and the fact that many mothers work part-time. **KvinnorKan** (070 629 77 88, www.kvinnorkan.se) works to enhance the empowerment of women.

It's unlikely that female visitors will face any kind of harassment; Stockholm is a safe city to walk around, although the normal precautions are recommended.

WORK

Work permits

All EU nationals can work in Sweden; non-EU citizens must apply for a work permit abroad and hand in the application to a Swedish embassy or consular representative. The rules for obtaining work permits vary for different jobs. EU citizens can stay in Sweden for three months, after which they must apply for a residence permit (which can take a month to process, so it's best to apply as soon as you arrive). Non-EU citizens must apply for a residence permit from outside Sweden. You'll need to produce a valid ID or passport and other documents depending on your status (employee, job-seeker, self-employed, student, etc). Contact the **National Immigration Authority** (Migrationsverket; 077 123 52 35, www.migrationsverket. se).

Useful organisations

The EU has a website (www. europa.eu) with comprehensive information on EU citizens' rights and useful numbers and addresses. The European Employment Services network, **EURES** (http:// ec.europa.eu/eures), provides a comprehensive database of job vacancies throughout the EU and information about working conditions. It's also worth registering at some of the many online recruiting companies, such as **Academic Search** (www.academicsearch. se), **Monster** (www.monster. se), **Stepstone** (www.stepstone. se) and www.careerbuilder.se. **The Hub** (https://thehub.se) lists start-up jobs, while **The Local** (www.thelocal.se) lists English-language careers opportunities.

If you're already living in Sweden, you can start looking for a job by going to the state employment agency, **Arbetsförmedlingen**; it has a lot of information and offers free guidance for people seeking work.

Arbetsförmedlingen

*Tunnelgatan 3, Norrmalm (077 141 64 16, www. arbetsformedlingen.se). **Open** Phone enquiries 8am-5pm Mon-Fri. Office 10am-4pm Mon-Fri. Self-service (use of computers) 8am- 4pm Mon-Fri. **Map** p80 M6.*

Vocabulary

Vowels

Swedish vowels include the standard a, e, i, o, u and sometimes y along with three additional vowels: å, ä and ö. Vowels are long when at the end of a word or followed by one consonant, and short when followed by two consonants.

- **å** – as in more
- **ä** – as in pet
- **ö** – as in fur
- **y** – as in ewe
- **ej** – as in late

Consonants

- **g** (before e, i, y, ä and ö), **j**, **lj**,**dj** and **gj** – as in yet
- **k** (before e, i, y, ä and ö), **sj**, **skj**, **stj**, **tj** and **rs** – all more or less like sh, with subtle differences
- **qu** – as kv (though q is hardly ever used in Swedish)
- **z** – as in so

Alphabetical order

Swedish alphabetical order lists **å**, **ä** and **ö**, in that order, after **z**.

Useful phrases

- **yes** ja (yah); **no** nej (nay); **please/ thank you** tack; **hello** hej (hay); **goodbye** hej då (hay daw); **excuse me** ursäkta (ewr-shekta); **I'm sorry** förlåt (furr-lawt); **do you speak English?** pratar du engelska? (prat-ar dew engelska?); **how are you?** hur mår du (hewr more dew?)

Sightseeing

- **entrance** ingång (in-gawng); **exit** utgång (ewt-gawng); **open** öppen (ur-pen); **closed** stängd (staingd); **toilet** (women/men) toalett (too-a-let) (kvinnor/män); **where** var; **when** när (nair); **near** nära (naira); **far** långt (lawngt); **(city) square** torg (tohrj); **church** kyrka (chewr-ka); **art gallery** konstgalleri; **town hall** stadshus; **street/road** gata/väg; **palace** slott; **metro** tunnelbana; **ticket to...** biljett till... (bill-yet till); **how much is this/that?** hur mycket kostar den/det? (hewr mewkeh costar den/det?); **which way to...?** hur kommer jag till...? (hewr comer yah til...?)

Accommodation

- **hotel** hotell; **youth hostel** vandrarhem; **I have a reservation** jag har beställt ett rum (yah har bes-telt ett room); **double room** dubbelrum; **single room** enkelrum; **double bed** dubbelsäng; **twin beds** två sängar; **with a bath** med bad; **with a shower** med dusch

Days of the week

- **Monday** måndag; **Tuesday** tisdag; **Wednesday** onsdag; **Thursday** torsdag; **Friday** fredag; **Saturday** lördag; **Sunday** söndag

Numbers

- **0** noll; **1** ett; **2** två (tvaw); **3** tre (trea); **4** fyra (few-ra); **5** fem; **6** sex; **7** sju (shew); **8** åtta (otta); **9** nio (nee-oo); **10** tio (tee-oo); **11** elva; **12** tolv; **13** tretton; **14** fjorton (fyoor-ton); **15** femton; **16** sexton; **17** sjutton (shew-ton); **18** arton; **19** nitton; **20** tjugo (chew-goo); **21** tjugoett (chew-goo-ett); **30** trettio (tretti); **40** fyrtio (fur-ti); **50** femtio (fem-ti); **60** sextio (sex-ti); **70** sjuttio (shew-ti); **80** åttio (otti); **90** nittio (nitti); **100** hundra (hewndra); **1,000** tusen (tews-sen); **1,000,000** miljon (milly-oon)

Eating out

- **have you got a table for...?** har ni ett bord för...? (hahr nee ett boord furr...?); **bill** notan (noo-tan); **menu** meny (men-ew); **lunch** lunch (lwench); **dinner** middag (mid-daag); **main course** huvudrätt (hew-vew-dret); **starter** förrätt (fur-et); **bottle** flaska; **glass** glas; **restaurant** restaurang

Basic foods & extras

- **egg** ägg; **bread** bröd; **cheese** ost; **potatoes** potatis; **rice** ris; **mustard** senap; **butter** smör; **sandwich** smörgås; **sugar** socker

Swedish specialities (husmanskost)

- **split pea and pork soup** ärtsoppa; **fish soup** fisksoppa; **gratin of anchovies and potatoes** Janssons frestelse; **stuffed cabbage rolls** kåldolmar; **meatballs** köttbullar; **pork dumpling with smoked salmon** lufsa; **potato salad** potatissallad; **fried meat and potato hash with a fried egg and pickled beetroot** pytt i panna; **lightly salted brisket of beef** oxbringa; **assortment of herring dishes** rimmad sillbricka; **typical self-service buffet** smörgåsbord

Fruit & veg (frukt & grönsaker)

- **orange** apelsin; **peas** ärtor; **lemon** citron; **raspberry** hallon; **cloudberry** hjortron; **strawberries** jordgubbar; **cabbage** kål; **lingonberry** lingon; **onion** lök; **carrots** morötter; **nuts** nötter; **peach** persika; **wild strawberries** smultron; **mushrooms** svamp; **grapes** vindruvor; **garlic** vitlök

Meat & game (kott & vilt)

- **elk** älg; **beef** biff; **pork** fläsk; **veal** kalvkött; **sausage** korv; **chicken** kyckling; **lamb** lammkött; **roe deer** rådjur; **reindeer** ren; **ham** skinka

Fish (fisk)

- **eel** ål; **mussels** blåmusslor; **trout** forell; **pike-perch** gös; **lobster** hummer; **crayfish** kräftor; **salmon** lax; **prawns** räkor; **sole** sjötunga; **herring (pickled/blackened)** strömming/sill (inlagd/sotare); **fermented Baltic herring** surströmming; **cod** torsk

Cakes/desserts (bakverk/ desserter)

- **ice-cream** glass; **cake** kaka/ tårta; **saffron bun** lussekatt; **Swedish cheesecake** ostkaka; **gingerbread biscuits** pepparkakor; **miniature pancakes served with jam and cream** plättar; **whipped cream and almond paste buns** semla

Drinks (drycker)

- **schnapps** brännvin; **fruit juice** fruktjuice; **fortified mulled wine** glögg; **milk** mjölk; **beer** öl; **arak-like sweet spirit** punsch; **red wine** rödvin; **hot chocolate** varm choklad; **white wine** vitt vin

Further Reference

BOOKS

Society, politics & history

Lola Akinmade Åkerström *Lagom, The Swedish Art of Living well* (2017) A detailed yet accessible unpacking of the concept of *lagom* (Swedish for 'just right'), featuring stunning photos by the author.

Elisabeth Åsbrink *Made in Sweden: 25 ideas that created a country* (2018) A presentation of core Swedish icons and concepts that debunks Swedish stereotypes.

Peter Berlin *The Xenophobe's Guide to the Swedes* (2008) An amusing book explaining the complex rules that govern Swedish social interaction.

Michael Booth *The Almost Nearly Perfect People: The Truth about the Nordic Miracle* (2014) A wry look at what really makes the Scandinavians tick.

Julien S. Bourelle *The Swedes: A Happy Culture of Scandinavia* (2018) Entertaining illustrations of Swedish cultural traits and unwritten social rules.

Sofi Tegsveden Deveaux (ed) *Six Weeks Holiday* (2018) 17 immigrants to Sweden explore the myths and realities of Swedish society and working culture.

Matz Erling *Glorious Vasa: The Magnificent Ship and 17th-century Sweden* (2001) An insight into what life was like in 17th-century Stockholm.

Istvan Hargittai & James Watson *The Road to Stockholm: Nobel Prizes, Science and Scientists (2002)* Discusses the selection process for the scientific laureates and the ingredients for scientific discovery and recognition.

Herman Lindqvist *A History of Sweden: From Ice Age to Our Age* (2006) An entertaining introduction to the history of Sweden.

Magnus Nilsson *Nordic: A Photographic Essay of Landscapes, Food and People* (2016) Photos by one of Sweden's most acclaimed chefs.

Byron J Nordstrom *The History of Sweden* (2002) Swedish history from prehistoric times to the 1990s.

Paul Rapacioli *Good Sweden, Bad Sweden* (2018) Explores the power of bad and fake news about Sweden, drawing on more than a decade of news coverage.

Jan Öjvind Swahn *Maypoles, Crayfish and Lucia: Swedish Holidays and Traditions* (1997) A guide to Swedish customs and festivals.

Kelsie Zaria *Swedish Death Cleaning Workbook* (2019) A cult guide to decluttering.

Architecture, art & design

Niki Brantmark *The Scandinavian Home: Interiors inspired by light* (2017) A peek inside classic and contemporary homes by an influential Swedish design and lifestyle blogger.

Courtney Davis *A Treasury of Viking Design* (2000) Scandinavian Viking design in ceramics, textiles, woodwork and so on.

Charlotte Fiell *Scandinavian Design* (2002) In-depth illustrated guide focusing on 200 designers and design companies.

Olof Hultin, Bengt Oh Johansson, Johan Mårtelius & Rasmus Waern *The Complete Guide to Architecture in Stockholm* (1999) This guide introduces the reader to 400 of the most notable buildings in the Stockholm area.

Lars & Ursula Sjöberg *The Swedish Room* (1994) Illustrated guide to interior design.

Ralph Skansen *Edenheim Traditional Swedish Style* (2002) Illustrated presentation of the interiors of Skansen's buildings.

Michael Snodin & Elisabet Stavenow-Hidemark (eds) *Carl and Karin Larsson: Creators of the Swedish Style* (1998) Numerous essays by experts.

Barbara Stoeltie, René Stoeltie & Angelika Taschen *Country Houses of Sweden* (2001) Coffee-table book with photos of Swedish country houses from various periods.

Angel Trinidad *Scandinavia Dreaming: Nordic Homes, Interiors and Design* (2016) Showcasing inspiring timeless interior projects from Sweden and Scandinavia.

Biographies, autobiographies & travelogues

Ingmar Bergman *The Magic Lantern: An Autobiography* (1989) Memoirs of the film master's career and childhood.

Maline Birger *Move and Work* (2014) Iconic interior and clothing designer takes the reader into her stylish life and homes.

Andrew Brown *Fishing in Utopia: Sweden and the Future that Disappeared* (2011) Reflections on Sweden's social demographic model, told through the eyes of a British immigrant.

Maaret Koskinen *Ingmar Bergman* (2007) An overview of the late, great filmmaker.

Zlatan Ibrahimovic *I am Zlatan Ibrahimovic* (2013) Sweden's biggest footballer in history shares his story.

Sharon Linnea *Raoul Wallenberg: The Man who Stopped Death* (1993) Biography of the famous Swedish diplomat who saved the lives of 100,000 Hungarian Jews during World War II and then disappeared in Soviet custody.

Eivor Martinus *Strindberg and Love* (2001) In-depth biography of the dramatist, focusing on the four most important women in his life.

Måns Mosseson *Avicii* (2020) A much-hyped book about Stockholm-born house DJ and producer Avicii (real name Tim Bergling), who died in 2018.

Carl Magnus Palm *From ABBA to Mamma Mia: The Official Book* (2000) The first book published with the co-operation of the pop group, with lots of good photos.

Karen Swenson *Greta Garbo: A Life Apart* (1997) Insights into the life of Sweden's silver screen darling.

Mary Wollstonecraft *Letters Written during a Short Residence in Sweden, Norway and Denmark* (2004) Wollstonecraft describes her travels through Scandinavia in 1795.

Fiction

Fredrik Backman *A Man Called Ove* (2012) A heart-warming look at a grumpy old man, adapted for cinema in 2015.

Frans G Bengtsson *The Long Ships* (1945) A true Swedish classic, this novel enchants its readers with the adventures of a fictional Viking.

Karin Boye *Kallocain* (1940) A bleak vision of a future totalitarian world state.

Eyvind Johnson *Dreams of Roses and Fire* (1949) Novel by the winner of the 1974 Nobel Prize for Literature.

Jonas Jonasson *The Hundred- Year-Old Man Who Climbed Out the Window and Disappeared* (2012) Comic novel about a pensioner who escapes from his care home, adapted into a movie in 2013.

Jonas Hassen Khemiri *Everything I Don't Remember* (2015) Award-winning novel about a car crash that reflects on life in multicultural Stockholm.

Camilla Läckberg *The Girl in the Woods* (2018) One of Sweden's best-selling thriller authors mixes mysteries with reflections on modern relationships.

Selma Lagerlöf *The Wonderful Adventures of Nils* (1906) One of Sweden's best-loved modern folk tales, written to teach Swedish schoolchildren about the geography of their country.

Stieg Larsson *The Girl with the Dragon Tattoo* (2005) First part of the blockbusting Millennium crime trilogy, starring Mikael Blomkvist and Lisbeth Salander.

John Ajvide Lindqvist *Let the Right One In* (2007) A bestseller in Sweden, this is a unique fusion of social novel and vampire legend.

Henning Mankell *Faceless Killers* (1991) The first in the world-famous series of detective stories starring Inspector Kurt Wallander.

Vilhelm Moberg *The Emigrants* (1949) Moving story about what it was like to emigrate from Sweden to the US in the 19th century.

Mikael Niemi *Popular Music* (2004) A witty, compelling coming-of-age story set in northern Sweden in the 1960s.

August Strindberg *Miss Julie and Other Plays* (1998) Contains some of the dramatist's key works.

FILM

The Best Intentions *(Bille August, 1992)* The story of Ingmar Bergman's parents, written by Bergman himself.

Border *(Ali Abassi, 2018)* Award-winning fantasy movie about a woman and a man who connect over shared facial deformities.

Elvira Madigan *(Bo Widerberg, 1967)* Beautiful-looking film about a doomed love affair.

The Emigrants *(Jan Troell, 1970)* First of two films dealing with Swedish emigrants to America.

Evil *(Mikael Håfström, 2004)* Oscar-nominated film about a young rebel in a Swedish private school in the late 1950s.

Fanny and Alexander *(Ingmar Bergman, 1982)* Family saga seen through the eyes of a young boy.

The Father *(Alf Sjöberg, 1969)* Film version of Strindberg's play about marriage, madness and death.

Force Majeure *(Ruben Ostlund, 2014)* Comedy drama about family tensions following an avalanche during a ski trip.

Four Shades of Brown *(Tomas Alfredson, 2004)* Black comedy interweaving four lives.

Fucking Åmål (Show Me Love) *(Lukas Moodysson, 1998)* All-girl twist to the high-school romance genre, which won multiple awards.

House of Angels *(Colin Nutley, 1992)* Prejudice and conflict in rural Sweden.

I am Curious: Yellow *(Vilgot Sjöman, 1967)* Sexually frank but morally involved tale.

Jalla! Jalla! *(Josef Fares, 2000)* Culture clash comedy.

Let the Right One In *(Tomas Alfredson, 2008)* Vampire horror set in the suburbs of Stockholm.

My Life as a Dog *(Lasse Hallström, 1985)* A witty and touching story of a young boy in 1950s rural Sweden.

Persona *(Ingmar Bergman, 1966)* An actress refuses to speak, while her nurse chats away about her sex life.

A Pigeon Sat on a Branch Reflecting on Existence *(Roy Andersson, 2014)* Bizarre, internationally acclaimed black comedy about two travelling salesmen.

Sami Blood *(Amanda Kernell, 2016)* Raw, coming-of-age drama about a teenage girl from northern Sweden's indigenous Sami community.

Songs from the Second Floor *(Roy Andersson, 2000)* Loosely connected vignettes deal with traffic jams and redundancy in a surreal black comedy.

The Square *(Ruben Ostlund 2017)* Oscar-nominated satirical drama centred around the curator of a fictional Stockholm gallery.

Together *(Lukas Moodysson, 2000)* Comedy about life and love in a 1970s commune.

Tsatsiki, Mum and the Policeman *(Ella Lemhagen, 1999)* Engaging story of a young

Stockholmer who longs to meet his Greek father.

We are the Best! *(Lukas Moodysson, 2013)* Tale of 1980s teen rebellion in Stockholm.

Wild Strawberries *(Ingmar Bergman, 1957)* Warm story of an academic who rediscovers his youth.

Wings of Glass *(Reza Bagher, 2000)* A Swedish-Iranian family's conflict between their Muslim roots and Swedish environment.

MUSIC

Classical

Hugo Alfvén *(1872-1960)* Composer of the ballet *Bergakungen*, five symphonies and numerous songs.

Franz Berwald *(1796-1868)* Wrote operas, chamber music and four symphonies.

Daniel Börtz *(born 1943)* Composer whose contemporary chamber music and solo pieces reflect earlier periods.

Anders Eliasson *(born 1947)* Composer of complex works.

Anders Hillborg *(born 1952)* Most famous for his *Celestial Mechanics* for solo strings.

Wilhelm Peterson-Berger *(1867-1942)* Composer of operas and piano miniatures with a folk influence.

Allan Pettersson *(1911-80)* Composer most renowned for his *Symphony No.7*.

Hilding Rosenberg *(1892-1985)* Wrote numerous string quartets.

Jan Sandström *(born 1954)* Renowned for his *Motorbike Concerto* for trombone and orchestra.

Sven-David Sandström *(born 1942)* Composer of complex orchestral works, ballets and percussion pieces.

Wilhelm Stenhammar *(1871-1927) Composed chamber music, operas and orchestral pieces.*

ABBA Phenomenally successful albums by Sweden's most famous group include *Waterloo* (1974) and *Super Trouper* (1980).

Avicii Internationally-acclaimed house DJ and producer who died in 2018. His albums include *True* and *Stories*.

The Cardigans Pop band formed in 1992. *Life* is probably their best-known album.

Cherrie Young R'n'B sensation from troubled Stockholm suburb Rinkeby. By 2019 she had released two albums *Sherihan* (2016) and *Araweelo* (2018).

The Concretes *Hey Trouble* (2007) was the third album from eccentric Stockholm-based rockers.

Europe Remembered for their iconic cheesy 1986 hit 'The Final Countdown'.

First Aid Kit Folk-pop duo who've had global success with albums including *The Lion's Roar* (2012).

Jose Gonzalez Songwriter made famous by his cover of Swedish band The Knife's 'Heartbeats', featured on his 2003 album *Veneer*.

The Hellacopters US-tinged Swedish rock.

The Hives Successful punk fivesome; albums include *Your New Favourite Band*, *Barely Legal* and *Tyrannosaurus Hives*.

Hov1 Clean-cut hip-hop quartet from Stockholm, wooing Swedish teenagers since 2015.

Lykke Li Hypnotic indie star, whose album, *So Sad So Sexy*, was released in 2018.

Petter Veteran Swedish-language rapper best known for his 2006 album *P*.

Robyn Hugely popular popster experiencing a resurgence after releasing long-awaited album *Honey* in 2018.

Seinabo Sey Soul-pop sensation who rose to international fame following her track 'Younger', first released in 2013.

Silvana Imam Rapper known for political songs featuring themes including racism and homophobia.

Soundtrack of Our Lives Successful six-piece rock outfit hailing from Gothenburg.

Tove Lo Electro-pop artist with hit albums including *Blue Lips* (2017).

Zara Larsson Achieved global fame after her single 'Lush Life' was released in 2015, later featured on her album *So Good* in 2017.

WEBSITES

City of Stockholm *www.stockholm.se* Official information on the city's government, services and history.

The Local Sweden *www.thelocal.se* News stories and regular features about life in Sweden.

Nobel Prizes *www.nobel.se* Everything you ever wanted to know about the Nobel Prize.

Radio Sweden *sverigesradio.se/radiosweden* Daily Swedish news updates in English.

Routes North *www.routesnorth.com* Useful travel tips and events in Sweden and the Nordics.

Scandinavian Design *www.scandinaviandesign.com* The products and personalities of Nordic design, plus museums, magazines and design schools.

Slow Travel Stockholm *www.slowtravelstockholm.com* Eclectic insights on Stockholm from a wide range of perspectives.

Stockholm Guide *www.visitstockholm.com* Official tourism site with good information on events and attractions.

Study in Sweden *https://studyinsweden.se* Information on life as an international student in Sweden.

Sweden *www.sweden.se* Well-written articles and fact sheets on Swedish culture.

Swedish Institute *www.si.se* Promotes Sweden around the world. Information on culture, education, science and business.

Index

INDEX

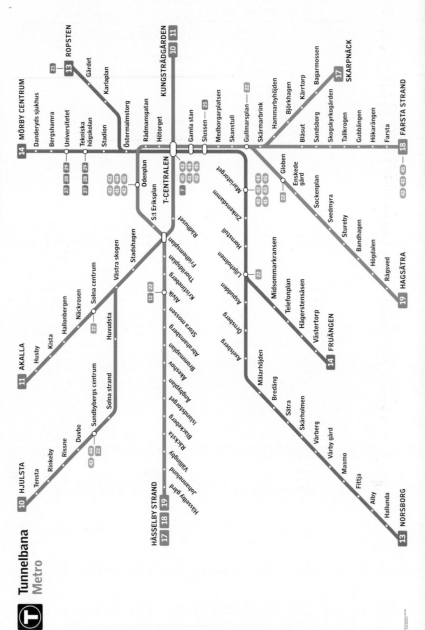

Tunnelbana
Metro

Picture credits

Inside front cover, 90, 234 (right) Downtown Camper; Inside front cover (right), 12 (bottom), 42 (bottom), 137 (bottom) jann@lipka.se/Meatballs for the People; 2 (top left), 17 (bottom), 19 (left), 51 Patrik Linden; 2 (top right) Mikhail Markovskiy/Shutterstock.com; 2 (bottom), 221 Stefan Holm/Shutterstock.com; 5, 29 (bottom) Oleksiy Mark/Shutterstock.com; 6, 56 Nikolay Antonov/Shutterstock.com; 11 (top) Adisa/Shutterstock.com; 11 (bottom), 15 bottom, 18 (bottom), 154, 163 Nadezhda Kharitonova/Shutterstock.com; 12 (top) anse/Shutterstock.com; 13 (top), 22 (top left), 139 (bottom) Fotografiska; 13 (bottom), 127 (bottom) Tatyana Bakul/Shutterstock.com; 14 (top) Catcha Snap/Shutterstock.com; 14 (middle) Alizada Studios/Shutterstock.com; 14 (bottom) Robin Hayes; 15 (top) SMM/Anneli Karlsson/Vasa Museum; 16 (top) Roman Sigaev/Shutterstock.com; 16 (bottom) a40757/Shutterstock.com; 17 (top), 123, 181 Pernille Tofte/Skansen; 18 (top), 54 (top), 111 Svenskt Tenn; 19 (middle) Goncharovaia/Shutterstock.com; 19 (right), 23 (top) Rasmus Lindahl/Urban Deli; 20, 70 Mistervlad/Shutterstock.com; 21 (left), 127 (top) Rolf_52/Shutterstock.com; 21 (right) B.Forenius/Shutterstock.com; 22 (top right) A. Aleksandravicus/Shutterstock.com; 22 (bottom) PhotoFires/Shutterstock.com; 23 (middle), 194 Thomas Telford/Debaser Strand; 23 (bottom), 31 Aliaksandr Antanovich/Shutterstock.com; 24 (top) Uwe Aranas/Shutterstock.com; 24 (middle & bottom), 41 Mio Sallanto/Falafelbaren; 25 (top), 130, 160 Kiev.Victor/Shutterstock.com; 25 (bottom), 199 Radiokafka/Shutterstock.com; 26 (top) Mokkasin/Nordiska Museet; 26 (middle) Tommy Pedersen/Skansen; 26 (bottom) Roman Vukolov/Shutterstock.com; 27 (top), 114 Anna Gerdén/Tekniska Museet; 27 (middle) Bengt Wanselius/Kulturhuset Stadsteatern; 27 (bottom), 203 Matilda Rahm/Kulturhuset Stadsteatern; 28 (top) Elena Pominova/Shutterstock.com; 28 (middle) Linus Strandholm/Shutterstock.com; 28 (bottom), 220 Mikael Damkier/Shutterstock.com; 29 (top) Viacheslav Savitskiy/Shutterstock.com; 29 (middle) Katriina Makinen/Stockholm International Film festival; 32, 33 Liv Oeian/Shutterstock.com; 34 (top) Volker Rauch/Shutterstock.com; 34 (bottom) iuliia_n/Shutterstock.com; 35 Fabio Kianek/Shutterstock.com; 36 Stephanie Kenner/Shutterstock.com; 37 Per-Boge/Shutterstock.com; 39, 46 (top) Magnus Skoglöf/TAK; 42 (top) Meatballs for the People; 43 Café Pascal; 44 (top), 107 (top & middle) Erik Olsson Photography/Gastrologik; 44 (bottom) Hobo; 45 Mälarpaviljongen; 46 (bottom) Grand Hotel; 47 Petter Bäcklund/Café Pascal; 49 www.loellaphotography/Designtorget; 50 (top) Carl Ander/Sandqvist; 50 (bottom), 137 (top) Grandpa; 52 Stutterheim; 53 Nordiska Galleriet; 54 (bottom) Granit; 55 David Thunander/NK; 59 SvetlanaSF/Shutterstock.com; 60 Popova Valeriya/Shutterstock.com; 63 trabantos/Shutterstock.com; 67 Heracles Kritikos/Shutterstock.com; 68 Mario Savoia/Shutterstock.com; 73 Predrag Jankovic/Shutterstock.com; 74 www.imagebank.sweden.se, Gösta Florman/The Royal Library; 77 Melissa A. Barton/Science Fiction Bokhandeln; 79, 95 Tupungato/Shutterstock.com; 82 Zabotnova Inna/Shutterstock.com; 85 Asa Liffner AB/At Six; 87 canadastock/Shutterstock.com; 89 (top) TAK; 89 (bottom) Wingalrdhs/TAK; 94 phichack/Shutterstock.com; 99 alljoh/Shutterstock.com; 101, 227 Roberto La Rosa/Shutterstock.com; 105 Sturebadet; 107 (bottom) Erik Olsson Photography/Speceriet; 109 Rasmus Malmstrøm/Mikkeller; 115 Photo: Mia Olvång/Bergius Botanic Garden; 117 Nordiska Museet; 121 Love Strandell/ABBA The Museum; 122 Karin Bernodt/Skansen; 125 Karolina Kristensson/SMM/Vasa Museum; 129 Per Erik Adamsson/Spritmuseum; 133 Sun_Shine/Shutterstock.com; 139 (top) Margita Ingwall/Fotografiska; 143 Urban Orzolek/Urban Deli; 144 ROT Butik &Kok; 149 Reuber Duarte/Shutterstock.com; 150 Daniel Lagerborn/Stikki Nikki; 153 Werner Lerooy/Shutterstock.com; 155 allanw/Shutterstock.com; 157 Tennessee Witney/Shutterstock.com; 161 Wizard8492/Shutterstock.com; 162 AG Restaurang; 165 Naturkompaniet; 167 Roland Magnusson/Shutterstock.com; 171 Hellas Storstugan; 174 Samuel Lind/Artipelag; 175 Kraeva Olga/Shutterstock.com; 176 Tiberiu Stan/Shutterstock.com; 177 ArtMediaFactory/Shutterstock.com; 178 Kungliga Operan; 182 Kulturnatt/Stockholm Stads; 185 Gather/Izabella Englund; 187 Åke Blomquist / SvD - Bild från Stockholmskällan/Wikicommons; 188 (top) Bio Rio; 188 (bottom) Jimmy Sileo/Wikicommons; 190 Zita Folkets Bio; 193 Slakthuset; 196 Leon Jiber Photography/Stockholm Under Stjärnorna; 200 Claes Helander/Södra Teatern; 205 Markus@markusgarder.se; 208 JeniFoto/Shutterstock.com; 211 Publicerad av Centrum för Näringslivshistoria/Wikicommons; 213 Vladimir Mucibabic/Shutterstock.com; 215 Attributed to David Klöcker Ehrenstrahl - www.nationalmuseum.se/Wikicommons; 216 Govert Dircksz Camphuysen - Stadsmuseet i Stockholm/Wikicommons; 218 Wikicommons; 219 SAS Scandinavian Airline/Wikicommons; 223 Carl Larsson - nationalmuseum.se/Wikicommons; 225 Lasse Olsson/Studio B3; 228 Lydmar Hotel; 230, 234 (left) Beatrice Graalheim/Hotel Skeppsholmen; 231 Oscar Söderlund/Miss Clara by Nobis; 254 Courtesy of www.sll.se.

Credits

Crimson credits
Author Maddy Savage
Listings editor Grace McCallum
Copy editor Felicity Laughton
Proofreader Ros Sales
Cartography Gail Armstrong

Series Editor Sophie Blacksell Jones
Production Manager Kate Michell
Production Designer Emilie Crabb
Print Manager Patrick Dawson
Design Mytton Williams

Chairman David Lester
Managing Director Andy Riddle

Advertising Media Sales House
Marketing Sophie Shepherd
Sales Lyndsey Mayhew

Publis
Time (,
© TIM
Janua

ISBN ⁹
CIP DA
availab

Published by Crimson Publishing
21d Charles Street, Bath, BA1 1HX (01225
584 950, www.crimsonpublishing.co.uk) on
behalf of Time Out England.

Distributed by Grantham Book Services
Distributed in the US and Canada by
Publishers Group West (1-510-809-3700)

Printed by Replika Press, India.

Acknowledgements

This edition of *Time Out Stockholm* was
researched and updated by Maddy Savage
and Grace McCallum. Stockholm Today,
Itineraries, Shopping and Getting Started
were written by Maddy Savage. Other
chapters were written by Maddy Savage and
by contributors to previous editions of *Time
Out Stockholm*. The author would like to thank
Kevin Adams, Lola Akinmade Åkerström,
Stephanie Ankarvall, Barry's Bootcamp,
Dejan Bojanic, Sandra Carpenter, Benoit
Derrier, Sara Edvinsson, Lisa Espinoza, The
Framfielders, Heather Hampshire, Elice
He, Ellie Hjelm, Oliver Gee, Anna Elizabeth
Gustafsson, Hus24, International Parents in
Sweden, Iona McLachlan, Dierdre McTiernan,
Momondo, Malin Nyberg, The Park Södra, The
Pintmen, Claire Pryde, Diego Planas Rego,
Routes North, Iain and Alison Savage, Maeva
Schaller, Malin Siegbahn, Signalfabriken, Slow
Travel Stockholm, Ssideline City Run Club,
That's Up Stockholm, Visit Stockholm and
contributors to previous editions of *Time Out
Stockholm* whose work forms the basis of
this guide.

Photography credits

Front cover Martin Wahlborg/iStock
Back cover left: Liv Oeian/shutterstock.com;
centre: JeeJantra/shutterstock.com; right:
Elena Pominova/shutterstock.com
Interior Photography credits, *see p255*.